Christopher M. Blumhofer is Visiting
Assistant Professor of New Testament at
Fuller Theological Seminary.

THE GOSPEL OF JOHN AND
THE FUTURE OF ISRAEL

The Gospel of John is renowned for the challenges it presents to interpreters: its historical complexity, theological and literary unity, and its consistently critical stance toward characters known as "the Jews." There is abundant scholarly literature on each of these challenges, and yet there are very few studies that consider the Gospel as a whole in light of these pressing issues. Christopher Blumhofer offers a fresh approach to understanding the Fourth Gospel, one that draws together the insights of scholarship in all of these areas. He shows that a historically sensitive, ethically attuned, and theologically and literarily compelling reading of the Fourth Gospel lies before us in the synthesis of the approaches that have long been separated. Unlike studies that consider only a narrow portion of the Gospel, Blumhofer's unique approach draws on most of the Gospel and shows how common themes and interests run throughout the narrative of John.

CHRISTOPHER M. BLUMHOFER is Visiting Assistant Professor of New Testament at Fuller Theological Seminary.

SOCIETY FOR NEW TESTAMENT STUDIES

MONOGRAPH SERIES

General Editor: Edward Adams, *Kings College, London*

177

THE GOSPEL OF JOHN AND THE FUTURE OF ISRAEL

The Gospel of John and the Future of Israel

CHRISTOPHER M. BLUMHOFER

Fuller Theological Seminary

CAMBRIDGE
UNIVERSITY PRESS

CAMBRIDGE
UNIVERSITY PRESS

University Printing House, Cambridge CB2 8BS, United Kingdom

One Liberty Plaza, 20th Floor, New York, NY 10006, USA

477 Williamstown Road, Port Melbourne, VIC 3207, Australia

314–321, 3rd Floor, Plot 3, Splendor Forum, Jasola District Centre, New Delhi – 110025, India

79 Anson Road, #06–04/06, Singapore 079906

Cambridge University Press is part of the University of Cambridge.

It furthers the University's mission by disseminating knowledge in the pursuit of education, learning, and research at the highest international levels of excellence.

www.cambridge.org
Information on this title: www.cambridge.org/9781108493550
DOI: 10.1017/9781108656122

© Cambridge University Press 2020

First published 2020

Printed in the United Kingdom by TJ International Ltd, Padstow Cornwall

A catalogue record for this publication is available from the British Library.

Library of Congress Cataloging-in-Publication Data
Names: Blumhofer, Christopher (Christopher Mark), 1983– author.
Title: The Gospel of John and the future of Israel / Christopher Blumhofer.
Description: Cambridge ; New York, NY : Cambridge University Press, 2020. |
    Series: Society for New Testament studies monograph series | Includes bibliographical
    references and index.
Identifiers: LCCN 2019035746 (print) | LCCN 2019035747 (ebook) | ISBN 9781108493550
    (hardback) | ISBN 9781108737432 (paperback) | ISBN 9781108656122 (epub)
Subjects: LCSH: Bible. John–Criticism, interpretation, etc. | Bible. John–Criticism,
    Narrative. | Israel (Christian theology) | Jews in the New Testament. |
    Christianity and other religions–Judaism. | Judaism–Relations–Christianity.
Classification: LCC BS2615.52 .B55 2020 (print) | LCC BS2615.52 (ebook) |
    DDC 226.5/06–dc23
LC record available at https://lccn.loc.gov/2019035746
LC ebook record available at https://lccn.loc.gov/2019035747

ISBN 978-1-108-49355-0 Hardback

For Stephanie

CONTENTS

Contents

ACKNOWLEDGMENTS

During my doctoral studies, I had the opportunity to describe this work while it was still in progress to a senior New Testament scholar who was visiting Duke University. After stumbling through an effort to summarize my project to her in academic terms, I tried a personal approach: "Basically, it's an attempt to read John in a way that holds together what I've learned from Richard Hays, Joel Marcus, and Kavin Rowe – although I'm not quite sure any of them believe it is possible to hold the three of them together!" We laughed, and she affirmed the importance of trying. Whatever the success of my thesis, it traces its beginnings to classes and conversations with these three remarkable teachers. Any student of the New Testament would be fortunate to be shaped by one of them. It is a blessing to have been shaped by them all.

But this is too general. When this project was in its dissertation phase, my advisor, Richard Hays, encouraged, challenged, and corrected me with his exacting insight and seemingly inexhaustible generosity of spirit. A mentor once told me that your advisor leaves a "thumbprint" on your life and scholarship. I can only hope so. For the better part of a decade, Joel Marcus pressed me toward historically sensitive exegesis that follows the evidence of our texts where it leads. He demonstrated this commitment in all of his work; nowhere did I learn it more clearly than among the reams of essays that he turned back to me with red markings pressing me to go back to the text and grapple further with its (often uncomfortable) logic. I am grateful for that extended lesson in interpretive honesty. I have learned from Kavin Rowe the importance of philosophical and methodological clarity, both in numerous classes and also in many conversations on his front porch. I cannot – and would not want to – approach the scholarly life or the Christian life apart from his wisdom and influence. In addition to these three mentors, two others, Stephen Chapman and Daniel Boyarin, helped shape this project in its earliest stage. I have often thought that Stephen Chapman knows my field better than I do – and rightly so: he is a Bible scholar who models a respect for the integrity of the Old and New Testaments as distinct parts of the same Bible, and he strives to understand the parts and the whole. His wisdom and insight are matched only by his kindness and good humor. Daniel Boyarin generously agreed to serve on my dissertation committee despite never meeting me. When we did meet in person, his brilliance and creativity as a scholar were complemented by his warm support and encouragement. I am grateful for both his willingness and patience to consider how his ideas might unfold in the work of another. To come full circle: the senior New Testament scholar who once visited Duke and listened to my stammering attempts to articulate this project is now my dean, Marianne Meye Thompson. Like these teachers above, Marianne's scholarly insight and personal support are among the many gifts for which I am deeply grateful.

A generation of peers in Duke's Graduate Program in Religion sustained and sharpened my work through their friendship and engagement. Zack Phillips – one step ahead of me in seemingly every way – is an invaluable conversation partner and friend. Away from Duke, the community at Blacknall Presbyterian Church deserves thanks, and especially Allan Poole, who nurtured my sense of vocation for nearly a decade, and also the team of women at Blacknall who included my work in their weekly prayers for the church. At one point, they interceded for my dissertation under the heading "prayers for healing"; it was a tremendous encouragement when they felt comfortable recategorizing my work. Two friends deserve special thanks: Griff Gatewood, whose kindness, hospitality, and wisdom sustain me; and Daryl Ellis, whose support and friendship are a gift beyond words. If the act of thinking cannot be separated from the act of living, then Daryl shows just how deeply and faithfully one can think and live.

My parents, Edith and Edwin Blumhofer, support us through their generosity and love. The courage and faithfulness that mark their lives are an inspiration and a witness to the gospel. I could not be a more grateful son. My parents-in-law, Jennifer and Greg Wheatley, love and inspire us. Our family has thrived these past years thanks in many ways to these parents.

Our daughters, Chloë and Marika, ground our lives, work, and faith. They are a limitless source of joy and silliness, and also of thoughtful observation. This work is dedicated to my wife,

Stephanie. Above all, Stephanie is my encourager and conversation partner. She inspires me every day with her work ethic and wisdom; she supported this project and continues to support my vocation with some of the most costly gifts imaginable: her time, her energy, and even the shape of her life. It is a humbling thing to be loved by someone who is willing to lay down so much for another. My gratitude far exceeds my words, but the words are indispensable: thank you.

1

INTRODUCTION

Nearly a century ago, Rudolf Bultmann described two basic problems that beset the study of the Fourth Gospel: (1) the place of the Gospel in the development of early Christianity and (2) its central idea.[1] Simply put, from what conceptual, social, and historical situation does the Gospel of John emerge? And how can we characterize the central theological claim of the Gospel? Whether stated or not, these two questions – the historical and the theological – and their corresponding answers are bound up with all exegesis of John.[2] The present study will propose an approach to the Fourth Gospel that sheds light on both problems: The Gospel of John ought to be read as a narrative argument about how Israel might embrace its future. The Gospel consistently demonstrates how Israel's worship of God and obedience to God find their fulfillment through Jesus Christ. John's concern for the future of Israel means that it is incorrect to view John as interested in *replacing* or *superseding* Judaism. It is incorrect to read John as a document that looks back on a decisive break with Judaism. Rather, John seeks to demonstrate the fundamental continuity that runs toward Jesus through the Scripture and history of Israel, and through the practices and convictions of first-century Judaism. John claims that this Scripture and history, those practices and convictions, find their home in Jesus and the people who believe in him. Nearly half a century ago, Nils Dahl called this a "peculiar" continuity.[3] He was surely right, about both

---

[1] Rudolf Bultmann, "Die Bedeutung der neuerschlossenen mandäischen und manichäischen Quellen für das Verständnis des Johannesevangeliums," *ZNW* 24 (1925): 100–146 (see esp. 100–102).

[2] See John Ashton, *The Interpretation of John*, 2nd ed. (Edinburgh: T&T Clark, 1997), 7–25. My categorization of Bultmann's two questions as "historical" and "theological" is indebted to Ashton.

[3] Nils Dahl, "The Johannine Church and History," in *Jesus in the Memory of the Early Church*, ed. Nils Dahl (Minneapolis: Augsburg, 1976), 119.

the continuity and its peculiarity. Be that as it may, the Gospel of John presents its reader with a theological vision for the way in which Israel might move into its future in continuity with its past. Reading the Gospel from this perspective sheds light on the historical context of the Gospel and its theological center.[4]

The burden of this entire study is to make this case. But before presenting this reading, a few clarifications are in order: First, while John is obviously a narrative, the statement that John is a *narrative argument* is not as clear. The claim of this study is that the theological vision of the Gospel of John derives from and speaks into a set of historical and theological concerns that were present within Second Temple Judaism. To read John historically is to read it within a particular "context of expectation," one that is alert to the question of how the Jewish tradition can live in fidelity to its past and anticipation of its future. In formal terms, the Gospel is a narrative that works within the generic conventions of its day, but it is implicitly an argument for a particular (and in its context, an alternative) understanding of Jesus' significance vis-à-vis the Jewish tradition.[5] We will consider this in much more detail in the pages that follow. A second clarification to make is that to state that John's narrative is also an argument does not mean to deny that John is also (and primarily) a gospel – good news. It is to claim, however, that a

---

[4] The methodological implications of the text's theological coherence and historical context, as well as the complex theological and historical developments that preceded the final form, are considered in M. C. de Boer, "Historical Criticism, Narrative Criticism, and the Gospel of John," *JSNT* 47 (1992): 35–48. My aim to read John as a *historically situated argument* attempts to build on de Boer's criticisms and proposals without accepting that a full reconstruction of the redaction history of the Gospel is a prerequisite to an account of its coherence. Similarly, see Jörn-Michael Schröder, *Das eschatologische Israel im Johannesevangelium: Eine Untersuchung der johanneischen Israel-Konzeption in Joh 2–4 and Joh 6* (NET 3; Tübingen/Basel: A. Franke Verlag, 2003), 26–28.

[5] Frank Kermode (*The Genesis of Secrecy: On the Interpretation of Narrative* [Cambridge, MA: Harvard University Press, 1979], 162–163) describes genre as "a context of expectation ... a set of fore-understandings exterior to a text which enable us to follow that text." This study proposes that the context/fore-understanding necessary to read John well is not only generic (John as a *bios*, novel, etc.) but also the urgent historical and theological questions facing John's Jewish tradition. As an "argument," I mean that the narrative of John is, as a whole, a kind of *reason* or *proof* that supports a particular proposition. (On this, see *OED, ad loc.*) The description of John as a narrative argument can be coordinated with many other approaches to the genre of the Fourth Gospel; see, e.g., the essays in Kasper Bro Larsen, ed., *The Gospel of John as Genre Mosaic*, SANt 3 (Göttingen: Vandenhoeck & Ruprecht, 2015).

theological vision for the future of Israel is basic to the good news of John. To miss John's vision for Israel is to miss something significant about the Gospel. Third, the meaning of the terms "*Ioudaioi*," "Jewish," and "Israel" requires clarification.[6] I will show in this study how a theological frame of reference for these terms must be added to their oft-noted sociological frames of reference. For now, it will suffice to note that in this study *Ioudaioi*, "Israel," and "Judaism" are not used allegorically.[7] Fourth, John's vision for the future of Israel correlates with the Gospel's critical stance toward the *Ioudaioi*. John is arguing not only *for* a particular vision of the future of Israel but also *against* a competing vision for the future of Israel. The positive argument and the negative argument belong together. Many studies falter when they reduce or underplay one side of the argument – as if John is primarily positive and only minimally critical, or vice versa.

My aim is to demonstrate John's commitment to the future of Israel as a theme that runs through the entire Gospel. This thesis draws on several streams of scholarship, and it has been anticipated by a number of studies of John. The streams that contribute to this reading include those that shed light on what C. K. Barrett aptly named "Johannine Judaism."[8] These include the significant studies of Wayne Meeks,[9] J. Louis Martyn,[10] Raymond Brown,[11] Klaus

---

[6] In this study, the transliterated "*Ioudaioi*" will refer to the group that is commonly referred to as "the Jews" (oftentimes including quotation marks) in other studies of the Fourth Gospel. It is my hope that the transliteration preserves some of the historical distance that is vital to reading John as a historically situated narrative argument.

[7] They are not allegorical in the way that is often attributed to Bultmann, where "Jews/*Ioudaioi*" = the unbelieving world. (Bultmann is more nuanced than this common summary of his position. See Bultmann, *The Gospel of John: A Commentary* [trans. G. R. Beasley-Murray; Philadelphia: Westminster Press, 1971], 86–87, esp. 87n2).

[8] C. K. Barrett, *The Gospel of John and Judaism*, 1st American ed. (Philadelphia: Fortress Press, 1975), 19.

[9] Wayne A. Meeks, *The Prophet-King: Moses Traditions and the Johannine Christology*, NovTSup 14 (Leiden: Brill, 1967); "The Man from Heaven in Johannine Sectarianism," *JBL* 91.1 (1972): 44–72; "Am I a Jew? – Johannine Christianity and Judaism," in *Christianity, Judaism and Other Greco-Roman Cults*, ed. Jacob Neusner and Morton Smith (Leiden: Brill, 1975).

[10] J. L. Martyn, *History and Theology in the Fourth Gospel*, 3rd ed. (Louisville: Westminster John Knox, 2003).

[11] Raymond Brown, *The Community of the Beloved Disciple: The Life, Loves and Hates of an Individual Church in New Testament Times* (New York: Paulist Press, 1978).

Wengst,[12] and John Ashton.[13] Focused studies on the Gospel of John that have attempted to sustain similar ideas in their exegesis include the works of Stephen Motyer,[14] Andreas Köstenberger,[15] and John Dennis.[16] Daniel Boyarin's important contributions to New Testament studies in general and Johannine scholarship in particular open up space for the thesis I will pursue.[17]

In order to set up a reading of the Fourth Gospel that can appreciate its vision for the future of Israel, this introduction proceeds in four steps: (1) a brief sketch of recent scholarship on this topic and a clarification of my approach in light of prior studies; (2) a review of the diversity of Second Temple Judaism, with particular attention to the theologically significant ways that Jewish groups could narrate their identity vis-à-vis "Israel"; (3) a conceptual account of this diversity – here we will turn from a historical mode to a philosophical mode in order to gain perspective about how Jewish writers, including the Fourth Evangelist, could understand the distance between their present way of life and their future as the restored and re-gathered people of God; and (4) a review of the *Ioudaioi* in the Gospel and how John's characterization of them informs the Gospel's vision for the future of Israel.

---

[12] Klaus Wengst, *Bedrängte Gemeinde und verherrlichter Christus: der historische Ort des Johannesevangeliums als Schlüssel zu seiner Interpretation* (Neukirchen-Vluyn: Neukirchener Verlag, 1981).

[13] John Ashton, *Understanding the Fourth Gospel*, 2nd ed. (Oxford: Oxford University Press, 2007).

[14] Stephen Motyer, *Your Father the Devil? A New Approach to John and the Jews* (Carlisle: Paternoster, 1997); "The Fourth Gospel and the Salvation of Israel: An Appeal for a New Start," in *Anti-Judaism and the Fourth Gospel*, ed. R. Bieringer et al. (Louisville: Westminster John Knox Press, 2001), 83–100.

[15] Andreas Köstenberger, "The Destruction of the Second Temple and the Composition of the Fourth Gospel," in *Challenging Perspectives on the Gospel of John*, WUNT 2/219, ed. John Lierman (Tübingen: Mohr Siebeck, 2006), 69–108.

[16] John A. Dennis, *Jesus' Death and the Gathering of True Israel: The Johannine Appropriation of Restoration Theology in the Light of John 11.47-52*, WUNT 2/217 (Tübingen: Mohr Siebeck, 2006).

[17] Daniel Boyarin, "The Gospel of the Memra: Jewish Binitarianism and the Prologue to John," *HTR* 94.3 (2001): 243–284; "The IOUDAIOI in John and the Prehistory of 'Judaism,'" in *Pauline Conversations in Context: Essays in Honor of Calvin J. Roetzel*, JSNTSup, ed. Janice Capel Anderson, Philip Sellew, and Claudia Setzer (London: Sheffield Academic Press, 2002), 216–239; "What Kind of Jew Is the Evangelist?" in *Those Outside: Noncanonical Readings of the Canonical Gospels*, ed. George Aichele and Richard Walsh (London: T&T Clark, 2005), 109–153.

Locating This Study on the Map of Johannine Scholarship

The question of the relationship between John and Judaism has dominated much of twentieth- and early twenty-first-century scholarship on the Gospel, but there are only a few studies of John's vision for the future of Israel. Three recent, sustained arguments for such a reading can be found in the works of Stephen Motyer, John Dennis, and Jörn-Michael Schröder. Motyer argues for a reading of John that rejects the specific historical background that many scholars have assumed in order to make sense of John (i.e., the alienation of the Johannine community following expulsion from the synagogue/ Jewish life by the Jamnian authorities). Instead of finding meaning in a murky history, Motyer attends to the "points of sensitivity" that any reader can find in the text of John.[18] For Motyer, these include the temple, the festivals, and the interpretation of Torah. The evangelist engages these central symbols of Jewish identity as a means of engaging his readers. When John is read with these points of sensitivity in mind, and within the tumultuous world of Judaism just after the destruction of the temple in 70 CE, interpreters are equipped to understand John as an appeal for fellow Jews to recognize how the symbols of Jewish life that were threatened by the crisis of the temple's destruction might be maintained in Jesus.[19]

There is much to affirm in Motyer's reading, particularly his interest in understanding the whole narrative of John and its particular emphases within the historical context of post-70 Judaism – a context about which nearly all ancient and modern interpreters of the Fourth Gospel agree. But at a number of points Motyer's interpretation requires critique as well as further application. First, Motyer's reading of the Gospel essentially ends at John 8:59 due to his focus on understanding the polemic of John 8 (esp. v. 44, ". . . your father the devil") within the framework of his wider thesis. (For Motyer, John 8 is part of a prophetic critique of John's coreligionists.)[20] Readers can infer how the whole Gospel might come under Motyer's thesis, but this is left largely undone.

---

[18] Motyer's language about "points of sensitivity" is from James D. G. Dunn, "Let John Be John," in *Das Evangelium und die Evangelien: Vorträge vom Tübinger Symposium 1982*, WUNT 1/28, ed. Peter Stuhlmacher (Tübingen: Mohr Siebeck, 1983), 309–339.

[19] See Motyer, *Your Father the Devil?*, 214.

[20] See Motyer, *Your Father the Devil?*, 141–159. Motyer's proposal that John's polemic is best understood as "prophetic" and *therefore* has a missionary purpose is strained. On the role of prophetic critique to circumscribe a community, see Marianne

Second, Motyer argues that the purpose of John is to serve as a missionary document for Jews.[21] Klaus Wengst, among others, has rightly shown that this is unlikely: the Gospel presupposes a knowledge of the basic Christian narrative (e.g., the evangelist takes for granted knowledge of the Twelve in 6:67, and Mary as the one who had anointed Jesus in 11:2); it assumes fundamental theological ideas (e.g., what it means to "abide" in Jesus, 6:56 et passim); and it tells the story of Jesus with devices of misunderstanding and irony that suggest an audience already converted to faith in Jesus.[22] Limited though it is, the glimpse of the Johannine community that we encounter in the epistles of 1, 2, and 3 John offers one important set of witnesses for the reception and use of the Fourth Gospel within a community that engages the core ideas of the Gospel *not* primarily in their outreach to unbelievers but in the task of understanding the significance of Jesus for the common life they share.[23] The evangelist would likely rejoice if nonbelievers came to faith through his gospel, but we have no reason to think of John as a kind of late first-century missionary tract.[24]

Third, it will be helpful to note a conceptual problem in Motyer's argument: in pursuing a reading that recognizes John's particular emphases, Motyer argues against J. Louis Martyn's proposal that a conflict with nascent rabbinic Judaism is also important for understanding the Fourth Gospel. Thus, he asks interpreters to accept a

Meye Thompson, *John: A Commentary*, NTL (Louisville: Westminster John Knox, 2015), 194; Andrew Lincoln, *Truth on Trial: The Lawsuit Motif in the Fourth Gospel* (Peabody: Hendrickson, 2000), 179–180.

[21] See esp. Motyer, 211–220. Here Motyer follows Karl Bornhäuser, *Das Johannesevangelium: Eine Missionsschrift für Israel* (Gütersloh: C. Bertelsmann, 1928).

[22] On this point, see Klaus Wengst, *Bedrängte Gemeinde und verherrlichter Christus: Der historische Ort des Johannesevangeliums als Schlüssel zu Seiner Interpretation* (Neukirchen-Vluyn: Neukirchener Verlag, 1981), 34–36; Meeks, "Man from Heaven," 70. Francis Moloney, "Who Is 'the Reader' in/of the Fourth Gospel," ABR 40 (1992): 20–33; Richard Bauckham, "John for Readers of Mark," in *The Gospel for All Christians*, ed. Richard Bauckham (Grand Rapids: Eerdmans, 1998), 147–171.

[23] On the relationship of the Gospel to the Epistles, I agree with Raymond Brown that the Epistles correct possible misreadings of the Gospel. On these points, see Brown, *Community of the Beloved Disciple*, 93–144 (esp. 93–109); *An Introduction to the New Testament*, ABRL (Doubleday: New York, 1997), 383–405.

[24] I read John 20:31 as an expression of the Evangelist's goal to build up the faith of his readers regarding how Jesus is, in fact, the Messiah, the Son of God. The difficult critical decisions about this text are best deferred to arguments about the nature of the whole Gospel – what kind of narrative is it? – and thus there is an important way that this entire study is an argument for how to understand this particular verse. On this question, see Maloney, "The Gospel of John and Evangelization," in Francis J. Maloney, *The Gospel of John: Text and Context*, BIS 72 (Leiden: Brill, 2005), 3–19.

false dichotomy: either a relationship of conflict between John and the Jews (Martyn et al.) *or* John's constructive vision for Jewish worship finding its fulfillment in Jesus (Motyer). Motyer's thesis and historical reconstruction cannot balance John's particular emphases on temple, worship, and Scripture with the sustained criticism of the *Ioudaioi* in the Fourth Gospel and the possible historical scenario that would make sense of it. Thus, he asks his readers to follow him in denying the conflict with Judaism that Martyn described. While there are reasons to be cautious in adopting and deploying Martyn's thesis, readers should not need to make a decision between John's "points of sensitivity" on the one hand and the specific historical conflicts that would fit in post-70 Judaism on the other.

John Dennis's study of restoration theology in the Fourth Gospel interprets John 11:47–52 within the broad context of first-century Jewish restoration theology. Dennis argues that the ingathering of the scattered children of God spoken of in 11:52 denotes the scattered people of Israel.[25] Thus, the Gospel of John presents Jesus' death as fulfilling Israel's expectation for the people to be gathered by God in the last days. The plight of Israel is brought to an end by Jesus' death for (ὑπέρ) the nation.[26] After showing how the specific concerns of a restored nation and place of worship fit within Second Temple and post-70 Judaism,[27] Dennis surveys the Fourth Gospel's presentation of Jesus as, among others, the new temple (1:14; 2:13–22), the one who gathers the scattered people lest they perish (6:11–14), the shepherd of Israel prophesied in Ezek 34–37 (John 10:1–18), and the one who defeats the devil, the cosmic foe who leads astray the people of Israel (12:31; cf. 8:44).[28] John 11:47–52 is the crystallization of John's understanding of Jesus' death: he dies on behalf of the nation in order to bring about Israel's eschatological restoration.

There are several ways in which my focus on *the future of Israel* differs from Dennis's argument about Jesus' *gathering the true Israel*. First, although the implications of his findings move in many directions, Dennis's major contribution is to clarify how Jesus'

---

[25] In John 11:52, Jesus death is ἵνα καὶ τὰ τέκνα τοῦ θεοῦ τὰ διεσκορπισμένα συναγάγῃ εἰς ἕν. On the relevant Scriptural context for such "scattering," see Deut 30:1–5; Neh 1:8; Ps 106:26–27; Jer 9:16; 10:21; 23:1–4; Ezek 5:10; 11:16; 12:15; 20:23; 20:24; 28:25; 29:13; Dan 9:7; Zech 1:21; Sir 48:15, and esp. Isa 56:8.

[26] Dennis, *Jesus' Death and the Gathering of True Israel*, cf. esp. 46.

[27] Ibid., 80–116.

[28] Ibid. See, respectively, ibid., 136–177, 188–200, 200–201, 205–209.

death functions in John from within a Jewish frame of reference, specifically how Jesus' death brings about the long-anticipated restoration of the people of God.[29] Dennis's study demonstrates the significance of Jesus' death by examining various motifs and images in the Gospel and in contemporary literature and then locating those motifs within the broader framework of Jewish restoration theology. The present study aims to show how a particular interest in eschatological fulfillment runs through nearly every pericope in the Gospel. To put the differences most sharply, where Dennis's driving interest is restoration theology, mine is Christology, focusing on John's portrayal of Jesus as the one who fulfills the hopes of Israel. To be sure, some aspects of John's depiction of Jesus derive from restoration theology, but not all. Moreover, this study will attend in a more sustained way than Dennis's to the presence of polemic in John's Gospel – how the Gospel both casts a vision for Israel's future in Jesus and rejects alternative proposals. Thus, I hope to demonstrate how several pressing questions lie behind the Gospel's presentation of Jesus: How can Israel faithfully live into its future? Around what (or whom) should it organize its life? I propose that John is an argument for a particular answer to these questions. The difference, then, is that I am trying to locate the whole narrative of John within a broad hermeneutical context. The question is not: *What do we understand when we understand Jesus's death as "for the nation" (11:52)?* – although the answer is critical, and the motifs, images, and expectations of contemporary Jewish literature are indispensable. The question for this study aims at the broader narrative: *What do we understand when we understand the Gospel according to John?*[30]

Jörn-Michael Schröder's *Das eschatologische Israel im Johannesevangelium* argues that in the Gospel of John Jesus establishes the eschatological people of God in continuity and discontinuity with the Jewish and Old Testament tradition.[31] In John, the vision for this newly established eschatological Israel informs both the salvation-historical message of the Gospel and illuminates the contextual

---

[29]   Against Bultmann et al., see Dennis, 13–14, 351–353.

[30]   There may of course be multiple ways of answering this question. My contention is that a historically and theologically rooted reading of John will lead to the conclusion that the future of Israel is one such thing that readers are meant to understand.

[31]   Jörn-Michael Schröder, *Das eschatologische Israel im Johannesevangelium: Eine Untersuchung der johanneischen Israel-Konzeption in Joh 2–4 und Joh 6*, NET 3 (Tübingen/Basel: A. Franke Verlag, 2003).

strategy of the Gospel as it serves a community in conflict with its local religious community. Schröder demonstrates his thesis by studying every pericope in John 2–4 and 6, and then reading the imagery of these pericopae against the eschatological expectations of the Old Testament and, especially, within the Fourth Gospel's own eschatologically loaded terminology.

The aim of the project is striking similar to my own: to demonstrate that John's eschatological vision stands in strong continuity with the traditions of Scripture and expectation that were long nurtured within Judaism, and that John also breaks with those traditions in order to characterize Jesus as the one who fulfills the hopes of Israel.[32]

The major differences between Schröder's work and my own are hermeneutical. First, as will become clear below, I approach the continuity/discontinuity between John and the Jewish tradition as one that is grounded in a more robust account of Judaism as a tradition that, in its various expressions, is sensitive to the question of how its current form (Hasmonean Judaism, Pharisaic Judaism, "common" Judaism, etc.) approximates its ultimate form (the restored Israel). This framing provides a broader historical context for understanding the Gospel of John, one that removes the necessity of reading the Gospel as a text that is generated primarily as a reaction to the exclusion of Johannine Christians from their parent religious group.[33]

Second, Schröder sees John's commitment to eschatological Israel as so thoroughgoing that it becomes the allegorical key to understanding the narrative. So, in John 2, the mother of Jesus should be understood an ideal "Jew" – one who does not understand Jesus but commits to trusting him.[34] Nicodemus should be seen not as the text presents him – a ruler of the *Ioudaioi*, a Pharisee – but rather as a representative of a late first-century synagogue adherent convinced of Jesus' signs but unwilling to fully entrust himself to Jesus.[35] Jesus' walking on the sea in John 6 should be seen as transparent to God's presence and preservation of his beleaguered eschatological people (following, it seems, Bornkamm's reading of Matthew

---

[32] Cf. Schröder, 351–354.   [33] Ibid., 12–17; cf. 316–317.
[34] Ibid., 42–43 and passim.
[35] Ibid., 83–88. Note that the representative function of Nicodemus is not a problem (he speaks in the first person plural), only the strained profile that Schröder creates.

14:22–33).[36] When John writes "it was dark" (6:17), we should read, "there was demonic opposition to the post-Easter church," because in John 8, 12, and in the letter of 1 John, σκοτία implies an era in or realm of history in which Jesus is not present in the world.[37] Taken individually, each of these proposals is interesting and possible, but taken together they reflect Schröder's broader hermeneutical approach, which views the eschatological fulfillment of God's promises to Israel as so thoroughly enclosed within the argument of John that individual terms are often shoehorned to fit his readings.[38] I am interested in pursuing the fulfillment of God's promises to Israel in the Gospel of John, but I see John making this argument by means of a much deeper engagement with specific traditions and expectations of Scripture and Second Temple Judaism. In other words, while Schröder's approach is heavily *intratextual* (within John) but requires the re-signification of common terms and a level of reading-in that strikes me as problematic, my approach is weighted toward *intertextuality* – reading John as an engagement with a historically situated set of texts and the arguments that they served.

Finally, Schröder consistently presents John's vision of the eschatological Israel as one that "transcends" the earthly level for the heavenly. For instance, the *Ioudaioi* and the crowds are left behind as Jesus offers an interpretation of the manna miracle that transcends its original, earthly frame of reference. In their earthly way of thinking, the *Ioudaioi* signify the problem of any religious practice without transcendent reference.[39] The problem here is the idea that in John the eschatology of Jesus is out of reach to the *Ioudaioi* because it transcends what they could think or imagine. This is off point: the gap between Jesus and the *Ioudaioi* is not the ability to think metaphorically or to imagine a transcendent reality (for instance, that God's word could sustain a person like bread – Deut 8). Rather, the gap between Jesus and the *Ioudaioi* in John is the unwillingness of the *Ioudaioi* to recognize *Jesus* as the one who mediates the transcendent reality that they both affirm. The gap of understanding is specifically Christological. The point of difference is not the ability to think eschatologically. It is the ability/willingness to

---

[36] Cf. 222. Cf. Bornkamm's "The Stilling of the Storm in Matthew," in *Tradition and Interpretation in Matthew*, ed. G. Bornkamm, G. Barth, and H. J. Held (Philadelphia: Westminster, 1963), 52–57.
[37] Schröder, 221–224; cf. 263.
[38] Schröder has a brief discussion of key terms on pp. 321–324.
[39] Cf. Ibid., 306–307.

think of Jesus as the Christ, the Son of God, and therefore to think eschatologically about *him*.

Students of John will know of several article-length studies suggesting theses like mine.[40] Two things distinguish my work from these. First, a brief study cannot make this argument in a convincing way. Too many texts need to be considered and too many exegetical decisions need to line up for an article to prove the point. Second, John's vision for the future of Israel needs to be coordinated with its polemic toward the *Ioudaioi*. This is critical. In order to understand the Fourth Gospel's vision for Israel, readers need to make sense of both John's constructive engagement with Israel's traditions and its polemic toward the *Ioudaioi,* and readers need to make sense of these two lines of the Johannine narrative as they play out across the whole Gospel.[41]

If Motyer, Dennis, and Schröder are readers of John who offer interpretations similar to mine, then from which interpretations of John does this study differ significantly? A list of scholars and explanation of all the differences would endlessly delay the task of actually reading John. Nevertheless, my understanding of the social, historical, and theological context of the Fourth Gospel differs from prior explorations of these topics, and so a basic sketch of the Jewish context in which John appeared will help situate this study within the broader scholarly discussion of the Gospel and its relationship to Judaism.

The Diversity of Second Temple Judaism, and Identification with "Israel" as a Theological Claim

First-century Judaism was diverse, but not endlessly so.[42] Within and alongside of a large center ("common Judaism") existed various

---

[40] See esp. Motyer, "The Fourth Gospel and the Salvation of Israel"; Andreas Köstenberger, "The Destruction of the Second Temple and the Composition of the Fourth Gospel," in *Challenging Perspectives on the Gospel of John*. Several specialized studies point in this direction without opening up their arguments to the Gospel as a whole, e.g., Hans Förster, Dorit Felsch, and Gerry Wheaton.

[41] Rightly noted by Schröder, *Das eschatologische Israel*, 31.

[42] The paragraphs that follow build on Shemaryahu Talmon, "The Emergence of Jewish Sectarianism in the Early Second Temple Period," in *Ancient Israelite Religion: Essays in Honor of Frank Moore Cross*, ed. Patrick D. Miller, Jr., Paul D. Hanson, and S. Dean McBride (Philadelphia: Fortress Press, 1987), 587–616. See also Boyarin, "What Kind of Jew Is the Evangelist?" (cited in n. 17); Joseph Blenkinsopp, "The Development of Jewish Sectarianism," in *Judah and the Judeans in the Fourth Century*

parties, sects, and schismatic groups. The roots of this diversity stretch back to the destruction of the first temple by the Babylonians in 586 BC. Up until that time, the land of Israel, the Jerusalem temple, the religious and cultic leadership of prophets and priests, and the political leadership of the king worked to center the identity of Israel and to ground the people in their shared history and ethnic identity. There were, of course, religious, political, and economic disagreements. Some of these disagreements ran very deep, for instance, to charges of syncretism, idolatry, and illegitimate claims to authority or social status. Nevertheless, a basically cohesive understanding of "Israel" existed: Ephraim and Judah, the Northern and Southern Kingdoms, shared a sense of peoplehood and commitment to the same basic social structures. The twelve tribes of Israel were distinct from all the other nations. Their differences never overcame the agreements that provided them with a common identity.[43]

The loss of the temple, the cult, the role of the priests, the leadership of the royal family, and the deportation of the upper strata of Judean society changed all of this. In the Babylonian conquest, beginning with the deportation of 597 BC and then after the destruction of the temple in 586, Judeans were settled in compact communities in Babylon (Ezek 1:1–3; 3:15; Ezra 8:15–20; Neh 1:1). In these exilic communities, Judeans worked to preserve their distinct identities, and they looked to the future for the restoration of the nation of Israel. The Judean vision for restoration and their particular understanding of religious identity, both of which were cultivated in exile, spurred an important shift in Israelite history.

Israelites who remained in the land, whether Judea or Samaria, did not develop the same understandings of their identities as the Judeans in Babylon. Some remained after the conquest and kept up their identities as Israelites but now under the religious, social,

---

B.C.E., ed. Oded Lipschits, Gary N. Knoppers, and Rainer Albertz (Winona Lake: Eisenbrauns, 2007), 385–404. My argument builds toward an image of Second Temple Judaism that balances the contributions of Gabriele Boccaccini on the one hand and E. P. Sanders on the other (see Gabriele Boccaccini, *Middle Judaism: Jewish Thought 300 B.C.E. to 200 C.E.* [Minneapolis: Fortress, 1991]; E. P. Sanders, *Judaism: Practice & Belief 36 BCE–66 CE* [Philadelphia: Trinity Press International, 1992]. Cf. Richard Bauckham, "The Parting of the Ways: What Happened and Why," in *The Jewish World in and around the New Testament* [WUNT 2/233; Tübingen: Mohr Siebeck], 175–192).

[43] Talmon, "The Emergence of Jewish Sectarianism in the Early Second Temple Period," 591–593.

political, and economic pressures imposed on them by their conquerors (see, e.g., 2 Kings 17; Ezra 4:1–4; 2 Chron 30:10–12). Others moved to Egypt: some settled in Upper Egypt, where they maintained their religious identity at the Jewish garrison in Elephantine;[44] others settled in Lower Egypt, where, according to Jeremiah, they abandoned the Lord to worship the Queen of Heaven (Jer 41–44). The critical observation about this moment in Israel's history is the emergence of a variety of "centers" for Israelite identity – some in Babylon, others in Palestine, perhaps others in Egypt. This "multicentricity" among Israelites was unprecedented.[45] Not all of these centers were of equal importance, and we need not envision them all in competing relationships.[46] Still, their development is what proves decisive. The Babylonian conquest robbed all of the people of Israel (both those in the South and those that remained in the North) of the land, temple, and cultic and political sovereignty that once circumscribed their shared, if also contested, identity. The conquest fragmented Israel by creating social, historical, and conceptual conditions in which communities of Israelites would cultivate independent understandings of their identity and the norms by which to maintain that identity. This fragmentation also catalyzed groups to fill the voids within Israelite identity and the corresponding structures of leadership for Israel. It is in this context, with the establishment of exilic communities and the return of some exiles to Palestine following Cyrus's decree in 538 BC, that readers of the Bible first encounter the terms *Ioudaios/Ioudaioi* as terms referring to a group marked by both a regional and a confessional identity.[47]

[44] On the Jewish community at Elephantine, see Abraham Schalit and Lidia Matassa, "Elephantine," *Encyclopedia Judaica* 6:311–314. Cf. also Talmon, "The Emergence of Jewish Sectarianism in the Early Second Temple Period," 596.

[45] The term is from Talmon, "The Emergence of Jewish Sectarianism in the Early Second Temple Period," 594 et passim.

[46] See, e.g., A. E. Cowley, *Aramaic Papyri of the Fifth Century B.C.* (Oxford: Clarendon Press, 1923). See esp. papyrus nos. 30–32.

[47] E.g., Ez 4–6; Neh 1, 4, 6; Esth 2. The terms Ἰουδαῖος/ יהודי occur in other biblical contexts as well (e.g., Jer 32:12; 38:19; 40:11); the point that I will demonstrate here is that post-exilic literature uses the terms with a particular range of meaning. Importantly, "Jews/Judeans" could refer to communities of Judeans resettled in places other than Babylon, e.g., the community at Elephantine referred to themselves as *Yahudiya* (יהודיא); Cowley, *Aramaic Papyri of the Fifth Century B.C.*, 112–119.

I am aware of the debates about when it becomes appropriate to translate "Jew" rather than "Judean." My preference for *Ioudaioi* reflects my sustained engagement

In Ezra, the term *Ioudaioi* refers clearly to the community whose identity was forged in the Babylonian exile.[48] In Ezra 4, "the adversaries of Judah" (4:1), who are synonymously referred to as "the people of the land" (4:4), approach the "returned exiles" and offer to help in the rebuilding of the temple.[49] The people of the land claim to have been worshipping God since the days of Esar-Haddon (i.e., the immediate successor to Sennacharib, the Assyrian conqueror of the Northern Kingdom). Zerubbabel and "the heads of the families of Israel" rebuff their offer for help. The logic of their rejection follows 2 Kings 17: the people of the land know only an illegitimate form of worship to Israel's God. But the people of the land do not take this rejection well. They write to the king and denounce the returned exiles: "The *Ioudaioi* who came up from you to us have gone to Jerusalem. They are rebuilding that rebellious and

with Boyarin, particularly his attention to the way in which the *Ioudaioi* are not inherently co-extensive with Israel (see his essay, "What Kind of Jew Is the Evangelist?"; cf. also Blenkinsopp, n. 54 in this chapter); Steve Mason, "Jews, Judeans, Judaizing, Judaism: Problems of Categorization in Ancient History," *JSJ* 38 (2007): 457–512. (This article is discussed in more detail below.) My use of "*Ioudaios*" in the period under discussion here is meant to draw out how the particular vision of the Babylonian exiles represents one understanding among others about the qualities that define Israelite peoplehood. Cf. also Seth Schwartz, "How Many Judaisms Were There? A Critique of Neusner and Smith on Definition and Mason and Boyarin on Categorization," *JAJ* 2 (2011): 208–238; for a helpful account of ethnicity in the first century, see Philip Esler, *Conflict and Identity in Romans: The Social Setting of Paul's Letter* (Minneapolis: Fortress, 2003), 62–74. (Again, my concern that "*Ioudaios*" might reflect a particular way of being "Judean" prevents me from reaching Esler's conclusion of translating Ἰουδαῖος as "Judean," despite his concern that the translation "Jew" is "morally questionable" [p. 68]. One wonders: Would *Ioudaios* be similarly morally questionable, or is it redeemed by its strangeness?) On recent trends in the translation of these terms, see Adele Reinhartz, "The Vanishing Jews of Late Antiquity," *Marginalia*, June 24, 2014. Online: http://marginalia.lareviewofbooks .org/vanishing-jews-antiquity-adele-reinhartz/; for John in particular, see the recent important work of Ruth Sheridan, "Issues in the Translation of οἱ Ἰουδαῖοι in the Fourth Gospel," *JBL* 132.3 (2013): 671–695.

[48] I am aware that Ezra and Nehemiah represent reality in a way that stands at some distance from what a critical history offers. The reconstruction offered here proceeds on the assumption that *for John (and many other writers up through the first century of our era) these writings were received as accurate representations of the past.* For modern works that clarify the gap between history and the representation of reality in this literature, see Morton Smith, *Palestinian Parties and Politics That Shaped the Old Testament,* 2nd ed. (London: SCM Press, 1987); Peter R. Bedford, *Temple Restoration in Early Achaemenid Judah* (JSJSup 65; Leiden: Brill, 2001) (and see: Victor Hurowitz, "Restoring the Temple – Why and When? Review of Peter Bedford, *Temple Restoration in Early Achaemenid Judah,*' *Jewish Quarterly Review,* 93.3–4 [2003]: 581–591); Sara Japhet, "The Temple in the Restoration Period: Reality and Ideology," *Union Seminary Quarterly Review* 44: 3–4 (1991): 195–251.

[49] Cf. Josephus, *Ant.* 11.84–115, where the adversaries are named the Samaritans.

wicked city. . ." (4:12). The people of the land lose their case and, in the end, the *Ioudaioi* are vindicated and their leadership receives the support of Darius (5:5; 6:6–12, 14). The remnant community then reestablishes worship and specifically undertakes sacrifice for the sins of the entire nation, offering "twelve male goats, according to the number of the tribes of Israel" (6:16). Passover follows six weeks later, observed by "the people of Israel who had returned from exile, and also by all who had joined them and separated themselves from the pollutions of the nations of the land to worship the Lord, the God of Israel" (6:21).

How should we understand these dynamics after the fragmentation of the Babylonian conquest and the prophetic vision for the reunification of Israel that was proclaimed in Babylon? The text suggests this: The book of Ezra narrates a particular segment of Israel, that is, the *Ioudaioi*, returning from exile and establishing worship on behalf of the larger nation of Israel. "The *Ioudaioi*" and "Israel" are not exactly co-extensive. Rather, the *Ioudaioi* are the mechanism by which Israel's national life is authentically reestablished.[50] If they will give up their idolatrous or syncretistic ways and identify with the *Ioudaioi*, then all the scattered people of Ephraim and Judah will again participate in Israel.

Before continuing, it is important to note that the transliterated term "*Ioudaios*" is preferable in these contexts to the terms "Jew" or "Judean." The strangeness of the transliterated term reminds modern readers that to be a *Ioudaios* in the ancient world meant to identify oneself with a particular stream within the broader Jewish tradition. While many today would consider the "people of the land," the Qumran community, and the Pharisees in John as groups

---

[50] This seems to be the reason for the use of *twelve* sacrifices (Ezra 6:17) and *twelve* priests (8:24). N.B. The "Ezra narrative" of Ez 7–10 prefers "Israel" to "*Ioudaios*" (e.g., 7:7, 11, 28; 9:1). A similar preference for "Israel" appears in 2:1, 3:1, and 4:3. This makes sense because, unsurprisingly, the book of Ezra is convinced of its own message, viz., that Israel will now be grounded in the faithful life of the returned exiles. In other words, in Ezra, the use of the term "Israel" presupposes *at least* religious alignment and *at times* historical identification with the Judean exiles who returned from Babylon at Cyrus's decree (1:5). Commentaries on Ezra do not contradict the approach I am outlining; the approach offered here also works when one considers the complicated history of redaction in Ezra. See further H. G. M. Williamson, *Ezra, Nehemiah*, WBC 16 (Waco: Word Books, 1985), l–lii; Jacob M. Myers, *Ezra, Nehemiah: Introduction, Translation, and Notes*, AB 14 (Garden City: Doubleday, 1964); Juhu Pakkala, "The Exile and the Exiles in the Ezra Tradition," in *The Concept of Exile in Ancient Israel and Its Historical Contexts*, ed. Christoph Levin and Ehud Ben Zvi, BZAW 404 (Berlin: de Gruyter, 2010), 91–101.

populated by "Jews," it is, as we will see, not the case that in their own historical contexts the members of these various groups would have all identified themselves with the term *Ioudaioi*. It is, however, also true that they each recognized themselves as sharing something in common. Thus, this study opts for the transliterated term *Ioudaioi* as a way of retaining some of the specificity of the ancient term (though, as we will see, there were also internal differences among those who designated themselves *Ioudaioi*); this study retains the adjective "Jewish" as a way of referring to the broader tradition that looks back to Israel, which a variety of groups (Qumran, people of the land, Pharisees, etc.) held in common.

An alternative to the choice made above would be to follow the reasoning of Steven Mason, who has argued at length for the central importance of *place* in designating an *ethnos* in the ancient world. This leads into a preference for translating Ἰουδαῖος as "Judean" by Mason and many other scholars when translating this terminology, especially in literature from this early period. But insofar as each group of "*Ioudaioi*" in the exilic period represents a particular option for how to live out "Judean" identity, it is helpful to retain the terms "*Ioudaios*"/"*Ioudaioi*" because the latter terms capture the way in which each group of Judean exiles represents a unique understanding of the qualities that define Israelite peoplehood. In the Gospel of John, as in this earlier literature, the *Ioudaioi* embody a particular way of life that is an argument for how to live faithfully as God's people. The term *Ioudaios* is not reducible to the constellation of beliefs and practices that define the "Judean" *ethnos* because, in addition to designating a historic connection to a place (a position that I have no quarrel with), the term also possesses the particularity of a specific vision for Israel.[51] Thus, the preference in this study for the term *Ioudaios*/*Ioudaioi* in the period under discussion is meant to draw out how the particular vision of the Babylonian exiles represents one understanding among others about the qualities that define Israelite peoplehood.

Coming back to portrayals of the *Ioudaioi* in the Scriptures of this early period, the usage of the book Ezra holds for the other texts that are expressly concerned with the return of the Judean exiles and the rebuilding of the temple (i.e., Nehemiah, Zechariah, and

---

[51] One way to say this by employing Mason's terminology would be to say that for John, the "*Ioudaioi*" represent a particular option about how to be "Judean." For more on this point, see n. 47.

Haggai).[52] In Nehemiah, the *Ioudaioi* are "those who escaped the captivity" (1:2)[53] and are actively engaged in resettling Jerusalem and repopulating the land (2:16; 4:1–2, 10–12; 5:1, 17; 6:6; 13:23). Like Ezra, Nehemiah uses "Israel" with reference to the returned exiles. This is because the *Ioudaioi* are the vanguard of the restored people of Israel. In the worship and resettlement of the land by the *Ioudaioi*, Israel is reconstituted (7:73; 8:17; 9:1; 10:33, 39; 11:3, 12:47; 13:1–3). But again the two terms are not identical. Nehemiah uses "*Ioudaioi*" to refer to the particular historical community that is engaged in the task of reestablishing the broader historical and theological reality of "Israel." Nehemiah can slip from one term to the other – to oppose the *Ioudaioi* is to oppose what is good for Israel (2:10) – but this slippage is *exactly* the point of how Nehemiah uses the language (Ezra too). The *Ioudaioi* are at the center of the reestablishment of Israel and its worship. The interchangeable use of *Ioudaioi* and "Israel" is not based on a simple historical identification, but rather on the theological aims of the story. Insofar as the identification "*Ioudaioi* = Israel" becomes historical, it demonstrates the acceptance of this theological claim.[54]

Haggai is simpler because it does not employ the terms "*Ioudaios*," "*Ioudaioi*," or "Israel." Yet it does add one noteworthy element to our picture of the resettlement. In Ezra and Nehemiah, the "people of the land" are aligned against the rebuilding of Jerusalem (cf. Ezra 4:4; 9:1–2; et passim; Neh 10:28–31). In Haggai, the people of the land are exhorted to join with Zerubbabel and Joshua in the work of

---

[52] For overviews of the historical, social, and theological contexts of these works, see Carol L. Meyers and Eric M. Meyers, *Haggai-Zechariah 1–8*, AB25B (Garden City: Doubleday, 1987), xxix–xliv; Carol L. Meyers and Eric M. Meyers, *Zechariah 9–14*, AB25C (New York: Doubleday, 1993), 15–29.

[53] This verse could refer to two groups, but the syntax of v. 2 suggests they stand in apposition, and the answer Nehemiah receives in v. 3 suggests this too: "I asked them about the *Yahudim* that survived, those who had escaped the captivity, and Jerusalem."

ואשאלם על־היהודים הפליטה אשר־נשארו מן־השבי ועל־ירושלם

αἱ ἠρώτησα αὐτοὺς περὶ τῶν σωθέντων, οἳ κατελείφθησαν ἀπὸ τῆς αἰχμαλωσίας καὶ περὶ Ιερουσαλημ (Note that the LXX lacks the word "*Ioudaioi*." The αὐτούς in the LXX refers back to Nehemiah's brother and certain men of Judah [ἄνδρες Ιουδα/ ואנשים מיהודה].

[54] For nuanced treatments of these themes, cf. Gary N. Knoppers, "Nehemiah and Sanballat: "The Enemy without or within?" in *Judah and the Judeans in the Fourth Century B.C.E.*, ed. Oded Lipschits, Gary N. Knoppers, and Rainer Albertz (Winona Lake: Eisenbrauns, 2007), 305–331 (esp. 320). See also Joseph Blenkinsopp, "Judeans, Jews, Children of Abraham," in *Judah and the Judeans in the Achaemenid Period: Negotiating Identity in an International Context*, ed. Oded Lipschits, Gary N. Knoppers, and Manfred Oeming (Winona Lake: Eisenbrauns, 2011), 461–482.

building the temple (2:4; cf. 1:12; 2:2). This may suggest a perspective in which Israelites who remained in the land (but who were still, technically, non-*Ioudaioi* /non-Judeans) have a role in reconstituting Israel. Or "people of the land" may simply refer to resettled Judeans (cf. Neh 11:3, 20). Either way, Haggai supports the basic perspective of Nehemiah and Ezra: The Lord himself orders and blesses the work of the returned exiles under the leadership of Zerubbabel and Joshua.

Zechariah's prophecies align with those of his contemporary, Haggai. The Lord calls his people to return to the land: "I have returned to Jerusalem with compassion ... my cities shall again overflow with prosperity; the Lord will again comfort Zion and again choose Jerusalem" (Zech 1:16–17). The first eight chapters of Zechariah focus on Jerusalem and Judah (e.g., 1:14, 16, 17, 21; 8:1–8, 15). They address the community under Zerubbabel's leadership (4:6–10), and they call the exiles in Babylon to leave their captivity and take part in God's reestablishment of Zion (2:6–13). With Zechariah's focus on the rebuilding of Jerusalem and its temple, and its message to the Jerusalem community and to the Judean exiles in Babylon, it is entirely fitting that the book's eight visions conclude with this promise: "In those days ten men from nations of every language shall take hold of a *Ioudaios*, grasping his garment and saying, 'Let us go with you, for we have heard that God is with you'" (8:23).[55] Here, as in Ezra and Nehemiah, the *Ioudaioi* (i.e., the Judeans who have been exiled in Babylon) are in the privileged position of participating in the restoration of the people and the blessings of the nations that will again come from Israel (8:13).

A shift occurs in Zechariah 9–14.[56] Jerusalem and Zion remain in focus, but Zechariah now introduces a wider frame of reference for "Israel." In a departure from Ezra, Nehemiah, Haggai, and even Zechariah 1–8, the pronouncements of Zechariah 9–14 introduce a concern for gathering all the tribes of Israel (9:1), for God's recompense on the oppressors of both the Northern Kingdom and the Southern (9:10, 13). God turns against the leaders of his people

---

[55] In Zech 8:23, *Ioudaios* is in the genitive sg. (Ἰουδαίου). I have altered the text in keeping with my consistent practice of using *Ioudaios/Ioudaioi* without inflection when they are transliterated.

[56] Critical scholarship recognizes here the beginning of "Second Zechariah." See Meyers and Meyers, *Zechariah 9–14*, 15–50.

(10:3) and promises to care personally for all of his people, both Ephraim/Joseph and Judah (10:6–10). The pronouncements of chapters 11–14 describe God's strong commitment to Judah, Jerusalem, and Israel, but they shift away from the emphasis on Zerubbabel, Joshua, or the *Ioudaioi*/Judeans and into a different emphasis on the initiative that God, rather than specific human actors, will take to establish Jerusalem as the place from which God reigns over the earth (14:9). This shift that occurs in Zechariah is a shift between two ways of thinking about Israel: The first, Zechariah 1–8, lines up with Ezra, Nehemiah, and Haggai in envisioning the *Ioudaioi* as the center of Israel; the second way of thinking about Israel in Zechariah 9–14 has in mind the same goal (Israel, and its center in Jerusalem and Judah) but approaches this goal with no commitment to the particular historical actors of the *Ioudaioi* (e.g., Ezra, Nehemiah, Zerubbabel, Joshua).[57]

This overview sheds light on an important development in the conceptual world of ancient Judaism: the way in which the distinction between the term "*Ioudaios/Ioudaioi*" and Israel arose and also the way in which that distinction contained within it the possibility for ongoing debates about how particular historical communities might relate to the biblical vision of "Israel." Observing these social realities and the impact of the returned Judean exiles on the larger makeup of the people, Shemaryahu Talmon writes:

> [O]nce this new form of communal life [i.e., communities constituted by their particular confession] had come into existence, it would not be discarded even when the conditions that brought it about were seemingly reversed or attenuated by the return to the land, which did not, however, put an end to the existence of an exilic community … When the returning exiles reconstituted the political framework of Judah in the early Persian period, there evolved a symbiosis of creedal community with nation. After that time, Jewish peoplehood would embrace communities that accentuate their national-religious heritage differently.[58]

---

[57] See here Meyers and Meyers, *Zechariah 9–14*, 29. See also Gary N. Knoppers, "Did Jacob Become Judah? The Configuration of Israel's Restoration in Deutero-Isaiah," in *Samaria, Samarians, Samaritans: Studies on Bible, History and Linguistics*, ed. József Zsengellér, SJ 66 (Berlin: de Gruyter, 2011), 39–67.

[58] Talmon, "The Emergence of Jewish Sectarianism in the Early Second Temple Period," 598.

The main lines that we have been observing offer this picture: In Babylon, the *Ioudaioi* developed a strong communal identity that was reinforced by particular norms and by prophetic teachings and pronouncements about the exile and the coming restoration.[59] The strong sense of identity, vocation, and emphasis on normative ways of being *Ioudaioi* (=Judeans) that were developed in exile persisted even when the exiles returned to their homeland. Once back in Palestine, however, the norms began to have an effect *within* the broader community: they began to separate not only the *Ioudaioi* from the Babylonians and other Gentiles, they also began to demarcate *Ioudaioi* from other Israelites (even "*Ioudaioi*" from other groups with a historical connection to Judea – for instance, the "people of the land"). Talmon pictures the varying ways of relating to the nation thus:

creedal-national	inner-group	[=*Ioudaioi*]
national	in-group	[=Israelite people broadly understood]
creedal-ethnic-foreign	out-group	[=Gentiles][60]

This model is helpful for understanding the distrust in Ezra and Nehemiah for "the people of the land" and concern for separation from people of mixed or foreign descent (Ezra 10; Neh 13:1–3). The separation enforces a distinction within the people of God, one in which the normative ways of living associated with the *Ioudaioi* from Babylon are necessary in order to claim participation in the theological reality of "Israel." This model also accounts for the conceptual shift between Zechariah 1–8 and Zechariah 9–14. In the former, the inner-group (i.e., the *Ioudaioi*) is the means of salvation; in the latter, the in-group (Israel broadly understood) is in view. This model accounts for the distinction between two groups of Israelites as, alternatively, "the wicked" and "those who fear the Lord" in Mal 3:13–18.[61] In a different way, it accounts for the rift between Samaritans and *Ioudaioi*: both groups claim a heritage going back to a pre-exilic people (the Northern and Southern tribes, respectively), and both groups put the Torah at the center of their communal life,

---

[59] On this paragraph, cf. also ibid., 599–604.

[60] Ibid., 599. The bracketed additions are mine.

[61] N.B. The identification of the groups mentioned in this passage is important for scholars who undertake historical reconstructions of Jewish life during this period. For in-depth discussion, see Andrew E. Hill, *Malachi*, AB25D (New York: Doubleday, 1998), 51–84, 357–363; Ralph L. Smith, *Micah-Malachi*, WBC 32 (Waco: Word Books, 1984), 298–299.

yet their particular visions of "Israel" preclude their unity. Although a decisive break between *Ioudaioi* and Samaritans may not have occurred until the Hasmonaean period (second century BC), the fundamental disagreement between the groups emerged out of these conditions in the Persian and Hellenistic periods of the fifth and fourth centuries BC.[62]

When these observations are taken together, the question that rises to the surface from this period in Israel's life is not only *Who's in and who's out?* (That question is important but can be too sharply focused on in-group/out-group relationships.) In the triad of possible relationships described earlier, the question that must now also be asked is this: *Who has a rightful claim to "the center" of Israel – and to the name "Israel" itself?* That is, *Who determines the inner-group and those who might participate in it?*

"*Ioudaioi*" and "Israelites" in the Later Second Temple Period

Within intertestamental literature, "*Ioudaioi*" and "Israelites" continue as distinct but overlapping entities. It is not the case, as a previous generation of scholarship argued (whose voice can still be heard today), that in Jewish literature outside of Scripture "Israel" is a term employed by insiders and "*Ioudaios*" a term used by outsiders.[63] Such a view cannot adequately account for the use of Ἰουδαῖος in literature written by and for *Ioudaioi* (e.g., 2 Macc 1:1–9).

---

[62] On the dynamics of this "schism" and its development, see Gary N. Knoppers, *Jews and Samaritans: The Origins and History of Their Early Relations* (Oxford: Oxford University Press, 2013); see also James D. Purvis, *The Samaritan Pentateuch and the Origin of the Samaritan Sect*, Harvard Semitic Monographs 2 (Cambridge, MA: Harvard University Press, 1968), 1–15, 88–118; Robert T. Anderson and Terry Giles, *The Samaritan Pentateuch: An Introduction to Its Origin, History, and Significance for Biblical* Studies, SBLRBS 72 (Atlanta: Society of Biblical Literature 2012), 7–23, 105–136; Gary N. Knoppers, "Samaritan Conceptions of Jewish Origins and Jewish Conceptions of Samaritan Origins: Any Common Ground?" in *Die Samaritaner und die Bibel: Historische und literarische Wechselwirkungen zwischen biblischen und samaritansichen Traditionen*, ed. Jörg Frey, Ursula Schattner-Rieser, and Konrad Schmid, Studia Samaritana 7 (Berlin: de Gruyter, 2012) 81–118. See also the discussion of John 4 in Chapter 2.

[63] Most importantly here, cf. K. G. Kuhn's statement in the *TDNT*: "ישׂראל is the name which the people uses for itself, whereas יהודים -Ἰουδαῖος is the non-Jewish name for it [i.e., the people]." Idem, "Ἰσραήλ, Ἰουδαῖος, Εβραῖος in Jewish Literature after the O T," *TDNT* 3.359–369. For a contemporary presentation of a similar view, see Peter J. Tomson, "'Jews' in the Gospel of John as Compared with the Palestinian Talmud, the Synoptics, and Some New Testament Apocrypha," in *Anti-Judaism and the Fourth*

As in the Persian period, so also in the following centuries, the distinction between the terms is better explained theologically. In the intertestamental period, "*Ioudaioi*" continues to refer to a particular segment of the broader people of Israel. Often the term refers specifically to a segment that stands in historical continuity with the people who left Judea during the time of the Babylonian conquest. Thus, as in Ezra and Nehemiah, so also in this literature, *Ioudaioi* can view themselves as the theological and sociological center of Israel. But by making such a claim they do not necessarily limit to themselves the meaning of "Israel." Nor does usage of the term "*Ioudaios*" designate a static understanding of how to organize religious and social life vis-à-vis Israel. The precise meaning of "*Ioudaios*" would certainly shift between Egypt, Palestine, and Babylon. The *Ioudaioi* at Elephantine certainly did not construe the implications of Judean identity in exactly the same way as their kin who returned to Jerusalem from Babylon. Yet the terms "*Ioudaios*"/"*Ioudaioi*" could nevertheless identify groups that lived differently yet still oriented themselves toward the same basic place and beliefs.[64] The term "Israel," however, is not used with such variety. "Israel/Israelites" continues to refer to the Northern Kingdom in the biblical past as well as to the unified people of God in the biblical past or in the prophesied future.[65] Numerous studies support the conclusion that in this period "Israel" refers to a biblical and theological entity that

Gospel, ed. R. Bieringer et al. (Louisville: Westminster John Knox, 2001), 176–212; Peter J. Tomson, "The Names 'Israel' and 'Jew' in Ancient Judaism and the New Testament," *Bjdr* 4 7.2–3 (1986): 120–140, 266–289. Cp. Maurice Casey, "Some Anti-Semitic Assumptions in the *Theological Dictionary of the New Testament,*" *NovT* 40.3 (1999): 280–291 (esp. 280–286).

[64] Thus, not all "*Ioudaioi*" in this literature have the same relationship to Judea or the same understanding of "Judaism" (a term that appears for the first time only in 2 Macc). Consider, for instance, how the Egyptian *Ioudaioi* addressed in 2 Maccabees conceive of their Judaism differently from the Palestinian *Ioudaioi* from which the work arises. Cf. Jonathan A. Goldstein, "Biblical Promises and 1 and 2 Maccabees," in *Judaisms and Their Messiahs at the Turn of the Christian Era,* ed. Jacob Neusner, William Scott Green, and Ernest S. Frerichs (Cambridge: Cambridge University Press, 1987), 70; for an account of such disagreements that considers the broader period, see Timothy Wardle, *The Jerusalem Temple and Early Christian Identity,* WUNT 2/291 (Tübingen: Mohr Siebeck, 2010).

[65] Second Temple writers envisioned Israel in a striking variety of ways. The variety is important, but the consistent place "Israel" holds as the entity of the biblical past that provides the substance for the eschatological vision is what is central to my argument. See Michael E. Fuller, *The Restoration of Israel: Israel's Re-gathering and the Fate of the Nations in Early Jewish Literature and Luke-Acts* (Berlin: de Gruyter, 2006), 13–101.

existed in the past and will exist again when God acts to restore the fortunes of the twelve tribes of Israel.[66] Space does not permit an exhaustive survey of the evidence, but it will be helpful to observe the linguistic differences that mark the usages of "*Ioudaios*" and "Israel" in some of the literature of the Second Temple period and thus to appreciate the kind of gap that existed between the terms. We will do this by considering briefly the distinctions between "*Ioudaios*" and "Israel" in three bodies of literature: 1 and 2 Maccabees, the Qumran scrolls, and Josephus's *Antiquities*.[67]

1 Maccabees demonstrates the success of the argument first made by Ezra and Nehemiah.[68] The history records a grave threat to the identity of Israel. Renegades from Israel make a covenant with the Gentiles, set up a citadel in Jerusalem, and Israelites are subjected to violent persecution (1 Macc 1:11, 34–36, 58). The nadir of this situation occurs when a *Ioudaios* from Modein steps forward to apostatize (2:23). In this situation, Mattathias and his sons become leaders in the leaderless Israel. The subsequent battles under Judas, Simon, and Jonathan are all narrated in terms of their significance for "Israel" (e.g., 3:2, 8, 10, 43 et passim). Close attention to the use of the terms "*Ioudaios*" and "Israel" in 1 Maccabees demonstrates that beginning in 4:1, and thereafter (e.g., 10:23, 25–45; 11:30–37, 45–51; 13:41–42; 14:47, etc.) the narrative of 1 Maccabees presents the community of warriors fighting on behalf of the whole people

---

[66] The significance of "Israel" as an eschatological entity is treated by Brant Pitre in *Jesus, the Tribulation, and the End of the Exile: Restoration Eschatology and the Origin of the Atonement*, WUNT 2/204 (Tübingen: Mohr Siebeck, 2005), 31–40. See also Jason Staples, "Reconstructing Israel: Restoration Eschatology in Early Judaism and Paul's Gentile Mission," PhD Diss., University of North Carolina at Chapel Hill, 2016, 64–461; Joel Marcus, "'Twelve Tribes in the Diaspora' (James 1.1)," *NTS* 60 (2014): 433–447.

[67] A stream of NT scholarship would emphasize the strained *social* relations between Judea and the *Ioudaioi* on the one hand and Galilee and Samaria on the other. For these writers, the regions were divided by economic, cultural, and religious distinctions that by the first century hardened into a situation in which Jews/*Ioudaioi*/Judeans were the bourgeoisie whose culture ran up hard against that of the Galilean/Samaritan proletariat. The regional differences between these groups are important, but I would argue for the need to find a way to view theological and social differences together, rather than attempting to explain one by the other. For a study of John that errs too much to one side, see Tom Thatcher and Richard Horsley, *John, Jesus & the Renewal of Israel* (Grand Rapids: Eerdmans, 2013).

[68] For introductory and critical issues relating to 1 and 2 Maccabees, see Jonathan A. Goldstein, *1 Maccabees: A New Translation with Introduction and Commentary*, AB 41 (Garden City: Doubleday, 1974), 3–36, 62–89.

of Israel as the *Ioudaioi*.[69] The text thus makes an important connection between Israel as a theological entity and the *Ioudaioi*, under Hasmonaean leadership, as the historical (and of course also theological) entity that protects and establishes Israel against threats inside and out. The two terms are not simply identical, but all the *Ioudaioi* in the narrative are vigorously engaged in the task of restoring the integrity of Israel's life among the nations.

In 1 Maccabees, readers encounter a text that identifies its actors with the historic and future people of "Israel." In stark contrast to 1 Maccabees, 2 Maccabees narrates the events of Judas Maccabeus and his campaigns with an overwhelming preference for describing the people as "*Ioudaioi*" and the way of life they are fighting for as "Jewish" (Ἰουδαϊσμός, 2 Macc 2:21; 8:1).[70] In 1 Maccabees, "Israel" and its cognates occur sixty-three times; in 2 Maccabees the term occurs six times, and each of these six occurrences come in instances of prayer or recollection of God's commitment to Israel in the past.[71] By contrast, the term "*Ioudaios*" (Ἰουδαῖος) and cognates appear fifty-nine times in 2 Maccabees – nearly twice the rate "*Ioudaios*" is used in 1 Maccabees.[72]

Why does the writer of 2 Maccabees not narrate the campaigns of Judas in terms of their significance for Israel as the author of 1 Maccabees does? An answer lies at hand if we follow Jonathan Goldstein's argument about the writer's theological assessment of his historical situation: The author of 1 Maccabees believed that the worst part of the "Age of Wrath" was past, and that "God had chosen the Hasmonaean dynasty to bring permanent victory to Israel."[73] But the writer of 2 Maccabees was ambivalent about the achievements of the Hasmonaeans in terms of ushering in a new age. Thus, even as he celebrates Judas, the narrator "discredits all other

---

[69] In strictly narrative terms, it is possible to consider that the low point of *Jewish* apostasy in 2:23 (i.e., apostasy in the "inner group") catalyzed the zeal of Mattathias.

[70] N.B. An ancient reader would not turn the page on 1 Maccabees and immediately begin 2 Maccabees. The books were composed with differing commitments and aims. See the work of Goldstein (n. 68) for further discussion. The significance of this point is that the differences we observe in this discussion likely reflect broader commitments.

[71] See 2 Macc 1:25, 26; 9:5; 10:38; 11:6; 15:14.

[72] On these statistics, and for an argument similar to this one, see Staples, 229–236.

[73] See Goldstein, "Biblical Promises," 81. Cf. also Staples, 219–236. See further Jonathan A. Goldstein, *2 Maccabees: A New Translation with Introduction and Commentary*, AB 41A (Garden City: Doubleday, 1983), 3–27.

Hasmonaeans."[74] Instead of following 1 Maccabees and presenting Mattathias and his sons as the actors through whom God began the restoration of Israel, the writer of 2 Maccabees prefaces his work with an appeal for the Egyptian *Ioudaioi* to join him in a prayer that acknowledges Israel's restoration as unfulfilled and awaiting God's action (2 Macc 1:24–29). The lack of "Israel" terminology in 2 Maccabees thus corresponds to the book's overarching theological *Tendenz*, which resists attributing eschatological significance to the Hasmonaean dynasty and looks to divine intervention for the future reconstitution of Israel.[75] 2 Maccabees refers to "Israel" when it describes the Lord's commitment to his people and how that commitment in the present stands in continuity with his commitment in the past, but the book does not characterize the success of Judas and the *Ioudaioi* who fight with him as the restoration of Israel through these particular *Ioudaioi*. In this way, the persistent use of the term "*Ioudaios*" reinforces the modest position of the book's eschatology vis-à-vis other possible presentations of the history: in 2 Maccabees, God actively preserves the *Ioudaioi* through Judas and the Jewish way of life for which he fought, but the restoration of Israel has not yet begun. This reading makes sense of the call for the reader of 2 Maccabees to join with other *Ioudaioi* in continuing to pray for the restoration of Israel (1:24–29).[76] For our purposes, the critical point is the distinction between "Israel" and "*Ioudaios*." The terms are loaded with historical and theological significance. They are not inherently coextensive, but the extent to which they overlap (or do not) corresponds to a broader assessment of the relationship between a particular historical and theological community and an idealized theological and historical people, Israel.

Josephus's *Antiquities* offers another body of literature in which to recognize the distinction between the terms "*Ioudaios*" and "Israel." In a way similar to the use of these terms in 2 Maccabees, Josephus shows an awareness of the gap between the people of the present moment and the biblical ideal of Israel that encompasses them. In a survey of Josephus's use of these terms, Jason Staples notes that Josephus shifts from using "Israel/Israelites" in the first 11 books of

[74] Goldstein, "Biblical Promises," 87; Goldstein, *2 Maccabees*, 17–19.

[75] See Goldstein, "Biblical Promises," 87, 96nn89–90.

[76] Robert Doran in *2 Maccabees: A Critical Commentary*, Hermenia (Minneapolis: Fortress, 2012), 13–14 lists "fidelity to ancestral laws" (e.g., 2 Macc 6:1, 6) as an aim of the narrative. This comports with the broader sketch offered here.

his *Antiquities* to a preference for the term Ἰουδαῖος at precisely the point in the narrative that he begins to speak of the return of the Babylonian exiles. According to Staples, there are 188 uses of "Israel" and cognates before *Antiquities* book 11, and none after it. Of just over 1,200 uses of Ἰουδαῖος and cognates in *Antiquities*, 1,190 occur *after* book 10.[77] Importantly, Josephus is self-aware in how he employs these terms, as he explains:

> This name [i.e., Ἰουδαῖοι] by which they have been called from the time when they went up from Babylon, is derived from the tribe of Judah; as this tribe was the first to come to those parts, both the people themselves and the country have take their name from it. (*Ant.* 11.173, LCL trans. Marcus)

> Then he [Ezra], read the letter in Babylon to the Jews [τοῖς... Ἰουδαίοις] who were there ... But all the Israelite people remained in the country. In this way it has come about that there are two tribes in Asia ... while until now there have been ten tribes beyond the Euphrates – countless myriads whose number cannot be ascertained.   (*Ant.* 11:132–133)

Josephus's use of terminology stems from his understanding that Israel encompasses the biblical past and the future expectation of the people of God.[78] In his time, however, he uses the term *Ioudaios* to designate an ethnic and religious group whose history is bound up with the exiled-and-returned people of the Southern Kingdom of Judah, and he notes how the "Israelite people" are not identical with the returnees.[79] Josephus is aware of the distinction that first arose in Ezra and Nehemiah, and he preserves it.

When we turn to the Qumran Community, we find a group that refers to itself with the term "Israel" as well as designations such as "the community," "the remnant" (often with "of your people" or "of

---

[77] See Staples, "Reconstructing Israel," 82–84.

[78] Ibid., 300–303 (= "Israel's Restoration in Josephus"), and note Staples's comment on early post-exilic literature: "[A]t the root of exilic and postexilic Judaism we find not a *redefinition of Israel limited to Jews/Judahites* but *restoration eschatology* – a theology looking backwards to biblical Israel and forward to a divinely orchestrated future restoration of Israel far exceeding the small return of Ἰουδαῖοι/יהודים in the Persian period" (p. 127).

[79] Staples, "Reconstructing Israel," 84–85.

your inheritance"), and "sons of light" (or "truth").["80] But even as the Qumran community uses these terms, it also retains an understanding of "Israel" that is bigger than the community itself. The Community Rule presents the group as the harbinger of the fully restored people of Israel. The community lays "a foundation of truth for Israel" and acts on behalf of "the house of truth in Israel" (1QS 5.5–6). In its faithfulness to the covenant, the community "is the tested rampart, the precious cornerstone that does not shake . . . it will be a house of perfection in Israel" (1QS 8.7–9), the place in the desert to which God's people may go to prepare the way of Lord (8.12–14; cf. 4Q398 Frag 14–21.7). To this new cornerstone of Israel the community calls out those people of the House of Judah who resist the illegitimate leadership of Judah's "Wicked Priest" (1QpHab 8.1–3; 11.10–12.10). The striking reticence to use terms like "*Ioudaios*" as well as the scrolls' ambivalence toward "the house of Judah" reflect the history of the group, which (likely) retreated into exile (perhaps to join in symbolic exile with the other tribes) after losing influence in Jerusalem.[81] Perhaps no other body of literature reveals in such a sustained way how the alignment of the terms "*Ioudaios*" and "Israel" (or the refusal to do so) constitutes a theological and historical claim about the authentic makeup of the people of God. The Qumran community struggled against (what it understood to be) a "Judean" inner-group and attempted to place itself as the inner-group of the people of Israel. Talmon's model of the inner-group, in-group, and outer-group can help us recognize how each of these texts considers "Israel" as the entity that did, and some day will again, comprehend all the people of God. Until that day, however, various groups posture to become the "inner-group" that might help the nation draw close to its true identity.

The conclusion of this survey can now be drawn: The terms "*Ioudaios*" and "Israel" were not inherently coextensive in the Second Temple period. Rather, the relationship between these terms hinges on theological convictions about the relationship of a particular historical and theological entity (a Judaism) to a broader, idealized historical and theological entity (Israel). The identification of

---

[80] These terms are ubiquitous across Qumran literature. On "the community" and "Israel," see, e.g., 1QS et passim; on "the remnant," see e.g., 1QM 14.8–9 et passim; on "sons of. . .," see 1QS 3.13–25, 1QH[a] 3.11.

[81] See 1QHab 7–13, and the well-documented discussion in Staples, "Reconstructing Israel," 403–410.

these terms as coextensive begins in the Bible itself (Ezra, Nehemiah), and in the Second Temple period that identification was at turns reasserted (1 Maccabees), challenged (Qumran), or modestly put to one side in anticipation of God's action to vindicate and restore his people through whatever means he would choose (Josephus, 2 Maccabees; cf. Zech 9–14). Admittedly, many who belonged to the "common Judaism" of these periods likely took for granted the continuity between their way of life and the "Israel" from which and toward which it grew. At no point in any of this literature, however, does opposition to or ambivalence about a particular form of Judaism necessarily signify a broader rejection of the people of Israel as a historical and theological entity. In fact, the opposite is the case: a commitment to Israel can motivate resistance by a Jewish group to an alternative, competing, and still Jewish vision of Israel.[82]

Judaism as a Tradition in Transformation and Crisis

Before we move to the Gospel of John, it will be helpful to offer a conceptual clarification of the dynamics observed above. How do we understand the relationships of various Jewish groups? How might a reader account for the variety of ways in which Jewish groups presented the continuity between particular historical communities and the people of the biblical past and prophesied future to which they laid claim? The returnees from Babylon, the Samaritans, the "people of the land" in Ezra, the Hasmonaean dynasty, the *Ioudaioi* who worshipped at Leontopolis, the Teacher of Righteousness – how do we conceptualize their agreements and disagreements?

Following Alasdair MacIntyre, we should see them as related to one another within a broader tradition, a narratively dependent way

---

[82] Helpfully, cf. Jacob Neusner: "*A Judaism is a religious system comprising a theory of the social entity, the 'Israel,' constituted by the group of Jews who sustain that Judaism;* a way of life characteristic of, perhaps distinctive of, that group of Jews; and a world-view that accounts for the group's forming a distinctive social entity and explains those indicative traits that define the entity." Neusner, "What Is "a Judaism?"" in *Judaism in Late Antiquity: Part 5: The Judaism of Qumran: A Systematic Reading of the Dead Sea Scrolls,* Volume 1: *Theory of Israel,* ed. Alan J. Avery-Peck, Jacob Neusner, and Bruce D. Chilton (Leiden: Brill, 2001), 3–21 (here 9–10, my emphasis). My only criticism of this definition as a description of ancient Judaism would be that it is drained of the eschatology that animates the meaning of "Israel" in literature from the period.

of thinking and living that extends through time.[83] Traditions possess their own rationalities, their own internal logic, their own standards of excellence. Participants in traditions are tutored in how to think and live in ways appropriate to their tradition. All traditions transform over time as participants live out the logic of the story they find themselves in. Traditions undergo changes when a conflict or argument creates a rupture in the conceptual world of the tradition and thereby uncovers various inadequacies. As they transform, and propose and work out new solutions, traditions "embody continuities of conflict."[84]

According to MacIntyre, we can recognize three stages within the enquiry of a tradition: the first stage is marked by a moment in which beliefs, texts, and authorities are recognized but not yet questioned; the second stage reveals inadequacies in the tradition that have not yet been resolved; and the third stage records the response to those inadequacies by means of reformulating, reevaluating, or reinterpreting the relationship of the tradition to its basic commitments.[85] If anyone can look back at her tradition and contrast her "new beliefs" with her "old beliefs," then she is able to recognize an inadequacy in her tradition and an attempt to resolve it.[86] To occupy a position whereby a new belief is (purportedly) true in contrast to an old belief is to take up and embody an argument: I claim that my new way of understanding our tradition and living it out overcomes the challenges of the past in a way that maintains continuity with our basic convictions.[87] Recognizing these inadequacies and the arguments they extend from, and then proposing resolutions to these inadequacies, results in a process that MacIntyre calls "transformation."[88]

---

[83] "A living tradition then is an historically extended, socially embodied argument, and an argument precisely in part about the goods which constitute that tradition. With a tradition the pursuit of good extends through generations, sometimes through many generations." Alasdair MacIntyre, *After Virtue: A Study in Moral Theory,* 3rd ed. (South Bend: Notre Dame University Press, 2007), 222.

[84] MacIntyre, *After Virtue,* 222.

[85] MacIntyre, *Whose Justice? Which Rationality?* (South Bend: Notre Dame University Press, 1989), 355.

[86] Ibid., 356.

[87] Cf. MacIntyre: "The test for truth in the present, therefore, is always to summon up as many questions and as many objections of the greatest strength possible; what can be justifiably claimed as true is what has sufficiently withstood such dialectical questioning and framing of objections" (ibid., 358).

[88] Ibid., 355–356.

But there is another phenomenon, which MacIntyre names an "epistemological crisis." An epistemological crisis occurs when a tradition stalls in terms of its ability to resolve the problems and issues that it faces. The resources of transformation are inadequate to the new challenge. "Its [i.e., the tradition's] trusted methods of inquiry have become sterile. Conflicts over rival answers to key questions can no longer be settled rationally."[89] In such crises, the presenting issue may uncover a range of problems in the modes of reasoning that led to that point. Thus, the "dissolution of historically-founded certitudes is the mark of an epistemological crisis."[90]

The path through such a crisis is the path of conceptual innovation. This innovation must have a particular character. First, an innovation must "furnish a solution to the problems which had previously proved intractable in a systematic and coherent way."[91] Second, the conceptual innovation must explain "just what it was which rendered the tradition … sterile or incoherent or both."[92] Third, the innovation must be able to exhibit fundamental conceptual and theoretical continuity with the beliefs that had defined the tradition before the crisis.[93] A solution need not emerge linearly. In fact, a crisis and its resolution might be grasped only in retrospect.[94] But looking back the tradition will be able "to rewrite its history in a more insightful way" – a way that traces previously unrecognized threads through the long fabric of its story.[95]

What if a tradition lacks the resources within itself to innovate? What if its way of reasoning is exposed as so deeply flawed that it cannot adapt? In such a state of epistemological crisis, adherents face two options. First they can live in the crisis and wait for a solution to emerge. The risk here is atrophy. Second, a tradition that cannot innovate may continue by recognizing the cogency of an alternative tradition. This new tradition would be cogent insofar as it could offer an account of the failure of the first tradition and a demonstration of how it, the new tradition, was capable of overcoming the conceptual challenges that overcame the first tradition. But embracing a new

---

[89] Ibid., 361–362.   [90] MacIntyre, *Whose Justice?* 362.   [91] Ibid., 362.
[92] Ibid.   [93] Ibid.
[94] Ibid., 362–363. The new conceptual structure will often have required "imaginative innovation" and will be "in no way derivable from those earlier positions [i.e., the theses that were central to the tradition before the crisis]." Ibid., 362. Continuous – yes. Derivable – no.
[95] Ibid., 363.

tradition would require something like conversion, the dramatic reorganization of a person's whole life around a new conceptual world, the language of that world, its beliefs and authority structures, and the practical ways of life that correspond to the new tradition. A new tradition would place a person in a new existential location.[96] The difference between a tradition overcoming a crisis by innovation and by conversion to a new tradition is this: conversion to a new tradition admits the failure of the old tradition; innovation within a tradition admits deeply rooted problems but overcomes them while maintaining basic continuity.

We have stepped off the path of Second Temple Judaism, but we have done so only to frame the issues considered above. Second Temple Judaism is our modern term for the tradition as a whole during one long historical period. It is the tradition that exists in historical continuity with the patriarchs of Israel, the monarchies of David, Solomon, the Northern and Southern Kingdoms, the cultic leadership of priests, and the heritage of Torah, prophets, and writings that underwrite all of this. Its various streams of sects, schools, schisms, and its large center in a "common Judaism" embody various efforts to live out the logic of the tradition, and each of these efforts offers its own account of the adequacy of the tradition and the various problems that await resolution. As we have seen, one important way of relating the present life of the tradition to its past and its future – that is, one way of assessing the presence and urgency of inadequacies – was by the coordination of one's present group in the tradition with the idealized entity that names the overall tradition's origin and goal – that is, Israel. Does the Hasmonaean dynasty close the gap between the *Ioudaioi* and Israel, or does the gap remain? Does the current organization of national leadership – especially temple leadership, priesthood, and calendar – lead the people into a way of life that is congruent with its storied past and promised future? In short, where do we stand in relation to Israel?

John's vision for the future of Israel stands within this tradition. The Gospel is at pains to demonstrate continuity between Jesus and

---

[96] Ibid., 364–367. See also C. Kavin Rowe, *One True Life: The Argument of Rival Traditions* (New Haven: Yale University Press, 2016): "Short of conversion, we are literally shut out of one [tradition] by the life we live in another" (p. 204); "Each tradition argues both that the truth of all things is that which it teaches and that one has to live the tradition to know this truth. They are existentially exclusive claims of the same, universalizing sort" (p. 235).

the traditions of Scripture and Second Temple Judaism. But its continuity is, as Dahl observed, "peculiar." How then do we account for John's distance from Judaism – the fact that "the Fourth Gospel is most anti-Jewish just at the points it is most Jewish"?[97]

Many studies of John answer this question by way of history and sociology, citing the traumatic expulsion of the Johannine community from the synagogue and the resulting development of a sectarian consciousness within the community.[98] Without negating these approaches, I would like to frame John's relationship to Judaism in a way that will draw out the logic that is at work in the Gospel's approach to Israel and "the *Ioudaioi*": From the perspective of the Gospel of John, Judaism is in an epistemological crisis. For John, the true sign of crisis is Christological – the failure of the *Ioudaioi* to recognize their messiah.[99] The logic of the tradition as it stands holds no promise for the future. The tradition must innovate or face failure. John's solution – its "innovation" – is Christological. As we will see, this is why John takes up Torah, Wisdom, Moses, temple, Passover, Booths, and Hanukkah, and uses the terms "Israel" and "the *Ioudaioi*" as it does. In taking up these basic ways of configuring Jewish life and identity, John presents Jesus as the fulfillment of (and at times, the alternative to competing ways of configuring) Jewish life. In each of these moves John is casting a vision for the future of Israel, a way of closing the gap between the people's present life and the eschatological identity of God's people. John is arguing that the gap between Judaism and Israel is bridged Christologically.

---

[97] Meeks, "Am I a Jew? – Johannine Christianity and Judaism," 172.

[98] This is an important aspect of the *Wirkungsgeschichte* of the works of, among others, Martyn (*History and Theology*) and Meeks ("The Man from Heaven in Johannine Sectarianism"). For more in this vein, see Kåre Sigvald Fuglseth, *Johannine Sectarianism in Perspective: A Sociological, Historical, and Comparative Analysis of Temple and Social Relationships in the Gospel of John, Philo and Qumran*, NovTSup 119 (Leiden: Brill, 2005); Raimo Hakola, *Identity Matters: John, the Jews and Jewishness*, NovTSup 118 (Leiden: Brill, 2005); Jaime Clark-Soles, *Scripture Cannot Be Broken: The Social Function of the Use of Scripture in the Fourth Gospel* (Boston: Brill, 2003).

[99] This is widely noted but helpfully summed up in Leander Keck's "Jesus and Judaism in the New Testament," in *Why Christ Matters: Towards a New Testament Christology* (Waco: Baylor University Press, 2015), 57–72: "So in John the issue between Jesus and Judaism is not the right way to obey Moses and achieve righteousness, as in Matthew... The issue between them is Jesus himself" (p. 66). Of course, the ruins of the temple were likely an important – though in John suppressed – confirmation of this crisis.

But three qualifications are necessary. First, as an account of the crisis within Judaism and its solution in Jesus, the Gospel of John is a historically situated argument. Presupposed by the argument is the perception that there is a crisis at all – that the structures of contemporary Jewish life are fundamentally inadequate to the task of faithfully embodying a witness to the God of Israel. John recognizes that these inadequacies have not always been present. Salvation is "from the *Ioudaioi*" (John 4:22). But it resides there no longer.[100] The Gospel of John is *a late first-century argument* about how Israel might embrace its future.

Second, what John presents as fulfillment will look like supersessionism, displacement, and/or apostasy to those members of the tradition who do not accept the Gospel's account of the crisis and its innovative solution. John tells us as much (see 7:20; 8:48; 9:22; 12:42; 16:2; 19:21). Related here is the historical observation that John's account of contemporary Judaism, its problems and solutions, occurred alongside of the early development of rabbinic Judaism, which did not frame the problems facing Judaism or their solutions in terms as innovative as John.[101] It does not seem to be the case that the rabbis saw the epistemological crisis that John did.[102] Where

---

[100] See John 8:24. Consider also the words of C. K. Barrett: "The eschatological fulfillment of the biblical tradition is now at hand (ἔρχεται ὥρα, verse 21), and the disputes and privileges of Judaism are alike left behind in realization. The privileges had been real ... We worship what we know ... Hence it is salvation that proceeds from the Jews to the world at large." Barrett, "Christocentric or Theocentric? Observations on the Theological Method of the Fourth Gospel" in C. K. Barrett, *Essays on John* (Philadelphia: Westminster Press, 1982), 14–15.

[101] The many studies that trace continuity, even if it is a complex continuity, from the Pharisees to the rabbis are evidence of this. See here Shaye J. D. Cohen, *From the Maccabees to the Mishnah*, 2nd ed. (Louisville: Westminster John Knox, 2006); Shaye J. D. Cohen, "The Significance of Yavneh: Pharisees, Rabbis, and the End of Jewish Sectarianism," *HUCA* 55 (1984): 27–53. See also Philip S. Alexander, "What Happened to the Priesthood after 70," in *A Wandering Galilean: Essays in Honor of Seán Freyne*, ed. Zuleika Rodgers et al., JSJSup 132 (Leiden: Brill, 2009), 5–33; and Philip S. Alexander, "'The Parting of the Ways' from the Perspective of Rabbinic Judaism," in *Jews and Christians: The Parting of the Ways A.D. 70 to 135*, ed. James D. G. Dunn (Grand Rapids: Eerdmans, 1992), 1–26.

[102] It would be interesting, but it would not change this argument, if nascent rabbinic Judaism did conceive of such an epistemological crisis (even as early as John did) and propose its own innovation. For arguments that this could be inferred from, see Jacob Neusner, "Emergent Rabbinic Judaism in a Time of Crisis: Four Responses to the Destruction of the Second Temple" (in Jacob Neusner, *Early Rabbinic Judaism: Historical Studies in Religion, Literature, and Art* (Leiden: Brill, 1975), 34–49; Jacob Neusner, *First Century Judaism in Crisis* (Nashville: Abingdon, 1975), 48–53, 160–175; Daniel Boyarin, "Masada or Yavneh? Gender and the Arts of Jewish Resistance," in *Jews and Other Differences*, ed. Jonathan Boyarin and Daniel Boyarin

John saw the fundamental incoherence of Judaism outside of its Christological reorientation, the rabbis saw a rupture, an inadequacy, and the need to transform Jewish life based on the resources that were available to them from within their tradition.[103] The judgment of apostasy or fidelity is a theological judgment that requires an assessment of the crisis facing Judaism.

Third, we should allow this model to render the complex relationship between John and the *Ioudaioi* in the text of the Gospel. We have already observed that the terms "*Ioudaioi*" and "Israel" are not coextensive. And we have seen how one Jewish community could distance itself from another, as for example the Qumran Community embraced its identity as the center of Israel while marking itself off from the House of Judah, or in the way that the *Ioudaioi* of Jerusalem argued for the legitimacy of their temple to the *Ioudaioi* of Egypt (2 Macc). The Gospel of John belongs in this milieu. It is a Jewish text – a document that simultaneously presupposes and attempts to resolve a fundamental problem in its tradition. When Raimo Hakola argues that the Gospel of John emerges from a *Sitz im Leben* that has "passed over the boundary between being Jewish and Christian" because of the Gospel's ambivalence to various institutions of Jewish life, he has rightly noted John's ambivalence toward a particular way of organizing Jewish life, but he has missed the conceptual, theological, and sociological situation by a wide margin.[104] In its specific references to "Israel" and in its many engagements with the writings and traditions of Judaism, the Gospel of John exploits the gaps between the *Ioudaioi* and Israel because it (1) belongs to the broad

(Minneapolis: University of Minnesota Press, 1997), 306–329; Daniel Boyarin, *Border Lines: The Partition of Judaeo-Christianity* (Philadelphia: University of Pennsylvania Press, 2004).

[103] Members of the Jewish tradition (including "the *Ioudaioi*") had precedent for this: the Babylonian exile had given them a clear paradigm for navigating a crisis like the destruction of the temple in 70.

At this point, we are facing the difference between referring to John's community as a "sect" (a group that is essentially an introversionist recovery movement) and a "cult" (a group that is innovating in the direction of becoming a new religion). I find these categories imprecise for studying the text of John. Insofar as John makes an argument, it makes efforts at both recovery *and* innovation, but the nature of its innovations (e.g., its re-understanding of important symbols) must be understood in the context of its placement within the broader tradition of Judaism. For nuanced reflections on these terms in Johannine scholarship, see Fuglseth, *Johannine Sectarianism in Perspective*, 45–65, and esp. 353–374.

[104] Hakola, *Identity Matters*, 228 (here quoting Alan Segal, *The Other Judaisms of Late Antiquity* [Atlanta: Scholars Press, 1987], 31).

tradition of Judaism and its vision for Israel and (2) it is seeking an innovative solution to a perceived crisis. John reads like a text that is "beyond the boundaries of Judaism" because it is innovating, but it is doing so within the tradition of Judaism. The Fourth Gospel thus vigorously opposes the *Ioudaioi* and their particular vision for the future of Israel while simultaneously casting its own vision from within the broader tradition.[105] This is the way in which, as Daniel Boyarin has written, the Gospel of John is "a non-canonical Jewish text."[106] To place John "beyond" Judaism would represent a failure to read the text historically – that is, to place John "beyond" Judaism would be to fail to read it as an argument that is set within the particular historical, social, and epistemological conditions of late first-century Judaism.

Several conclusions follow after recognizing John's relationship to Judaism as one of engagement on the basis of an epistemological crisis. Importantly, the "trauma" of an expulsion from the synagogue, whether real or merely perceived/feared, is a necessary but not sufficient explanation for why John engages the *Ioudaioi* as it does.[107] The trauma explanation can be sketched as follows: The Johannine community felt alienated because they had been rejected by their parent-community. Therefore, the Fourth Gospel narrates the story of Jesus in order to reclaim key aspects of Jewish identity for the socially-beleaguered and psychologically-wounded community. In this vein, and in an uncharacteristic moment of

---

[105] Although originally developed to characterize Justin Martyr's relationship with Trypho, Kavin Rowe's term "dis-agreement" agreement captures well John's relationship to the *Ioudaioi*. The orthographic awkwardness reinforces the simultaneity of both agreement (same God and Scripture) and disagreement (Jesus Christ offering an ἐξήγησις of God, 1:18; Jesus as the one to whom the γραφή bear witness, 5:39). See Rowe, *One True Life,* 166–170.

[106] Boyarin, "What Kind of Jew Is an Evangelist?" 131.

[107] The main proponent of the expulsion as real is, of course, Martyn (*History and Theology*). An effort to relegate that expulsion to the symbolic world of the Johannine community is in Hakola, *Identity Matters,* 41–86. The argument of Hakola (and to an extent Reinhartz) that the Gospel manufactures fear of persecution seems strained to me. On the historical situation, see Joel Marcus, "*Birkat Ha-Minim* Revisited" *NTS* 55 (2009): 523–551.

It must also be noted that the expression "the synagogue" can be very misleading: it can mean a local place of assembly, or it can mean an emerging institution. The present study tends to avoid this term in order to prevent the inference that John means anything more than the locally organized religious community known to its readers. "The synagogue" is not shorthand for Judaism as an organized religious institution.

psychologization, Margeret Daly-Denton suggests that the Christological fulfillment of the Psalms works to "console" the Johannine
community.[108] Mary Coloe leads off her study of the temple theme
in John suggesting that the presence of temple imagery would
"soothe" the painful break between the Johannine community and
the *Ioudaioi*.[109] Gale Yee's classic study *Jewish Feasts and the Gospel
of John* argues that John's nullification and replacement of Jewish
liturgical practice extends from "much hurt and bitterness" over the
loss of those institutions "in its divorce from the synagogue."[110]

The imagery of "trauma" and even "divorce" can helpfully characterize an intense historical moment; however, such language
cannot sufficiently account for Johannine theology or even the
deployment of all of the images or themes taken up in the narrative.[111] The Gospel of John presents belief in Jesus as the innovation
that will save Judaism from its current situation of blindness
(9:39–41; 12:40), deafness (12:28–30), and being scattered among
the nations (11:52–53). Jesus is the one who can rightly orient God's
people around their Scripture (5:39–47) and give them life (20:31;
3:16–17). The Psalms, temple, and festivals all point to Jesus not
simply because of the wounds of the community but because
according to John, Jesus literally embodies the deepest logic of these
aspects of Israel's life. We will see this in much detail in the chapters
that follow. For the moment it is enough to recognize that reading

---

[108] Margaret Daly-Denton, *David in the Fourth Gospel: The Johannine Reception of
the Psalms,* AGJU 47 (Leiden: Brill, 2000), 120.

[109] Mary Coloe, *God Dwells with Us: Temple Symbolism in the Fourth Gospel*
(Collegeville: The Liturgical Press, 2001), 7.

[110] Gale Yee, *Jewish Feasts and the Gospel of John* (Wilmington: M. Glazier, 1989),
25–26.

[111] Note, for instance, that nearly all of these works follow the historical reconstruction of Raymond Brown (*The Community of the Beloved Disciple,* 36–47), who
located key Christological developments *before* expulsion from the synagogue (and
thus theological developments precede psychological developments as explanations of
social and historical conditions). For an example of the alternative from which
I dissent, see Robert Kysar, "Anti-Semitism and the Gospel of John," in Robert
Kysar, *Voyages with John: Charting the Fourth Gospel* (Waco: Baylor University
Press, 2005), 147–159. "[T]he posture of the church was that of defensiveness amid
the self-doubt of uncertain identity . . . The vitriolic attack on Judaism is nothing more
or less than the desperate attempt of the Johannine Christians to find a rationale for
their existence in isolation from Judaism" (154–155).
For recent bibliography and helpful reappraisal of this approach (one that views the
trauma *not* as expulsion but as incarnation), see Adele Reinhartz, "Incarnation and
Covenant: The Fourth Gospel through the Lens of Trauma Theory," *Int* 69.1 (2015):
35–48.

John as a "non-canonical Jewish text," and one that seeks to overcome an epistemological crisis, will lead us to prioritize the Christological claims of the Gospel as the basis for the Gospel's stance toward the *Ioudaioi*. The Gospel of John does not make strong claims against the *Ioudaioi* due primarily to a sense of alienation. It does so because a theological commitment to the future of Israel underlines what is at stake.[112]

Additionally, John's engagement with the *Ioudaioi* on the basis of an epistemological crisis renders the question of John's anti-Judaism more complex, as we have seen, and also more serious. More complex because it occurs within the banks of the tradition. More serious because it cannot be accounted for without recognizing that John's vision for the future of Israel presents Jesus as the way in which to bring the people of God into their identity as Israel while simultaneously presenting Jesus in a way that will counter an alternative vision for the future of Israel – the vision of formative Judaism. John's argument that Jesus brings near the future of Israel puts a question mark (if not an *X*) over rival visions for the future of Israel, and particularly the one represented by the *Ioudaioi*.[113] The Fourth Gospel narrates this basic theological difference between (what we call) emergent Christianity and the forms of late first-century Judaism that were coalescing into the rabbinic movement – that is, between those who seek the future of Israel in Jesus and those who seek it in a different construct.[114] The final section of this

---

[112] I hasten to add that the programmatic comments of this paragraph are intentionally framed in terms of the Gospel in its final form. I have no intention to sweep aside the insights of form- or redaction-criticism related to the Johannine community and the way in which particular aspects of the Gospel reflect back particular experiences. I do believe, however, that identifying formative contexts for individual parts is not the same thing as accounting for the narrative whole.

[113] Though writing about a different text (Galatians), Joel Kaminsky rightly notes that the establishment of an intra-Jewish context for NT polemic does not remove the challenges of these claims: "Once one recognizes that Galatians contains part of Paul's critique of Judaism, it becomes quite clear why later Christian writers felt compelled to expel the Jews. It seems that christological exclusivism creates only enough dialogue space to accommodate those Jews who abandon their religion." (Citation from Joel S. Kaminsky, review of Jeffrey S. Siker, *Disinheriting The Jews: Abraham in Early Christian Controversy, CH* 63 [1994]: 82–83.)

[114] I see this late first-century context as one marked by competing authorities. This context is also one in which the nascent rabbinic movement was probably the best-organized alternative for the challenges facing the Jewish community in Palestine. This claim draws together the works of several historians and theorists of this historical moment: Philip Alexander, "What Happened to the Priesthood after 70"; idem, "'The Parting of the Ways' from the Perspective of Rabbinic Judaism"; Daniel Boyarin,

introduction will demonstrate how John narrates this basic theological difference. We will consider John's characterization of the
Ioudaioi in order to bring into focus how the Gospel casts a vision
for the future of Israel while also implying that believers in Jesus
must resign alternative visions for Israel, specifically the vision of the
Ioudaioi.

John, the *Ioudaioi*, and the Narration of an Epistemological Crisis

The opening scenes of the Fourth Gospel (1:19–4:54) present readers
with *Ioudaioi* who are inquisitive, perplexed, and at times uncompre-
hending about Jesus. At first, the *Ioudaioi* send priests and Levites to
John the Baptist to inquire about his identity. "Who are you?" they
ask (1:19). The Baptist's witness to Jesus is unrestrained, but the
initial curiosity and lack of understanding among the *Ioudaioi* per-
sists – "Who are you?" "Why, then, are you baptizing?" (1:19, 25).
When Jesus begins to interact with the *Ioudaioi* directly in the temple
court, they do not dispute his actions, but they question his legitimacy ("What sign will you give us?" 2:18). Jesus' death and resurrection are supplied as the sign (2:19), and the *Ioudaioi* are again placed
in a position of incomprehension (2:21–22). This continues with
Nicodemus. This "ruler of the *Ioudaioi*" addresses Jesus as his first
disciples did – "rabbi" (2:2; cf. 1:38) – but Jesus' teaching about how
one might see the Kingdom of God outpaces Nicodemus' best
attempts at understanding. "How can these things be?" he asks
(3:10). For Jesus, the question represents the profound inadequacy
of Nicodemus to his role: "You are a teacher of Israel and you do
not know these things!?!"
    Questions continue to mark the interactions as Jesus moves on.
"A *Ioudaios*" (sg.) inquires about the growing popularity of Jesus'
baptisms instead of John the Baptist's (3:25–26). The Samaritan
woman tries to relate Jesus' actions to his Jewishness, but Jesus does
not fit her image of a *Ioudaios* (4:9; cf. 4:22). Galilee is then marked
out as a place in which Jesus is received (4:44–45, 54), almost to

Border Lines; idem, *Dying for God: Martrydom and the Making of Christianity and
Judaism* (Stanford: Stanford University Press, 1999); Shaye J. D. Cohen, *From the
Maccabees to the Mishnah;* Jacob Neusner, *First Century Judaism in Crisis: Yohanan
ben Zakkai and the Renaissance of Torah* (Nashville: Abingdon, 1975); E. P. Sanders,
Judaism: Practice and Belief; and Klaus Wengst, *Bedrängte Gemeinde.*

suggest (it will become more explicit later) that a person cannot simultaneously center her worship around Jerusalem and follow Jesus.[115] Together, these opening scenes characterize the relationship of Jesus to the *Ioudaioi* with a strong sense of curiosity and perplexity about Jesus, and intimations of the incompatibility of following Jesus and belonging to the *Ioudaioi*. In what follows (John 5:1–10:41), curiosity is replaced by hostility, and intimations of incompatibility become open disagreements.

A Sabbath-day healing catalyzes the antagonistic relationship between Jesus and the *Ioudaioi*, but the disagreement quickly settles on the claims of Jesus' relationship to his Father (5:16–18), the honor due Jesus (5:43–44), and the legitimacy of his work as "the one sent by God" (5:30).[116] The failure to recognize Jesus signifies that the *Ioudaioi* have never heard the voice or seen the form of God (5:38), that they do not have the love of God (5:42), that the Scriptures are opaque to them (5:39, 46–47), and that Moses is against them too (5:45). These charges challenge the coherence of the worldview of the *Ioudaioi*. This challenge continues in John 6, where the *Ioudaioi* take offense at Jesus' claim to be "the bread that came down from heaven" (6:41). Jesus quotes Isaiah – "They will all be taught by God" (Isa 54:13; John 6:45) – in order to bind up together belief in Jesus with the will of God to draw people into the truth. The rich imagery of this chapter will come under discussion later in the book, but for understanding John's position vis-à-vis the *Ioudaioi* it is enough to note here that John raises the question, "Who is 'taught by God'"? John traces the thread that runs from Moses (6:14) to Passover (6:4) to the wilderness generation (6:31) to the eschatological day of divine teaching (6:45; Isa 54:13) and the nourishment that God gives (Isa 55:1–3) – and the thread leads to Jesus. Hearing these claims is difficult (σκληρός ἐστιν ὁ λόγος οὗτος; 6:51). But the stakes at least are clear: Continuity with the Israel of the biblical past and the prophesied future can only be found by belief in Jesus. This view is crystalized in the closing words of John 5: "If you believed in Moses, you would also believe in me – for he wrote about me. But

---

[115] See W. D. Davies, *The Gospel and the Land* (Berkeley: University of California Press, 1974), 288–335.

[116] The strong overtones to Moses are relevant in Jesus' repeated references to the "Father who sent me" (John 5:23–24, 30 et passim; cf. Ex 3:13–15; 7:16; Num 16:28–29). See also Meeks, *Prophet-King*, 301–303.

if you do not believe his writings, how will you believe my words?" (vv. 46–47).

John sustains these questions and the conviction that in his own person Jesus provides continuity between the biblical past and the prophesied future of Israel for the Jewish tradition. The *Ioudaioi* seek Jesus at the Festival of Booths (7:11), and they question the source of his learning (7:15). Jesus argues for his own legitimacy even as he lodges a criticism against his opponents: "The one who speaks from himself seeks his own glory, but the one who seeks the glory of the one who sent him is true and there is no unrighteousness in him" (7:18). Having framed his conflict with the *Ioudaioi* on the basis of legitimate motives and authority, Jesus defends his action to heal on the Sabbath (7:19–24). A key turn of events happens next: many people believe in Jesus (7:31; cp. 2:23). Divisions open between the Pharisees and chief priests in leadership (7:32 = "the *Ioudaioi*," 7:35) on the one hand and the crowds and Jerusalemites who are drawn to Jesus on the other. Jesus' appropriation of the imagery of living water deepens the division between those who recognize Jesus as prophet or messiah and those who see him as misleading the people (7:40–49). Here we can see the struggle developing between Jesus and the *Ioudaioi*: Jesus' teaching comes from God; the teaching of the *Ioudaioi* comes from themselves. Jesus is the anticipated prophet and messiah; the *Ioudaioi* see him as misleading the people (7:12; cf. 7:47). Jesus claims that Scripture bears witness to him; "look and see," say the Pharisees, that Scripture marks this out as impossible (7:52).

Chapter 8 develops this further. Jesus again appropriates the imagery of the festival to himself ("I am the light of the world," 8:12). The Pharisees criticize the insufficiency of his testimony, but the exchange that ensues reveals what John understands to be the profound inadequacy of the criticism: The Torah's requirement for two witnesses is fulfilled by the Father and Jesus (8:13, 17–18). What other witnesses could one ask for? As irrational as Jesus' answer might sound, it is in fact the rejection of Jesus and the Father by the *Ioudaioi* that is, in John's view, truly absurd: Jesus' opponents are looking at God's enfleshed word and asking for a human witness. Their inability to be taught by God renders them completely inadequate to their role as leaders of the people or interpreters even of the imagery of the festival they celebrate. Next, for the second time at the festival, many believe in Jesus (8:30). But Jesus does not accept the belief unchecked. He addresses "the *Ioudaioi* who believed in him" and claims himself as the locus of true freedom. This is too much for them, and the ensuing conversation about paternity (Abraham, God, the devil; 8:33, 41, 44) moves "the *Ioudaioi* who believed in him" back into a state of disbelief.[117] The priority of Jesus over Abraham is nonnegotiable (8:56–59). For John, those who would believe in Jesus must do so entirely on his terms.

Jesus' healing of the man born blind depicts the growing rupture between Jesus and the Pharisees (9:13, 15, 40 = "the *Ioudaioi*," 9:18, 22). As in the previous scene, a division occurs within the ranks of the *Ioudaioi* (9:16). For the *Ioudaioi*, uncertainty about Jesus' origins nullifies any claim to legitimacy: "*You* are a disciple of that one, but *we* are disciples of Moses. *We* know that God spoke to Moses, but *this one*, we do not know where he is from" (9:29–30). For John, to pit Moses against Jesus is to create a false alternative. Moses precedes and bears witness to Jesus (cf. 1:17; 5:45–47). But the Pharisees/the *Ioudaioi* cling to this distinction.[118] The continuity between Jesus and the heritage of Israel becomes the sticking point. To see it, or not, is a matter of vision or blindness (9:39–40).

The healing of the blind man spills over into chapter 10. Jesus describes his own identity as "the good shepherd" in a way that draws on the rich Scriptural images of God shepherding, or providing a shepherd for, his people, and at the same time he also criticizes those who illegitimately occupy the position of leading God's people.[119] Jesus' characterization of himself as the shepherd again causes a division among the *Ioudaioi* (10:19–21). As John has shown before, however, Jesus responds to the division among the *Ioudaioi* concerning his identity not by simply embracing those who are open to him but by challenging them further. In 10:22–39, Jesus insists on the connection between his messiahship and sonship (10:25–30). If those who once received the word of God were called gods, is it

---

[117] It is hard to understand John 8 with "the *Ioudaioi* who believed in him" (τοὺς πεπιστευκότας αὐτῷ Ἰουδαίους) being understood in a pluperfect sense (i.e., the *Ioudaioi* who *had* believed but had since fallen away). John 7–10 describes various groups believing and doubting Jesus' identity, and also being divided over it, and thus it seems most likely that the characters referred to in 8:31 refer to a group of *Ioudaioi* who had begun to believe in Jesus but had done so without adequately orienting their world-view around him. For further discussion, see Hoskyns, *The Fourth Gospel* (London: Faber and Faber, 1956), 338–340; cf. Thompson, *John*, 189–194, esp. 189n178. For a reading similar to my own, see Lincoln, *Truth on Trial*, 82–83.

[118] Relatedly, the synagogue becomes the social space that signifies this distinction (9:22; cf. 6:59–60).

[119] Cf. esp. Ps 80:1–2; 2 Sam 5:2; Mic 7:14; Jer 3:15; 23:1–8; Ezek 34:1–34.

blasphemy for the one sanctified and sent into the world by God to also claim that status (10:34–36)?[120] As at Booths, so at Hanukkah, Jesus responds to the growing interest of the *Ioudaioi* by pushing their beliefs to the breaking point. In the process, they turn against him (10:39). Jesus' speech in John 10 moves from a proclamation of the inability of the *Ioudaioi* to believe ("You do not believe because you are not of my sheep," 10:26) to an appeal for them to believe ("If I am doing [the works of my Father], then even if you do not believe me, believe in the works, in order that you might know and recognize that the Father is in me and I in him," 10:38). The logic of this movement is the conviction that the only way to recognize Jesus, to come under the good shepherd, is by believing in him on his terms. Specifically, this means believing in Jesus and his relationship to the Father. The *Ioudaioi* cannot reason their way into this. One enters this hermeneutical circle by belief in the words of Jesus. In MacIntyre's terms, we can see here that only if the *Ioudaioi* are willing to accept the innovation of Jesus as the one sent by God – that is, even God's son – will they be able to grasp the coherence of Jesus as the one who will truly shepherd Israel.

The striking development in John 11–12 in terms of the relationship between Jesus and the *Ioudaioi* is that "many of the *Ioudaioi* who had accompanied Mary saw the things he did and believed in him" (11:45). In raising Lazarus, Jesus had, of course, exercised the power over life and death that the Father had given him (5:24–29, 11:21–27). What interpreters often overlook, however, is that the *Ioudaioi* who believed are those who embraced Jesus' appeal of 10:38: they saw the works and believed in Jesus and his relationship to the Father. (See esp. 11:42–43, where Jesus performs the raising of Lazarus *in the context of a prayer to his Father.*) Jesus does not rebuff these new believers. They have come to him on his terms and recognized him correctly as the son of the Father. But the threat that Jesus represents to the Pharisees is clear: If many believe in Jesus, then the Romans will "take away from us, the place [i.e., temple], and the people" (11:48). John thus offers a passing glimpse of *Ioudaioi* coming to belief in Jesus, but as soon as the Gospel presents the possibility, it also shows the Pharisees recognizing the threat that Jesus poses to life as they know it. Chapter 12 carries the narrative forward while also repeating the new elements in

---

[120] My reading here follows that of Jerome H. Neyrey, "I Said: 'You Are Gods': Psalm 82:6 and John 10," *JBL* 108 (1989) 647–663.

Jesus's relationship to the *Ioudaioi.* As they witness Jesus and Lazarus together, many are again "leaving the *Ioudaioi* and believing in Jesus" (12:11). The Pharisees look at Jesus, however, and see a man whose popularity has become a risk (12:19; cf. 11:48). As the chapter goes on, John records the inquiries of the crowd, the belief of many "rulers" and also the nature of the Pharisees' coercive power (12:42). Isaiah foresaw it all – both the particular glory of Jesus and obstinacy of the people to whom he came. But John 12 does not end on a note of the permanent rejection of Jesus by his people. Jesus cries out again, appealing for those who have seen and heard him to recognize that they have, in truth, seen and heard the Father (12:44–50).

In John 13–17, the *Ioudaioi* appear in backward glances (13:33) and in predictions that the hostilities of the present will continue in the future (15:18–16:4). They appear indirectly as Jesus' references to "the world" allude to prior interactions with the *Ioudaioi* (14:17; cf. 5:37). Once John's Passion Narrative begins, the characterization of the *Ioudaioi* continues as a major element in the narrative. Officers sent from the chief priests and Pharisees (18:3 = the *Ioudaioi;* cf. 18:12) arrest Jesus and lead him to Pilate. While the chief priests and their officials are at times specified as the actors, John slips easily into describing Jesus' antagonists as the *Ioudaioi.*[121] Yet, even as John's Passion Narrative refers to Jesus' opponents as the *Ioudaioi,* it also raises the question of the distance between Jesus and the *Ioudaioi.* "Are you the King of the *Ioudaioi?*" says Pilate to his prisoner (18:33); "Your nation and chief priests handed you over to me" (10:35); "Hail! King of the *Ioudaioi!*" cry the soldiers (19:3); "Behold, your King!" says Pilate to the *Ioudaioi* (19:14); "Jesus of Nazareth, King of the *Ioudaioi,*" writes Pilate (19:19); "Do not write, 'The King of the *Ioudaioi,*' but that *he claimed,* 'I am King of the *Ioudaioi*'" say "the chief priests of the *Ioudaioi*" (19:21). Even as John describes the *Ioudaioi* pledging allegiance to another – "Our only king is Caesar" (19:15) – he also tells the story of the crucifixion in

---

[121] N.B. John's passion narrative slips from specific descriptions of Jesus' opponents (officers of the chief priests) into labeling them "the *Ioudaioi.*" (e.g., 18:35, 36). This happens also in John 9 and 11. The Jewish leaders are the only opponents who could be meant by the term "the *Ioudaioi*" in John's passion narrative. But limiting "the *Ioudaioi*" to "the leaders," while fitting the narrative, reduces the range that is implied in 18:20 ("I always taught in the synagogue and in the temple, where all the *Ioudaioi* gather.") The *Ioudaioi* thus seem to include not just specific leaders but the movement they constitute and, therefore, the adherents to that movement.

such a way that the *Ioudaioi* cannot escape the possibility – or the irony – that Jesus is their would-be king. Why does John develop the story in this way? Is Jesus "the King of the *Ioudaioi*" or not? And how does the appellation "King of the *Ioudaioi*" square with Jesus' view of kingship (18:36–37; 6:15)? In a narrative so rife with misunderstanding, it would be a mistake to accept the words of Pilate or the *Ioudaioi* at face value. The narrative of the Gospel consistently measures Jesus' kingship in terms of Israel (1:49; 12:13) and the way in which Jesus, in his own person, embodies the deep logic and significance of the tradition's Scripture, belief, expectation, and practice. The *Ioudaioi* deny this, recognizing a different logic and significance in the same tradition's core commitments. When the *Ioudaioi* witness the crowd's acclamation that Jesus is "King of Israel" (12:13), they perhaps hear a claim that Jesus is "King of the *Ioudaioi*" *simpliciter* (12:19; 19:21). But in John's view they would be wrong to do so. Jesus' kingship can be rightly recognized only by belief in Jesus and his relationship to the Father. In John, the worldview of the *Ioudaioi* precludes this. Thus, insofar as Jesus lays claim as shepherd and teacher to the heritage of Israel and offers in himself the fulfillment of its promises and vision for the future life of God with his people, he is the king over all of those who find themselves in the same tradition and claiming the same heritage. But he is also *not* the King of the *Ioudaioi*. He is incapable of being absorbed into the preexisting worldview of the *Ioudaioi*, incapable of sharing primacy of place with Abraham or Moses. This is why, for John, belief in Jesus coincides with "departing" from the *Ioudaioi* (πολλοὶ δι' αὐτὸν ὑπῆγον τῶν Ἰουδαίων καὶ ἐπίστευον εἰς τὸν Ἰησοῦν; 12:11).

This summary shows that the characterization of the *Ioudaioi* shifts throughout the narrative of John. The *Ioudaioi* begin as inquisitive, transition to hostile, and then the hostility of some is overcome by faith. This is short-lived, however. The Pharisees and chief priests, who speak as leaders of the *Ioudaioi,* perceive in Jesus a threat to the integrity of the tradition and the very concrete forms that it takes – the people, the place, their own leadership (11:48).[122]

---

[122] Although his work has largely been dismissed because of its untenable thesis that John is a "Missionschrift für Israel," Bornhäuser's discussion of the identity of the *Ioudaioi* in John and the way that an understanding of that identity situates the conflict of the Gospel is valuable. Admittedly, Bornhäuser's treatment is at times uncomfortably polemical against those whom he reconstructs as "Thorafanatiker" (Bornhäuser, *Das Johannesevangelium*, 19–23; 139–152).

Taken together, in the account of Jesus' relationship to the *Ioudaioi*, John has narrated the alternatives that compete for the claim of representing the future of Israel. How can the people of God live in accord with Scripture? How can they experience God's presence (an especially poignant question after AD 70)? How can they weigh the insights of those who have purportedly "seen God"? How might God's people experience the realization of all that the festivals signify? What will it look like when the words of the prophets and psalmist are fulfilled? What will it look like when "they will all be taught by God"? John's presentation of Jesus presupposes these questions and places him as their answer. The *Ioudaioi* disagree about the answer, but not the questions.

In all of this, the alternatives that readers of the Fourth Gospel encounter are those that stand within the same tradition of thinking and living – they both stand within the tradition of Second Temple and late first-century Judaism. For both alternatives, the logic of the world and its basic structures are, in this broad sense, Jewish. Though they both belong to the same Jewish tradition, however, the ways in which Jesus and his followers structure their thinking and living stands at a distance from how the *Ioudaioi* and their followers would structure theirs. Thus, for John, a new linguistic and conceptual problem faces the Jewish people after Jesus. John has taken the conceptual gap that could exist between the *Ioudaioi* and "Israel," that is, between a particular historical community within this tradition and the idealized theological and historical people to whom they belong – and John has stretched the gap into a chasm. In philosophical terms, John has taken a distinction and "perfected it" – carried it through to its conceptual limit.[123] A possible incongruity (to be a *Ioudaios* need not entail a privileged position vis-à-vis "Israel") has become in John a necessary incongruity (*Ioudaios* does not correspond to "Israel"). John does not resolve the linguistic problem that this creates; nor does the Gospel take up the word

---

[123] The philosophical "perfection" of a concept has nothing to do with the morality of that perfection but rather with the way in which a person develops out a concept (or here, a distinction) to its teleological limit. For a helpful application to New Testament studies, cf. John M. G. Barclay's comments:
"Perfecting a theological motif may constitute an implicit or explicit claim to theological correctness, discrediting those who understand (and even perfect) the concept in a different way. Where such conceptual perfection is matched by social practice, it becomes the ideology of a distinctive pattern of life, and can prove enormously powerful in legitimating a religious tradition." John M. G. Barclay, *Paul and the Gift* (Grand Rapids: Eerdmans, 2015), 69.

"Christians" as an alternative to "*Ioudaioi.*"[124] Nevertheless, the Gospel creates the problem because the continuity that joins the living tradition of first-century Judaism to its foundation is at stake.

This survey of the characterization of the *Ioudaioi* in the Fourth Gospel illustrates the three implications of reading John's vision for Israel sketched in the previous section. The argument above was that John's Christology is an innovation that intends to argue for a way in which the tradition of Judaism might enter its future in continuity with its basic beliefs, traditions, and practices. Returning to those implications in light of this overview, we can see, first, that John's argument for the future of Israel is *historically situated.* It presents a vision for the future that touches down within the particular debates and points of sensitivity that belonged to late first-century Judaism. Second, John's argument for the future of Israel *looks like supersessionism, displacement, and/or apostasy to those who do not accept it.* This does not mean that John's claims vis-à-vis Judaism are inherently illegitimate. It means, rather, that the only way to state a position on John's supersessionism, displacement, and/or loyalty to the traditions of Israel is to do so by taking a theological position. Is Jesus the one sent by God or not? The one who brings Israel into its future or not? Finally, John's argument for the future of Israel *renders the relationship between believers in Jesus and the Ioudaioi more complex and serious.* Nearly everyone in the Gospel is Jewish, in the sense that they belong to the broad tradition of Second Temple Judaism. But John pushes the distinction between Jesus and the *Ioudaioi* to the point that belief in Jesus implies the reorganization of one's conceptual and linguistic (and by implication social) world away from the particular construal of the *Ioudaioi* that John knew.[125]

---

[124] Cf. Boyarin, *Dying for God* (esp. 6–19, 92, 123–124) and his correct rejection of an early "reified Judaism" (or "reified Christianity"). This perspective sheds important light on the Fourth Gospel, but also note that habits of speech guided by the Gospel of John would move in the direction of a new linguistic innovation and reification of "*Ioudaioi*" and, eventually, "Jews") as one thing and believers in Jesus as another. Jacob Neusner notes the broad linguistic challenges that this situation creates for those who inquire into this field (Jacob Neusner, "Review of *Dying for God*," *Review of Rabbinic Judaism* 6.2–3 [2003]: 379–380).

[125] Of course, what John meant for a particular, historically situated group of *Ioudaioi* has been transposed onto innumerable other Jews by Christians through the reception history of the Fourth Gospel. Insofar as a form of Christianity (or Judaism) stands in historical and conceptual continuity with this founding form of Christianity (or formative Judaism), the problem of John's characterization of the *Ioudaioi* possesses contemporary relevance. It cannot be reduced to a historical or rhetorical moment; it cannot be passed over as a "moment" of intolerance. The argument in

Conclusion

As this study now turns toward the text of the Gospel of John, it will be helpful to review the four major claims of this introduction:

1. Participation in the Jewish tradition includes debating and proposing understandings of continuity between the people of the present and their storied past and prophesied future.
2. The terms "*Ioudaioi*" and "Israel" are not inherently coextensive. Their connection is the result of a theological argument – one that was widely accepted but also contestable.
3. The Gospel of John takes up major aspects of the Jewish tradition in order to demonstrate how continuity with the past and future of Israel is achieved in Jesus. This task extends from a perceived "epistemological crisis."
4. The Gospel's specific polemics against the *Ioudaioi* represent, in John's logic, not a break with the tradition itself but with an alternative, historically embodied argument by the *Ioudaioi* about how to connect the contemporary members of the Jewish tradition to their historic and eschatological identity.

The following chapters trace the constructive claims that the Fourth Gospel makes about how Jesus opens up a future for Israel in himself. Where possible, this study will sketch how others in the Jewish tradition drew on similar texts and traditions to present their own visions for how to live in continuity with the central themes and commitments of the tradition. But a clear mirror image about what the *Ioudaioi* believed is not available for every claim John makes, so the attention in what follows will be on the Gospel of John as an argument for the future of Israel, and specifically an argument that offers an innovative solution to a tradition that is perceived to be in crisis. In all of this, it is my hope that attention to John's vision for Israel will add a layer of complexity and clarification to treatments of the Gospel of John that attempt to understand how its forceful argument worked in the past and still works today.

the Fourth Gospel between Jesus and the *Ioudaioi* is *still an argument* insofar as there is continuity between the originating and the contemporary participants in this debate. Of course, the continuity bears the complexity of 2,000 years of historical development. One hopes that the intervening centuries have taught Christians in particular to approach this argument in a way that is consonant with the fundamental claims of the larger tradition, namely nonviolently.

2

ANNOUNCEMENT: JOHN 1–4

The opening chapters of the Gospel of John characterize Jesus in terms that are rooted deeply in the biblical past and that look forward to the future foreseen by Israel's prophets. This chapter offers a close reading of several key sections in these opening chapters of John, specifically 1:1–18; 1:19–51; 2:13–22; 3:1–21; and 4:4–42. The readings offered here will show the Gospel's sustained interest in presenting Jesus as the fulfillment of Israel's eschatological expectations in a way that also grounds Jesus' significance in the major symbols and commitments of the Jewish tradition. While presenting Jesus in these ways, John's characterization of Jesus also closes down alternative visions for how God's people might be faithful to their past as they anticipate God's promised future. John presents Jesus and his significance through dense allusions, evocative scenes, and carefully constructed dialogues. As we examine John's presentation of Jesus, it will be important to keep in mind throughout the following exegesis the primary claim of this study: that John consistently portrays Jesus as the one who provides an innovative continuity that links Israel's past to its promised future.

John 1:1–18: "The Word Became Flesh"

According to John, a proper understanding of Jesus Christ begins with a reflection on the way of God's Word in the world. Although many questions about the source- and form-critical background to the prologue remain, several basic aspects of this text are clear. The prologue functions as an introduction to the character of Jesus and the plot of the Gospel.[1] Here John presents the character and

---

[1] On source- and form-critical questions, see Michael Theobald, *Im Anfang war das Wort: textlinguistische Studie zum Johannesprolog,* SBS 106 (Stuttgart: Verlag Katholisches Bibelwerk, 1983). See also Rudolf Schnackenburg, *The Gospel according to*

mission of Jesus in terms that derive from Jewish theological reflection on God's Word and God's wisdom.[2] By beginning in this way, John demonstrates the significance of Jesus Christ: To understand who Jesus is, one should view him as the enfleshed Word of God that has, like wisdom, sought a home among God's people. John thus presents a modified version of a narrative about God's wisdom in the world in order to portray Jesus as the unique revealer of God. In taking up these terms, John binds the Gospel's presentation of Jesus to several basic theological forms of expression that were available within first-century Judaism. Yet, as we will see, John also develops in a new direction these theological commitments and the narratives from which they extend. We begin by considering the broad wisdom discourse that provides a setting for John's prologue, and then we will turn to a more detailed exegesis of the prologue.

In book 2 of 1 Enoch (37–71), the seer is in heaven observing the mysteries of creation and the judgment of God. In his vision, Enoch sees wisdom. Strikingly, she does not – cannot – dwell on earth but only in heaven:

> Wisdom could not find a place in which she could dwell;
> but a place was found (for her) in the heavens.
> Then wisdom went out to dwell with the children of people,
> but she found no dwelling place.
> (So) wisdom returned to her place
> and she settled permanently among the angels.
> (1 En 42:1–2)[3]

As Enoch sees it, heaven is wisdom's home. Fountains of wisdom flow there (48:1), and they do so before the Chosen One, the Son of Man, who himself embodies wisdom (49:1–3). The abundance

---

St. John, 3 vols. (New York: Crossroad, 1981–1990), 1.224–229; Brown, *John*, I.2–4, 18–23; Boyarin, "The Gospel of the Memra"; R. Alan Culpepper, *Anatomy of the Fourth Gospel* (Philadelphia: Fortress, 1983), 86–98. Michael Theobald, *Die Fleischwerdung des Logos: Studien zum Verhältnis des Johannesprologs zum Corpus des Evangeliums und zu 1 Joh*, NTAbh 20 (Münster: Aschendorff, 1988), esp. 296–373.

[2] In the following discussion, wisdom will be put in lowercase, even where the term refers to a personified figure.

[3] Quoted from 1 (Ethiopic Apocalypse of) Enoch, trans. E. Isaac, *OTP*, vol. 1. However one resolves the text- and tradition-critical problems regarding the Similitudes, 1 Enoch's presentation of wisdom as an eschatological gift runs through the entire document, e.g., 1 Enoch 5:8, 32:3–6, 91:10–11, 93:8, 94:1–5, 99:10, 104:12–105:2.

of wisdom in heaven contrasts with its absence on earth – after searching for a home among humans, she retreated to heaven. For 1 Enoch, wisdom is absent from the earth and will remain so until the day of the Son of Man. Until then, righteous people live under the oppression of rulers, kings, and those who possess the land. The significance of the message is clear: The restored people of God will experience this wisdom in the eschatological future, but for now it remains remote.[4] Wisdom's absence reflects the distance at which Israel stands from its eschatological hopes. Importantly, 1 Enoch's presentation of wisdom's current absence and future presence dates to the same period as the Fourth Gospel.[5]

In describing the remoteness of wisdom, 1 Enoch draws on several streams of biblical tradition such as Job 28:12–28 (e.g., vv. 12–13, "But where shall wisdom be found? ... Mortals do not know the way to it, and it is not found in the land of the living") and Proverbs 1:23–33 (e.g., vv. 28–29, "...they will seek me diligently, but will not find me, because they hated knowledge [σοφίαν] and did not choose the fear of the Lord"). 4 Ezra also envisions wisdom along these lines. In 4 Ezra 5 the angel Uriel describes wisdom's retreat: In the confusion of the last days, "wisdom shall withdraw into its chamber, and it shall be sought by many but shall not be found" (4 Ez 5:9–10). The words of Ezra offer a momentary experience of this wisdom (15:45–48) but amount to nothing like the disclosure that is to come. Similar to 1 Enoch, the image of wisdom's absence in 4 Ezra likely dates to the final years of the first century.[6] In these texts, wisdom's absence reflects a judgment about the faithfulness of God's people and the eschatological conditions in which they live. To describe the inaccessibility of wisdom is to highlight the gap that separates Israel from its promised future.

In contrast to its remoteness in these texts, wisdom is an ever-present figure for Israel in other Jewish traditions. For instance, as Baruch wrestles with Israel's defeat by its enemies, the book explains the roots of the exile as the consequence of forsaking wisdom:

---

[4] My use of "remote" is indebted to Ashton, *Understanding the Fourth Gospel*, 378–383.

[5] See here E. Isaac in Charlesworth, *OTP* I.5–89; M. A. Knibb, "The Date of the Parables of Enoch: A Critical Review," *NTS* 25 (1979): 345–359; Gabriele Boccaccini, ed., *Enoch and the Messiah Son of Man* (Grand Rapids: Eerdmans, 2007), 415–491.

[6] This is *almost* transparent in the opening words of 4 Ezra 3. For further discussion, see Metzger's introduction (*OTP* I.520) and Michael Edward Stone, *Fourth Ezra,* Hermeneia (Minneapolis: Fortress, 1990), 9–10.

Hear the commandments of life (ἐντολὰς ζωῆς), O Israel;
    give ear, and learn wisdom (φρόνησις)!
Why is it, O Israel, why is it that you are in the land of your
    enemies,
that you are growing old in a foreign country,
that you are defiled with the dead,
that you are counted among those in Hades?
You have forsaken the fountain of wisdom (σοφίας).

        (3:9–12)

The close alignment of the "commandments of life" with wisdom is
critical to the logic of Baruch, which presents Israel's violation of
God's law as an abandonment of wisdom.[7] If Israel will return to the
way of wisdom, the people may reclaim the life and vocation to
which God has called them. The way of wisdom is always available
to Israel:

    [God] found the whole way to knowledge (ἐπιστήμης)
    and gave her to his servant Jacob
    and to Israel, whom he loved.
    Afterward she appeared on earth
    and lived with humankind (συνανεστράφη).
    She is the book of the commandments of God (ἡ βίβλος τῶν
    προσταγμάτων τοῦ θεοῦ),
    the law that endures forever (ὁ νόμος ὁ ὑπάρχων εἰς τὸν
    αἰῶνα).
    All who hold her fast will live,
    and those who forsake her will die.

        (3:37–4:1)[8]

For Baruch, wisdom resides among God's people in the book of the
commandments and the eternal law. God is committed to comforting his people, and their proper response is an embrace of the way of
wisdom:

---

[7] The text uses φρόνησις interchangeably with σοφία; see 3:12, 23.

[8] There are text critical problems related to Bar 3:37 See Rudolf Bultmann, "The
History of Religions Background of the Prologue to the Gospel of John," in *The
Interpretation of John*, ed. John Ashton, 2nd ed. (Edinburgh: T&T Clark, 1997),
27–41, here 31; see also Anthony Saldarini, "The Book of Baruch," *NIB* 6; ed.
Leander E. Keck (Nashville: Abingdon, 2001), 968.

Take courage, my children, and cry to God,
for you will be remembered by the one who brought this
    upon you.
For just as you were disposed to go astray from God,
return with tenfold zeal to seek him.
For the one who brought these calamities upon you
will bring you everlasting joy with your salvation.
(4:27–29)

By writing in these terms, Baruch calls Israel to conform its life to the wisdom that God has already set in its midst in the Torah. Wisdom is not only an eschatological goal for Baruch, as it is in 1 Enoch. It is an option for today. Israel's pursuit of wisdom – that is, its conformity to Torah – is its fitting response to God's own restorative work.

Baruch's presentation of wisdom echoes the viewpoint we find in Sirach.[9] In his book, Jesus ben Sirach introduces the Torah and prophets as the unique heritage of instruction and wisdom that God had given Israel. Torah and wisdom exist in harmony. Thus, after setting out his task as one that aims to instruct those who seek to live lawfully (ἐννόμως βιοτεύειν), Sirach commends the life of wisdom: "All wisdom is from the Lord (Πᾶσα σοφία παρὰ κυρίου), and with him it remains forever" (1:1). As the Torah is available to Israel, so also is wisdom.

Wisdom praises herself,
and tells of her glory in the midst of her people.
In the assembly of the Most High she opens her mouth,
and in the presence of his hosts she tells of her glory:
I came forth from the mouth of the Most High,
and covered the earth like a mist ...
Alone I compassed the vault of heaven
and traversed the depths of the abyss.
Over waves of the sea, over all the earth,
and over every people and nation I have held sway.
Among all these I sought a resting place;
in whose territory should I abide?
Then the Creator of all things gave me a command,

---

[9] Fixing a date for Baruch is difficult. On this, see Doron Mendels, "Baruch, Book of," *ABD* I.618–620; and Saldarini, "Baruch," *NIB* 6.931–933. Sirach dates in the early to mid-second century BC (see Patrick Skehan and Alexander A. Di Lella, *The Wisdom of Ben Sira,* AB 39 [New York: Doubleday, 1987], 8–10).

and my Creator chose the place for my tent (τὴν σκηνήν μου).
He said, 'Make your dwelling in Jacob, (Ἐν Ἰακωβ
κατασκήνωσον)
and in Israel receive your inheritance . . .'
and so I was established in Zion . . .
Thus in the beloved city he gave me a resting place,
and in Jerusalem was my domain.
I took root in an honored people,
in the portion of the Lord, his heritage . . .
Come to me, you who desire me,
and eat your fill of my fruits.
For the memory of me is sweeter than honey,
and the possession of me sweeter than the honeycomb . . .
All this is the book of the covenant of the Most High God,
the law that Moses commanded us as an inheritance for the
congregations of Jacob (συναγωγαῖς Ἰακωβ).

(Sir 24:1–3, 5–8, 10–12, 19–20, 23)

For Sirach, as for Baruch, wisdom's presence in Israel is nothing other than the law. This view is also taken up in Qumran literature, which records that "God has given her [i.e., wisdom] to Israel, and like a good gift, gives her" (4Q185 2:10). For Baruch, Sirach, and the Qumran community, to live in wisdom is to follow the law, and to follow the law is to embrace the life of wisdom. Considered together, we encounter in 1 Enoch, 4 Ezra, Job, Proverbs, Baruch, Sirach, and 4Q185 striking visions of the way of God's wisdom in the world.

Rudolf Bultmann, when he studied these texts, reconstructed an ancient wisdom myth, a story of wisdom's presence in the world, her frustrated efforts to find acceptance, and her eventual retreat.[10] 1 Enoch, 4 Ezra, Proverbs, and traces of wisdom's voice in other New Testament texts (e.g., Lk 11:49–51; cf. Matt 23:34–37) exemplify this myth in its classic form. Baruch and Sirach offer a development of this myth, one in which a select few (i.e., [some in?] Israel) recognize wisdom and give her a dwelling place on earth. Bultmann's efforts to reconstruct a single myth and its subsequent development moves his focus away from the specific claims of each text within the arguments of the books in which they stand. Rather

---

[10] Bultmann, "The History of Religions Background," in Ashton, *Interpretation,* 30–35. For his discussion of Luke 11 and Matthew 23, see Bultmann, *History of the Synoptic Tradition* (Oxford: Blackwell), 114–115.

than reconstructing a single myth, it is helpful to linger with one of the basic problems with which each of these texts is concerned and how the way of wisdom contributes to a theological vision of Israel. Each of these texts correlates the presence of wisdom with a vision of Israel living faithfully. In this way, reflections on wisdom's way in the world are simultaneously statements about the ability of Israel to live into its vocation. This is the case when the context is an appeal for the realignment of Israel's present life with the ways of wisdom (Baruch; cf. Sirach). It is also the case that Israel's proximity to, or distance from, its eschatological identity is in view when a text offers a vision of wisdom's current absence but future presence with the coming of the Son of Man (1 Enoch). Wisdom's retreat can reflect the way in which Israel currently lives in a penultimate condition and will require divine intervention in order to live fully into its hope (4 Ezra). Alternatively, wisdom's retreat may be the divine response to those who have spurned her ways (Proverbs). In these ways, the dwelling place of wisdom reflects the essential terms of Israel's relationship to its God. Is wisdom present in Israel? In its law? If so, then the people may live into their eschatological vocation even now. Is wisdom remote, concealed, confined to heaven? If so, then Israel's calling is to fidelity and also to patience, as the people of God await the fullness of wisdom that will come only in the last days.

This extended consideration of the role of wisdom in several important Jewish texts secures a simple but seldom-considered perspective: by echoing this tradition, John's prologue enters into a discourse concerned with the history and identity of Israel. John's entry into this discourse is particularly timely: the Gospel stands as one late first-century Jewish text among others in offering an account of Israel's situation by narrating the way of wisdom in the world. John thus taps into the basic concerns of such a discourse. Is the life of wisdom, that is, the life to which God calls Israel, available or remote? If wisdom was once far off, is it now at hand – signaling a new moment in Israel's history? As John Ashton has noted, the Gospel's answers to these questions are nuanced.[11] Even so, this nuance should not distract readers from the Fourth Gospel's eloquent and timely contribution into a discourse that is concerned primarily with the possibility of Israel's faithfulness and how it might

---

[11] See esp. Ashton, *Understanding*, 378–386.

approximate that faithfulness. John makes numerous modifications to the tradition's reflections on wisdom's way in the world, yet the prologue continues to "rhyme" with the discourses considered above and with their overarching concern to consider wisdom's presence or absence as a way of exhorting Israel into an awareness of its vocation and fidelity to that vocation. This broader discourse situates the specific concerns that the prologue evokes. For our purposes, the issue of central importance is the way in which the prologue emphasizes the continuity of Jesus Christ's identity and mission with the activity of Israel's God, or God's agent, among his people. John uses the *form* of a narrative that is concerned with wisdom's way in the world. But John fills in this form *not* with an account of wisdom but of God's Word. By beginning the Gospel in this way, the Evangelist presents Jesus in terms of his significance for the basic question of how Israel might move into its future in continuity with its past but also shifts the question of faithfulness away from the specific role of wisdom (and/or Torah) and toward the presence of God's Word.[12] Thus John begins:

1. Ἐν ἀρχῇ ἦν ὁ λόγος, καὶ ὁ λόγος ἦν πρὸς τὸν θεόν, καὶ θεὸς ἦν ὁ λόγος.

2. οὗτος ἦν ἐν ἀρχῇ πρὸς τὸν θεόν.

3. πάντα δι᾽ αὐτοῦ ἐγένετο, καὶ χωρὶς αὐτοῦ ἐγένετο οὐδὲ ἕν.

[4.] ὃ γέγονεν[13] ἐν αὐτῷ ζωὴ ἦν, καὶ ἡ ζωὴ ἦν τὸ φῶς τῶν ἀνθρώπων·

5. καὶ τὸ φῶς ἐν τῇ σκοτίᾳ φαίνει, καὶ ἡ σκοτία αὐτὸ οὐ κατέλαβεν.

John's opening words (Ἐν ἀρχῇ) signal exactly what kind of story the Gospel will tell. It is a biblical story, one that takes unto itself the title and opening words of the first book of Torah (Ἐν ἀρχῇ; בראשית; Gen 1:1) and the imagery of creation that Genesis recounts (i.e., light

---

[12] In this vein, see Luc Devillers, "Le prologue du quatrième évangile, clé de voûte de la littérature johannique," *NTS* 58.3 (2012): 317–330. N. T. Wright proposes a reading of John 1 that draws on these traditions in *The New Testament and the People of God*, Christian Origins and the Question of God, vol. 1 (Minneapolis: Fortress, 1992), 413–417.

[13] Here I follow the punctuation preferred, among others, by Brown and Theobald (see, respectively, *John*, I.6–7; *Im Anfang*, 19–21; for the alternative, see John McHugh, *A Critical and Exegetical Commentary on John 1–4*, ICC [New York: T & T Clark, 2009], ad loc.).

[e.g., Gen 1:3–4], darkness [1:2], shining [1:15], life [1:20; 2:7]). John reimagines the scene of creation but does so with the addition of a new agent, "the Word."[14] The presence of another agent at the side of God (πρὸς τὸν θεόν) and one who is, in fact, God suggests an account of creation in Genesis similar to the vision of wisdom offered in Proverbs. There, wisdom speaks: "The Lord created me as the beginning of his ways, for the sake of his works. Before the present age he founded me in the beginning" (ἐθεμελίωσέν με ἐν ἀρχῇ; Prov 8:22–23). Wisdom recounts her presence at the establishment of the earth, waters, and nations, and she appeals to her listeners for obedience and blesses those who follow her. "For my paths," she says, "are the paths of life" (αἱ γὰρ ἔξοδοί μου ἔξοδοι ζωῆς) (Prov 8:35).

John attributes to the Word the prerogatives of wisdom but does not stop there. It is never said of wisdom, καὶ θεὸς ἦν ἡ σοφία. In the broader Jewish tradition, wisdom can be the privileged witness to God, a reflection of God's divine light, a breath or emanation from God, and a mediator for God.[15] But σοφία is not a predicate for God. The case is different, however, with Jewish reflection on God's Word. In the Targums, an Aramaic-speaking stream of the Jewish tradition developed the practice of narrating God's presence among his people in terms of God's word (Memra; מימרא). Targum Onkelos to Genesis, for example, narrates the presence of the Lord in the Garden with the words, "They heard the voice of the Memra of the Lord God walking in the Garden" (3:8). Later, when God pledges to protect Abraham, the targumist substitutes the MT's "I am a shield to you" with a different pledge: "Fear not ... my Memra shall be your strength ... And he believed in the Memra of the Lord, and he accounted it to him as merit" (15:1, 6).[16] A similar pledge is echoed in Onkelos's version of Exodus 3:12: God promises

---

[14] See Theobald, *Im Anfang*, 41–42; there is precedent for this in Ps 33:6 (32:6 LXX).

[15] See, e.g., Prov 8:22–31; Wis 7:24–26; Sir 24:3. In Philo, the λόγος embodies many attributes of wisdom: for a suvery of the range of representations, see *QE* 124; *Somn.* 241; *Fug. Conf.* 41; *QE* 2.68; *Mig.* 102–103; *Fug.* 94–98, 100–101, 137–138; *Somn.* 1.228–230. On the relationship of Philo to the targumic traditions of the Memra, see Robert Haywood, *Divine Name and Presence: The Memra* (Totowa, NJ: Allanheld, Osmun & Co, 1981), 137–139.

[16] Examples could be multiplied (see e.g., Gen 9:13; 17:2; 20:3; 22:16–18). See also Moses Aberbach and Bernard Grossfeld, *Targum Onkelos to Genesis: A Critical Analysis Together with an English Translation of the Text* (New York: Ktav, 1982), 35 n7.

his presence to Moses by stating, "My Memra will support you."[17]
These examples are drawn largely from the Targum that is widely
considered to be the earliest and most conservative in its renderings
of the Hebrew (Onkelos).[18] As we will see, however, other manu-
scripts of the Palestinian Targum tradition develop the practice of
envisioning God's Word as an intermediate figure who bridges
the divide between Creator and creature, all while existing on the
Creator's side of the equation.[19]

In recent years, Daniel Boyarin has revived the argument that
Memra does more work in these texts than as a simple circumlocution for the name of God.[20] The term denotes God's immanent
presence in creation. (Note, for example, this immanence in the
examples above.) In the Palestinian Targums Neofiti and the Fragmentary Targum, God's Memra speaks (e.g., "let there be light")
and acts ("the Memra of the Lord divided between the light and the
darkness").[21] The Memra appears as an agent who at once is distinct
and yet inseparable from God. Along these lines, the targums can
gloss the divine name with the term Memra and the allusion to its
activity in creation. In the Palestinian Targums, the one who spoke
"let there be . . ." in Genesis 1:3, that is, the Memra of the Lord, is
also the God of Israel in the revelatory moment of Exodus 3:14:

> And the *memra* of the Lord said to Moses: "The One Who
> said to the world in the beginning: 'Come into being!' and it
> came into being, and Who will eventually say to it: 'Come

---

[17] Quoted from Martin McNamara, Robert Haywood, and Michael Maher,
Targum Neofiti I: Exodus and Targum Pseudo-Jonathan: Exodus, AramBib 2 (Collegeville: The Liturgical Press, 1994).

[18] For issues of dating, provenance, and other considerations relevant to drawing
on the Targums at this point, see Paul V. M. Flesher and Bruce Chilton, *The Targums:
A Critical Introduction* (Waco: Baylor, 2011); Martin McNamara, *The New Testament
and the Palestinian Targum* (Rome: Pontifical Biblical Institute, 1966); Martin
McNamara, *Targum and Testament* (Shannon: Irish University Press, 1972); Stephen
A. Kaufman, "Dating the Language of the Palestinian Targums and Their Use in the
Study of First Century CE Texts" in *The Aramaic Bible: Targums in Their Historical
Context,* D. R. G. Beattie and M. J. McNamara, ed., JSOTSup 166 (Sheffield:
Sheffield University Press), 118–141.

[19] On the dating of these texts and traditions, see Flesher and Chilton, *The Targums,*
151–166, 172, 178–200.

[20] Boyarin, "The Gospel of the Memra," 255–261; *Border Lines,* 112–127. For a
history of the question, see Haywood, *Divine Name and Presence,* 1–14.

[21] Cf. Genesis 1:3–4 in Michael L. Klein, *The Fragment-Targums of the Pentateuch
according to Their Extant Sources,* 2 vols, AnBib 76 (Rome: Biblical Institute Press,
1980). I.43 (cf. English trans. II.7); Martin McNamara, *Targum Neofiti 1: Genesis,*
AramBib1A (Collegeville: The Litrugical Press, 1992), 52–53.

into being!' and it will come into being"; and he said this to the Israelites: 'It is He, Who sent me to you.'"[22]

In another text in the Palestinian Targum, the writer uses the Passover vigil as a prompt for considering God's redeeming actions in history. Here, the Memra takes on an active role in creation and redemption, and the dramatic moments of salvation are imagined as occurring on four nights of the Memra's activity:

> A night of vigil: It is a night that is preserved and prepared for salvation before the Lord, when the Israelites went forth redeemed from the land of Egypt. For four nights are written in the Book of Memories: The first night: when the *memra* of the Lord was revealed upon the world in order to create it; the world was unformed and void, darkness was spread over the surface of the deep; and the *memra* of the Lord was light and illumination [or, and it (or "he") shone]; ... The second night, when the *memra* of the Lord was revealed upon Abraham between the pieces ... The third night, when the *memra* of the Lord was revealed upon the Egyptians in the middle of the night; His left hand was slaying the firstborn of the Egyptians and his right hand was rescuing the firstborn of Israel; to fulfill that which Scripture says, "Israel is my firstborn son." ... The fourth night: when the world will reach its fixed time to be redeemed; the evildoers will be destroyed, and the iron yokes will be broken and Moses will go forth from the midst of the wilderness and the King Messiah from the midst of Rome: this one will lead at the head of the flock, and that one will lead at the head of the flock; and the *memra* of the Lord will be between both of them; and I [i.e., not the *memra*] and they will proceed together.[23]

---

[22] See Boyarin, "The Gospel of the Memra," 259; Klein, I.164 (II.123). This reference is to the Vatican ms., of the Fragmentary Targum (FT); it agrees here with the Paris ms. (Klein, I.71; II.36).

[23] Klein, I.166–167 (the translation is Klein's, including the distinction between the *memra* and "I" in the last sentence, ibid., cf. II.126). The text also occurs in T. Neofiti. Cf. McNamara et al., *Targum Neofiti 1: Exodus, 51–53;* McNamara, *Targum and New Testament: Collected Essays,* WUNT 2/279 (Tübingen: Mohr Siebeck, 2011), 441. See also Bruce Chilton, *Targumic Approaches to the Gospels: Essays in the Mutual Definition of Judaism and Christianity* (Lanham: University Press of America, 1986), 113–135. For an exhaustive study, see Roger Le Déaut, *La nuit pascale: Essai sur la*

This text depicts the Memra as the initial revelation of God. It is the Memra that is the object of the verb (it *was revealed*). In contrast to the Targum on Exodus 3:14, the Memra is not depicted as the speaker who said, "Come into being," but instead as identical to the light of creation ("the *memra* of the Lord was light"). It is important to observe that these usages of Memra in the Palestinian Targum do not add up to a systematic account of the role of the Memra.[24] But in these texts, and in usages of the Memra more broadly, the transcendent presence of God is distinguished from the immanent presence of God and, as Boyarin rightly notes, if the term Memra has any significance at all, then its significance is the way in which it enabled people within the Jewish tradition to affirm God's real presence in the world in a form that was continuous with but not identical to God's transcendent self.[25]

Thus, the preference for defining Memra as a circumlocution (e.g., Strack-Billerbeck and G. F. Moore) should not stand. The issue at stake is not, *Did Aramaic-speaking participants in the Jewish tradition posit a hypostasis and then write that hypostasis into the various Targums?* but rather *What view(s) of God does use of the Memra allow? Do distinct ways of speaking about God's transcendence and immanence create the conceptual conditions that allow for thinking/ speaking of the Memra as a mediator/deuteros theos/hypostasis, particularly when certain other texts (Dan 7, 1 Enoch) enable these ways of thinking about God?*[26]

The traditions considered above offer a suggestive Jewish theological context from which to consider John's prologue as a text that draws on and develops the conceptual possibilities from this broader tradition. Seen from within this stream of the tradition, the striking claim of John 1:1–5 here *is not* the existence or creative activity of God's Word, but rather the repeated mention of the

signification de la Pâque juive à partir du Targum d'Exode XII 42, AnBib 22 (Rome: Pontifical Biblical Institute, 1963).

[24] For discussion of the identity of the *Memra*, see Haywood, *Divine Name and Presence*, 1–26.

[25] Boyarin, "Gospel of the Memra," 255.

[26] Cf. Alan Segal's view regarding the rabbinic ambivalence toward the term Memra: "The best we can say is that ideas like this [i.e., *memra, shekhina, yekara*] might have been seen as heretical in some contexts. More importantly, they certainly formed the background out of which heresy arose." Alan Segal, *Two Powers in Heaven: Early Rabbinic Reports about Christianity and Gnosticism* (Leiden: Brill, 1977; reprint, Waco: Baylor University Press, 2012), 183.

uniqueness of the Word in relation to God.[27] No Targum emphasizes (or argues for) the simultaneous proximity and distinctiveness
between God and the Word in the way that the prologue does. John
emphasizes the nearness of the Word to God (πρὸς τὸν θεόν), and
John underlines that nearness by means of a poetic repetition of
claims that were thoroughly Jewish, though (as far as we know)
not a point of common theological development. To lose John's
poetry but to underline its point, the opening words of the prologue
might be paraphrased thus:

> In the beginning was the Word – the one you have heard
> about and that you know of as the Word that spoke at
> creation, to Abraham, to Moses, to Israel[28] – and the Word
> was very close to God. And the Word *was* God. This Word
> was, in the beginning, *with* God.[29] All things came to exist
> through it. Without it, not one thing that exists has come to
> pass. That which was in it was life, and this life was the light
> of humankind. The light is shining in the darkness, and the
> darkness has not grasped it.[30]

The persistent focus of the prologue here is on the distinctiveness of
the Word, how it relates both to God and to creation in such a way
that, as Bultmann observed, in the Word "God is really encountered,
and yet ... God is not directly encountered."[31] For John – like the
targumist who envisioned the Word of the Lord present on the nights
of creation, Abraham's covenant, Israel's Exodus, and the Messiah's
advent – the identity of the Word is bound up with God's act of
creation, ongoing presence in the world, and the covenant of God to
Israel. As the Memra called forth light and living creatures in the
Targum, so also the prologue describes the Word as the source of
light and life. The shift into the present tense connects this storied

---

[27] This characterization is one of the more compelling reasons to stake one's claim
with traditions related to the Memra, rather than with a more general account of
God's Word or Wisdom.

[28] For similar connotations accompanying the term Memra, cf. Neotifiti I on
Genesis 1:1: "In the beginning, before the material world was created, there existed
the Word of God, the Compassionate, the All-merciful."

[29] See de la Potterie's elegant translation: "Le Logos était tourné vers Dieu" (de la
Potterie, L'emploi de eis dans S. Jean et ses incidences theologiques,' *Biblica* 43.3
[1962]: 379–384).

[30] Several of the phrasings in this paragraph are indebted to McHugh's commentary (*John*, 5–20).

[31] Bultmann, *John*, 34.

past to the community's present: "The light (of the Word) is shining in the darkness, and the darkness has not grasped it."

The introduction of John the Baptist in 1:6–9 strengthens the connection of the work of the Word to the community's present. The Evangelist introduces John with a familiar biblical idiom, "there was a man sent from God" (cf. "there was a man from Zorah," Judg 13:2, see also Judg 19:1, 1 Sam 1:1).[32] In place of a geographical origin, however, the Evangelist states John's divine commission. The entire work of John is characterized as one of bearing witness to the light in order that all might believe because "the true light – the one that gives light to all people – was coming into the world" (1:9). To follow the logic of the prologue, then, is to recognize John the Baptist as the privileged witness to one who was present at creation and who has been shining in the darkness ever since.

Importantly, there is strong continuity between creation and salvation in John 1:1–9. The Word that shines in the world is the Word of Israel's God, the Word whose history intersects specifically with the people of God in moments of creation, covenant making, instruction, and deliverance. This Word is the source of life and light. Because the Gospel draws on a rich scriptural and theological context for the Gospel's presentation of the Word in these opening verses, the specific character of the Word as the bearer of life and light should be considered in terms of this same context. In Scripture, the Lord is the creator of life and the giver of eschatological life (cf. Ezek 37; Dan 12:2).[33] Light is the eschatological gift of God and a sign of Israel's deliverance: As the psalmist declares, "With you is life's fountain, in your light, we see light" (Ps 36:9 MT).[34] Or as Isaiah exhorts Israel, "Arise, shine, for your light has come … darkness shall cover the earth … but the Lord will arise upon you; his glory will appear over you" (Isa 60:1–2);[35] "The people who walked in darkness have seen a great light; those who lived in a land

---

[32] Bultmann (*John*, 48–49) helpfully notes the source-critical implications of the presence of Hebraism at this point. See also Brown, *John*, I.27–28; McHugh, *John*, 21–22.

[33] Cf. John McHugh, "In Him Was Life," in *Jews and Christians: The Parting of the Ways A.D. 70–135*, ed. James D. G. Dunn (Tübingen: J.C.B. Mohr, 1992), 123–158.

[34] Later writers would explicitly connect the Law with this imagery – e.g., CD 6:4–5.

[35] Quoting here from the MT. Cp. the specification of Jerusalem in the LXX: Φωτίζου φωτίζου, Ιερουσαλημ, ἥκει γάρ σου τὸ φῶς.

of deep darkness (LXX: "in death's darkness") – on them light has shined" (Isa 9:1 MT).

For a reader who is attending to the biblical context of these images, the witness of John the Baptist to the light possesses the specificity of such scriptural visions. The light that is coming is the light of Israel's God. It is for all people (πάντα ἄνθρωπον), but it comes through the blessing and deliverance of Israel.[36] It is not the case that the witness of the Baptist is broader than Israel in the prologue and then exclusive to Israel in the subsequent narrative, where John states, "I came baptizing with water that he might be revealed to Israel" (1:31). While the emphasis of the prologue is on the significance for all people of the Word's way in the world, the imagery is consistent with the broader biblical expectation that through the blessing of Israel the entire world will be blessed. The Evangelist knows, of course, that not all of Israel recognized the Word, and it is that story to which the prologue now turns.

In vv. 10–13, the Word undertakes a journey similar to the path of wisdom summarized above.[37] Though the Word is the source of all things, its presence in the world is unrecognized. ("Then wisdom went out to dwell with the children of people, but she found no dwelling place" [1 En 42:2].) Even the presence of the Word in its own territory (τὰ ἴδια) and people (οἱ ἴδιοι) is largely ineffective. (Contrast Sir 24:8: "... my Creator chose the place for my tent [κατέπαυσεν τὴν σκηνήν μου]. He said, 'Make your dwelling in Jacob [κατασκήνωσον], and in Israel receive your inheritance.'") But instead of retreating when it is not recognized or received, the Word persistently seeks a dwelling place: "But to as many as received him – to those who believe in his name – he gave to them the ability to become children of God" (1:12). John's vision for the way of God's Word in the world does not follow here the storyline considered above wherein wisdom is either available or remote. The Word does not find a home among its own people, but neither does it retreat. It will not be equated with the law, nor will it be locked up out of human reach. For John, the light of the Word is present (v.10) but unrecognized except by the children of God (v. 12).

---

[36] The abundance of "light" imagery in the Old Testament, and the marked increase of this imagery in Isa 40–55, supports this. See, e.g., Isa 2:25; 51:4, Zech 14:6–19.

[37] The parallelism between the λόγος in John and σοφία in wisdom traditions accounts for why some commentators see vv.10–12 as a narrative about the Word's actions *before* the incarnation. Cf. McHugh, *John*, 17, 31–32.

Belonging to the "children of God" (τέκνα θεοῦ) results from divine begetting (οἳ . . . ἐκ θεοῦ ἐγεννήθησαν, v. 13). Alan Culpepper has ably demonstrated the rich resonance of John's phrase "children of God" with biblical and other Jewish texts. "You are sons of the Lord your God" (Υἱοί ἐστε κυρίου τοῦ θεοῦ ὑμῶν; בנים אתם ליהוה אלהיכם, Deut 14:1), says Moses to Israel.[38] He speaks God's word to Pharaoh, "My firstborn son is Israel" (Ex 4:22). A strong tradition of Jewish interpretation takes up this language of Israel as the child of God. But John stands in a stream of Judaism that understands the children of God in primarily ethical rather than simply ethnic terms – not in a way that would exclude ethnic Israel, but in a way that identifies the key element of belonging to Israel in a person's way of life. This is obviously the case in 1 John, which uses ethics to identify people as children of God or the devil (e.g., 1 John 3:10). It is also on display in John's assertion that it is those *who do* the truth (ὁ δὲ ποιῶν τὴν ἀλήθειαν) who show that their deeds are done in God (John 3:21). Beyond John, the first Christians were eager to articulate this view. Thus Paul writes, "Those who are 'by faith' are children of Abraham" (Gal 3:7). And John the Baptist says in Luke, "Do not begin to say among yourselves, 'We have Abraham for a father.' For I tell you that God is able to raise up from these stones children for Abraham (τέκνα τῷ Ἀβραάμ)" (Matt 3:9; Luke 3:8). Others within the broader Jewish tradition articulated a similar view. The Qumran community emphasized the moral aspect of sonship: "In the hand of the Prince of Lights is dominion over all the sons of justice; they walk on paths of light. And in the hand of the Angel of Darkness is total dominion over the sons of deceit; they walk on paths of deceit . . . The God of Israel and the angel of his truth assist all the sons of light" (1QS 3.20–25). The Babylonian Talmud, although it ultimately opposes such a view, records a similar viewpoint from two teachers: "How do they interpret the verse, 'Ye are sons [etc.]'? . . . When you behave as sons you are designated sons; if you do not behave as sons, you are not designated sons" (*b.* Kidd 36a).[39]

Like these others, the earliest believers in Jesus found precedent for this view in Scripture itself, particularly in moments in which Israel's sin jeopardizes its sonship. Thus, Moses denies the sonship of Israel due to idolatry when he says, "blemished children, not his (οὐκ

---

[38] The use of υἱός in the LXX should not obscure that both υἱός and τέκνον render the Hebrew term בן. See Culpepper, "Pivot," 17–19.

[39] For further discussion, see Culpepper, "Pivot," 20–23.

αὐτῷ τέκνα/לא בנ‏), have sinned ... Do you thus repay the Lord these things?" (Deut 32:5–6). Hosea insistently refers to God's people as "sons of Israel" (τέκνα/בנים) while also placing the privilege and status of sonship in the balance of God's judgment (cf. Hos 1:8–11, 3:4–4:6). Yet, while unfaithfulness endangers Israel's sonship, Israel's restoration is envisioned as the restoration of the children of God.[40] Hosea implores Israel to return to the nurturing care of the one who called his children (τὰ τέκνα αὐτοῦ/בני‏) out of Egypt (Hos 11:1). The book of Isaiah begins with a declaration of sonship lost: "I begat children (υἱοὺς ἐγέννησα) and raised them up, but they rebelled against me" (1:2).[41] Later, when Isaiah envisions the restoration of the people to the land, he pictures Mt. Zion as a woman observing the gathering of sons and daughters in her midst and then asking, "Who has begotten me these (Τίς ἐγέννησέν μοι τούτους)?" (Isa 49:21; cf. 49:18). Within the arc of Isaiah's prophecy, the answer is clear: God has begotten them. Jeremiah also envisions the restoration of Israel and Judah as a restoration to Israel of the status of children of God: "I will make you as children (τάξω σε εἰς τέκνα)... You will call me Father and will not be turned away from me" (Jer 3:19 LXX; cf. 3:21). Standing in line with this scriptural vision, John's prologue presents belief in the Word as a divine begetting into a new relationship, particularly the relationship that Scripture envisions for Israel at the moment when God will restore its fortunes and the people may reclaim their status as the children of God.[42]

Following on this striking promise, the prologue continues by specifying the way in which the Word came into the world and in which belief and divine begetting become possible. These nine words encapsulate the innovation that John proposes for the Jewish tradition: Καὶ ὁ λόγος σὰρξ ἐγένετο καὶ ἐσκήνωσεν ἐν ἡμῖν (v. 14a).[43] Going beyond the traditions about the Memra, John claims that the Word crossed the ontological divide that separates the Creator from creation. The Word of God, the Word that *is* God, became human

---

[40] For a full discussion of this, see John A. Dennis, *The Death of Jesus,* 278–284.

[41] The MT's "I reared and brought up" (בנים גדלתי ורוממתי) offers a clear hendiadys where the LXX opts for a more sequential logic (I begat and brought up).

[42] Note how the Septuagint moves in this direction as it pluralizes "son" into "sons/children." Cp. Schnackenburg (2.350 [writing on John 11:52]): "It is not the tribes of Israel who are to be gathered out of the dispersion, but the 'children of God.'" If one reviews the prophecies of Isaiah, Jeremiah, and Hosea, it becomes clear that Schnackenburg is laboring to establish a distinction where there is no difference.

[43] This point is also stressed by Boyarin ("Gospel of the Memra," 261).

flesh. Going against the wisdom traditions that could view the Torah as the encapsulation of divine wisdom dwelling in Israel, and going beyond the presentation of the Memra as the immanent presence of God in the targums, John presents the journey of God's Word in the world as one that comes to rest in the incarnate Word dwelling among God's people.

John's phrase, "he dwelled among us," suggests also that in the Word God acts to fulfill a further set of biblical promises. In particular, ἐσκήνωσεν ἐν ἡμῖν evokes a biblical tradition about God's presence in Israel beginning with the tabernacle. God commands Moses: "Build for me a sanctuary, and I will dwell in the midst of them [ושכנתי בתוכם] (Ex 25:8).[44] This promise, "I will dwell in the midst of you" (or "of them" or "of the children of Israel") is restated at the conclusion of Moses' instructions for the tabernacle (Ex 29:45–46). It is spoken to Solomon at the construction of the temple (1 Kings 6:13). After the exile, Ezekiel's vision of the new temple comes with a renewal of the promise: "I will dwell in the midst of the children of Israel . . . I will dwell in their midst forever" (Ezek 43:7, 9). Zechariah also envisions the day of restoration as one in which God reinstates his dwelling among the people: "Sing and rejoice, O daughter Zion! For lo, I will come and dwell in your midst (ושכנתי בתוכך), says the Lord. Many nations shall join themselves to the Lord on that day, and shall be my people; and I will dwell in your midst (ושכנתי בתוכך)" (Zech 2:14–15; cf. 8:3). John's language evokes these, and other, visions of God's past and future presence among his people.[45]

When considered within the dual streams of the wisdom tradition and the targumic Memra, John's claim "The Word became flesh and dwelt among us" offers a stark alternative to the narratives of God's wisdom dwelling (κατασκηνόω) in Israel as the law of Moses (Sir 24:8, 23) or as an inaccessible heavenly reality (1 En 42:1–2). In contrast to these depictions, John presents the Word dwelling

---

[44] Cp. LXX: "Make me a sanctuary, and I will be seen among you (ὀφθήσομαι ἐν ὑμῖν)."

[45] These examples of *to dwell + in the midst (of you/them)* are those that closely correspond to John's phrasing. If one were to cast the net more broadly and consider the idea of God dwelling within Israel, then the root שכן (κατασκηνόω/κατοικέω) would offer common ground to the variety of expressions that are used in MT and LXX to express this expectation (see, e.g., Pss 74:2; 135:21; Jer 7:3, 7; Joel 4:17 MT; Ezek 37:27); other formulations express the same hope (e.g., Zeph 3:15, "the Lord is in your midst" [ἐν μέσῳ σου/בקרבך]). For related images, see e.g., Lev 26:12; Rev 21:3; 2 Cor 6:16–18.

among people in human flesh – in the inescapable simplicity and frailty of "sheer humanity."[46] As a use of the Memra, the prologue's formulation of the Word becoming flesh is unprecedented. But it accomplishes two purposes for John. First, it binds the incarnation of the Word to the fundamental biblical images that describe the relationship between God and Israel, particularly the relationship that God will bring about in the last days. In the Word-become-flesh, God has fulfilled Scripture's promise that he will dwell in the midst of his people. Again, as described above, in the Word-become-flesh, the eschatological re-gathering (or "begetting") of God's children is taking place.[47] And finally, the life and light that God promised his people at their restoration have now become available. The enfleshing of the Word, as it is both identifiable with God and yet distinct from God, allows John to set these claims before his readers and to insist that these eschatological promises are now present realities due to the human life of the Word of God in the midst of its people.

A second implication of John's claim that the Word, the Memra, became flesh, is that it allows John to present the revelation of God in Jesus in a term that has theological priority over the Torah. In the Fragmentary Targum to Genesis 2, for example, the Memra of the Lord "took Adam and confined him to the Garden of Eden in order to toil in the [study of the] Torah and to keep its commandments."[48] After the Fall, the Memra of the Lord establishes the Torah as the means for mortal humans to partake of the fruits of the tree of life and thus to prepare for the life to come.[49] In Deuteronomy, the Memra of the Lord gives the Torah to the Israelites, and when they receive it the Israelites respond by saying, "Everything that the Memra of the Lord speaks, we shall do, and we shall accept."[50] The Palestinian Targum thus presents the Torah as extending from

---

[46] Bultmann, *John*, 63.

[47] Cf. Isaiah Targum 49:15, 18, 21: "Is it possible that a woman can forget her son ... Even if these may forget, my Memra will not reject you ... Lift up your eyes round about, O Jerusalem, and see all the sons of the people of your exile ... Then you will say in your heart, 'Who has brought me these?'" Quoted from Bruce D. Chilton, *The Isaiah Targum*, AramBib 11 (Wilmington: Michael Glazier, Inc, 1987), 97–98. See also Gal 4:29–31.

[48] Ibid., P. Gen 2:15; V. 2:15. T. Neofiti contains the same commitment to Torah but the Memra is referred to only in the margin (where it would replace "the Lord God." T. Onkelos makes no reference to either Torah or Memra.

[49] See Klein, *Fragment-Targum,* (P) Gen 3:24, II.8; cf. also the expansions of these ideas in the text of the Vatican ms. on the same passage (II.91–92).

[50] Ibid., P Deut 33:3 (II.87–88) and cf. V Deut 33:2 (II.187–188), and T. Neofiti (Deut 33:2). This expansion is lacking in T. Onkelos.

and witnessing back to the Memra of the Lord. There is no tension, no competition, in these texts between Torah and Memra. The Memra is the source of the Torah; it gives the Torah through Moses.[51] For a tradition that organized its thinking and living around the Torah, the claim that God's Word, the Memra, had "become flesh and dwelt among us," would have profound epistemological, hermeneutical, and ethical implications. To put it simply, the Torah's existence and theological witness would need to be rethought it terms of a particular person. This is, of course, the claim that John makes. Those who recognize Jesus see in him the one about whom Moses wrote in the law – and the prophets too (1:45). Those who search the Scripture for life, and who place their trust in Moses, should recognize Jesus as the one to whom Scripture bears witness (5:39, 45–46). The theological priority of Memra over Torah in the targums provides a valuable analogy for John's argument about how Scripture bears witness to Jesus.[52]

A cascade of biblical references follows John's declaration that "the Word became flesh and dwelt among us." The first, "we have seen his glory" (1:14b), records the community's experience of Jesus in language that draws on the revelation of the Lord to Israel. The children of Israel, and particularly Moses and Aaron, witnessed the glory of the LORD in the wilderness (Ex 16:10), at Sinai (24:17), and at the completion of the tabernacle (40:28–29). As with the images considered above, God's past presence informs the expectation for God's future presence. Isaiah prophesied a day in which, "The people shall see the glory of the Lord" (35:2) and "The glory of the Lord shall appear" (40:5). In the climactic chapters of Ezekiel's vision, the prophet saw "the glory of the Lord" take up residence in the new temple in the same context in which he described the Lord dwelling in the midst of the people (43:4–5).

The prologue describes the glory of the enfleshed Word as the glory of one who is "full of grace and truth" (1:14).[53] This latter formulation continues John's pattern of describing the Word's

---

[51] Cf. T. Onkelos Lev 26:46: "These are the statutes and judgments and laws which the Lord appointed between His Word [Memra] and the sons of Israel, in the mountain of Sinai, by the hand of Mosheh." (Etheridge trans.)

[52] My choice of "analogy" is intentional. I do not claim that John depended on a targum, but I do claim that the precedent of Word over Torah in John is paralleled in the roughly contemporary conceptualities within the targum.

[53] On μονογενής: I follow Brown (*John*, I.13–14) and McHugh (*John*, 58–59); See also Büchsel "μονογενής," *TDNT* 4.737–741.

presence in terms that derive from Israel's experience of God's presence in the wilderness. Here the allusion is to the self-declaration of God's name in Exodus 34:6: "The Lord, the Lord, a God compassionate and gracious, slow to anger, and great in steadfast love and truthfulness." John does not take up the Septuagint's rendering of God's character (i.e., καὶ πολυέλεος καὶ ἀληθινὸς/cp. ורב־חסד ואמת) but instead describes the Word as "full of grace and truth" (πλήρης χάριτος καὶ ἀληθείας). This preference for the term χάρις over πολυέλεος renders uncertain John's goals with this phrase. If John wants to draw a direct connection between the Word and the God of Israel at this critical moment of self-revelation, why does the prologue offer an independent translation at this point?

There are numerous reasons to hold that John 1:14 echoes Exodus 34:6, but also that John's echo is intentionally indirect. On the likelihood that John choses to echo Exodus 34:6, we should note that although the Septuagint regularly translated ἔλεος for the Hebrew חסד, this translation was eventually contested, and later Greek translators opted to depart from the Septuagint practice and use χάρις in translating חסד.[54] (Though it is important to note that there is no textual evidence of Exodus 34:6 being brought into Greek with the term χάρις, thus the textual tradition makes this possible, but not inevitable.) In addition to the Greek textual tradition coming to embrace χάρις as a translation of חסד, we should also note that the targums occasionally offer טב (=good/goodness) as a translation for חסד in moments where the Greek rendering of "mercy" would be inadequate to the context.[55] But beyond the evidence that χάρις existed as an apt and available term for translating חסד, there are further reasons to read John's πλήρης χάριτος καὶ ἀληθείας as an invocation of this solemn declaration from Israel's past. John's broader context supports this when, in 1:18, John records that "no

---

[54] Lester Kuyper, "Grace and Truth: An Old Testament Description of God, and Its Use in the Johannine Gospel," *Int* 18 (1964): 3 n1. For LXX texts that use χάρις to translate חסד, see Esther 2:9, 17, although this happens also in Sirach 7:33, 40:17. Edward Schillebeeckx cites Symmachus (e.g., 2 Sam 2:6), Theodotian (Prov 31:26), and Philo as translations/writers who prefer χάρις to ἔλεος in passages where the LXX opts for ἔλεος. See Schillebeeckx, "New Testament Theology of the Experience of Grace" in *Christ: The Christian Experience in the Modern World, Collected Works of Edward Schillebeeckx*, vol. 7 (London: Bloomsbury, 2014), 75–101, esp. 94. See also Alan R. Kerr, *The Temple of Jesus' Body: The Temple Theme in the Gospel of John*, JSNTSup 220 (Sheffield: Sheffield Academic Press, 2002), 117–119.

[55] E.g., Psalms Targum (Ps 36:11). For further discussion, see James A. Montgomery, "Hebrew Hesed and Greek Charis," *HTR* 32 (1939): 97–102.

one has ever seen God." As A. T. Hanson points out, this statement is very likely a reference to Exod 33:18–20, which records Moses' request to see God's glory, and the response that "no one can see my face and live."[56] John 1:14–18 is concerned with exactly the same problem: the vision of God and the revelation of glory that comes from God. More immediately to John 1:14, the clear designation of the Word as truthful relates directly to both the Hebrew and Greek descriptions of God's character in Exodus 34:6. John's πλήρης captures the Hebrew רב ("great") and allows it to govern both qualities of God's character. This is lost in the Septuagint's πολυέλεος.

Most importantly, the effort to identify John's χάρις as an independent translation likely owes something to the obvious preference among the earliest believers in Jesus for descriptions of their experience of God, and particularly Jesus Christ, with the word "grace."[57] If this is the case for John, then the prologue witnesses a moment of daring poetic freedom: The Word is God, is near to God, is from the Father. Like the Lord in the wilderness, the Word dwells among his people, and they see his glory. But the disclosure of the Word has also exerted pressure on the Bible's traditional formula for describing the character of God. For this reason – and in a way that tracks with other early believers in Jesus – John creates room for the particular Christian experience of God's covenant love and faithfulness to his promises in Jesus Christ by employing a word that was increasingly capable of expressing the early Christian experience of God's action through Jesus Christ: "grace." And John then boldly inserts this fully scriptural but also particularly Christian shorthand into Scripture's solemn declaration of the Lord's identity by replacing πολυέλεος with χάρις. A first-century hearer of this text who was familiar with the Septuagintal disclosure of God's name in Exodus 34 might have been startled by John's willingness to insert the "wrong" word at this place. For John, however, χάρις is a "wrong" word, but it is in exactly the right place.[58]

---

[56] Cf. A.T. Hanson, "John 1:14–18 and Exodus XXXIV," *NTS* 23.1 (1976): 90–101.

[57] Here I am developing a suggestion in Thompson, *John*, 34.

[58] For an account of this use of Scripture, cf. E. D. Freed's comments: "In every instance his quoted text appears to be adapted to its immediate context, to his literary style, and to the whole plan of the composition of his gospel ... His method presupposes and reveals a thorough training in the Jewish scriptures and tradition and a thorough knowledge of their content." E. D. Freed, *Old Testament Quotations the in the Gospel of John*, NovTSupp 11 (Leiden: Brill, 1965), 129. See also Jörg Frey, "Wie Mose die Schlange in der Wüste erhöht hat..." in Frey, *Die Herrlichkeit des*

After another description of John the Baptist's testimony to Jesus, the prologue continues to witness to the glory of the Word: "We have all received from his fullness, grace in place of grace" (1:16). The reference to the fullness of the Word (ἐκ τοῦ πληρώματος αὐτοῦ) refers back to the glory of the Word, "full of grace and truth" (πλήρης χάριτος καὶ ἀληθείας, v. 14). The experience of the enfleshed Word and the vision of it constitute for this community an encounter that is analogous to the revelation of the Lord to Moses on Mt. Sinai. But it is also more. For if the revelation of God to Moses was grace, then the grace John speaks of exceeds it as "grace in place of grace."[59]

If John is still working in terms derived from Exodus 34, then it is likely that Moses' pleas for God to show favor (χάρις) to him and to the people of Israel in Exodus 33–34 offer a helpful background to John's χάριν ἀντὶ χάριτος (1:16).[60] In the immediate context of Exodus, the Lord demonstrates grace in the declaration of his name and revelation of his glory to Moses (33:12, 13, 16, 17); he also demonstrates grace in the covenant that he makes with the people (34:9–10). These past acts of grace are the foundation of John's understanding of grace. The grace of seeing and dwelling with the enfleshed Word of God corresponds to these experiences of grace given to Israel. Yet insofar as the grace of the enfleshed Word is immediate and direct, visible instead of veiled, the present experience of grace stands in place of the former. John does not deprecate the grace of the past – indeed, it is *grace*. In agreement with many witnesses in Scripture, however, John considers the grace of the past neither final nor ultimate but rather typological. For John, the fullness of God's gracious self-revelation to Moses and biblical Israel was genuinely gracious but also penultimate, and it has found a fulfillment in the experience of the enfleshed Word.

John goes on to qualify the way in which the present grace stands in place of the former: "For the Law was given through Moses, grace and truth came through Jesus Christ" (1:17). John's word choice, "it was given" (ἐδόθη) upholds the divine source of the Torah and

Gekreuzigten, WUNT 2/307 (Tübingen: Mohr Siebeck, 2013), 89–145 (esp. 130–140, 143–145).

[59] On this translation of ἀντί, see McHugh, *John*, 64–67; Brown, I.15–16; Gerald Wheaton, *The Role of Jewish Feasts in John's Gospel*, SNTSMS 162 (New York: Cambridge University Press, 2015), 13–82.

[60] Note, for instance, the density of usages of the terms χάρις/חן in Ex 33:12, 13, 16, 17; 34:9.

therefore resists an antithetical relationship between Moses, Torah, and Jesus Christ.[61] What John does insist on, however, is that the fullness of God's revelation, that is, of "grace and truth," is present in Jesus Christ. If John has been echoing God's self-declaration in Exodus 34:6, then the emphasis of John's claims here must fall on the availability of God's gracious presence among his people in Jesus Christ.[62] The Torah necessarily stands in a secondary position to this revelation of God's self-identity. From the perspective of John, the revelation of grace and truth in Jesus Christ brings with it a climactic experience of the fulfillment of promises that stretch from Exodus to Ezekiel. In the enfleshed Word – that is, in Jesus Christ – the glory of God now dwells among his people. God's promises to Israel have been realized. From this perspective, the secondary position of the Torah is not one of dishonor; yet, even if not dishonored, the Torah's place in Israel's life will need reappraisal in light of Jesus the Messiah.[63]

The closing words of the prologue pull the cords through on the difference that John develops between Jesus and Moses and the implications of those differences. "No one has ever seen God," claims John (1:18). Here the prologue makes another direct allusion to Exodus 33–34, and an indirect allusion to a host of close encounters with God.[64] When Moses said, "Show me your glory" (Ex 33:18), God resisted and instead declared: "You cannot see my face, because no person can see me and live" (Ex 33:20; see also Deut 5:23–29). What was denied to Moses has been granted to those who "have seen his glory." Specifically, God has been made known (ἐξηγήσατο) by the "unique God." The vision of God that was withheld from Moses is accessible now by this other one. Here John returns to the earlier statements of the prologue about the Word which *was* God and was *with God* (v.1) and offers them again them in light of the glory that was made manifest by the "unique God"

---

[61] Indeed, the Gospel repeatedly resists the creation of such a false alternative (see 1:45; 5:45–46; cp. 9:28–29).

[62] Theobald (*Im Anfang*, 61–62): "die neue und einzigartige *Qualität der Vermittlung* der göttlichen 'Gnadenwirklichkeit.'"

[63] Of course, this is a prime example of decision that will look different depending on which side of the answer one is on.

[64] Cf. Num 12:8; Gen 32:30; Isa 6:1. For how Jewish writers navigated these theophanies in terms of the invisibility of God ("No one may see me and live," Ex 33:20), see Craig Keener, *The Gospel of John: A Commentary*, 2 vols. (Grand Rapids: Baker Academic, 2010), 1.422–424; Thompson, *John*, 35–36.

(μονογενὴς θεὸς), who is "at the bosom of the Father" (εἰς τὸν κόλπον τοῦ πατρὸς).

In this way, John's prologue ends by contrasting two of God's agents and the revelation of God that they experienced and facilitated. Moses sought out God's glory but was denied a vision of God. He heard God proclaim his name and glimpsed the back of God's glory, but he could not witness the full glory of Israel's God. By contrast, the Word was with God, and the Word was God. The Word was utterly unique, offering the light of its life in the world. And the Word became flesh. Its glory participated fully in the glory of the God of Israel, such that to speak of it meant to speak in terms of God's long-promised presence among his people and the reconstitution of the children of God. Again, Bultmann's words are apposite. In the Word "God is really encountered, and yet ... God is not directly encountered."[65] In contrast to Bultmann, of course, we have seen that all of these terms derive from the Bible's presentation of Israel's celebrated past and anticipated hopes. And all of these terms are, for John, the proper way of introducing Jesus Christ.

To summarize this long and dense study of John 1:1–18: the prologue as a whole uses *the form* of a narrative about wisdom's way in the world and then fills in that form with an account of God's Word. Both the form of the prologue and its narrative content connect to broader discourses in Jewish theology about the nature of Israel's existence and the proximity of Israel's present way of life to its deepest hopes about the presence of God in the midst of his people. According to John, the first words of the Good News about Jesus Christ should invoke this story in vivid, cosmic terms. Just as wisdom undertook a journey into the world, so also the Word of God came into the world. For some, wisdom became available in the Torah; for others, it remained distant. For John, the Word sought a dwelling place and, where it found acceptance, it granted to men and women the fulfillment of Israel's deepest hopes. These hopes are the hopes that were sparked in Exodus and carried on through the prophets – the hopes of seeing God's glory, of being called God's children. But the Word's presence also challenged the priority of Moses and the Torah. For someone speaking in the terms that John speaks, nothing could be more logical. After all, it is the Word that has priority over Moses, and it is the Word that gave the Torah.

---

[65] Bultmann, *John*, 34.

There is nothing inherently difficult about speaking in vague terms of the priority of God's Word and its power to renew Israel and bring about its hoped-for future. Yet the Fourth Gospel does not use vague terms. Instead, John's bracing decision is to introduce the life of Jesus with a narrative that directs onto a particular Galilean Jewish man the prerogatives and significance of the Word of God and its wisdom-like descent into the world. In doing this, John's prologue introduces the high stakes that are involved in belief in Jesus. For John, to speak of Jesus is to speak of the glory, grace, and truth of the Word of God. It is to speak of creation, life, and light. It is to claim a revelation of God that is more immediate than the one given to Moses. It is to claim that the source of the Torah has taken on flesh and come into Israel, and thus Torah itself must be understood anew. To speak of Jesus is to speak of the way in which God has fulfilled the promise to beget children in the last days and to dwell in the midst of his people. By beginning in this way, John has marshaled a series of potent images available within the first-century Jewish tradition from Scripture and contemporary theological reflection, and John has ordered those images around Jesus. All of these images invoke the rich stories and promises that lie at the root of the Jewish tradition. To bring up this past and to claim the fulfillment of these promises is to call up Israel's foundational story in order to cast a vision for the future of Israel in Jesus Christ.

John 1:19–51: Jesus and Eschatological Hopes of Israel

After the prologue, the Fourth Gospel records the beginning of Jesus' public ministry as the Synoptic Gospels do – with the witness of John the Baptist, a figure whose significance has already been sounded (1:6–8, 15). As we will see, the Fourth Gospel orients the role of John the Baptist around the revelation of Jesus to Israel. John is a witness whose vocation is not primarily a call to repentance but rather a summons – a voice crying in the wilderness – for Israel to recognize Jesus as the lamb and son of God (1:29, 34). The opening of Jesus' public ministry presents John the Baptist as a figure whose confession declares to Israel the salvific presence of its God and the arrival of the one who ushers in the new age.

The Gospel focuses its account of the Baptist's ministry almost entirely on the question of John's identity. "Who are you?" is the question at the center of the story. Yet when the priests and Levites come to him, the Baptist preempts their question by denying that he is the Christ (1:20; cf. 1:8; Lk 3:15), and then he responds negatively to the possibilities offered by his interlocutors. He is not Elijah (cf. Mal 3:23); he is not the prophet (Deut 18:15–19). He claims, instead, in a quotation of Isaiah 40:3, "I am the voice of one crying out in the wilderness, prepare the way of the Lord."[66]

Isaiah 40 is, of course, an oracle proclaiming the restoration of Israel in general, and offering a message of comfort to Jerusalem in particular. In the LXX, the voice that Isaiah describes is presented standing in the wilderness but directing its message to the priests in the city ("Priests, speak to the heart of Jerusalem; comfort her!" Isa 40:2). The opening narrative of the Gospel describes a similar scene. John is in the wilderness beyond the Jordan (πέραν τοῦ Ἰορδάνου, 1:28), bearing witness to the authorities of Jerusalem by addressing the priests and Levites who have come to inquire of his message (1:19). The substance of John's message is the presence in the midst of God's people of a coming figure, one who is greater than John but whose presence is as yet undetected. Such a figure was associated in the evangelist's day particularly with the messiah (see John 7:27; Mal 3:1-2, 4 Ezra 13:51–52; *Dial.* 8.3, 110.1). The witness of the Baptist is, therefore, that the day Isaiah saw has come; a deliverer has arrived on the scene.[67] John the Baptist announces the fulfillment of Isaiah's vision, and the figure at the heart of Isaiah's proclamation is God himself (εἰπὸν ταῖς πόλεσιν Ιουδα Ἰδοὺ ὁ θεὸς ὑμῶν).[68]

The Gospel describes the inquirers of John as "the *Ioudaioi* from Jerusalem" (οἱ Ἰουδαῖοι ἐξ Ἱεροσολύμων), who have commissioned priests and Levites to determine the identity of the Baptist (1:19). In 1:24, these envoys are described as "from the Pharisees" (ἐκ τῶν Φαρισαίων).[69] Thus, the identification of the *Ioudaioi* at this early moment is relatively secure: the Fourth Gospel initially presents the *Ioudaioi* as a body of leaders based in Jerusalem, identified with

---

[66] John alters the wording from the LXX, most notably by replacing the verb Ἑτοιμάσατε of Isa 40:3 LXX (also in Mark 1:3 and pars.) with εὐθύνατε. This may reflect the intentionality of the evangelist (cf. e.g., Bruce G. Schuchard, *Scripture within Scripture: The Interelationship of Form and Function in the Explicit Old Testament Citations in the Gospel of John*, SBLDS 133 [Atlanta: Scholars Press, 1992], 2–15).

[67] So also Schuchard, 4.   [68] Cf. McHugh, *John,* 124–125.

[69] Schnackenburg suggests that the ἐκ is partitive ("some of these were from the Pharisees"); others read this as a repetition of 1:19. For text-critical matters related to this text, see Schnackenburg, *The Gospel according to St. John*, 1.292; Bultmann, *John*, 90n7.

the Pharisees, and who have the capacity to commission other Jewish religious leaders to act on their behalf. Moreover, they are at this early moment in Jesus' ministry defined by their questions: first, "Who are you?" (1:19, 21, 22); and second, "Why are you baptizing?" (1:25). The answer to their first question is given in vv. 19–25: John is not the Christ, Elijah, or the prophet, but rather a voice in the wilderness heralding the Lord's coming among his people. The answer to their second question – Why are you baptizing? (1:25) – is the focus of vv. 26–34.

John baptizes, he claims, in order to witness to the coming one, who is unknown but already "among you" (1:26–27). John reiterates this vocation after seeing Jesus in v. 29. "This is the one about whom I spoke ... I myself had not known him, but for this reason I came, baptizing in water – that he might be revealed to Israel" (κἀγὼ οὐκ ᾔδειν αὐτόν, ἀλλ' ἵνα φανερωθῇ τῷ Ἰσραὴλ διὰ τοῦτο ἦλθον ἐγὼ ἐν ὕδατι βαπτίζων; 1:30–31). Although it is the first of only five uses of the term "Israel" in the Fourth Gospel, the presentation of John's ministry as the revelation of Jesus to Israel is noteworthy.[70] There is no hint at this point in the Gospel that "Israel" denotes anything other than the people of God whose history and identity are rooted in Scripture and whose future is bound up with the restoring action of God.[71] Indeed, the Gospel so far has presented Jesus in terms that are fully consonant with this history and identity. Importantly, however, the significance of Jesus has also been concealed. The questions that the priests and Levites bring from the *Ioudaioi* demonstrate as much, and the Baptist not only affirms this ignorance on behalf of the authorities (μέσος ὑμῶν ἕστηκεν ὃν ὑμεῖς οὐκ οἴδατε, 1:26) but also admits that he himself was ignorant of Jesus' identity (κἀγὼ οὐκ ᾔδειν αὐτόν, 1:31). Without the revelation of God, no one in Israel – neither those with charismatic authority nor those

---

[70] Cf. John 1:49; 3:10; 12:13; Ἰσραηλίτης is used in 1:47.

[71] I take this hoped-for restoration to be independent of the question of whether or not all members of the Jewish tradition believed themselves to be "still in exile" (and in what sense they might affirm such a claim). Importantly, the nature of such claims would be dramatically different for a post-70 text. On these topics, see Brant Pitre, *Jesus, the Tribulation, and the End of the Exile;* Fuller, *The Restoration of Israel in Luke-Acts;* N. T. Wright, *The New Testament and the People of God*, Christian Origins and the Question of God (Minneapolis: Fortress, 1992); on Wright's view of exile in particular, see Richard B. Hays, *Echoes of Scripture in the Gospels* (Waco: Baylor, 2016), 16–20, 371 n2.

with traditional or institutional authority – would recognize the one whom God has sent.[72]

The remainder of John 1 records the beginnings of recognition and the way that Jesus' identity is adumbrated, if not in each case fully captured, by means of the traditional categories of authoritative Jewish figures. The narrative of 1:19–51 ascribes eight titles to Jesus. The first three are spoken by the Baptist, "Look, the lamb of God, who takes away the sins of the world" (1:29); "This one is the son of God" (1:34); and "The lamb of God" (1:36). The next two titles occur on the lips of the first disciples. They address him initially as "Rabbi/teacher" (1:38), but as Andrew describes Jesus to his brother, he modifies the description: "We have found the messiah," he says (1:41). The final three titles occur in the interactions between Philip, Nathanael, and Jesus: Philip says, "We have found the one whom Moses wrote about in the law – and also the prophets" (1:45); Nathanael declares, "Rabbi, you are the son of God, you are king of Israel" (1:49); and Jesus speaks the last word, "You will see heaven opened and the angels of God ascending and descending upon this Son of Man" (1:51).

This cascade of titles has at least three functions in presenting Jesus as the way for Israel to move faithfully into its future. First, the significance of Jesus needs to be measured in the terms of major figures who secure for Israel a future with God. The Baptist's description of Jesus as "the lamb (ἀμνός) of God who takes away the sin of the world" calls upon an array of possible backgrounds: The significance of Passover throughout the Gospel suggests that John intends to identify Jesus as a new eschatological paschal lamb.[73] The reference to Jesus taking away sin (ὁ αἴρων τὴν ἁμαρτίαν) – odd for Passover which, strictly speaking, was not a sacrifice for sin – likely aligns Jesus also with Isaiah's suffering servant, silent like a sheep (πρόβατον; Isa 53:7) and bearing the sins of others (ἀναφέρω/סבל/נשׂא; Isa 53:11, 12).[74] Jesus' removing the sin "of the world" may also look back to the servant of Isaiah, who bore sin as a spectacle for the nations so that they might understand God's

[72] On traditions related to the hidden messiah, cf. Marinus de Jonge, "Jewish Expectations about the 'Messiah' according to the Fourth Gospel," *NTS* 19 (1973): 246–270, esp. 254–257.

[73] See John 19:14, 24, 36(?); Wengst, *Bedrängte Gemeinde und verherrlichter Christus*, 108 n. 324.

[74] Cf. C. K. Barrett, "The Lamb of God," *NTS* 1 (1955): 210–218. McHugh, *John*, 126.

new deliverance of Israel (52:15). Beyond these often noted frames of reference for the title "the lamb of God." Mary Coloe compiles significant rabbinic evidence suggesting that the Gospel alludes here to Jesus as an eschatological embodiment of the *Tamid* sacrifice (Ex 29:38–42; Num 28:3–8).[75] Sandra Schneiders traces important links between this title for Jesus and the promise spoken by Abraham: "God himself will provide the sheep (πρόβατον)" (Gen 22:1–18).[76] C. H. Dodd argues that the words of the Baptist align Jesus with the deliverers of Israel who are described as lambs in Revelation 5:6 and Testament of Joseph 19:1–10.[77] While the first two possibilities – paschal lamb and suffering servant – seem particularly strong, any identification of Jesus as "the lamb of God, who takes away the sin of the world" activates these further possibilities, all of which derive from Jewish Scripture and tradition. The Gospel describes Jesus from within that matrix of symbolism in order to cast him as the initiator of a new phase in the life of God's people, one who embodies and fulfills one of Israel's most basic cultic symbols and who, doing so, brings about the possibility of a new relationship between Israel and its God and, through the fulfillment of promises made to Israel, brings about the further possibility, also attested in Scripture, of Israel's restoration opening out onto the reconciliation of the broader Gentile world to God as well.

The other titles of John 1:19–51 suggest this as well: Son of God (1:34, 49) carries with it the royal and messianic expectations associated with David, Solomon, and others. "King of Israel" (1:49) draws on the same background to name Jesus as the ruler over the whole people of God; "messiah" (1:41) denotes the figure that would usher

---

[75] Cf. Mary Coloe, "'Behold the Lamb of God': John 1:29 and the Tamid Service," in *Rediscovering John: Essays on the Fourth Gospel in Honour of Fréderic Manns,* ed. Lesław Daniel Chrupcała (Milano, Italy: Edizioni Terra Santa, 2013), 337–350. Cf. McHugh, *John,* 126–134 (esp. 127–128); Bultmann, *John,* 96–97.

[76] Sandra M Schneiders, "The Lamb of God and the Forgiveness of Sin(s) in the Fourth Gospel," *CBQ* 73.1 (2011): 1–29. Schneiders (p. 18) helpfully quotes Geza Vermes (*Scripture and Tradition in Judaism: Haggadic Studies,* 2nd ed., SPB 4 [Leiden: Brill, 1973], 225): "For the Palestinian Jews, all lamb sacrifice, and especially the Passover lamb and the Tamid offering, was a memorial of the Akedah with its effects of deliverance, forgiveness of sin and messianic salvation."

[77] C. H. Dodd, *The Interpretation of the Fourth Gospel* (Cambridge: Cambridge University Press, 1965), 230–238. Rev 5:6 employs ἀρνίον, not John's ἀμνός. See also Per Jarle Bekken, *The Lawsuit Motif in John's Gospel from New Perspectives: Jesus Christ, Crucified Criminal and Emperor of the World,* NovTSup 158 (Leiden: Brill, 2015), 249–250.

in God's promised deliverance.[78] "The one whom Moses wrote about in the law, and also the prophets" suggests the "prophet like Moses" (Deut 18:15, 18–19) as well as a host of expectations for a coming ruler that were rooted in both the Pentateuch and in the prophetic corpus of the Jewish Scriptures (e.g., Gen 49:9–12; Num 24:17–19; Mic 5:1; Isa 9; 11–12; Ezek 34).[79]

The final title of the chapter – and all the more significant because it is the one Jesus ascribes to himself and addresses to an audience wider than Nathaniel (λέγω ὑμῖν) – identifies Jesus as "the [or 'this'] Son of Man." The title asserts the humanity of Jesus while also relating Jesus to the eschatological ruler of Daniel 7, who has a throne in heaven and to whom the Ancient of Days grants authority over the people of the earth (7:13–14). Nathaniel and those whom he represents stand in the position of Jacob (Israel!): they are promised not a vision of new ladder whose location sanctifies a plot of earth, but rather a vision of heaven opened for angels to ascend and descend upon this Son of Man. A complex web of interpretive traditions can be called in to explain Jesus' statement.[80] Regardless of how one traces the prehistory of these ideas, however, readers can be sure of this: John records here a bracing promise that, first, underlines the humanity of Jesus (he is a son of man, cf. John 1:14). Second, it claims for him the significance of a divine eschatological ruler (one *like* a Son of Man, Dan 7:13). The apocalyptic setting of "the heavens opened" suggests that this claim needs to be included with the affirmation of Jesus' humanity. Third, the words

---

[78] Cf. the combination of similar ideas 4QFlor 1:11 and 4Q246 2:1.

[79] Indeed, Bultmann (among others) notes that the phrase could encompass the whole of Scripture. On the particular expectations, cf. William Horbury, *Jewish Messianism and the Cult of Christ* (London: SCM Press, 1998).

[80] For helpful discussion of this passage, see John Ashton, *Understanding the Fourth Gospel*, 2nd ed. (Oxford: Oxford University Press, 2007), 241–251; Daniel Boyarin, *The Jewish Gospels* (New York: The New Press, 2012), 25–101; Christopher Rowland, "John 1.51, Jewish Apocalyptic, and Targumic Tradition," *NTS* (1984): 498–507; Jerome H. Neyrey, "The Jacob Allusions in John 1:51" *CBQ* 44 (1982): 586–605; Kerr, *The Temple of Jesus' Body*, 136–166; Hugo Odeburg, *The Fourth Gospel: Interpreted in Its Relation to Contemporaneous Religious Currents in Palestine and the Hellenistic-Oriental World* (Uppsala: Almqvist & Wiksells Boktryckeri; 1929), 33–42; Francis J. Maloney, *The Johannine Son of Man* (Rome: LAS, 1976), 23–41, esp. 40–41; Francis J. Maloney, "The Johannine Son of Man Revisited," in Francis J. Maloney, *The Gospel of John: Text and Context* (Leiden: Brill, 2005), 66–92. For a discussion of the importance of the humanity of "the Son of Man" in John, see Thompson, *John*, 57–58. (I distill the strengths of many of these studies to be the various ways that they emphasize the [1] humanity, [2] suffering, and [3] authority of the Johannine Son of Man.)

John records suggestively associate the soon-to-be-narrated ministry of Jesus with the manifestation of God's presence to Israel (Jacob). He is the one who mediates the relationship between heaven and earth. The significance of Jacob's vision anticipates the climactic significance of Jesus' ministry.

As is widely recognized, the Fourth Gospel will make a long arc from the titles of John 1:19–51 to its closing description of Jesus as "the Christ, the Son of God" (20:31). The fact that nineteen chapters are required to return to some of the same titles suggests that while each of these titles is rightly ascribed to Jesus they are also all vulnerable to misinterpretation without the intervening narrative of Jesus' ministry.[81] Thus the concentration of the titles for Jesus early on in the narrative prompts readers to ask the same question of Jesus that the priests and Levites brought to John: Who are you? How can one person bear the significance that all of these titles require? What the Gospel begins by calling up these titles – Jesus as a Passover lamb, suffering servant, sign for the world, royal deliverer, son of God, eschatological judge – it will go on to do with other aspects of Jewish life: Jesus will be the bread from heaven, the light of the world, the source of living waters. John does not argue for the bracing possibility that all of this symbolism could be concentrated onto a single person. Instead, in this opening narrative John signals to the reader the course that the rest of the Gospel will pursue: the capacity of one person, Jesus, to mediate through himself the basic terms of Israel's identity and the key images of Israel's eschatological future.

The titles of John 1:19–51 perform an additional task beyond identifying Jesus as an eschatological figure who can embody within himself a vast array of Israel's hopes. The titles also create contrasts that fund the Gospel's polemics, primarily directed against the *Ioudaioi*. As noted above, the hiddenness of the messiah has biblical and traditional precedent, but it also functions in this narrative to distance the *Ioudaioi* (and the priests, Levites, and John the Baptist) from any privileged authority regarding the one who fulfills the hopes of Israel. Ever so subtly, John introduces the gap between the *Ioudaioi* and Israel that the Gospel will pursue. The Evangelist further emphasizes the significance of Jesus when the disciples first address him in a term that would initially link him with the *Ioudaioi* – "rabbi/teacher," they call him (1:38). But the disciples quickly adjust

---

[81] For a helpful study of these titles, see Schnackenburg, *The Gospel according to St. John*, 1.507–514.

their address to "messiah" as they realize who he is (1:41).[82] Like some of the *Ioudaioi*, Jesus is a teacher (3:2; cf. 3:10), but unlike his contemporaries, he is a teacher with singular authority, the one through whom the words of Isaiah will be fulfilled: "they will all be taught by God" (Isa 54:13, John 6:45). The Gospel of John employs the title "rabbi" for Jesus more than any other Gospel, but it does so with an eye to this singular authority.[83] Contrasts with Moses signal an additional polemic in John 1:19–51. It is Moses whom Jesus' opponents will claim for authority (5:45; 9:28), but as John has already described Jesus in terms that surpass Moses (1:14–17), so here Moses is cast as a witness to Jesus (1:45).[84] Finally, the description of Jesus as the focal point of angelic ascents and descents suggests that other places of intercourse between heaven and earth are at least redundant and more likely that they belong to another time altogether.[85]

Taken together, the titles of Jesus in John 1 concentrate a startling significance onto a single person. The terms of description for Jesus derive from Scripture and Jewish tradition and portray him as the fulfillment of the eschatological promises and hopes of Israel. Indeed, Jesus is intelligible only within the particular hopes, images, and expectations of this tradition. Jesus is the one who brings the promises of Israel's future into the present. Jesus is the one through whom Israel's ongoing fidelity to God may occur. This affirmation suggests a negation, however. It rejects any alternative vision for Israel's life organized around expectation but not fulfillment, fidelity to Moses without recognition of the one about whom he wrote, commitment to the temple (even in an era when its functions have been suspended) without a vision of the Son of Man who now mediates access between heaven and earth. John 1 presents Jesus as a figure who embodies innovative continuity with the past and who

---

[82] This realization of Jesus' true significance is a central insight of Martyn, "Glimpses," 149–155.

[83] See Bruce Chilton, "The Gospel according to John's Rabbi Jesus," *BBR* 25.1 (2015): 39–54.

[84] It is even possible that the reference to Jesus as "lamb of God" (1:29, 36) draws a subtle contrast between Jesus and other traditions that imagined Moses as lamb sent by God. See Renée Bloch, "Quelques aspects de la figure de Moïse dans la tradition rabbinique" in *Moïse: L'homme de l'alliance* (Tournai: Desclée & Cⁱᵉ, 1955), 93–167 (esp 104–107). Cf. Meeks, *Prophet-King,* 286–319.

[85] By "suggest" I mean that this is a reasonable inference, rather than proposing that John 1:51 encapsulates a polemic against the temple (see Kerr, *The Temple of Jesus' Body,* 136–166).

offers a path into Israel's hoped-for future. In this affirmation of Jesus, as well as in the direct and indirect negation of other forms of continuity, John is casting a vision for the future of Israel.

John 2:13–22: Jesus and the Dwelling Place of God

Jesus appears in the temple at Passover after revealing his glory at a wedding "on the third day" (John 2:1–12). Nearly all commentators recognize in the miraculous provision of wine a reference to the eschatological abundance of wine foreseen by Amos (9:13) and Isaiah (Isa 25:6–8) and with it the arrival of God's long-promised deliverance (Gen 49:11; Isa 55:1–3). Francis Maloney has argued that the timing of John's narrative of the wedding at Cana is modeled on the revelation of God's glory to Israel *on the third day* (Ex 19:9–17; cf. John 2:1).[86] Much debate surrounds what significance, if any, readers should attribute to other features of the text (e.g., the six jars, the identity of the bridegroom).[87] Nevertheless, it is clear that Jesus' public ministry in John begins with a sign that, at least for the disciple with eyes to see, announces the arrival of a new era of fulfillment in Israel's history.

John's description of Jesus' appearance in the temple at Passover (2:13–22) sustains this announcement and offers a glimpse of the way in which John's vision for the future of Israel draws on Scripture and the temple as witnesses of Jesus. To see this, readers must attend to two questions: First, how are Jesus' actions on behalf of the temple (vv.14–16) related to expectation of his death (cf. Ps 69:10 in John 2:17)? Second, how does Jesus' clearing of the temple relate to the portrayal of his body as the dwelling place of God (2:18–22)? The exegesis below will argue that John 2:13–22 presents Jesus' action in the temple as a sign that is meant to illuminate the eschatological significance of Jesus.

John describes Jesus entering the temple and immediately opposing the commercial practices that are basic to its functions. As in

---

[86] Francis J. Maloney, *Belief in the Word: Reading the Fourth Gospel: John 1–4* (Minneapolis: Fortress, 1993), 83–84; Francis J. Maloney, *John,* Sacra Pagina 4 (Collegeville: The Liturgical Press, 1988), 50–51.
[87] For discussions of these symbols, see, e.g., Barrett, *The Gospel according to St. John,* 2nd ed. (Philadelphia: Westminster Press, 1978), 188–194; Maloney, *John,* 65–74; Jocelyn McWhirter, *The Bridegroom Messiah and the People of God: Marriage in the Fourth Gospel,* SNTMS 138 (Cambridge: Cambridge University Press, 2006), 46–50.

Matthew and Mark, John's Jesus takes particular aim at those who provide sacrifices for the poorest worshippers, the pigeon sellers. Jesus justifies the interruption of sacrifice by saying: "Take these away! Do not make my Father's house a house of commerce (οἶκον ἐμπορίου)!" (2:16). It is important to note what is missing in this command. Jesus does not criticize the temple as a "hideout for robbers" (Jer 7:11) or as a place that is out of step with Isaiah's vision of it as "a house of prayer" (Isa 56:7; Mk 11:17, Mt 21:13; Lk 19:46). Jesus' words and actions come across as an effort to safeguard the temple as the house of God in a way that commerce somehow endangers. But how would commerce jeopardize the temple's status as the Father's house?

An answer is at hand if we consider how Jesus' actions evoke the image of the temple presented in Zechariah 14:21.[88] There the prophet describes the restored Jerusalem. God is present as king (14:9); living water flows from the city (v.8); Israel and the nations gather annually to observe the great pilgrimage festival (Booths; vv.16, 19); and "no longer will there be traders (כנעני/Χαναναῖος) in the house (οἴκῳ) of the Lord Almighty" (v. 21). Zechariah thus envisions a day of when Israel's cultic life flourishes apart from moneychangers and animal merchants.[89,90] It is this image that John evokes with Jesus' actions to drive out the animals, moneychangers, and his call for an end to commerce in the temple.[91] Jesus indicts those in the temple *not* for their immorality, financial exploitation of worshipers, or exclusion of the Gentiles; rather, he indicts them for the incongruity of the temple's operations vis-à-vis the eschatological

---

[88] The importance of Zechariah for the eschatological expectations of the Fouth Gospel should not be overlooked. John often refers to Zechariah, e.g., Zech 1:5 (John 8:52); 9:9 (John 12:15); 12:10 (John 19:37); 13:7 (John 16:32); 14:8 (John 4:10; 7:38); 14:21 (John 2:16). Cf. William Randolph Bynum, "Quotations of Zechariah in the Fourth Gospel," in *Abiding Words: The Use of Scripture in the Gospel of John*, Alicia D. Myers and Bruce G. Schuchard, eds. (Atlanta: SBL Press, 2015), 47–74.

[89] Possibly because the need for offerings due to sin and impurity are suspended(?).

[90] On this "mercantile" interpretation of "Cananites," see Joel Marcus, "No More Zealots in the House of the Lord: A Note on the History of Interpretation of Zechariah 14:21," *NovT* 55.1 (2013): 22–30. The term ἔμπορος is used with a negative valence in Rev 18, and it occurs often in the LXX with reference to Tyre or other oppressive economic powers. Against Kerr (79–81), however, the term does not have a clear negative valence, and so we should not import one here.

[91] The characterization of John evoking images is critical to this reading. See further Richard B. Hays, *Echoes of Scripture in the Gospels* (Waco: Baylor, 2016), 288.

moment in which Israel lives. Jesus announces the beginning of the time of fulfillment – the glory of God visible among the people, the presence of the messiah, and the first tastes of an eschatological banquet. Merchants in the house of the Lord have no place in the era of fulfillment.

John takes the reader aside to explain Jesus' statement about the Father's house: "His disciples remembered that was written, 'Zeal for your house will consume me'" (2:17). As elsewhere in the Gospel, with the mention of the disciples remembering John refers to a recollection of Jesus that is enabled by the Holy Spirit.[92] The Spirit enables the disciples to remember the words of Psalm 69:10 (68:10 LXX), although John modifies the quotation to denote a future event: zeal for your house *will consume* me.[93] The future tense, along with the other applications of this Psalm to Jesus in John and throughout the New Testament, strongly implies that Ps 69:10 has become for the disciples a prophecy of Jesus' passion and death.[94] This fits with the action of the scene: first, Jesus clears the temple (2:14–16); second, the disciples connect this zealous action on God's behalf to Jesus' suffering (2:17); third, the *Ioudaioi* (who will eventually be responsible for Jesus' death, 11:47–50; 19:7) challenge Jesus' authority to take such action (2:18–21). In the narrative of John, Jesus speaks for a passing moment with the voice of a righteous, Davidic sufferer, a man who is tragically alienated from his brothers (לאחי; τοῖς ἀδελφοῖς μου; Ps 69:9) and who proleptically describes the consequences of that alienation. Jesus has cleared the temple and, if only for a moment, dramatically transformed it into the place that resembles what it will one day be, the house of the Lord without any merchants within its walls. In narrating Jesus' strong commitment to bringing the temple closer to its prophesied future, John also intimates the consequences of this commitment: zeal for God's house – for the Father's house – will consume the righteous sufferer who is marked out for rejection by his compatriots.

As an eschatological action, Jesus' clearing of the temple expresses a strong identification with the temple and a concern that Israel

---

[92] See esp. John 14:26. For a discussion of the timing of this memory, see Kerr, *The Temple of Jesus' Body*, 82. For a reading that does not envision this as a post-resurrection form of memory, see M. J. J. Menken, *Old Testament Quotations in the Fourth Gospel*, 42.

[93] On the form of the quotation, see Menken, *Old Testament Quotations*, 37–45.

[94] John 15:25 (Ps 69:10), John 19:28–29 (Ps 69:22).

recognize that its future hopes have become present. But this concern for the temple is fleeting. Initially, the *Ioudaioi* evince no confusion about Jesus' action. Perhaps they recognize the claim Jesus is making; perhaps not. What they do, however, is to ask Jesus for a sign that would vindicate his claim.[95] Jesus tells them, "Destroy this temple (τὸν ναὸν τοῦτον), and in three days I will raise it" (2:19). The *Ioudaioi* are incredulous, able only to perceive the temple in which they stand and to think of its decades-long construction.[96] "But he spoke concerning the temple (τὸν ναὸν) of his body," writes John. Jesus describes the destruction and resurrection of his body; the *Ioudaioi hear* a threat against the building in Jerusalem. Readers must take care to follow the narrative at this point. There is no threat against the Jerusalem temple in this confrontation; indeed, a threat against Israel's temple would be incongruous with Jesus' action.[97] Jesus clears the temple in order to demonstrate what time it is in Israel's history. The eschatological moment signified by the cleared temple will be vindicated by the death and resurrection of Jesus.

The striking claim of John 2:18–22 is that Jesus' body represents τὸν ναὸν, the dwelling place of God.[98] The implications of this claim will become clear as the narrative unfolds. Jesus will take to himself the image of living waters flowing from the temple (John 7:38; Ezek 47:1–12 Zech 14:8). John has already characterized Jesus as the one who mediates access between heaven and earth (1:51). The Gospel will go on to envision an era (or hour) of worship in which the possession of the Spirit, not a person's presence on a particular mountain, will be the defining element in her worship of God (4:21–24). Jesus fulfills these promises – the giving of the Spirit, the place of God's indwelling presence, the source of living waters. He gives the blessing once expected of the temple. In a post-70 text, these characterizations of Jesus could not but evoke an awareness of what had been lost: the temple that took decades to build was destroyed;

---

[95] Such a demand for a sign would obviously invoke Moses (see esp. Ex 34:11), but would also have a precedent in the sign given to Hezekiah (2 Kings 20:8–11). Signs validate the message of the prophets but can also accompany false prophets (Deut 13:1–5; 18:15, 18–22).

[96] That is, for the *Ioudaioi*, τὸ ἱερόν (v.14) = ὁ ναὸς οὗτος (v. 20). (The interchangeability of these terms was common.) John upholds some distinction (v. 21).

[97] Cf. Mk 14:57–59.

[98] On ναός as "dwelling place," in contrast to the use of ἱερόν to refer to the whole temple structure, cf. BDAG 470, 666; Kerr, *The Temple of Jesus' Body*, 88–89.

the vision of it as the source of living waters must have seemed achingly distant.[99]

A reader unconvinced of John's eschatology could recognize replacement theology here: The temple is gone. Jesus stands in its place and declares that he will raise up a new one in its place. But a reader operating within the horizons of John's theology must offer an account of Jesus as the dwelling place of God and the temple of his body (2:18–21) that coheres with Jesus' zeal for the house of the Lord, the house of his Father (2:14–17). How can Jesus seem to act *on behalf of* the temple in 2:14–17 if he really anticipates its replacement in 2:18-21? Why narrate Jesus' loyalty toward that which he supplants? How can we read with the grain of this text?

The simplest resolution is this: Jesus' clearing of the temple brings into the present a glimpse of the future reality that his death will accomplish. The merchant-less temple calls to mind a vivid image of the future day of God's eschatological blessing. Jesus' disciples make this connection: they recognize Jesus as committed to the Lord's house in precisely this way, and their recollection suggests that the vision for Israel's future that Jesus enacts in the temple will lead to his death (i.e., it will "consume" him). The *Ioudaioi* ask Jesus to vindicate this announcement through a sign, and he offers them an inaccessible one – the destruction and raising up of his body. The death and resurrection of Jesus, whose body is τὸν ναόν, will accomplish the long-promised outpouring of the Spirit and the presence of living water; it will bring about judgment and life; it will effect the restoration of the people of God and embody the dwelling place of God. The zealous clearing of the temple signifies Jesus' total commitment to ushering in the future of Israel.

Yet this scene also draws out John's ambivalent view of the temple. On the one hand, Jesus' concern for the temple to embody now what it will one day be calls the evangelist to portray Jesus as zealous for the house of the Lord. On the other hand, John's understanding of Jesus as the dwelling place of God shows the limits of the evangelist's commitment to the temple built by human hands. John genuinely values the Jerusalem temple, but only as sign – a witness – that points to Jesus. It seems, therefore, that Jesus enacts Zechariah's

---

[99] See Zech 14:8, Ezek 47:1–12; W. D. Davies, "Aspects of the Jewish Background of the Gospel of John," in *Exploring the Gospel of John: Essays in Honor of D. Moody Smith,* ed. R. Alan Culpepper and C. Clifton Black (Louisville: Westminster John Knox, 1996), 43–64 (esp. 55–56).

prophecy as a parable. For a passing moment, the scene described by the prophet becomes reality: the merchant-less temple captures in a single image Jesus' proclamation that the eschatological hopes of Israel are fulfilled in him. The prophecy is transformed from an image of what Israel's ongoing life will look like and into a glimpse of a single moment that is pregnant with meaning for Israel. In the enactment of Zechariah's vision John presents Jesus as the one who announces the arrival of Israel's future, who will suffer because of the conflict his announcement elicits, and who will be vindicated by his rising from the dead. Zechariah's merchant-less temple thus witnesses to the future of Israel through Jesus.

This is, of course, an innovative appropriation of a prophet's vision and a bold subordination of the temple from its central place in the topography of eschatological Israel to a new place of witness to Jesus. But it is also a compelling interpretation of John 2:13–22. It is so, first, because it explains both Jesus' actions on behalf of his Father's house and his self-identification as the ναός of God. It holds these two aspects of the text together without forcing Jesus' action in the temple to be something it is not – that is, a rejection of the Father's house.[100] Second, this is a compelling reading of John 2:13–22 because it fits the logic of John's Gospel. If Jesus truly embodies the dwelling place of God in the world, then readers should expect the temple, and the prophecies about it, to bear witness to him.

John 3:1–21: New Birth and Living Water

Who has authority to instruct Israel? This is the question at the heart of Jesus' interaction with Nicodemus. The passage opens with Nico-demus' credentials: he is a man from the Pharisees, a ruler of the *Ioudaioi* (3:1). He speaks as a representative of a larger group, "Rabbi, *we know* (οἴδαμεν) that you are a teacher who has come from God" (3:2). The conversation that follows puts two leaders in conversation and exposes the impoverished knowledge of Nicode-mus and those for whom he speaks. For our purposes, a key aspect of the Nicodemus pericope is the utter failure of Nicodemus' eschatological vision. Jesus announces how several long-promised elements of Israel's life might be experienced in the present, and although he should be comprehending, Nicodemus is confounded.

---

[100] Similarly, Thompson, *John*, 73.

After Nicodemus recognizes Jesus as a teacher who has come from God (3:2), Jesus begins by saying that being born ἄνωθεν (from above, or again) is the precondition of seeing the Kingdom of God (3:3). Nicodemus inquires after rebirth from a human womb (τὴν κοιλίαν τῆς μητρός). Following this initial misunderstanding by Nicodemus, Jesus repeats the need for rebirth by water and spirit, differentiating a birth from flesh and a birth from the spirit (3:5–6). Jesus exhorts Nicodemus not to be surprised by his teaching – as the wind can be heard and felt, but not mapped or directed, so those who enter into the Kingdom of God do so by rebirth from the spirit, and not any other controllable phenomenon (vv. 7–8). Nicodemus responds, exasperated, "How can this be?" (3:9). Jesus' use of the title "teacher" in his response to Nicodemus exposes his shortcomings: "Are you the teacher of Israel (ὁ διδάσκαλος τοῦ Ἰσραήλ) and you do not know these things?" (3:10).

Both questions – Nicodemus' expression of incredulity and Jesus' response – serve as indictments of Nicodemus and the *Ioudaioi* and Pharisees for whom he speaks. Nicodemus repeatedly misunderstands what Jesus is talking about (vv. 4, 9), and Jesus' question highlights the theological failure at the root of Nicodemus' misunderstanding. He would occupy the role of "the teacher of Israel," and yet he is incompetent to discern either the necessity or the significance of rebirth by water and spirit. If Nicodemus cannot instruct Israel, then the question arises: Who can? And what will that teaching include?[101]

Jesus' speech is dense with meaning and terse formulations, but it is not opaque. The necessity of a new, qualitatively different birth draws on an image from Isaiah and Septuagint Ezekiel. As we saw in considering John 1:12, Isaiah records Zion observing her restored fortunes: "Then [in the day of the Lord's favor] you will say in your heart, 'Who has borne me these?'" (Τίς ἐγέννησέν μοι τούτους/ מִי יָלַד־לִי אֶת־אֵלֶּה; Isa 49:21). Ezekiel envisions the time of Israel's restoration by proclaiming, "I will beget upon you [the mountains of Israel] human beings – my people Israel" (γεννήσω ἐφ' ὑμᾶς ἀνθρώπους τὸν λαόν μου Ισραηλ; Ezek 36:12).[102] This latter passage offers a

---

[101] See also Thompson, *The God of the Gospel of John* (Grand Rapids: Eerdmans, 2001), 169–170.

[102] In Ezek 36:12, the MT reads, "I will lead out upon you [והולכתי] . . ." The LXX translator seems to have read the MT's והולכתי as והולדתי, thus using γεννήσω where he might have used instead a form of ἐξάγω or πορεύομαι. The context would encourage

particularly suggestive context for understanding Jesus' speech in John 3, moving as it does from assertions of God's commitment to restore Israel (Ezek 36:8–10), to beget a people (v. 12), to act entirely on the basis of a divine prerogative (vv.21–24), and finally to cleanse the people with clean water (ὕδωρ καθαρόν) and "a new spirit" ... "my spirit" (πνεῦμα καινὸν/ τὸ πνεῦμά μου; vv. 25–27).[103]

By casting the discussion between Jesus and Nicodemus in this way, John shows the wide gap of eschatological understanding that divides these two characters and the visions for Israel that they uphold. For John, Jesus envisions a clear moment of fulfillment – rebirth, water, spirit. Nicodemus cannot even grasp the terms under discussion. Jesus describes this failure as an inability to grasp even earthly realities: "We are speaking of that which we know and testifying to that which we have seen – and you do not accept our testimony! If I speak of earthly things and you do not believe, how will you believe if I speak heavenly things to you?" (John 3:11–12). Jesus here runs up against Nicodemus' basic unwillingness to admit what he should know to be true: That earthly things must be remade into things that are enlivened by divine power. Such rebirth is based, as we have seen, in prophetic visions of eschatological rebirth (Isa 49; Ezek 36), restoration and healing (Isa 35:5–10), in promises of new hearts and new spirits (Jer 31:33–34; Ezek 37:11–14), and also in the expectation that God will restore life within the created order (Isa 65:17–25). John's Jesus is fully at home in the basic categories of the Jewish tradition in describing the necessity for such rebirth.[104] The evangelist casts Nicodemus' confusion about these "earthly things" as a failure to grasp the basic contours of Jewish eschatology and thereby as an indictment of his position as "a teacher of Israel."

If the "earthly things" of which Jesus speaks refers to his declaration that people must be born ἄνωθεν, then the "heavenly things" that are beyond Nicodemus' reach are the specific means by which

---

such a "misreading" (e.g., "I will multiply people ... they will be fruitful and multiply," 36:11; and "no longer shall you be childless [ἀτεκνωθῆναι] by them," 36:12). See John W. Olley, *Ezekiel: A Commentary Based on Iezekiel in Codex Vaticanus,* Septuagint Commentary Series (Leiden: Brill, 2009), 480. I am grateful to Dr. Ross Wagner for helping me think through this striking variant reading.

[103] These are, of course, not the only Old Testament or Jewish texts that discuss rebirth, cleansing water, or a new spirit. Nevertheless, the concentration of these ideas in Ezek 36 is significant. See further, Ps 2:7; Joel 3:1–5; Isa 44:3; 1 QS 4:20–22.

[104] See Matt 19:28; Tit 3:5; 1 Cor 15:35–50 (esp. vv. 40, 50). For specific visions of people transfigured in the eschaton, see Dan 12:3, 2 Bar 51:10 (cp. Mk 12:25 and pars.), 1 Enoch 62:15–16.

God will accomplish this rebirth.[105] Jesus moves from what should be, in John's view, uncontroversial claims about the need for rebirth to a more controversial description of how God will give new life to humankind: "Just as Moses lifted up the snake in the wilderness, so it is necessary for this Son of Man to be lifted up, in order that everyone who believes in him might have eternal life" (3:14–15).[106] Here Jesus refers to the snake that Moses lifted up before the Israelites as a sign (Num 21:8, 9).[107] John draws on both the exaltation of the figure and its life-giving effects. However, in contrast to traditions that understood the exalted snake as a prompt for God's people to return to God's commands, particularly the law, the exalted snake now serves as a prompt for God's people to recognize another exalted, saving figure.[108] Moses' snake and the life that it brings anticipate Jesus on the cross and the life that belongs to those who believe in him. Here we see again how Moses and Jesus are in no competition – the former anticipates the latter, and the latter is comprehensible in the images and actions of the former.

But who is qualified to interpret the arrival of new birth by water and spirit as the eschatological fulfillment that it is? Who can tell the difference between "the Christ, the Son of God," and "a teacher sent from God" (20:31; 3:2)? Who can recognize the innovative continuity that would allow Moses' ministry in the wilderness to anticipate the crucified and exalted Jesus? As John presents him, Nicodemus cannot recognize the basic eschatological expectations spoken by Israel's prophets. Unsurprisingly, therefore, Nicodemus drops out of the scene as Jesus explains to him how new birth, spirit and water, and eternal life come to the believer. There is no debate about the interpretation of Moses' action in the wilderness because Nicodemus has failed the prior hermeneutical test: without understanding earthly

---

[105] Compare 4 Ezra 4, which records Ezra trying to understand the plight of his people with regard to earthly and heavenly things. Like Nicodemus, Ezra is not granted a satisfying explanation of heavenly things. Unlike Nicodemus, Ezra *can* make sense of earthly realities.

[106] My translation "*this* Son of Man" follows Thompson (*John*, 53–54) in emphasizing the humanity of the speaker.

[107] ἐπὶ σημείου; the Hebrew of Num 21:8 could also be translated as "sign," depending on how one vocalizes the term נס as either a noun or the direct object marker. See further Frey, "Wie Mose," 89–145.

[108] See Wisdom 16:5–14 (v. 6: "They received a symbol of salvation in order that they might remember the commandment of your law"/σύμβολον ἔχοντες σωτηρίας εἰς ἀνάμνησιν ἐντολῆς νόμου σου.) Cf. Frey, "Wie Mose," 95–114, 137; Schröder, 100–102.

things, how could he possibly comprehend the work of the one who has descended from heaven (ὁ ἐκ τοῦ οὐρανοῦ καταβάς; 3:13)?

John concludes the discourse by further summarizing the mission of Jesus (3:16–17) and highlighting the salvation and judgment that result from belief or unbelief (3:18–21). The text presents unbelief as the consequence of a wrongly ordered life: Evil deeds cause people to hate the light and to love the darkness. Nicodemus' inability to understand Jesus exposes the need for this would-be teacher of Israel to reorient his life and bring it into line with the vision of the prophets, the sign of Moses, and the exaltation of Jesus. To do this he would need to become a "doer of truth" (ὁ δὲ ποιῶν τὴν ἀλήθειαν, 3:21). For John, this certainly means believing in Jesus (John 6:29; 14:1, 10–11), but of course this belief is not a simple assent but rather a fully embodied way of ordering one's life in the world. (This is on vivid display in Jesus' confrontation of "the *Ioudaioi* who believed in him" in John 8:31: their belief is insufficient because it is not the ordering point of their thinking and living.) Such belief is the key to the future of Israel. Jesus announces it. Nicodemus is baffled by it. John's vision of the future, and its innovative continuity with the past, lies accessible on the far side of the reorientation of one's thinking and living around Jesus.

John 4:4–42: The Restoration of Judah and Samaria

The opening verses of John 4:4–42 frame Jesus' encounter with the woman at the well in terms of the location in which it occurs. "He had [Ἔδει] to pass through Samaria," John writes. "Therefore [οὖν] he came to a Samaritan city called Sychar" (4:4–5). As with every other use of δεῖ in the Fourth Gospel, the need to pass through Samaria in this instance derives from a theological necessity.[109] As we will see, numerous biblical expectations envision the people of God reunited into a single people in the last days. When John describes Jesus coming to Samaria, he is interested in how his messiah may bring this about.[110] Close attention to the narrative of John 4 will show that in Samaria Jesus announces the restoration of

---

[109] See (3:7, 14, 30; 4:4, 20, 24; 9:4; 10:16; 12:34; 20:9). The οὖν further supports this. On the routes between Judea and Galilee, see Josephus, *Life* 269; *Ant.* XX.118; *War* II.12.3.

[110] This is not to deny that John 4 sets out numerous contrasts with John 3 (man/ woman, "orthodox"/"heterodox," day/night, "his own [οἱ ἴδιοι]/ not his own," etc. It is to state, however, that the Samaritan setting is uniquely important.

Israel, including Samaria, that occurs through his ministry, but that Jesus' announcement to the Samaritan woman takes its bearings from within the mainstream of the Jewish tradition.[111]

The history of Samaria in the Bible begins with Abram, who upon arrival in the land of Canaan came to the city that would one day be at the center of Samaria, Shechem (Gen 12:5–6). Jacob later purchased a plot and built an altar at Shechem (Gen 33:18–20), and he pledged the land to his son Joseph (Gen 48:22; Josh 24:32). Later, the tribes of Joseph – Manasseh and Ephraim – inherited the land that comprised the region (Josh 16–17). During the monarchic period, the city and its surrounding area of Samaria became critical to the Northern Kingdom (1 Kings 12:25). In 721 BC, the fall of Samaria brought about the end of that kingdom and the exile of the ten tribes of Israel (2 Kings 17:1–6). At that time the Assyrians resettled the cities of Samaria with people from five cities – Babylon, Cuthah, Avva, Hamath, and Sepharvaim. Each group of settlers established in Samaria the cult of their home city (17:29–31) and they worshipped the Lord as well (17:32).[112] After recounting the fate of the Northern Kingdom, the author of 2 Kings issues a strong rejection of the inhabitants of Samaria: They are marked out as syncretists and foreigners who have turned their backs on the heritage they share in common with the other descendants of Jacob: "They do not fear the Lord, and they do not follow the statutes or the rules or the law or the commandment that the LORD commanded the children of Jacob, whom he named Israel" (2 Kings 17:34).[113] Later, in Ezra, Zerubbabel echoes this criticism when he refuses the assistance of the people of the land – that is, those people settled in the land by the Assyrians – in the task of rebuilding the temple (Ez 4:1–4).

The prophets and the Chronicler were not so quick to write off Samaria, however. Hosea prophesied the restoration of the Judah and Israel into one people (1:10–11; MT/LXX 2:1–2), and a day in

---

[111] For a discussion of this text with a different orientation but one that nevertheless makes many observations amenable to the following argument, see Marion Moser, *Schriftdiskurse im Johannesevangelium* (WUNT 2/380; Tübingen: Mohr Siebeck, 2014), 50–143.

[112] On these cults, see also Josephus, *Ant.* IX.14.3; McHugh, *John*, 281–282. The recurrent emphasis in 2 Kings – "they worshipped the Lord, but also served their carved images" (17:33; cf. v. 41) – offers a suggestive background for the woman's five husbands plus one (John 4:18).

[113] This translation follows the MT, which tends to heighten the aspect of *apostasy* among the new settlers in Samaria; for its part, the LXX highlights their *syncretism*.

which God, not the Baals, would be the husband of Israel (2:16–17; cf. 14:4–7).[114] Isaiah gives readers the words they will speak when Ephraim and Judah are restored: "I will bless you, O Lord, because you were angry with me, and [then] you turned away your wrath and comforted me" (Isa 12:1; cf. 11:10–12:6). Ezekiel takes two sticks – the stick of Joseph (= Ephraim) and the stick of Judah – and clasps them together in his hand in order to show how God will unite the people and cleanse them from their sin when he comes to dwell among them (Ezek 37:15–28).[115] Jeremiah's well-known oracle of a new covenant is deeply concerned with the possibility of renewed faithfulness for the ten northern tribes who are addressed together under the name "Ephraim" (see Jer 31:1–37). Finally, the Chronicler records the Judahite king Hezekiah and the levitical priests going to great lengths to include northerners in a Passover festival (2 Chron 30). Some resist this worship (30:10), but others from the north, including Samaria, humble themselves to participate in the worship of the Lord as a unified people (30:11–27; cf. 35:18). Later, when Josiah enacts reforms, some from Manasseh and Ephraim – that is, Samaria – turn back to the Lord and sponsor the renewed worship of the Lord in Jerusalem (2 Chron 34:6–7,9). For the Chronicler the message is clear: the northern tribes, including their remnant in Samaria, are only one act of repentance away from participation in the true worship of Israel.[116] Of course, for the Chronicler especially but also for several of these voices, the repentance of the northern tribes will lead to a way of life that aligns with the ways of the faithful in Judah.[117]

The centuries between the time of the Chronicler and the time of Fourth Gospel saw the divisions between Samaritans and mainstream Judaism grow, but the voices of the biblical prophets and writers were never silenced. Though the communities were, at times, hostile to each other, their common kinship was not forgotten. Josephus charges that Samaritans adapt their attitude toward the *Ioudaioi*

---

[114] This wordplay may surface in John 4 with the fivefold repetition of "husband" (ἀνήρ) in John 4:16–18. McHugh (*John*, 282) points out that in Aramaic (and Hebrew) a common term for husband is *ba'al* (cp. Hos 2:16; 2:18 ET).

[115] Cf. also Ezek 16 (esp. vv. 46–63). 36:16–38 (God cleansing Israel). Indeed, this concern for unity precedes the exile (cf. Josh 22).

[116] Cf. also 2 Chron 31:1–4 and Jer 41:5.

[117] For the Chronicler, salvation is ἐκ Ἰουδα. Ezekiel envisions Samaria, which was formerly Jerusalem's "elder sister," becoming a "daughter" of Jerusalem in the age of restoration (16:61).

in response to circumstance – claiming their common ancestry in times of convenience, but in hard times they disown the *Ioudaioi* in both "friendship and race" (εὐνοίας ἢ γένους; *Ant.* 9.290–291).[118] When Alexander the Great showed favor to the God of the Jews, the Samaritans worked to benefit from his favor: though they were (and are) "apostates from the Jewish nation," they "professed themselves Jews" (*Ant.* XI.340) – or, more accurately, "Hebrews" (11.344).[119] In the Maccabean period, John Hyrcanus deepened the division between Jews and Samaritans when he destroyed the Samaritan temple on Mt. Gerizim (13.254–257). Summarizing Josephus' views of the Samaritans, Reinhard Plummer argues that Josephus viewed the Samaritans as "a child of his time and people."[120] Occasionally Josephus presents them as the kin of the *Ioudaioi* (συγγενεῖς; cf. 2 Chronicles 30, 34); other times they are émigrés from Persia (ἄποικοι) who stand outside of his community (cf. 2 Kings 17).[121]

Josephus' ambivalence marks much of the evidence regarding the relationship between *Ioudaioi* and Samaritans. Samaritans were never something entirely "other" than *Ioudaioi*. They steadfastly claimed membership in Israel. In the second century BC, a Samaritan community on the Greek island of Delos referred to themselves as "Israelites in Delos."[122] Jesus ben Sira would dispute that claim: he refers to Samaritans as "the foolish people that live in Shechem" and says they are "not even a people" (50:25–26).[123] The author of 2 Maccabees, however, does not go so far: he holds together *Ioudaioi* and Samaritans when he depicts them as a single people (τὸ γένος) suffering under the decrees of Antiochus (2 Macc 5:22; 6:1–2).[124] In the New Testament, Samaritans and *Ioudaioi* are at times held apart: Jesus clearly distinguishes them from Israel in Matthew 10:5–6. Other times, they are much more closely joined to Israel: In the Third Gospel, a Samaritan rightly assesses the priority of neighbor love over purity concerns (Luke 10:25–37); another follows the law

---

[118] For examples of these shifting loyalties, see 12.257–261; 17.342. For more detailed treatment, see Reinhard Plummer, *The Samaritans in Flavius Josephus*, TSAJ 129 (Tübingen: Mohr Siebeck, 2009), esp. 281–285.

[119] See *Ant.* (11.344, 346–347).

[120] Plummer, *The Samaritans in Flavius Josephus*, 282.

[121] Ibid. Plummer draws the Greek terms from *Ant.* XII.257.

[122] For the texts and discussion, see Plummer, *The Samaritans*, 16–17.

[123] "The foolish people" likely echoes Deut 32:21. See Plummer, 9–12; T. Levi 7:1–4: "Shechem shall be called 'city of the Senseless,' because as one might scoff at a fool, we scoffed at them [for committing folly in Israel]."

[124] Ibid., 12–15. Cf. also Neh 6:6.

for lepers set out in Leviticus 14 (Luke 17:11–19). In Acts 8, Philip proclaims the message of Jesus in Samaria in terms that are rooted in Scriptural language and with a response that parallels the reception of the message in Jerusalem. Later than the New Testament, the rabbis debated the status of Samaritans. It was not permitted to say "Amen" to a Samaritan prayer until the speaker had concluded (*m.* Ber 8.8). Eating with them was contested (*m.* Sheb 8.10); their daughters conveyed a heightened degree of uncleanness (*m.* Nidd 4.1–2). But overall the Samaritans occupied a liminal space, clearly falling short of the commitments and comprehensive purity that should define Israel but also fringe members of the people of God. A minor tractate of the Talmud maintains this view: "The Samaritans in some of their ways resemble the Gentiles and in some resemble Israel, but in the majority they resemble Israel" (*b.* Kuthim 1.1); "When may they be received into the Jewish community? When they have renounced Mt. Gerizim and acknowledged Jerusalem and the resurrection of the dead" (ibid, 2.8).[125]

John narrates Jesus' entry into Samaritan territory, and therefore into this contested theological relationship, by establishing its connection to the patriarchs Jacob and Joseph. Jesus sits "at the well of Jacob" (πηγὴ τοῦ Ἰακώβ) near the field that Jacob gave to Joseph (ὃ ἔδωκεν Ἰακὼβ [τῷ] Ἰωσὴφ τῷ υἱῷ αὐτοῦ). Thus, the primary significance of this location is that it can be identified as the inheritance passed down from Israel's ancestors. In this place, tired from his journey, Jesus sits down on (or beside) the well (ἐπὶ τῇ πηγῇ; John 4:5–6). For the reader who has caught – and perhaps puzzled over – Jesus' likeness to Jacob in John 1:51, these references to Jacob and this setting at the well evoke the story of Jacob meeting Rachel (Gen 29:1–20).[126] But Genesis 29 is not a perfect type for John 4. Jesus is not Jacob *redivivus*. Instead, the relationship between Jesus and the patriarch is one of suggestive association: Jesus is like Jacob, but he also brings in fullness what Jacob only saw at a distance.[127] He

---

[125] Cf. also *m.* Dem 3.4; 4.9; Ned 3.10; Kidd 4.3; Nidd; 7:4–5; *b.* Kidd 75b–76a. The quotations are from A. Cohen, ed., *The Minor Tractates of the Talmud* (London: Soncino Press, 1965), 615, 621. The translator of tractate Kuthim, Maurice Simon, dates the core of its traditions before the third century (ibid., v.), though specific evidence for that claim is not offered.

[126] On the relationship of John 4 to these type scenes, esp. Gen 29, see McWhirter, 58–78, esp. 64–65. Cf. also Moser, *Schriftdiskurse*, 101–107.

[127] See Michael Theobald, "Abraham – (Isaak) – Jakob. Israels Väter im Johannesevangelium" in *Israel und seine Heilstradition im Johannesevangelium: Festgabe für Johannes Beutler SJ zum. 70 Geburtstag,* ed. Michael Labahn, Klaus Scholtissek, and

comes to the well not at the beginning of the story of Israel but rather at its climax. The themes of marriage due to this setting evoke not simply a repetition of the past but a long-awaited union.[128] Jesus' request for a drink (4:7) causes the woman to question the propriety of their association. She asks, "How are you – a *Ioudaios* – asking a drink from me – a woman of Samaria? For *Ioudaioi* do not associate with Samaritans" (4:9).[129] This protest introduces the conflict that *should* frame the story. But it does not. Jesus refuses to let the estrangement of *Ioudaioi* and Samaritans inhibit his message. He claims that if she knew God's gift and the person with whom she is speaking, then she would be the one seeking a drink of living water from him (4:10). She grasps the strangeness of this reply: not only is he ill-equipped to draw water (4:11), but the well where they are meeting was given by Jacob himself. Thus she appeals to the patriarch she and Jesus share in common: "Are you greater than our father Jacob?" she asks (μὴ σὺ μείζων εἶ τοῦ πατρὸς ἡμῶν Ἰακώβ) (4:12).[130]

Instead of a direct answer, however, Jesus offers water that will quench all thirst and become for the thirsty a spring of water welling up into eternal life (4:13–14). To assess Jesus' status vis-à-vis Jacob, one must understand what he offers. The greatness of the gift signifies the greatness of the giver.[131] The phrase Jesus uses – a spring of water welling up to eternal life (πηγὴ ὕδατος ἀλλομένου εἰς ζωὴν αἰώνιον) – would be puzzling to a Samaritan, as there are no

---

Angelika Strotmann (Paderborn: Ferdinand Schöningh, 2004), 171–172. I do not understand why for Theobald the abundant goodness of Jesus' gift would remove the possibility of a typology at this point (cp., e.g., Rom 5:12–21).

[128] For this reason, the marital themes than run through John 2:1–11, 3:25–30, and 4:4–42 call up the eschatological reconciliation of God and Israel. See Isa 54:5, 62:4; Jer 3:14; 31:32; Hos 2:14–20; cf. Schröder, 60–61. The "voice of the bridegroom" mentioned by John the Baptist (John 3:29) is an eschatological sign of restoration (Jer 40:11; cf. 7:34; 16:9; 25:10 [the only use of φωνὴ νυμφίου/ קוֹל חָתָן in Jewish Scripture]). See further Richard Patterson, "Metaphors of Marriage as Expressions of Divine-Human Relations," *JETS* 51/4 (2008): 689–702; Mirjam and Ruben Zimmermann, "Der Freund des Bräutigams (Joh 3,29): Deflorations- oder Christuszeuge," *ZNW* 90 (1999): 123–130.

[129] On conflicting interpretations of οὐ γὰρ συγχρῶνται Ἰουδαῖοι Σαμαρίταις, see Sir 50:25; David Daube, "Jesus and the Samaritan Woman: The Meaning of Synchraomai," *JBL* 69.2 (1950): 137–147.

[130] This is also noted in Hans Förster, "Die Begegnung am Brunnen (Joh 4.4-42) im Licht der Schrift," *NTS* 61 (2015): 201–218 (see esp. 209–215). For a catalog of Jewish and Samaritan traditions related to this text, see Jerome H. Neyrey, "Jacob Traditions and the Interpretation of John 4:10–26," *CBQ* 41 (1979): 419–437.

[131] My wording here is indebted to McHugh, *John*, 271. Cf. Moser, *Schriftdiskurse*, 57–58.

metaphorical references to wells or living water in the Pentateuch.[132] But outside of the Torah these terms resound with eschatological significance: "You will give them a drink (ποτιεῖς) from the brook of your delights, because with you is the spring of life (πηγὴ ζωῆς), and in your light we see light" (Ps 35:9–10 LXX; MT 36:9–10). Similarly, the life of wisdom is a spring of life (Prov 10:11; 13:14; 14:27; 16:22; 18:14).[133] In Jeremiah, the Lord bears witness against his unfaithful people – "they have abandoned me, the spring of life" (ἐγκατέλιπον πηγὴν ζωῆς τὸν κύριον/ מקור מים־חיים; Jer 2:13; cf 17:13). Life-giving water fills the prophetic visions of the restored and reconciled people (Ezek 47:1–12; Zech 14:8; cf. Hab 2:14; Isa 35:6–7), by this new water they are cleansed (Zech 13:1; cf. Ezek 36:25–27) and quenched (Isa 48:21; 55:1). On the day of the restoration of Ephraim and Judah, the people will draw water with joy from "the fountains (πηγῶν) of salvation" (Isa 12:3; cf. 11:1–12:6).[134]

John presents Jesus as the one who brings these conditions of eschatological life into existence.[135] But the vision Jesus offers and the terms in which it is rooted derive from biblical traditions that Samaritans deny. Thus, it is to the mainstream tradition of Judaism, shaped by the prophetic vision for the restored, reconciled, and blessed people of God – including Samaritans – that Jesus summons the Samaritan woman. With his offer of living water, Jesus implicitly invites her to recognize his gift as one that brings with it the promise of the restoration of north and south, Ephraim and Judah. Jesus' offer is made in terms of eschatological blessings, specifically *Jewish* eschatological blessings. In this important sense – which is shared also with the Chronicler, Ezekiel, Jeremiah, Isaiah, and Zechariah – the blessings of God are conceived within a Jewish frame of reference.[136]

The next step in Jesus' conversation with the Samaritan woman sustains his invitation for her to experience what he has to offer as well as the requirement that she reorient her beliefs to a new frame of

---

[132] McHugh, *John*, 273–274.

[133] Compare Sirach 21:13; 24:19–34. See also McHugh, *John*, 274–275, who cites 1QH 8. No single Hebrew phrase is used as consistently as this Greek expression.

[134] Isa 12:3: ἀντλήσετε ὕδωρ μετ' εὐφροσύνης ἐκ τῶν πηγῶν τοῦ σωτηρίου/ ושאבתם־מים בששון ממעיני הישועה. (Note that the Hebrew word for salvation in this line is *Yeshua*.)

[135] See Moser, *Schriftdiskurse*, 78–79, 111–123.

[136] See John Bowman, "Samaritan Studies," *BJRL* 40 (1958): 298–327. Bowman locates this reunification particularly in the visions of Ezek 36–37, an attractive hypothesis given the significance of Ezek 37 later in John (cf. John 10:1–20).

reference. Asked to call her husband, she responds that she has none; Jesus agrees – she has had five, and the one she has at present is not her husband (4:16–18). Interpreters divide on the question of whether Jesus speaks of her actual marital status or only a symbolic reality (namely, the five husbands represent the cults of the five cities that resettled Samaria in 2 Kings 17:29–32).[137] Likely, however, both readings are correct: The biography of the Samaritan woman embodies the history of her people.[138] When Jesus makes this connection, the woman recognizes Jesus' insight and raises a controversial question about proper worship (4:19–20). For the purposes of recognizing Jesus as the one who announces and inaugurates the future of Israel, there are three necessary observations about Jesus' identity in the interactions that follow (4:21–30, 39–42).

First, the woman confesses Jesus to be a prophet (θεωρῶ ὅτι προφήτης εἶ σύ, 4:19). The missing definite article and the subsequent dialogue (in which the woman continues to recognize Jesus as a *Ioudaios* – that is, not a Samaritan deliverer) suggests that she recognizes Jesus' insight but remains uncertain about his significance.[139] Nevertheless, the affirmation that Jesus is a prophet brings forward for the reader a rush of questions about Jesus' identity. Is he "the prophet like Moses" whom God will raise up from among his brothers (Deut 18:15–18)?[140] Are Jesus' words given to him by God?[141] Will he faithfully shepherd the people of Israel as Moses did?[142] This passing – and even equivocal – recognition of Jesus as a

---

[137] See the fuller discussion and variation on this proposal in Craig R. Koester, "'The Savior of the World' (John 4:42)," *JBL* 109 (1990): 668–674.

[138] See Otto Betz, "Reflections on John 4, 20–26," in *Standing before God: Studies on Prayer in Scripture and in Tradtion with Essays in Honor of John M. Oesterreicher,* ed. Asher Finkel and Lawrence Frizzell (New Yord: KTav, 1981), 57. Moser, *Schrift-diskurse,* 81–82; Koester, "'The Savior of the World' (John 4:42)," 665–680.

[139] So also in 3:2. In 4:29, the woman is still asking, "Could this be the messiah?" Cp. with the articular ὁ προφήτης in 1:21, 6:14, 7:40 (but inarticular in 7:52). Deut 18:15–18 describes this figure without the article.

[140] Samaritans had specific expectations for a figure called the *Taheb* (the title can mean either "the restorer" [transitive] or "the returning one" [intransitive]), and some sources merge expectations for God to raise up "a prophet like Moses" with the *Taheb.* In *Memar Marqah* (fourth century AD), the appearance of the *Taheb* brings peace, exposes darkness, and restores correct worship for Israel. See Josephus, *Ant.* 18.85–86; Meeks, *Prophet-King,* 246–254.

[141] Deut 18:18: "I will put my words in his mouth, and he will speak to them as I command him." Cf. John 7:16–18, where Jesus vigorously affirms that he speaks not from himself but from God.

[142] On this image, see Meeks, *Prophet-King,* 196–200. For an additional application to Jesus, see Rev 7:17.

prophet does not provide an easy category for interpreting Jesus' identity. It does, however, pique hopes, raise questions, and create associations. This question will rise to prominence again in John 6–7, and groundwork for those debates is laid here.[143]

Second, when confronted with the basic theological difference between the Samaritans and mainstream Judaism, Jesus makes two assertions. First he describes the time that it is in Israel's history; second he rejects the specifics of Samaritan belief. Taken together, Jesus calls this woman out of her wrongly ordered life and into the mainstream of Jewish tradition, and then beyond it – into a recognition that the foundational stories and hopes of the Jewish tradition signify him. We will consider these dynamics in turn.

Jesus' first assertion is that an hour (ὥρα) is coming and has arrived when the rivalry will be overcome: "You will worship the Father neither on this mountain nor in Jerusalem (4:21) . . . true worshippers will worship the Father in sprit and truth" (4:23). Worship in the spirit harks back to Jesus' discussion of rebirth by the Spirit in 3:5–8, and it draws on the expectation of the biblical prophets that when God restores Israel he will do so by giving the people a new spirit that enables fidelity and fellowship.[144] For John, because "God is Spirit" (4:24), worship in spirit describes a worship in which God enables people to come before him under the conditions of the new age, unobstructed by idolatry, and also without the need of places for its mediation.[145]

Worship in truth is a more perplexing assertion. The phrase might be simply epexegetical: "worship in spirit – that is, in truth."[146] Along these lines, it might point to the coherence of a person's spiritual and ethical life. In this vein, one might recognize the phrase in John 4 coming alongside similar terminology used by the Qumran

---

[143] Or rather, the emphasis on the faithfulness of the words Jesus speaks in John 4 actually *settles* the debate before it even begins in John 6–7.

[144] Isa 32:15; 44:3 (Isa 44 is a lengthy oracle about the vanity of false worship and God's promise to restore right worship); Ezek 36:25–27; 37:9–10; Joel 3:1–5 (LXX 2:28–29).

[145] In separating worship in spirit and truth from the eschatological vision of worship on Mt. Zion, Jesus breaks sharply from biblical prophecies that connect the Spirit's outpouring to life in the land (e.g., Ezek 36:28). This is not unprecedented; it might be implied, for instance, in Isa 66:1. It would, however, stand in contrast to the teaching of the rabbis who emphasized the significance of *Eretz Israel* during a time when emigration was widespread (see Davies, "Aspects of the Jewish Background of the Gospel of John," 54–56).

[146] See Brown, I.172, 180.

community, which described the Holy Spirit (also reckoned as the "Spirit of truth") as the one who directed and sanctified the life of the community and made it into "a house of perfection and truth in Israel" (1 QS 8.9), in which God will "sprinkle over [the member of the community] the spirit of truth like lustral water."[147] But perhaps ἐν πνεύματι καὶ ἀληθείᾳ is more than a hendiadys.

Otto Betz has suggested that Joshua's charge to the tribes of Israel at Shechem helpfully illuminates Jesus' phrase: "Now, therefore, fear the Lord and worship him in blamelessness and in truth (בתמים ובאמת). Turn away from the gods which your fathers served beyond the river and in Egypt and worship the Lord" (Josh 24:14).[148] Along these lines, Jesus stands on the same ground as his namesake Joshua (Ἰησοῦς/ יהושׁע), and he announces to the Samaritan woman the arrival of the kind of worship her fathers had sought but failed to enact (cf. Josh 24:19–28). The time of the Spirit has now come, however, and with it the long-awaited time of worship "in truth." When John's Jesus proclaims the necessity of worshiping the Father "in Spirit and truth," he proclaims the necessity of worshiping God under the conditions of the new age. In Samaria, the arrival of this new age signals the possibility for a fidelity that had been pledged but never realized.[149]

Sandwiched within Jesus' statements about true worship of the Father is a rejection of Samaritan theology: "You (pl.) worship what you do not know. We worship what we know – for salvation is from the *Ioudaioi*" (4:22). In the theological controversies between *Ioudaioi* and Samaritans Jesus calls this woman out of error and into truth. Samaritanism had separated itself from the mainstream of the Jewish tradition and ought to return. As we have seen, nearly every statement of Jesus in John 4 presupposes an eschatological vision rooted in the prophets of the Jewish tradition. In addition to calling

---

[147] 1 QS 3.6–12; 4:20–26. Notably, the Qumran community also envisioned faithful worship in Spirit/truth away from Jerusalem (1 QS 8.1–14). Cf. O. Betz, 62–65; Schnackenburg 1.436–40; see further Richard Bauckham, "John and Qumran: Is There a Connection?" in *The Scrolls and the Scriptures: Qumran Fifty Years After*, ed. Stanley E. Porter and Craig E. Evans, JSPSS 26 (Sheffield: Sheffield Academic Press, 1997), 267–279.

[148] Betz, 58–61. N.B. The LXX does not use ἀλήθεια to translate אמת but instead "righteousness." Thus, "worship him in uprightness and righteousness" (λατρεύσατε αὐτῷ ἐν εὐθύτητι καὶ ἐν δικαιοσύνῃ).

[149] See Ignace de la Potterie, "'Nous adorons, nous, ce que nous connaissons, car le salut vient de Jiufs': Historie de l'exégèse et interprétation de John 4,22," *Bib* 64.1 (1983): 74–115, esp. 110–114.

Samaritans out of error and into the knowledge of the *Ioudaioi*, Jesus also calls this woman to recognize the new eschatological moment in which she lives. Thus, there are two reconfigurations taking place here. The first is a call for Samaritans – and perhaps all non- *Ioudaioi* – to align their lives and expectations for God and Jesus according to that which is required of them by the Jewish tradition (even to the basic commitments of the tradition with which the *Ioudaioi* identify). The second reconfiguration is a call to recognize the time – the hour – that is coming and has arrived. It is the hour of the outpoured Spirit and the possibility of Samaria/Ephraim reunited with Judah in worship before God.

In the broader narrative of the Fourth Gospel, the identification of Jesus as a *Ioudaios* serves the purpose of locating Jesus' theological vision within the broader tradition of Judaism. For John, Jesus announces the arrival and actualization of God's eschatological promises in a way that comports fully with the texts that underlie this tradition. ἡ σωτηρία ἐκ τῶν Ἰουδαίων ἐστίν (4:22).[150] The *Ioudaioi* in John are the inheritors of this tradition. They posses the resources to recognize Jesus, to understand the terms in which he speaks, and to identify the coherence of his message with Moses and the prophets.[151] This clear affirmation of the *Ioudaioi* is an affirmation of the deep agreement that John finds between his gospel and the basic convictions of Judaism, and even of the group whose vision for Jewish life is the primary rival to John's.[152] It is also, however, an affirmation that reinforces John's presentation of Judaism in epistemological crisis. Salvation is from the *Ioudaioi*, and yet they cannot recognize Jesus as the one who would save them.[153]

---

[150] Reading the ἐκ here as a denoting derivation. (For a reflection on this usage, see Leander Keck, "Anthropology and Soteriology in Johannine Christology," in *Why Christ Matters: Toward a New Testament Christology* [Waco: Baylor, 2015], 73–89). For an opposing view, see Barret, *John,* 237. Schnackenburg is on the mark: "Converted Samaritans had to recognize that they were once schismatics and that it was only in Christ [i.e., the messiah whose identity is grounded in the tradition affirmed by the *Ioudaioi* –CMB] that they had been made part of the people of salvation" (1.436).

[151] John 1:45; 5:39.

[152] For a literary-critical development of this perspective, see Moser, *Schriftdiskurse,* 98, 131–132.

[153] Hengel (*Die johanneische Frage: Ein Lösungversuch,* WUNT 67 [Tübingen: Mohr Siebeck, 1993], 296–298, 301–302) argues that John 4 lays the groundwork for a Gentile mission: The Samaritans are "halben Heiden." In light of the exegesis in this section, it is more likely that John is working with the problem of Samaritans as "halben Juden."

Third, and finally, beginning with the woman and ending with her people, the Samaritans recognize Jesus as "a prophet" (4:19), the "messiah/Christ" (4:25–29), and "the savior of the world" (4:42).[154] As we saw with the titles of Jesus in John 1, so here the titles concentrate eschatological significance onto Jesus. The farthest reaching is the last – "savior of the world" (ὁ σωτὴρ τοῦ κόσμου; 4:42). A similar title was used of God by Philo (Spec. Laws 2.198), and in the broader Roman world it was used of Hadrian, among others emperors, as well as certain gods.[155] In John, the recognition of Jesus as "savior of the world" recalls most prominently the words of John 3:17: "God sent his son into the world not to condemn the world but to save the world through him" (ἀλλ᾽ ἵνα σωθῇ ὁ κόσμος δι᾽ αὐτοῦ). The Samaritans recognize what Nicodemus failed to see, and they affirm Jesus' ministry as a ministry that is bound to the identity of the God of Israel, that is, the one who is repeatedly acclaimed in Scripture as the "God of salvation."[156] Seen from within John's broader vision for Jesus as the one who announces and establishes the future of Israel, the Gospel's presentation of Jesus as the savior of the world implies a recognition of Jesus from within the expectations set out by the prophets of Israel and, thus, the reconfiguration of the Samaritan worldview *first* into a Jewish frame a reference and *second* into a version of that worldview that is capable of recognizing the arrival of eschatological fulfillment in Jesus.

Conclusion

The aim of the exegesis in this chapter has been to show John's sustained interest in portraying Jesus in terms that are defined by Israel's foundational stories and also rooted deeply in a concern for Israel's future. To read "with the grain" in these chapters is to see how John identifies Jesus as the enfleshed Word of God, who has persistently sought a dwelling place in the world. John presents Jesus

---

[154] Justin Martyr (*First Apology* 53.6), who spent his early life in Samaria, records that Samaritans and Jews have one Christ who will redeem both communities (see Marinus de Jonge, "Jewish Expectations about the 'Messiah' according to the Fourth Gospel," *NTS* 19 [1973]: 268).

[155] On the emperors, see Koester, "Savior of the World," 665–668; Adolph Diessmann, *Light from the Ancient East* (New York: Hodder and Stoughton, 1910), 368–369.

[156] Cf. Deut 32:15; Isa 17:10; 45:14–15; Pss 24:5; 25:5; 27:1 et passim. N.B. The biblical judges are regularly referred to as "saviors," but even their leadership was interpreted as an extension of God's salvation (1 Sam 10:19; Neh 9:27).

as the one whose identity is witnessed by John the Baptist, Moses, and (even) the temple. Jesus is, for John, the teacher who exposes the failure of others who would instruct Israel. He is the source of the waters that will refresh and restore Israel, and he is the source of the Spirit that signifies participation in the realities of the eschatological hour. He is the one whose identity can comprehend the vast array of titles and expectations for deliverance that exist within the Jewish tradition. In short, for John, Jesus is the one who brings Israel into its future life.

As the Fourth Gospel narrates the identity and actions of Jesus in terms that resound with significance from the biblical past and its expectations of the future, it affirms Jesus as the one who provides an innovative continuity that leads from one to the other. In short, the tradition of Judaism may faithfully bridge the gap between the past and the future through faith in Jesus. This is the theological vision John casts. In the shadow of this vision, however, is a negation of the alternatives. Moses and his ministry function as types for Jesus; Jacob's vision functions similarly; the Torah and the temple are called in as witnesses to Jesus. John portrays Nicodemus, the teacher of Israel, as incapable of understanding the Scriptures he should know. The Samaritan woman is offered the living water of eschatological life and is simultaneously called out of worshiping what she does not know. These affirmations and negations co-inhere, and together they represent the argument embedded in the opening chapters of John's Gospel: Jesus' ministry takes up the foundational stories and beliefs of the Jewish tradition; he offers a way into the future in continuity with these foundational commitments. Yet his way requires the reorganization of a person's thinking and living. In John 5–10, the controversial nature of John's innovation takes center stage.

3

DEBATE: JOHN 5–10

In chapters 5–10, John presents the identity and significance of Jesus in light of the principal feasts of the *Ioudaioi*, first at an unnamed feast (John 5), then around the time of Passover (John 6), then at the festival of Sukkot (John 7–10:21), and finally at the Festival of Dedication (10:21–42). These festivals organize the chronology of the narrative, and they provide a context for the symbols and expectations that illuminate Jesus' identity. The claims that John makes about Jesus in the context of these festivals also provoke increasing conflict between Jesus and the *Ioudaioi* (or, as John occasionally calls them, "the Pharisees," or "the chief priests and the Pharisees"). The aim of this chapter is to consider this section of John's Gospel as one that characterizes Jesus as one who offers innovative continuity between the past and the future for the people of God in terms of the specific observances that nurtured the memories of Israel and also shaped their expectations. How does Jesus relate to the past that these festivals recall? How does he fulfill the hopes they nurture? How do both innovation and continuity account for John's characterization of Jesus and the growing conflict with the *Ioudaioi*?

John 5: Healing on the Sabbath

The structure of John 5 follows the familiar Johannine pattern of first describing a dramatic sign and then following that sign with a discourse interpreting the identity of Jesus in view of the sign. The scene unfolds as follows: In Jerusalem, at a feast, Jesus seeks out a man who has been ill for thirty-eight years. He is lying near the pool called Bethesda when Jesus approaches him with a question: "Do you want to be made whole?" (5:6). The sick man offers an excuse for why he has not yet been made so: every time the water stirs, he fails to reach it. He has no man to bring him into the pool (5:7). Readers of John know that Jesus offers a water more potent than those that stir intermittently in Bethesda (cf. 4:10–14), and the sick man quickly experiences this power firsthand. Jesus commands him, "Get up, carry your mat, and go," and he does (5:8–9). "But that day was a Sabbath," John writes (5:9).

Mention of the Sabbath in this healing occurs almost as an afterthought, tacked on at the end of scene that otherwise resembles healings on the Sabbath and encounters between Jesus and paralytics in the Synoptic Gospels.[1] It is this detail of timing, however, that sets in motion all of the action that follows. Jesus' violation of the Sabbath engenders a debate about basic aspects of his identity – his authority, legitimacy, and how he might be known.[2] Through this sign and the discourse it provokes, the Evangelist takes an opportunity to lay bare the sweeping significance of Jesus as one whose identity is bound up with the identity of the God who named and blessed the Sabbath and as it is also the identity of a son with a commission to work as his father works.[3] This is why John can leave the festival unnamed without the portrayal of Jesus losing any power: It is the violation of the Sabbath (a festal Sabbath, to be sure) that provides the key setting for the claim that the Fourth Gospel makes in this chapter about Jesus as one who lives in a relationship of closest unity with the God of Israel.[4]

In what follows, we will take particular care to attend to four ways in which the presentation of Jesus healing *on the Sabbath* characterizes him as the one who authentically reveals God and as the one through whom God's people might faithfully relate to their past and experience the blessings of God's future. First, we will consider the way that Jesus' action provokes a debate about his identity; second, we will turn to the significance of Jesus' claim to exercise authority as the Son of Man (5:27); third, the witness of Scripture to Jesus will

---

[1] See Mk 3:1–6 and pars.; Lk 13:10–17; Mk 2:23–28 and pars.; Lk 14:1–6). See also C.H. Dodd, *Historical Tradition in the Fourth Gospel* (Cambridge: Cambridge University Press, 1963), 174–180; Hays, *Echoes of Scripture in the Gospels*, 424n2; Peder Borgen, "The Sabbath Controversy in John 5:1–18 and Analogous Controversy Reflected in Philo's Writings," *Studia Philonica* 3 (1991): 209–21.

[2] See here Jerome H. Neyrey, S.J., *An Ideology of Revolt: John's Christology in Social-Scientific Perspective* (Philadelphia: Fortress, 1988), 9–36; Nils A. Dahl, "'Do Not Wonder!' John 5:28–20 and Johannine Eschatology Once More," in *The Conversation Continues: Studies in Paul & John in Honor of J. Louis Martyn*, ed. Robert T. Fortna and Beverly R. Gaventa (Nashville: Abingdon, 1990), 322–336.

[3] Cf. Hoskyns, *The Fourth Gospel*, 255.

[4] On Sabbath observance in John, see John 5, 7, and 9; cf. also Philo, *Special Laws* II.XI.41, XV.56–XVI.70; *m.* Shab.

come under focus; fourth, we will consider how John accounts for the inability of the *Ioudaioi* to receive these claims. These four aspects work together in John 5 to present Jesus as the one who carries out the work of God in the world. Indeed, John 5 dramatizes what the prologue already stated: "No one has ever seen God; the unique God, who is at the bosom of the Father, this one has made him known" (1:18). Our first task is to consider how John 5 raises the issue of Jesus' identity.

The Implications of Jesus' Identity as the Son

In the Synoptic Gospels, Jesus justifies healing on the Sabbath with reference to saving a life, doing good, or, by a *qal vahomer,* rescuing an animal that has fallen into a pit.[5] If these acts be justified on the Sabbath, then surely it is appropriate to restore to wholeness one who is afflicted by sickness. In John 5, however, Jesus offers no such defense of his actions. Instead, it is his command to the healed man, "Get up, take your mat, and go," that draws a response from the *Ioudaioi.* This is the action they protest by saying, "It is not lawful for you to carry your mat" (5:10–11). And thus, with this setup, John centers the conflict surrounding Jesus' actions on a straightforward violation of Sabbath – the act of carrying a burden from one place to another.[6] Jesus' command stands in clear tension with a basic command issued by God through Jeremiah: "Thus says the Lord, guard your lives and do not bear a burden on the Sabbath" (Jer 17:21). In Jeremiah's teaching, the consequences for breaking the Sabbath include the destruction of the city (17:27). By contrast, Sabbath observance brings with it the promise of kings who sit on David's throne, as well as the prosperity of Jerusalem (vv. 24–26). The prophet charges the people to "carry no burden" (μὴ αἴρετε βαστάγματα/מַשָּׂא מָשָּׂא תִשְׂאוּ) and "do no work" (μὴ ποιεῖν πᾶν ἔργον/ וְאַל־תִּשְׂאוּ) on the Sabbath (17:21, 22, 24, 27).[7] Aware of

---

[5] Cf. Mark 3:4, Matt 12:11–12.

[6] In the Mishnah, this act of carrying a burden is inferred from the prohibition of Ex 16:29 ("A man should not go out [יֵצֵא] from his place [with a burden] on the Sabbath") when read with Jer 17:22 ("Do not carry out [תּוֹצִיאוּ] a burden from your houses on the Sabbath"). Cf. *m.* Shab. 1:1, 3; 7:2; 10:5.

[7] In Jer 17:22, 24 the Greek and Hebrew verbs change to ἐκφέρετε/תוֹצִיאוּ and εἰσφέρειν/הָבִיא. Cf. Lutz Doering, "Sabbath Laws in the New Testament Gospels," in *The New Testament and Rabbinic Literature,* ed. R. Bieringer et al., JSJSup 136 (Leiden: Brill, 2010), 243–248.

this context, we can recognize that in John 5:9–18 the *Ioudaioi* respond with hostility to Jesus not because of a priggish commitment to Torah observance above mercy, but because Jesus has provoked them by issuing an order that directly violates the words of God. "For this reason," John writes, "the *Ioudaioi* persecuted Jesus – because he was doing these things on the Sabbath" (5:16).[8] Jesus does not respond to this hostility by interpreting his action as analogous to saving a life on the Sabbath or as an inadvertent violation of the commandment.[9] He justifies his action by asserting his close relationship to God: "My Father is still working, and I am working" (5:17). The claim that God works every day of the week can be found in various contexts. Philo, for instance, observes that Genesis 2:2 uses a transitive verb to record that God rested (κατέ-παυσεν) on the Sabbath. He argues that by using the transitive form (and not the middle [ἐπαύσατο]), Moses signals that God caused creation to rest, though God himself "never ceases making."[10] Later than the Fourth Gospel, the rabbis argued that God's activity on the Sabbath does not violate the commandment because God occupies the earth as a man occupies his house. (It is not a violation of the commandment to carry an object in one's own house.) Thus, it is not work for God simply to be God.[11] It is on analogous reasoning – the reasoning that God's activity and authority obtain every day of the week – that Jesus justifies a command that violates the Sabbath. In the narrative of John, this claim is uncontested. Both Jesus and the *Ioudaioi* affirm in principle that God acts on the Sabbath. The controversy is rooted in what it means for Jesus to justify his work as an extension of the Father's.

The *Ioudaioi* immediately recognize that Jesus has done more than break the Sabbath – he makes himself equal to God (καὶ πατέρα ἴδιον ἔλεγεν τὸν θεὸν ἴσον ἑαυτὸν ποιῶν τῷ θεῷ, 5:18). They see this as a dangerous usurpation of divine prerogatives, and rightly so: In Scripture, God rebuked the prince of Tyre who claimed, "I am

---

[8] On distinctions related to Sabbath breaking, see *m.* Shab. 7:1; Num 15:32–36.

[9] Cp. John 7:23; see also *m.* Shab. 18:3, 19:1–6; Ned. 3:11; *m.* Yoma 8:6: "whenever there is doubt whether life is in danger this overrides the Sabbath."

[10] *Alleg. Interp.*, I.5–6, 16–18. Cf. also Dodd, *Interpretation*, 320–323; Per Karl Bekken, *The Lawsuit Motif in John's Gospel from New Perspectives: Jesus Christ, Crucified Criminal and Emperor of the World*, NovTSup 158 (Leiden: Brill, 2015), 148–164.

[11] See further Strack-Billerbeck, 2.461–462; cf. Mekhilta on Ex 20:11; Dodd, *Interpretation*, 321.

God [Θεός εἰμι ἐγώ/אל אני]; I dwell in the dwelling place of God" (Ezek 28:2). Pharaoh also came under judgment when he viewed himself as the maker of Egypt (Ezek 29:3) and one whose rule lay outside the authority of Israel's God (Ex 5:2). Closer to the time of John, the writer of 2 Maccabees recorded Antiochus IV Epiphanies confessing on his deathbed that he had claimed too much: "It is right to be subject to God – indeed no mortal should think himself equal to God" (καὶ μὴ θνητὸν ὄντα ἰσόθεα φρονεῖν; 2 Macc 9:12).[12] For all such offenses, the penalty for blasphemy looks back to Leviticus 24:10–16, which prescribes death for the one who blasphemes God.

In John's view, however, equality with God does not adequately summarize the claim of Jesus that "my Father is still working, and I am working." For Jesus, this statement implies the unity of the Son's will with the Father's will, the Son's dependence on the Father, and the Father's commission of the Son. In a word, Jesus' statement implies the fundamentally *relational* basis of his identity and actions. Everything for Jesus derives from this relationship. For the *Ioudaioi*, however, Jesus' statement makes an improper *ontological* claim. "They [the *Ioudaioi*] can only conceive of equality with God as independence from God, whereas for Jesus it means the very opposite."[13] Jesus reiterates the fundamental importance of the Father-Son relationship in the following statements:

> For whatever the Father does, these things the Son does likewise. (ἃ γὰρ ἂν ἐκεῖνος ποιῇ, ταῦτα καὶ ὁ υἱὸς ὁμοίως ποιεῖ, 5:19).

> For just as the Father raises the dead and gives life, so the Son likewise gives life to whom he wills. (ὥσπερ γὰρ ὁ πατὴρ ἐγείρει τοὺς νεκροὺς καὶ ζῳοποιεῖ, οὕτως καὶ ὁ υἱὸς οὓς θέλει ζῳοποιεῖ, 5:21)

> For indeed the Father judges no one, but he has given all judgment to the Son, that all might honor the Son like they honor the Father – the one who does not honor the Son does

---

[12] Cf. also Philo, *Embassy*, 114–118, 162–164; Jos. *Ant.* 19:344–347; Acts 12:22–23; Thompson, *John*, 123–124; Wayne A. Meeks, "Equal to God," in *The Conversation Continues: Studies in Paul & John in Honor of J. Louis Martyn*, ed. Robert Fortna and Beverly Gaventa (Nashville: Abingdon, 1990), 309–321. On "Blasphemy" in the Fourth Gospel, see Thompson, *John*, 235; Bekken, *The Lawsuit Motif in John's Gospel from New Perspectives*, 57–62.
[13] Bultmann, *John*, 245.

not honor the Father who sent him. (οὐδὲ γὰρ ὁ πατὴρ κρίνει οὐδένα, ἀλλὰ τὴν κρίσιν πᾶσαν δέδωκεν τῷ υἱῷ, ἵνα πάντες τιμῶσι τὸν υἱὸν καθὼς τιμῶσι τὸν πατέρα. ὁ μὴ τιμῶν τὸν υἱὸν οὐ τιμᾷ τὸν πατέρα τὸν πέμψαντα αὐτόν, 5:22–23)

Because of this dependence, Jesus is not like Antiochus, Pharaoh, or the prince of Tyre. He does not *make himself* equal to God. Jesus is, instead, a son who has been sent and thereby takes with him the authority of his father. Indeed, in a statement that echoes the words of Moses when he was confronted by a mob of hostile priests, Jesus argues that his claims are justified because he does nothing "from himself" (ὁ υἱὸς ποιεῖν ἀφ᾽ ἑαυτοῦ οὐδὲν, 5:19; cf. 5:30), but instead enacts the commission of another.[14]

By viewing John 5:1–23 as a presentation of Jesus in the temple, at a festival, on the Sabbath, purposefully violating the Sabbath, we can see that Jesus' provocative command to the paralytic carries forward the Gospel's agenda of portraying Jesus as a human being who exists in the closest possible relationship to God, that is, as the Son to the Father. Jesus violates the Sabbath in order to confront the *Ioudaioi* with the claim that he, like his Father, possesses the authority to enact divine prerogatives even on the Sabbath. Thus, the claims of this scene dramatize John's earlier statements that "the Word was with God, and the Word was God," and that the enfleshed Word bears glory "as of an utterly unique one from a father." Jesus' claim that the Son carries out the work shown to him by the Father (5:19) recalls the Gospel's earlier claim that "no one has ever seen God; the unique God, who is at the bosom of the Father, has made him known" (1:1, 14, 18).[15] In dramatizing these claims, however, John also demonstrates how vulnerable they are to another interpretation – that is, to an interpretation of these statements as presumptuous, even blasphemous self-representations. The penalty for such blasphemy would be death. By making these provocative claims in Jesus' initial conflict with the *Ioudaioi*, John shows both how Jesus should be understood and how his identity is

---

[14] Cf. Num 16:28, where Moses predicts the downfall of his opponents by claiming that the miracle they are about to witness will prove that he does the works of the Lord who sent him; they are not done from himself (ἀπ᾽ ἐμαυτοῦ, Num 16:28). The Hebrew phrase (מלבי) occurs in the MT only in Num 16:28 and 24:13; the Greek phrase (ἀπ᾽ ἐμαυτοῦ) only in Num 16:28 and 4 Macc 11:3.

[15] See C. H. Dodd, "A Hidden Parable in the Fourth Gospel," in C. H. Dodd, *More New Testament Studies* (Grand Rapids: Eerdmans, 1968), 30–40.

open to a serious misinterpretation – and John claims that a decision about Jesus' identity is unavoidable: to honor the Son is to honor the Father who sent him; to deny the Son honor is to deny it to the Father as well (5:23).

The Authority of Jesus as the Son

A shift in emphasis occurs as John moves further into the engagement between Jesus and the *Ioudaioi*. The legitimacy of Jesus' healing on the Sabbath moves from a claim about his identity (5:17–23) to the implication of that claim for the authority of Jesus. The two claims intertwine, but authority becomes the focal point in 5:24–30. This is the second aspect of John 5 that merits consideration: Jesus claims that the Father has shared with the Son the life that he has in himself (5:26). Further, he claims that hearing and believing the word of the Son is the means to the life that God has promised (5:24–25), and that those who hear and believe the human voice of Jesus are in fact listening to the voice and message of the Son of God who has the power to grant eschatological life. "For he [the Father] has given him [the Son] authority to enact judgment, because he is the Son of Man" (καὶ ἐξουσίαν ἔδωκεν αὐτῷ κρίσιν ποιεῖν, ὅτι υἱὸς ἀνθρώπου ἐστίν, 5:27).

Here we see Jesus disclose his identity as the life-giving Son of the Father and as the authoritative, judging Son of Man. The first claim, that Jesus is the life-giving Son of the Father, asserts that the singular attributes of Israel's God are shared with Jesus. Readers of John's opening chapters are familiar with these ideas (see John 1:4; 3:14–16; 4:14, 46–54). As they encounter them here, however, readers are pressed once more by the bracing proposal that a particular Galilean Jewish man mediates the life that God possesses in himself not as a miracle worker dispenses wonders or as a prophet announces God's impending action. No – Jesus mediates life as a co-possessor of it. The life that the Father has in himself (ὁ πατὴρ ἔχει ζωὴν ἐν ἑαυτῷ) is also the life that Jesus has in himself (οὕτως καὶ τῷ υἱῷ ἔδωκεν ζωὴν ἔχειν ἐν ἑαυτῷ, 5:26).[16] For John, these bold claims are entailed by the title "Son."

The general authority of the Son as one with whom God has shared (ἔδωκεν) divine prerogatives takes specific form with regard

---

[16] Cf. Thompson, *God of the Gospel of John*, 57–100 (esp. 73–80).

to judgment. As with giving life, the authority to enact judgment is an aspect of the Father's authority that he has given (ἔδωκεν) to Jesus.[17] But John uses a different title when referring to Jesus as one who enacts judgment. In other words, in *possessing* authority, Jesus is the Son to the Father. In *exercising* it, Jesus' authority is expressed not through the title "Son," but through the particular title "the Son of Man" – the human figure envisioned by Daniel who received authority from the Ancient of Days (καὶ ἐδόθη αὐτῷ ἐξουσία, Dan 7:14).[18] The two roles of Son and Son of Man are closely related, but they are not identical. Rather, the Son of Man title develops a particular aspect of Jesus' identity as the Son. Since Jesus is the Son (of God/the Father), he exists as the place of revelation, the place where God is encountered and made known.[19] Because Jesus embodies a revelation of God, an encounter with him occasions a judgment similar to those that occurred when God revealed himself in the past.[20] To accept or reject Jesus as the emissary of the Father is thus to occupy a position with regard to Jesus in his role as the Son of Man – marked either by his judgment (5:27) or the life that he has in himself (cf. 3:14–15).

It is because John presents Jesus' identity as a unity that judgment is both a present reality (5:25–27) and a future one (5:28–29). Or, to specify this claim in light of the exegesis of John 1–4, it is because Jesus embodies the presence of God and the conditions of eschatological life that had long been promised to Israel that he confronts his hearers with the claim that in the present moment they are responsible to an eschatological judgment – namely, to honor the Father or not (5:23). In John's view, it should not surprise his hearers that the judgment of the last days has already begun and will be

---

[17] John 5:27: καὶ ἐξουσίαν ἔδωκεν αὐτῷ κρίσιν ποιεῖν, ὅτι υἱὸς ἀνθρώπου ἐστίν. Note that in Dan 7:13, the vision of "one who comes as a son of man" (ὡς υἱὸς ἀνθρώπου) also lacks the Greek articles.

[18] In Dan 7:22, 26 judgment is enacted by the Ancient of Days on behalf of the holy ones, but this is not specifically assigned to the Son of Man figure. Such judgment is more closely related to 1 Enoch 69 (e.g., 69:29). The way in which the rule of the Son of Man in Dan 7:13–14 merges with the rule of the Holy Ones in Dan 7:18, 22, 27 is taken up in Daniel Boyarin, *The Jewish Gospels*, 145; Daniel Boyarin, "The Suffering Christ as Jewish Midrash," in *Religion und Politik: Die Messianische Theologien, Religionswissenschaften und Philosophien des zwanzigsten Jahrhunderts*, ed. Gesine Palmer and Thomas Brose, Religion und Aufklärung 23 (Tübingen: Mohr Siebeck, 2013), 209–224, esp. 214.

[19] Cf. John 1:18.

[20] See Francis J. Maloney, *The Johannine Son of Man*, Biblioteca di Scienze Religiose 14 (Rome: LAS, 1976), 83.

completed in the future. If Jesus lived on the earth as the Son of the Father, how could acceptance or rejection of him *not* entail the honoring or dishonoring of the one who sent him and the judgment that is concomitant to such an encounter?

Even as John claims that the judgment of the Son of Man is at work in the present encounter of Jesus with the *Ioudaioi*, the Gospel also describes Jesus as the one who will enact the resurrection of the last days. In 5:28–29, John paraphrases the expectation of Dan 12:2:[21]

Dan 12:2	John 5:28–29
Many of those who sleep	All who are
in the dust of the earthy	in the tombs
shall awake:	will hear his voice and come forth
those who have done good	some
to everlasting life,	to the resurrection of life,
and some	and those who have done evil
to shame and everlasting contempt	to the resurrection of judgment

The Gospel would have its readers recognize that the figure who dialogues with the *Ioudaioi* in the temple (5:14) also shares the life and authority of the God of Israel (5:17–23) as a Father shares what is his with his Son. For this reason, an encounter with Jesus in the present is simultaneously an encounter with one whom Scripture describes as having been given authority by God (καὶ ἐδόθη αὐτῷ ἐξουσία, Dan 7:14). To be sure, Daniel 12 does not specify as "the Son of Man" the figure who will enact the judgment it describes; the Evangelist reads the Son/Son of Man figure from Daniel 7 into Daniel 12. As he does, he presents the general resurrection as the "eschatological verification" of the ministry of Jesus.[22] The judgment of the last day will vindicate the accuracy of the judgment that takes place with a response to Jesus in the present (John 5:24 cf. 3:18–21). In making these claims, John affirms Israel's traditional hope of eschatological life and expectation of God's ultimate judgment. At the heart of this hope and expectation, however, John presents Jesus. We can see here how John's vision for how Israel will achieve its promised future in light of its storied past takes up the traditional expectations of the biblical past and Jewish tradition,

---

[21] The following chart and several points of discussion here are drawn from Dahl, "Do Not Wonder!" 326–327.

[22] The phrase is Dahl's ("Do Not Wonder!" 328).

while also positing both a bold eschatological claim ("the time of fulfillment has arrived") and a striking development related to the identity of God as well ("the God of Israel, and the promises of that God, must be conceived anew in terms of a Father and his Son – and that son is Jesus, who in fact was spoken of by Daniel"). This is, indeed, an innovative continuity.

Witnesses and the Legitimacy of Jesus

True to form, the Fourth Gospel asserts, rather than argues for, this view of Jesus and the revision of theological claims that it entails. But it is to the legitimacy of these assertions that the narrative turns next (5:30–47). The role of witnesses, and the witness of Scripture in particular, is the third aspect of this scene that merits attention as we consider how John 5 carries forward the Gospel's vision of presenting Jesus as the one who is both the revelation of God and the one who establishes continuity between Israel's past, present, and promised future. John marshals witnesses to demonstrate that Jesus' identity is genuinely continuous with the identity of God, the expectation of God's servants, and the witness of Scripture.

Just as Jesus and the *Ioudaioi* agree that God acts on the Sabbath, so they also mutually affirm the importance of witnesses to validate Jesus against the charge of blasphemy.[23] Thus Jesus reviews those who legitimate his claims, beginning with the witness of John the Baptist. To correctly characterize John's role, Jesus turns to the Psalms. The psalmist had long ago envisioned God coming to the temple, blessing it with abundance, and providing a ruler for the people. God had promised through the psalmist, "There [in the temple] I will cause a horn to rise up for David; I have prepared a lamp for my anointed one" (ἡτοίμασα λύχνον τῷ χριστῷ μου· ‏ערכתי נר למשיחי‎, Ps 131:17 LXX, see also vv. 11–18). Now, standing in the temple, Jesus offers John the Baptist as such a lamp, burning and shining (ἐκεῖνος ἦν ὁ λύχνος ὁ καιόμενος καὶ φαίνων). This, says Jesus, is what the *Ioudaioi* experienced when they encountered the ministry of John (John 5:35). Implicit in Jesus' words is the charge that the experience of John's light in the past ought to be complemented by a vision of the one whom John illuminated. (The

---

[23] On the role of witnesses in accusations of wrongdoing, see Deut 19:15; Num 35:30; Deut 17:6. Cf. Bekken, *The Lawsuit Motif in John's Gospel from New Perspectives*, 121–147.

lamp does not illumine itself!) The Baptist occupies an honored position, but that honor must be specified not as his charismatic or prophetic ministry, but rather as his (Isaiah-like) testimony to Israel that God is newly present among his people (cf. 1:19–36).

Jesus' second witness surpasses the first: the works of healing – even on the Sabbath – and giving life and judging bear witness to Jesus' uniqueness as Son of the Father (5:36; cf. 5:21–29).[24] As with the Gospel's presentation of the Baptist, no independent confirmation of the works of Jesus is available. For John it is simply true that Jesus' healing on the Sabbath confirms his freedom to live and work on that day in the same way that God lives and works on the Sabbath. Those who encounter Jesus are left with the bracing challenge: Is Jesus a deceiver and blasphemer who would work on the Sabbath and order others to do so too? Or is he free to work on the Sabbath because he is from God?[25]

Third, Jesus calls on the witness of the Father. The tone shifts, however, as Jesus cites his Father's testimony. Jesus' words now entail both defense and accusation. "This one," he claims of his Father, "has born witness to me (μεμαρτύρηκεν περὶ ἐμοῦ), though his voice you have never heard nor his image have you seen, and his word you do not have abiding in you – because you are not believing in the one whom he sent" (5:38). The immediate application of Jesus' word to the Scriptures of Israel in v. 39 – "they bear witness to me" – informs readers that, in John's view, *a true understanding of the revelation of God in Scripture ought to open out onto an acceptance of Jesus.* To oppose or reject Jesus is to cut oneself off from the true referent of Scripture. Thus, while seeing God was a defining experience for the major figures of Israel's past (Abraham, Jacob, Moses, Isaiah, Ezekiel),[26] those who deny Jesus lose claim to such experiences.

When Jesus denies that his opponents have seen God's form, he does not deny these visions of the past. (The charge is that *you* have not seen his form.) What Jesus does state, however, is that his opponents do not recognize what their ancestors have seen. The patriarchs and prophets of old saw not God himself but rather Jesus (John 8:56–58; 12:41).[27] Therefore, as they do not receive and believe

---

[24] See Thompson, *John*, 133.

[25] These questions – in nearly these exact terms – replay throughout Jesus' ministry (John 7:21, 31; 9:31–32; 10:20–21).

[26] See, e.g., Gen 18:1; 32:30; Ex 24:9–11; Num 12:8; Isa 6:1; Ezek 1:26; A.T. Hanson, "John 1:14–18 and Exodus XXXIV," 96.

[27] Cf. also John 1:18; 3:13, 32–34; 5:19–20; 12:45; 14:7; 9; 1 John 4:12.

in the Son, the *Ioudaioi* confirm that they are alienated from their own past and even from the theophanies of their forebears to which their own tradition ascribes such great import. In addition to formative moments of seeing God, God's people had been defined in the past by hearing God's voice. In Deuteronomy 4:12, when the Israelites receive the Law from God, they hear the voice of God (φωνὴν ῥημάτων ὑμεῖς ἠκούσατε) but do not see his likeness (ὁμοίωμα). More generally, the Scriptures of Israel characterize the voice of the Lord as a constant experience and hope within Israel. It is the voice of the Lord that Israel hears when it carries out the Torah, and it is the voice of the Lord that they seek in times of distress.[28] Moses, whom John will soon invoke directly as a witness to Jesus (5:46), is one who heard God's voice directly, face to face (Sir 45:1–5). As with the visions of God, Jesus' statement, "his voice you have never heard," does not deny this past experience. What Jesus does deny is the connection between the *Ioudaioi* in the present and this experience of past.[29] John will later portray the Father himself speaking from heaven and the crowds hearing an angel or a peal of thunder (12:28–30). That is similar to the kind of mishearing John portrays here: the inability of the *Ioudaioi* to signify correctly the experiences at the root of their own tradition.

John presses this accusation deeper in the next charge. By refusing to accept or believe in Jesus, the *Ioudaioi* expose their inability to have the words of God abiding in them. Although the language of John (τὸν λόγον αὐτοῦ οὐκ ἔχετε ἐν ὑμῖν μένοντα) alludes to no single Scriptural context, the almost certain reference of Jesus' words is the command for Israelites to keep the words of God in their hearts and souls.[30] Indeed, as the argument turns next to the Mosaic writings, John implies that hearing the voice of the Lord and abiding in his words means specifically recognizing Jesus as the witness of the Torah. To hear and abide in the words of God should lead those who hear the words of Moses to recognize and honor Jesus.

As John goes on in 5:39–47, it becomes clear that there is no neutral reading of the Scriptures that fund the basic commitments of the Jewish tradition. Even the love of the *Ioudaioi* for God – that

---

[28] E.g., Ex 15:26; 19:5; 23:21–22; Deut 4:33, 36; Pss 29; 95:7; Jer 42:1–6.

[29] Cf. Thompson, *John*, 134.

[30] See e.g., Deut 6:6; Josh 1:8; Jer 23:12; Pss 1:2; 119:10–19; Sir 6:37. Lori Baron identifies numerous points of contact between Jesus' claim here (and John 5 more broadly) and the Shema (cf. Lori Baron, "The Shema in John's Gospel," PhD Diss., Duke University, 2016, 306–316).

is, their faithfulness to the prescription at the heart of the *Shema* (Deut 6:4) – is thrown into question by their inability (or unwillingness) to recognize Jesus (John 5:42).[31] All of this reveals that, for John, the claim of the *Ioudaioi* to continuity with the historic past of Israel is seriously misguided. They *think* (δοκεῖτε) they can find life in Scripture without acknowledging the one about whom it witnesses (5:39).[32] For John Scripture does not contain life *in se;* rather, Scripture witnesses to the life of God that both precedes it (John 1:4) and serves as its eschatological goal (3:16, 4:14; 10:10). "If you believed Moses," says Jesus, "you would believe me, for he wrote about me" (5:46).[33]

John does not reveal how Scripture testifies so clearly on Jesus' behalf, but the Gospel does offer hints at its hermeneutic. We have seen how the opening chapters of the Gospel portray Jesus in terms that suggest his priority over Torah (see on John 1:1–18), (dis) continuity with Moses in terms of grace in place of grace (1:17), fulfillment of a host of titles and offices that find their meaning in God's past and promised presence with Israel (1:19–51), and as the one who ushers in the experiences of eschatological blessings such as water, Spirit, and life (John 3:1–9; 4:7–15). To these portrayals of Jesus, John 5 makes the further claim that Moses wrote specifically about Jesus (5:46). Wayne Meeks has shown that expectation for a Moses-like figure based on Deut 18:15–18 accounts for important aspects of John's portrayal of Jesus.[34] The prophet–king connection in the next pericope (esp. John 6:14–15) clarifies one important way in which John conceives of Moses's testimony to Jesus: Jesus exists as a successor to Moses, who is the figure through whom God accomplished defining acts of deliverance and provision for Israel in the past. Moses's words – indeed, all of the Scriptures – are teleologically oriented to Jesus: "They bear witness to me"... "he wrote about me" (5:39, 46).The continuity that John envisions between Jesus and the foundational aspects of the Jewish tradition is total. This continuity is recognizable, however, only to a reader who is willing to accept the innovative proposal that eschatological fulfillment is underway and that the tradition must be retrospectively

---

[31] So also Baron, "The Shema in John's Gospel," 310–311. On the desire to glorify God (lit., "the only God") as something that entails accepting Jesus, see 5:44.

[32] On finding life in the law, cf. 1 Baruch 4:1–2; *m.* Aboth 2:7.

[33] On the stinging portrayal of Moses as the accuser (ὁ κατηγορῶν) of the *Ioudaioi*, see Meeks, *Prophet-King,* 200–204.

[34] Cf. Meeks, *Prophet-King,* 67, 287–91, 301–02.

reconsidered in lights of this innovative solution. At the heart of John's proposal is the claim that the God whom the tradition calls "Father" also has a unique (μονογενής) son, who exercises the prerogatives of judgment and life, and whom one must recognize in order to fulfill the love of God to which Israel is called. This Son is none other than the man Jesus.

So far we have considered John 5 as a healing story that emphasizes (1) the identity of Jesus as the Son of the Father; (2) Jesus' identity not only as the Son but also as the divine, judging figure known as the Son of Man; and (3) the way in which John draws together the witnesses of the Baptist, the works and prerogatives of God, and the Scriptures of Israel. This characterization demonstrates the continuity of Jesus with the storied past and prophesied future of Israel and, to be precise, it sharpens the image of Jesus in the Gospel by binding his character and actions closely to the identity of God in terms of his freedom to act on the Sabbath, and to give life and enact judgment. Through Jesus, Israel encounters its God and the opportunity to embrace the blessings it has long expected. The Gospel recognizes, however, that this proposal and the characterization of Jesus provided in John 5 are judged inadequate by the *Ioudaioi*. Therefore, the fourth element of John 5 for us to consider is how John accounts for the rejection by the *Ioudaioi* of Jesus and the theological vision that his ministry announces.

Unbelief and Rejection

Although Jesus' opponents have been silent for the majority of the encounter, they are, in John's presentation of them, resistant to Jesus down to the final words of the scene. "If you will not believe what he [i.e., Moses] wrote," asks Jesus, "how will you believe in my words?" (5:47). This closing question draws together the challenges that Jesus has made to those who do not receive him. His opponents ought to believe in him not in spite of Moses but because of Moses. Here again we recognize John's fundamental concern to present Jesus as the one who can join the present and future of Israel to the past. But John's innovation is the blasphemy of the *Ioudaioi*. The Evangelist accounts for this disagreement by portraying the *Ioudaioi* as preoccupied with human testimony to the exclusion of the Father's. Thus, they (the *Ioudaioi*) sought the witness of John (5:33–34), but they do not accept the works of the Father as a greater witness (5:37–38). They accept those who come in their own names, but choose not to accept the one who comes in the Father's (5:40–44).[35] For John, the preoccupation of the *Ioudaioi* with human testimony and human glory characterizes the way in which the horizons of their knowledge and expectations are oriented in such a way as to exclude them from divine revelation (vv. 43–44). Similarly, for John, the approach to Scripture of the *Ioudaioi* is fruitless because they are devoted to Scripture as an end in itself rather than as a means – a witness – to something (and someone) beyond itself. A person can read the right text or law, know the right history, hear the right speakers, and witness the right actions, and yet be marked by an orientation that excludes him from recognition of God's revelation. John characterizes this orientation as a problem of the will – οὐ θέλετε ἐλθεῖν πρός με ἵνα ζωὴν ἔχητε (5:40; cf. 3:19–21) – and as such it is the act of the human will that corresponds to the blinding and hardening action of God (12:40).

Although the inability of the *Ioudaioi* to believe runs deep, it need not be total. This is a crucial and often overlooked point in the narrative of John 5. When Jesus spoke of the witness of John the Baptist, he said: "You sent to John, and he witnessed to the truth – not that I receive the witness of a man, but I am saying this that you might be saved – he was a lamp, kindled and shining, and you were willing to rejoice in his light for a time" (5:33–35). We have considered above how Jesus' description of John cast him as a figure who illumines God's anointed one (Ps 131:17 LXX). When we attend to the structure of this statement, we can see that here Jesus mentions the Baptist in order to interpret his (the Baptist's) ministry in a way that might expand the horizons of Jesus' opponents and allow them to recognize God's anointed one. This is why Jesus momentarily accepts the possibility of a human witness. We might paraphrase him thus: "Let me show you how to understand John so that you can be saved – you need to see him as lamp, kindled and shining, who illumines someone else. You were close to recognizing me when you were willing to hear the testimony of John." It is, therefore, the *willingness* to read the present moment in the Jewish tradition as a moment of decisive and innovative eschatological

---

[35] Bekken, *The Lawsuit Motif in John's Gospel from New Perspectives*, 144–145 cites Philo (*Leg.* 3:207–08) on the view that God can serve as a witness and that the divine word (λόγῳ θείῳ) is capable of bearing witness (μαρτυρεῖσθαι); additionally, God's sign (σημεῖον) can serve as a testimony (μαρτυρία; 2:263; in this case, the manna miracle).

fulfillment that stands between those who accept Jesus and those see him as guilty of blasphemy.

Taken as a whole, John 5 operates as an expression of the Gospel's thoroughgoing portrayal of Jesus as a figure who exists in the strongest possible continuity with commitments that are at the heart of the Jewish tradition. John claims that Jesus relates to God as a Son to the Father – and the Father is the God of Israel, who inhabits the world in freedom and undertakes work appropriate to the Creator and Judge every day of the week, who holds the power of life and judgment, and who was expected at the last time to give authority to the Son of Man. Moses and Scripture bear witness to Jesus, and truly understanding Scripture's witness to God (seeing and hearing God) and commands (loving God) entails accepting and believing in Jesus as the one toward whom all of these witnesses and expectations point. Seen as a whole, John makes Jesus' healing of a lame man to be the point of departure for a discourse that lays bare Jesus' significance for the Jewish tradition in terms of God, eschatology, Scripture (including Torah observance), and the patriarchs (viz., Moses and those who have seen and heard God). We have seen in the opening chapters of the Gospel an interest in portraying Jesus in terms of each of these aspects of the Jewish tradition, but here John concentrates them into a single discourse. The Sabbath and festival setting provide a uniquely charged context for these provocative claims. When viewed within the whole of John, the central concern of the miracle and the discourse of John 5 is best accounted for in terms of the Gospel's interest in presenting Jesus as the one who, because of his unique identity, can offer an innovative continuity linking the Jewish tradition of the present to its past and its future.

John 6: The Bread That Satisfies

As was the case in the previous section, the Gospel's aim to present Jesus as the one who opens a future for Israel unites the setting, miracles, and discourse of John 6.[36] Specifically, in John 6, the Gospel portrays Jesus as the substance of a meal that is eschatologically

---

[36] John 6 has an obvious history of composition and redaction. My argument is that this history serves, rather than undermines, the theological unity of this scene. On these issues, see R. Alan Culpepper, ed., *Critical Readings in John 6*, BIS 22 (New York/Leiden: Brill, 1997), and particularly the essay of Paul N. Anderson (pp. 1–59).

meaningful and, indeed, one that Scripture had long anticipated. The feeding miracle sets the stage for this (6:1–15), and the miracle of Jesus walking on the sea suggests the divine identity of Jesus (vv. 16–21), but it is the bread of life discourse (vv. 22–59) that most explicitly considers how Jesus makes available in the present the long-awaited conditions of Israel's future. The following exegesis considers, first, how the two miracles enable John's readers to appreciate this focus and, second, how Jesus, in the bread of life discourse, transmutes the image of eschatological food in order to show how it is now experienced in himself. We will see that John presents the events of this chapter in the terms of Exodus 16 (and Ps 78), and according to the theological vision of Isaiah 54–55. As the crowds and the *Ioudaioi* stumble in unbelief, Jesus announces that the purposes of God are accomplished in him and available to those who believe.

The Passover setting of John 6 provokes the themes that this passage explores. As we will see, however, John engages less with the specific imagery of the feast than with the broad context of the Exodus narrative – miraculous provision of food outside the land of Israel, expectations for a second (eschatological) deliverance, the peoples' struggle to entrust themselves to God's unlikely ways. It is impossible to know which Mishnaic and Talmudic traditions related to Passover circulated at the same time and place as the traditions present in John 6, and so the relation of this chapter to specific first-century Passover observances is uncertain.[37] Even so, some of the parallels are striking: The opening words of the Passover Haggadah, "This is the bread of oppression, which our fathers ate in the land of Egypt; everyone who hungers may come and eat; everyone who is needy may come and celebrate the Passover feast," offer a remarkable alternative to the words of the bread of life discourse: "I am the bread of life, the one coming to me will never hunger, and the one believing in me shall never thirst" (6:35).[38] Further, uncertainty about the particulars does not elide what should be broadly affirmed: Speaking at the time of Passover, John's Jesus offers to Israel an

---

[37] See Bertil E. Gärtner, *John 6 and the Jewish Passover,* ConBNT 17 (Gleerup: Lund, 1959), 14–52, esp. 27–28; see also the works of Joel Marcus and Joseph Tabory cited in the next note.

[38] The Haggadah is quoted from Gärtner, *John 6 and the Jewish Passover,* 27; see also Joseph Tabory, "The Passover Eve Ceremony – An Historical Outline," *Emmanuel* 12 (1981): 32–43; Marcus, "Passover and Last Supper Revisited," *NTS* 59.3 (2013): 317.

eschatological meal. Heard in a post-70 context, John's presentation of Jesus in this way would have circulated at nearly the same time that the early rabbis were reimagining Passover without Jerusalem or its temple.[39] As John 6 sets forward one aspect of the Gospel's vision for the future of Israel, it does so in a way that is mirrored in another community laboring to envision observances that are faithful to the past and the hopes of the future in light of Israel's dramatically altered present.[40]

John opens the scene describing Jesus and a large crowd on the far side of the Sea of Galilee and, consequently, in a place that is just outside of the land of Israel proper (6:1–3). Passover is near (6:4), and therefore a constellation of memories of deliverance and miraculous provision, as well as hopes for future deliverance and provision, are at hand as well.[41] Jesus recognizes in this setting an occasion to reveal himself, and thus he poses to his disciple Philip a loaded question – "Where will we buy bread so that these people might eat?" he asks, "but he said this to test him [or examine him; πειράζων αὐτόν], for he knew already what he would do" (6:6). As in the Synoptics, the specifics of the miracle are passed over quickly, and in place of this emphasis readers are struck by both the amount of bread that Jesus provides (twelve baskets from five loaves!) as well as (for an early Christian audience) the proximity of the language to the words of the Eucharist.[42]

Taken together, John's setting of the feeding of the 5,000 at Passover associates Jesus' actions with a variety of symbols and expectations that are deeply rooted in the memories of biblical Israel and Second Temple Judaism. It is not by mistake that *twelve* baskets abound with bread at the conclusion of the meal, nor that Jesus employs the biblical language of the restoration of Israel in his command to the disciples to gather (συνάγω) the fragments that

---

[39] Cf. M. J. J. Menken, "Die Feste im Johannesevangelium," in *Israel und seine Heilstraditionen im Johannesevangelium: Festgabe für Johannes Beutler SJ zum 70. Geburtstag,* ed. Michael Labahn (München: Paderborn, 2004), 269–286, esp. 285.

[40] This is the case no matter how hazy our understanding of late first-century Judaism is.

[41] We do not know how near, but see Michael Daise, *Jewish Feasts in the Gospel of John,* WUNT 2/229 (Tübingen: Mohr Siebeck, 2007).

[42] Cf. Did 9:4, 10:1, 5. Cp. John 6:11 (ἔλαβεν οὖν τοὺς ἄρτους ὁ Ἰησοῦς καὶ εὐχαριστήσας διέδωκεν; cf. John 6:23; Mark 8:6), Luke 22:19 (καὶ λαβὼν ἄρτον εὐχαριστήσας ἔκλασεν καὶ ἔδωκεν αὐτοῖς; cf. 1 Cor 11:24). The thanksgiving is also reflected Jesus' words in Mark 14:23 and pars. Cf. Brown, *John,* I.236–250.

none should perish (ἵνα μή τι ἀπόληται, 6:12).[43] Jewish literature contemporary with and later than John expected a recurrence of the manna miracle in the last days. For example, 2 Baruch records: "It will happen at that time that the treasury of manna will come down again from on high, and they will eat of it in those years, because these are they who will have arrived at the consummation of time" (2 Bar 29:8).[44] A variety of midrashic texts, many of which are attributed to third- and fourth-century rabbis, offer the expectation that "as with the first deliverer (i.e., Moses), so with the second (i.e., the messiah)" – including the miraculous provision of bread from heaven at the time of the messiah's revelation.[45] When considered in the context of these expectations, the crowd's desire to seize Jesus and make him king at the conclusion of the scene makes good sense: outside the land of Israel, near Passover, Jesus has taken on a role that is strikingly similar to the role of Moses when through him God brought forth bread for the hungry tribes of Israel. The crowd recognizes Jesus as "the prophet who is coming into the world" (οὗτός ἐστιν ἀληθῶς ὁ προφήτης ὁ ἐρχόμενος εἰς τὸν κόσμον; John 6:14), that is, the figure of whom Moses said: "the Lord your God will raise up among your brothers a prophet like unto me" (Deut 18:15).[46] The crowd in John 6 recognizes what we know from the later rabbis, that the messiah's deliverance would be typologically related to Moses'. Thus, John's setting of the feeding of the 5,000 associates Jesus' actions with Passover deliverance, the prophet like Moses, and God's miraculous provision of food for Israel in the last days. Nevertheless, the crowd's response to Jesus is misguided: they would seize and make king him whose kingdom is not of this world (6:14–15, 18:33–38). John sets forward a potent combination of images – Passover, Moses, abundant bread, all united in the person

---

[43] In the LXX, the object of ἀπόλλυμι is almost always a person or people who have been scattered (see Jer 23:1). In John, perishing designates the opposite of eternal life (3:16; cf. Isa 11:12). See Dennis, *Jesus' Death*, 188–198; cf. Gärtner, *John 6 and the Jewish Passover*, 20.

[44] Cf. also Rev 2:17; cf. Barrett, *The Gospel according to St. John*, 298; Schnackenburg, *The Gospel according to John*, 2:449. Eccl. Rab 1.128. On Torah as bread, see Prov 9.5; Gen R 70.5; Strack-Bill 2.483.

[45] Strack-Billerbeck gives dates from AD 280–340 for the Amoraim named in these traditions. T. F. Glasson (*Moses in the Fourth Gospel* [London: SCM, 1963], 21) argues that this was a popular (i.e., not specifically rabbinic) expectation because the messianic pretenders in Josephus attempted to align themselves with Moses' actions.

[46] See also 1 Macc 14:41.

of Jesus – but they await an interpretation of how the meal that Jesus oversees functions within this symbolism.

Between the feeding miracle and the discourse, John records Jesus' walking on the sea (6:16–21). What is the role of this miracle in the narrative argument of this chapter, beyond the traditional pairing of the feeding miracle with the walking on the sea (cf. Mark 6:32–52) or the need to reunite Jesus with his disciples in Gospel narrative?[47] If we hold together closely our reading of the sea miracle with the presentation of Jesus in the feeding of the crowd, then the contribution of this miracle to the Gospel's presentation of Jesus emerges in this way: In the feeding miracle, the Evangelist casts Jesus in terms charged with Passover, Mosaic, and messianic significance. When he walks on the sea, however, Jesus distances himself from his predecessor Moses. Jesus walks toward his disciples upon a sea that is tossed up by a great wind; his simple self-identification, ἐγώ εἰμι· μὴ φοβεῖσθε, recalls a common scriptural instruction to those who have encountered God.[48] The imagery of Jesus walking on water also recalls a handful of biblical visions of Israel's God treading upon the sea: "In the sea was your way, and your paths on the great waters" (Ps. 77:20);[49] the Lord, says Job, "walks on the sea as upon dry ground" (περιπατῶν ὡς ἐπ᾽ ἐδάφους ἐπὶ θαλάσσης, 9:8). Psalm 107:23–30 records God's self-revelation to sea travellers who survive a tempest and immediately arrive at their port, a striking development given the conclusion of the episode in the same way in John 6:21. Importantly, John does not develop the implications of this scene as a theophany – that is, the disciples do not worship Jesus as the Son of God when he enters the boat (cp. Matt 14:33). Instead, John allows this striking image of Jesus walking on the sea to remain underinterpreted for the moment as readers encounter the debate about who Jesus is in the subsequent dialogue (cf. 6:30, 41, 52).[50]

When readers consider them as a pair, the feeding miracle and the walking on the sea depict a single reality, even if they do so more as a diptych than an image within a single frame: In the first panel,

---

[47] Cf. C. H. Giblin, "The Miraculous Crossing of the Sea: John 6.16–21," *NTS* 29.1 (1983): 96–103; Maloney, *Signs and Shadows: Reading John 5–13* (Minneapolis: Fortress, 1996), 39–40.

[48] The ἐγώ εἰμι recalls Exod 3:14; the instruction by God not to fear is also common (see Gen 15:1, 28:13 [LXX], Josh 8:1; Isa 35:4, 40:9, 41:10, 43:1, Jer 1:8; Lam 3:57).

[49] Cf. Ps 76:20 LXX; I have translated the LXX's "many waters" (ἐν ὕδασι πολλοῖς) as "great" following the MT (במים רבים).

[50] See also Hays, *Echoes of Scripture in the Gospels,* 70–73.

readers recognize that Passover provides the context of memory and expectation for Jesus' action; the tribes of Israel are symbolically present in the disciples and the fragments they are ordered to gather; the abundance of bread (manna) signals the eschatological consummation as well as the authority of Jesus as a deliverer whose role is typologically related to Moses'. The crowds recognize as much (6:14–15). Away from the crowds, however, the second panel shows Jesus behaving in a way that recalls the activities of God himself striding upon the sea and delivering his people. As a pair of images, the feeding miracle and the walking on the sea envision a setting that looks back to the Passover and sea crossing of Exodus 12–15 (and the re-narration of these events Pss. 77–78). What is known to the readers (and, perhaps, the disciples) and *not* to the crowds, however, is that Jesus' walking on the sea has demonstrated that, while the identification of Jesus with Moses is necessary, it does not provide a sufficient measure of the significance of Jesus. In what follows, the bread of life discourse presses forward the unanticipated quality of the eschatological food that Jesus embodies and offers; those who have not experienced the vision of Jesus walking on the sea are challenged by assertions that Jesus offers a food different from what they have anticipated.

The discourse begins with a change of scene (6:22–25), and Jesus quickly confronts the crowd with their true motives. Instead of seeking to appease their present hunger, they should be working for the bread that endures to eternal life, which the Son of Man offers. They have seen a miracle, but they have not grasped its significance in terms of the eschatological life that God makes available in Jesus. The crowd then presses on: "What work can we do to obtain this bread that endures to eternal life?" it asks. "Believe in the one God sent," Jesus tells them. The work of belief in the one sent by God enables a person to receive the sustaining food of God (6:29). And what is that food? It is Jesus. "I am the bread of life," he says, "the one who comes to me will certainly not hunger, and the one who believes in me will certainly never thirst" (6:35). In this way, Jesus presents himself as the content of his own proclamation. Importantly, however, Jesus reveals his identity using imagery of bread from heaven and the satisfying food of God, all of which is specifically rooted in Israel's storied past and future hopes.

The crowd that seeks the bread of life asks Jesus to demonstrate who he is in terms of this past: "What sign are you doing so that we might believe in you? ... Our fathers ate manna in the desert, just as it is written, 'He gave them bread from heaven to eat'" (6:30–31). As we will see, Jesus will accept their question, but he will also press them to rethink their expectations so that the sign (the bread) and the person (Jesus) are no longer two distinct things, but one. *Jesus is* the bread of life. The argument moves this way as Jesus takes up their citation of Scripture. The quotation in 6:31 (ἄρτον ἐκ τοῦ οὐρανοῦ ἔδωκεν αὐτοῖς φαγεῖν) resembles a variety of biblical texts that describe God's provision of manna to the exodus generation, including Exodus 16 (esp. vv. 4, 15), Ps 105:40 (LXX 104:40), and Neh 9:15. It is Ps 77:24 LXX, however, that comes closest to the quotation of the crowd in John 6:[51]

> 21. Therefore, the Lord heard and was put out,
>   and a fire was kindled in Jacob,
>   and anger mounted against Israel,
> 22. because they had no faith in God (οὐκ ἐπίστευσαν ἐν
>   τῷ θεῷ)
>   nor did they hope in his saving power.
> 23. And he commanded clouds above
>   and opened heaven's doors,
> 24. and he rained down manna for them to eat (καὶ ἔβρεξεν
>   αὐτοῖς μαννα φαγεῖν),
>   and heaven's bread he gave them (καὶ ἄρτον
>   οὐρανοῦ ἔδωκεν αὐτοῖς).
> 25. Bread of angels man ate;
>   provisions he sent them in abundance.
>   (Ps 77:21–24, alt. from NETS)

Here the psalmist describes the Israelites as witnesses of the power of God to rescue and provide for his people, and yet they are remarkably persistent in their unbelief. Indeed, Psalm 77 goes on: "in all these things, they still sinned, and they did not believe in his marvels" (καὶ οὐκ ἐπίστευσαν ἐν τοῖς θαυμασίοις αὐτοῦ, 77:32). On the surface, the crowd's quotation of this psalm calls forward a clear image of a dramatic miracle. Can Jesus vindicate his teaching by similarly dramatic means? As their question draws in Psalm 77, however,

---

[51] Cf. Menken, *Old Testament Quotations in the Fourth Gospel;* Diana M. Swancutt, "Hunger Assuaged by the Bread of Heaven," in *Early Christian Interpretation of the Scriptures of Israel,* ed. Craig A. Evans and James A. Sanders, JSNTSup 148 (Sheffield: Sheffield Academic Press, 1997), 218–251, esp. 225–230.

the crowd in John 6 has implicitly (and ironically) invoked a broader context in which miraculous, heavenly provision is met by unbelief. Jesus responds to the crowd's request for a sign by reasserting the nature of the manna in the wilderness. "Truly, truly, I say to you, it was not Moses who gave you the bread from heaven; rather, my Father is giving to you the true bread from heaven" (6:32).[52] Jesus' gift of bread may resemble God's provision to Israel through Moses, but Jesus moves the imagery away from the Moses–Jesus typology. God was the giver of the manna in the past, and God is giving the true bread now. "For the bread of God is the one who comes down from heaven and gives life to the world" (ὁ γὰρ ἄρτος τοῦ θεοῦ ἐστιν ὁ καταβαίνων ἐκ τοῦ οὐρανοῦ καὶ ζωὴν διδοὺς τῷ κόσμῳ; 6:33).[53] With this statement, readers feel the ground shifting under their feet: the feeding miracle at the opening of John 6 presented Jesus as the host and provider of an eschatologically symbolic meal, but the discourse now casts Jesus as the substance of God's provision. He – the one who comes down from heaven – is the true bread. The earlier bread, both Moses' and Jesus', pointed ahead to the bread of Jesus as the bread of life.

Belief and Eschatological Fulfillment

After presenting Jesus as the bread of life, the discourse shifts next to the problem of belief, and it addresses this problem by describing believers in Jesus as those who partake in the conditions of Israel's fulfilled hopes. Jesus explains this, first, by accounting for the conditions that enable a true recognition of Jesus: those whom the Father has given to Jesus will come; others will see and not believe (6:36–37). The *Ioudaioi* grumble (ἐγόγγυζον) at the pretense of these claims (6:41–42), and Jesus accounts for their unbelief in terms of the Father. Only those whom the Father draws may come to Jesus. Indeed, Isaiah himself speaks to this effect: "It is written in

---

[52] My translation of ἀλλά as "rather" follows the logic of BDAG (see use 3) wherein the adversative particle transitions from a settled matter (it was not Moses, but God, who gave bread in the desert) to a new claim. Similarly, see John 7:49 ("None of the rulers has believed in him [=settled matter], ἀλλά this crowd that doesn't know the law is accursed.")

[53] The participial phrase could be rendered attributively ["The bread of God is that which is coming down from heaven ..."] or substantivally ["the bread of God is the one coming down from heaven ..."]. After John 3:13, however, the latter reading is to be preferred.

the prophets," says Jesus, 'They will all be taught by God' (καὶ ἔσονται πάντες διδακτοὶ θεοῦ). Everyone who has heard and learned of the Father comes to me" (6:45). By citing Isaiah in support of his identity, Jesus makes two important claims. First, although the quotation most closely approximates Isaiah 54:13 (καὶ [θήσω] πάντας τοὺς υἱούς σου διδακτοὺς θεοῦ), Jesus attributes the statement to the general witness of the prophets (ἔστιν γεγραμμένον ἐν τοῖς προφήταις).[54] Isaiah represents the broader prophetic expectation that the people of God will be divinely taught in the last days.[55] The claim of John 6:45 is simple: those who believe in Jesus embody the hopes of the prophets for Israel: they are "taught by God."

The second striking aspect of this quotation is the way that it communicates the eschatological time frame during which Jesus and his interlocutors speak. In Isaiah, God's declaration that "I will make all your sons taught by God" is set within a broader vision describing the eschatological restoration of Israel. It will be a time when the humbled, storm-tossed, and un-consoled people of God will be given a city built with precious stones and marked by lasting peace and righteousness (Isa 54:12, 14), a city in which proselytes may take up residence among the people of Israel (54:15 LXX only), and, as we have seen, in which the teaching of God will be ubiquitous (54:13). Jesus claims that those who hear and believe in him possess in the present one of the conditions of God's eschatological future. The last day has not fully arrived (e.g., the resurrection has not occurred, John 6:44), but the eternal life that characterizes the eschaton has begun already in those who have been taught by God to believe in Jesus (6:47, 50–51). Believers experience in themselves and bear witness to others of the conditions of the age toward which Israel had been told to hope. John 6 thus repeats a claim that we have heard before: the fulfillment of God's historic promises to Israel is so near at hand that a person can begin to experience that fulfillment now by believing in Jesus; such belief offers an unbroken continuity between the stories and promises of the past and the anticipated future of Israel.

---

[54] Cf. Menken, *Old Testament Quotations*, 67–77; Swancutt, "Hunger Assuaged by the Bread of Heaven," 230–234.

[55] E.g., Jer 31:33 (38:33 LXX); Isa 2:1–5; Isa 11:9; Jer 24:87; Hab 2:14; see also CD 20:4. The early Christians viewed themselves in these terms too (1 Thess 4:9, Barn 21:6; cf. 1 John 2:27).

As we have seen in previous contexts, the grumbling of the *Ioudaioi* responds to the unprecedented claim that this man, whose father and mother are known, might also be one who has descended from heaven (6:41–42). And, as we have also seen (e.g., with Nicodemus), John accounts for the distance between the *Ioudaioi* and Jesus as an eschatological difference: the *Ioudaioi* are unable to recognize the fulfillment of the promises that are at the heart of their tradition. In chapter 12, John will quote Isaiah and attribute such unbelief to divine hardening (12:39–40). Here in John 6, after quoting Isaiah, the Gospel explains that the Father draws some to faith in Jesus, but such faith – that is, the ability to recognize Jesus as the one sent and descended from God – is a matter of God's will (6:36–40, 44). Undeterred, however, the *Ioudaioi* continue to press questions about Jesus: "How is this one able to give us flesh to eat?" (6:52). They strive to understand, or at least challenge, what they cannot accept.

As they press their question, the *Ioudaioi* come no closer to agreement with Jesus, who now recasts his teaching in more challenging terms. Moving from his claim to be the bread of life that descends from heaven (6:33–35, 41, 48), Jesus asserts the importance of "eating" the bread that he gives: "The bread that I give is my flesh on behalf of the world" (6:52). The language paints a jarring picture: eating (ἐσθίω, 6:49–53) – even chewing or munching (τρώγω, 6:54, 56–58) – on this flesh, and drinking this blood (6:53–56), is the way to enter into the eternal life that Israel's God has long promised. "For my flesh is true food, and my blood is true drink," Jesus says (6:55). These jarring descriptions focus those who hear Jesus' words on the challenge of partaking of Jesus' flesh. The question that stands out then is this: How does one eat the bread of life?

Eating the Bread of Life

Diana Swancutt has convincingly demonstrated that the drama of John 6 is carried out with significant parallels to Isaiah 55, which in context is of-a-piece with Isaiah 54.[56] Isaiah 55 invites those who hunger and thirst to satisfy themselves on the food God will provide, specifically, the "food" of God's trustworthy promises to David.

---

[56] I have framed the following arguments in my own way, but I am indebted throughout the following discussion to the work of Swancutt (esp. 234–245). See also Hays's discussion in *Echoes of Scripture in the Gospels*, 321–323.

When read in light of Isaiah 55, various aspects of John 6 take on new significance as they reflect how John perceives the fulfillment of Isaiah's prophecy in the ministry of Jesus. Consider, for example, these various aspects of John 6 in light of Isaiah 55: Jesus begins this scene with a loaded question (πόθεν ἀγοράσωμεν ἄρτους ἵνα φάγωσιν οὗτοι; John 6:5); he feeds the people until they are satisfied (ἐνεπλήσθησαν)[57]; he urges the crowds to work not for that which perishes but that which endures to eternal life (ἐργάζεσθε μὴ τὴν βρῶσιν τὴν ἀπολλυμένην ἀλλὰ τὴν βρῶσιν τὴν μένουσαν εἰς ζωὴν αἰώνιον, ἣν ὁ υἱὸς τοῦ ἀνθρώπου ὑμῖν δώσει, 6:27). These elements of the narrative stand out when heard alongside of the opening invitation of Isaiah:

> You who thirst, go to water,
> and as many of you as have no money,
> go, buy (ἀγοράσατε), and drink wine and fat,
> without money and without price.

> Why do you set a price with money
> and your labor (τὸν μόχθον) for that which does not satisfy (πλησμονήν)?[58]
> Hear me, and you shall eat good things,
> and your soul shall revel in good things.

> Pay attention with your ears,
> and follow my ways; listen to me,
> and your soul will live in good things.
> I will make with you an everlasting covenant,
> the sacred things of David that are sure. (Isa 55:1–3, NETS)

Read with Isaiah's words in mind, John 6 appears to cast the feeding miracle as a fulfillment of Isaiah's vision, that is, a day in which the unsatisfying bread for which men and women labor is replaced by the abundance of God's provision. Additionally, John's vision moves in the same direction as Isaiah's: both authors elide distinctions between material food and divine teaching. Or, rather, both

---

[57] John's ἐνεπλήσθησαν (6:12) stands out from the term for "satisfied" used in other canonical accounts of the feeding miracle (ἐχορτάσθησαν; but see John 6:26); John's term derives from a different root than the term used in Isa 55:2 (πλησμονή), but there is an aural similarity between the terms.

[58] Swancutt notes that eating to satisfaction "εἰς πλησμονήν" resounds with the echoes from the Exodus story (Ex 16:3, 8; Lev 25:19; 26:5; see also Ps 77:25 LXX).

authors envision divine teaching as a kind of life-sustaining food.[59] "Listen to me, and you [or, your soul, ἡ ψυχή/נַפְשׁ] will live in good things" (Isa 55:3). After the opening invitation to partake of God's abundant food and to listen to his teachings, Isaiah continues with an urgent instruction: "Seek God, and when you find him, call upon him" (Ζητήσατε τὸν θεὸν καὶ ἐν τῷ εὑρίσκειν αὐτὸν ἐπικαλέσασθε, 55:6).[60] The prophet then calls sinners to forsake their ways and to entrust themselves to a God whose plans are not like human plans (55:7–8).

Again, there are noteworthy parallels to this language in John 6, in which the crowd seeks Jesus (ζητοῦντες τὸν Ἰησοῦν, 6:24, ζητεῖτέ με 26), but upon finding him (εὑρόντες αὐτὸν, 6:25) they resist what he offers.[61] Jesus' repeated references to the actions of his Father in this section (6:27, 36–40, 44–46) can easily be read as Johannine elaborations of Isaiah's teaching that the plans of the God are not like human plans, nor his ways like theirs (Isa 55:8–9).

Ultimately, it is the word of God that binds John 6 most firmly to Isaiah 55. The prophet had likened God's word to the rain and snow, which descends (καταβῇ) upon the earth and gives seed to the sower and bread for food (καὶ ἄρτον εἰς βρῶσιν; 55:10). Similarly, the word (ῥῆμά; דבר) of God goes out and does not return until it has accomplished the will of the one who sent it (οὐ μὴ ἀποστραφῇ, ἕως ἂν συντελεσθῇ ὅσα ἠθέλησα; לֹא־יָשׁוּב אֵלַי רֵיקָם כִּי אִם־עָשָׂה אֶת־אֲשֶׁר חָפַצְתִּי, 55:11). The parallels with Jesus in John are numerous, particularly the description of Jesus "descending" (see 6:33, 38, 41–42, 50–51, 58; cf. 3:13), the will of the father as the driving force behind his ministry (4:34; 5:30; 6:38–40; 7:17, et passim), and Jesus' own embodiment and proclamation of God's word (1:1–5, 14; 5:38, 47; 6:63; 8:31, et passim). As the word of God does not return until it finishes (συντελεσθῇ) its work, so Jesus characterizes his will as "finishing" the work of his Father (τελειώσω αὐτοῦ τὸ ἔργον, John 4:34; cf. 19:30). As Isaiah held out this nourishment to those who respond to the invitation "Come!" (πορεύεσθε/לְכוּ, 55:1) so the satisfaction

---

[59] This begins even in Deut 8:3: "And he fed you manna, which your fathers had not seen, in order make clear to you that a person does not live by bread alone, but a man lives by every word the comes from the mouth of God."

[60] The Hebrew reads "seek the Lord" (דִּרְשׁוּ יְהוָה). It is commonly suggested that the דרשׁ is implied in John 5:39 ("you search [ἐραυνᾶτε] the Scriptures …").

[61] See also John 7:34, 36.

that Jesus offers is for all who "come" to him (ὁ ἐρχόμενος πρὸς ἐμὲ οὐ μὴ πεινάσῃ κτλ., John 6:35).[62]

Now we can consider these observations together: Isaiah envisioned an eschatological day in which God's people would be taught by him. The prophet followed up that vision with an invitation for the hungry and thirsty to come and experience the abundant food of God (i.e., the good ways and teachings of God). Convinced that such an eschatological moment has arrived, the Evangelist portrays in John 6 a dramatic fulfillment of Isaiah 54–55: It is the day of divine teaching, the day in which the hungry may eat and drink at no cost. The feeding miracle signals this eschatological moment. As the first redemption came at the time of Passover/Exodus with abundant bread in the wilderness, so now Jesus signals the presence of eschatological redemption outside the land, at the time of Passover, and with a new provision of food. Yet, since the actions of Jesus are eschatologically oriented, the true food of John 6 is not material bread but rather, as Isaiah proclaimed, the word of God that will sustain the people for eternal life. As we have seen earlier in John, the scandal of a particular Jewish man claiming both to embody and proclaim God's word is too much for some (6:41–42, 52). But Jesus is uncompromising on this point: he himself, in his flesh and blood, is the true food of God (6:55). To "eat" Jesus in this context means primarily what it means in Isaiah 55, where "eating" and "delighting" in the food of God means "hearing," "listening," and turning in trust to the unlikely ways of God and God's word in the world.[63]

If the exegesis above correctly traces the logic of John 6, then how does this narrative presentation of Jesus function as an argument regarding the future of Israel? An answer to this question is at hand if we consider how the Jewish tradition before and after the Fourth Gospel related the ideas that the Gospel applies to Jesus in John 6. As we will see, the combination of texts and images employed in John 6 have a history within the broader Jewish tradition, and John's engagement with these texts and his presentation of Jesus in and through their imagery suggests that in John 6 the evangelist re-signifies the imagery of Passover/Exodus and thus constructs an

---

[62] Note also John 7:36. Cf. John V. Dahms, "Isaiah 55:11 and the Gospel of John," *EvQ* 53.2 (1981): 78–88.

[63] Note that the reading offered here resists a "sacramental" approach to this chapter, and particularly to such an interpretation of 6:51–58. For a summary of these, see Rensberger, *Johannine Faith and Liberating Community*, 65–86.

important interpretive frame that uses this tradition in order to demonstrate how to understand Jesus as the one who fulfills the hopes of Israel that had been nurtured in the Jewish tradition. A few examples will demonstrate how this works.

As Peder Borgen has shown, the imagery of bread from heaven in Exodus 16:4 sparked the imagination not only of the Fourth Evangelist but of Philo and the rabbis too. One noteworthy aspect of the imagery from Exodus 16 (and its recurrence in other biblical contexts, especially Ps 77 LXX) is its resonance with Isaiah 55. This occurs not only in terminology shared among these texts (e.g., "bread," "rain," "from heaven") but also in concepts that appear in both (e.g., abundant food, free of cost or labor). In imagery shared between Isaiah 55 and Deuteronomy 32, the "Song of Moses" describes Moses' teaching descending like rain, even as snow (ὡσεὶ νιφετὸς) upon grass (Deut 32:20). In Deuteronomy 8 and Isaiah 55, the satisfaction of physical hunger illustrates the more vital truth that trusting in God's word satisfies basic human needs ("one does not live by bread alone," Deut 8:3). Similarly, Philo draws on the manna miracle to illustrate that God's provision of manna in the desert witnesses to the deeper truth of God's generous care for his people. Thus, to understand God's feeding miracle in the past is to understand God's deeper commitment to human thriving in general:

> This [i.e., that "one does not live by bread alone ..."] is confirmed by the words that follow, "He fed thee with the manna." He who provided the food that costs no toil or suffering, the food which without the pains and cares of men came not from earth in the common way, but was sent a wonder and a marvel from heaven for the benefit of those who should use it ... should we not call him the author of thriving and prosperity and secure and ordered living.   (Cong. 173–174)[64]

Based on this passage, if a person were to grasp the truth of the manna miracle, she would recognize God's goodness in a way that runs remarkably parallel to Isaiah 55: the manna teaches that the God who graciously provides food at no cost or labor possesses a

---

[64] In this passage, Philo pivots to a discussion of manna from a context in which he had previously been discussing the bread of Passover. N.B. readers who are familiar with Borgen's book *Bread from Heaven* will notice that this and the following passage comprise two of the three Philonic texts to which he devotes extended discussion.

deeper wisdom that he makes available to those who trust in him and by which he offers to the people the good things for which they long. In another place, Philo envisions God's self-sufficiency with an illustration of manna, but with a logic that moves along the same path as Isaiah 55. In both cases, God's provision of physical food illustrates the availability of a truly divine food – that is, instruction (or wisdom). Philo writes:

> The earthly food is produced by the co-operation of husbandmen, but the heavenly is sent like the snow by God the solely self-acting, with none to share his work. And indeed it says, "Behold, I rain upon you bread from heaven." Of what food can he rightly say that it is rained from above, save of heavenly wisdom . . .?   (*Mut.* 258–260)[65]

Philo's description of heavenly food sent "like snow," his easy shift from manna to divine wisdom, and perhaps even the contrast between food produced in cooperation with laborers and the word of God that grows on its own all resonate with the intertextual field that we have been considering, but they strike a particular chord with Isaiah 55. The significance of Philo's casting of the manna miracle in terms that invoke imagery and ideas from Isaiah 55 emerges in the way in which it suggests that in John 6 the Fourth Evangelist is working within an established set of connections that bind together Exodus, Deuteronomy, Psalms, and Isaiah.[66]

When considered alongside these texts, the lines that connect the biblical traditions at work in John 6 are unlikely to be original to the Fourth Gospel. In fact, it is the case that the Gospel's presentation of Jesus is more likely to achieve its purpose if the traditional and intertextual connections stood in place before the Gospel was written, because in that case readers might grasp more fully John's innovative re-presentation of Jesus. If this is so, the Gospel deviates from the traditional logic in which manna opens up the possibility of more fully grasping the significance of God's word, namely Torah or wisdom – a logic implied both in Deuteronomy 8 and Isaiah 55, and later picked up by Philo and the rabbis. Having already established

---

[65] N.B. Philo's term for snow (νίφει) never appears in the LXX, which prefers χιών (but νιφετός, "snowfall," occurs four times in the LXX, including the aforementioned Deut 32:2).

[66] Cf. also Wis 16:20; Sir 24:21; *b.* Baba Kama 82a. The latter includes this striking statement: "Water means nothing but Torah, as it says, 'Ho, everyone that thirsteth cometh for water.'" Cf. also *b.* Avodah Zarah 5b.

Jesus as the λόγος, a figure with priority over Torah and wisdom, John 6 acts as a demonstration of what it would mean to read an established tradition with the innovative re-signification of "the words that come from God." It is as if John argues: When scripture says "words [of God/from God]" do not infer "Torah" or "wisdom," but rather "Jesus," the one who speaks the words of God (cf. John 5:47) and who even embodies that word (1:14).[67]

If the reading offered above is correct, the central concern of John 6 is to present Jesus as the bread of life, the true and living bread that imparts God's eschatological blessings to those who come and partake of what he offers. Though the claim itself is simple, its power lies in the way that it concentrates onto Jesus the significance of being the one whose identity is grounded in the foundational stories, commitments, and hopes of Israel. With this image of bread, John can cast Jesus and the crowds in terms of deliverance at Passover, provision through Moses, and the grumbling of the Israelites in the wilderness. John can also call up Isaiah's vision of eschatological blessing ("they will all be taught by God") and the prophet's invitation for the hungry to partake of food that finally satisfies. In describing Jesus in these ways, the Gospel engages not only expectations rooted in Scripture but also the particular hopes that had been (and would continue to be) nourished within the Jewish tradition. As John would have its readers believe, Jesus is the one who carries the hopes of Israel from the past and into the future. What is required to live in continuity now with these hopes of this past is the willingness to re-signify the meaning of the "word" of God and the act of divine speech as it is encountered in the scriptures of Israel. The word of God, that is, the true bread, which comes down from heaven and nourishes humanity, refers neither to Torah nor wisdom, but Jesus.

John 7–10:21: Jesus: The Hope of Sukkot/The Deceiver of the People

The festival of Sukkot provides a setting for the narrative of John beginning at John 7:1 and running until 10:21. In this section, the

---

[67] Cp. the Isaiah Targum on Isa 55 (expansions in italics): "Ho, everyone who *wishes to learn, let him* come and *learn*; and he who has no money, come, *hear* and *learn*! Come, *hear* and *learn*, without *price* and *not with mammon, teaching which is better than* wine and milk … Incline your ear, and *attend to my Memra*; hear, that your soul may live" (trans. Chilton, 107–108).

Gospel sustains its characterization of Jesus as the one who opens for Israel a way into its future by presenting Jesus as the one signified by the practices and expectations of Sukkot. Alongside this character-ization, however, another thread of John's narrative that relates to Jesus and the future of Israel rises to the surface: Jesus' actions and statements at Sukkot divide the *Ioudaioi* and the Jewish crowd. Thus, the Gospel begins to draw out not only how Jesus ushers in the future of Israel (e.g., as the living word of God, the source of the Spirit, the future judge speaking in the present, the light of the world) but also what his uncompromising claims mean for the people of God and the ways in which they orient their lives vis-à-vis the revelation of God within the tradition of Second Temple Judaism. To track these aspects of John's narrative, it will be helpful to change approaches in the following pages, from considering one scene at a time to now considering how John's presentation of Jesus plays out across these three-and-a-half chapters. We will first consider the interplay and significance of John's presentation of Jesus in view of the imagery and themes of the festival. Then we will consider three ways in which John describes and accounts for the growing conflict with the *Ioudaioi* that accompanies belief in Jesus.

Jesus and the Imagery of Sukkot

John's presentation of Jesus at Sukkot picks up a number of images and themes that would have stood out prominently to readers famil-iar with the observance of the festival. The scriptural story of Sukkot begins in Leviticus 23:33–43.[68] It is the fall harvest festival. The first and eighth days of the festival are designated days of rest (v. 39); the people live in booths as they did when God brought Israel out of Egypt (vv. 42–43); and they are instructed to observe the festival with joy (23:40). These themes of joyful celebration and recognition of God's saving power recur throughout the biblical and traditional portrayals of the festival. Deuteronomy repeats twice the command to celebrate the festival with joy (16:14, 15), and it emphasizes the festival as an opportunity for the people to remember and to

---

[68] It is referred to as the "festival of ingathering" in Exodus 23, 34. For background on Sukkot, see Håkan Ulfgard, *The Story of Sukkot,* BGBE 34 (Tübingen: Mohr Siebeck, 1998); Seth Klayman, "Sukkot from the Tanakh to Tannaitic Texts: Exeget-ical Traditions, Emergent Rituals, and Eschatological Associations" PhD Diss., Duke University, 2008.

celebrate the blessing and provision of God. Deuteronomy also anticipates the centrality of the temple and altar in later observances of the festival, as it stipulates its observation at the place "the Lord will choose" (16:15). According to Deuteronomy, every seventh year – in the year of remission – the law is to be read to the entire people of Israel during the festival (31:10–11).

Extending from these foundational texts, scriptural tradition dates the dedication of Solomon's temple to the time of Sukkot (1 Kings 8:2).[69] In Ezra, the exiles return to the land in the month of the festival and observe Sukkot around the rebuilt altar (the foundation for the temple had not yet been laid; Ezra 3:1–5). Nehemiah, in what seems to be a fulfillment of the command of Deuteronomy, records the occasion of Sukkot as the setting of the reading and interpretation of the law to the people, as well as the heartfelt repentance and recommitment to the law that follows (7:73–8:18; cf. 9:1–10:39; cf. Deut 31:10–11). In view of the return of the exiles from Babylon and observance of Sukkot in Ezra and Nehemiah, it is striking that Zechariah envisions a gathering of survivors from many nations streaming to Jerusalem to celebrate Sukkot (Zech 14:16–21). Zechariah's announcement of continuous light (14:7) and living water flowing out from Jerusalem (14:8) associates with the festival images of God's provision of water in the desert (cf. Ex 17), rain upon crops (Deut 28), as well as God's anticipated eschatological provision of life-giving water and endless light (cf. also Ezek 47; Isa 12, 55). Taken together, the biblical account of Sukkot unites Israel around God's deliverance from Egypt (Lev) and from Babylon (Ezra, Neh); God's sustaining provisions, both agricultural (Deut) and eschatological (Zech); Torah, temple, and altar play prominent roles (Deut, 1 Kings, Ezra, Neh); great joy marks the festival's various ways of remembering and looking forward to God's presence with Israel (cf. Lev, Deut, Neh).

Post-biblical Jewish tradition developed these themes too. Jubilees records Abraham as the first celebrant of Sukkot when, after the birth of the promised child, Isaac, he builds an altar beside the Well of the Oath (at Beersheba) and celebrates the festival with rejoicing (Jub 16:20–31). In 2 Maccabees, the festival marking the reconsecration of the temple and altar is modeled on Sukkot – "They celebrated it for eight days with rejoicing, in the manner of the

---

[69] For further references to Sukkot in Scripture, see Klayman, "Sukkot from the Tanakh to Tannaitic Texts", 19–117.

festival of booths ..." (2 Macc 10:6).[70] Both the Mishnah and the Tosefta record the joyous celebration of Sukkot, complete with daily processions around the altar with the branches of various trees, a water libation that originated at the pool of Siloam and was poured out on the altar, and the recitation of the Hallel psalms (113–118).[71] The Mishnah envisions dramatic declarations of faithfulness to God as part of the festival:

> At the close of the first holy day of the Festival of Taber-nacles they went down to the Court of Women where they had made an important rearrangement. And golden candle-sticks were there with four golden bowls at their tops and four ladders to each one and four youths from the young priests with pitchers of oil ... which they used to pour into each bowl ... And there was no courtyard in Jerusalem that was not lit up with the light at the Libation Water-Well ceremony.
>
> Pious men and men of good deeds used to dance before them with burning torches in their hands and sang before them songs and praises ... [The Mishnah details the singing of the Psalms of Ascent and the blasting of trumpets.] They kept up prolonged blasts and proceeded until they reached the gate that led out to the east, when they arrived at the gate that led forth to the east they turned their faces to the west [i.e., toward the sanctuary] and said, "Our ances-tors when they were in this place turned with their backs unto the temple and their faces toward the east and the prostrated themselves eastward towards the sun [Ezek 8:16], but as for us our eyes are turned to the eternal."[72]

The early rabbis thus sustained the biblical and Second Temple themes that marked Sukkot: joyous celebration, commitment to the altar and the temple, recollection of God's past faithfulness and expectation of future deliverance.[73] The recitations of the Psalms assured this dual orientation of memory and expectation. The night-long light rituals anticipated the experience foretold by Zechariah:

---

[70] Cf. also 2 Macc 1:9, 18; 1 Macc 4:36; Josephus, *Ant.* 12:323–326.

[71] See *m.* Sukk 3:9, 4:1, 5, 8–10.

[72] *m.* Sukk 5:2–4 (trans. Blackman). I have altered spelling and capitalization.

[73] Cf. *m.* Sukk 4:5, with the prayer for future deliverance that quotes Ps 118:25: "Save us, we beseech you, O Lord."

"at evening time there shall be light" (14:7). The water poured over the altar and flowing onto the ground affirmed the future expectation of "living water" flowing from Jerusalem (Zech 14:8).[74] This joyful recollection of the past and its vivid anticipation of coming deliverance illustrate why the Mishnah records that a person who has not observed Sukkot has "never seen rejoicing in his life."[75]

When the Fourth Gospel depicts Jesus standing up and crying out on "the last day – the great day – of the festival," it envisions him appealing to a crowd of worshippers who are keenly aware of the contexts outlined above. This context suggests that Jesus' words are rightly interpreted in terms of the eschatological hopes nurtured and affirmed through the practices of the festival.

The most forthright assertion of Jesus' identity occurs in 7:37–38. Jesus cries out, "If anyone is thirsty, let him come to me, and let the one who believes in me drink – just as Scripture says – rivers of living water will flow from within him" (ἐάν τις διψᾷ ἐρχέσθω πρός με καὶ πινέτω ὁ πιστεύων εἰς ἐμέ, καθὼς εἶπεν ἡ γραφή, ποταμοὶ ἐκ τῆς κοιλίας αὐτοῦ ῥεύσουσιν ὕδατος ζῶντος).[76] Interpreters of John have long divided over the punctuation of this verse and the implications of that punctuation for an understanding of the source of the living waters about which Jesus speaks. If readers encounter a full stop after "let him come to me and drink," then the following translation that presents the believer as the source of living water could result:

> If anyone is thirst, let him come to me and drink.
> And whoever believes in me – as Scripture says – from within him will flow rivers of living water.

---

[74] Cf. Ezek 47:1–12. Cf. *t.* Sukk 3:18; Wheaton, *The Role of Jewish Feasts,* 131–58.

[75] *m.* Sukk 5:1. In the second century, the festival had a particular political importance, as evidenced by the importance of its symbolism on coins dating from the time of Bar Kosiba (cf. Ya'akov Meshorer, *Jewish Coins of the Second Temple Period,* trans. I.H. Levine [Am Hassafer and Massada: Tel-Aviv, 1967]). And see the letters from the time of Bar Kosiba in Robert K. Sherk, *The Roman Empire from Augustus to Hadrian,* Translated Documents of Greece and Rome, volume 6 (Cambridge: Cambridge University Press, 1988), 152.

My reasoning for using these texts in light of one another, despite the later dates for the rabbinic texts, is the cautious admission that even though the Mishnah belongs to the century after the Fourth Gospel, it nevertheless records observances, symbols, and themes that are all present in earlier texts. John corroborates the scene sketched out in the Mishnah and Tosefta.

[76] On the translation here, see Brown, *John,* I.321–329.

But if Jesus' first two statements stand in parallel and thus make one claim (come/believe) not two (come; believe and thus be the source of living water), then the translation offered here would result:

> If anyone is thirsty, let him come to me,
> and let the one who believes in me drink
> – just as Scripture says – rivers of living water will flow from within him."

All together, no resolution is possible on the basis of grammar or syntax alone.[77] The context of this statement within the Fourth Gospel, however, strongly suggests that Jesus is speaking of himself as the source of living water, extending the invitation of John 6 for his hearers to come to him, eat and drink, and be satisfied by the eschatological food he has to offer.[78] Moreover, although it is likely that a mélange of biblical traditions is in view in Jesus' appeal to Scripture, the majority of biblical traditions that envision living water going forth view Jerusalem, or specifically the temple, as the source of these waters. God's people are the recipients, not the initiators, of the eschatological blessings that living water will bring.[79]

Written after 70, and thus with the temple in ruins (at least temporarily), and with the joyful observance of Sukkot's water libation and light ritual a thing of the past (whether the real or imagined past), the Gospel of John envisions Jesus as the one who offers in full the blessings toward which Sukkot was oriented. Jesus does not claim to replace the observances of the festival (i.e., he is not an embodiment of the water libation.) His claim is, instead, that the eschatological blessings toward which Sukkot looked are available in him. He is the object, the aim, of the festival: If anyone is thirsty (hear esp. Isa 55), let him come to Jesus, for he is the source of the living waters that Israel has been expecting. For John, to accept the invitation to come, drink, and experience Jesus as the source of living water is to draw a line of continuity that runs from Israel's

---

[77] For extended discussion, see Menken, *Old Testament Quotations*, 187–203.

[78] See esp. 6:35 and 53. The repeated use of seeking/finding language in 7:34–36 and the presence of "grumbling" about Jesus (7:32) strengthens the connections between John 6–7; these ties suggest that John's indebtedness to Isa 55 does not end in Chapter 6.

[79] In addition to Menken, see also Joel Marcus, "Rivers of Living Water from Jesus' Belly (John 7:38)," *JBL* 117 (1998): 328–330. Note that even John 4:14 is no exception to this proposal, because the spring inside of the person is not generated by the believer. See also Barrett, "The Old Testament in the Fourth Gospel," *JTS* 48.2 (1947): 156.

foundational stories and practices, into the observance of Sukkot in its traditional forms and even in the recent past, and then to complete the line at Jesus himself and the experience of eschatological blessing that he offers to those who believe in him.

Importantly, however, John qualifies Jesus' invitation by transmuting the image of eschatological living water into a promise of the Holy Spirit (7:39). This move has solid biblical grounding, as Scripture often envisions the Spirit as a substance that pours down upon people: "I will pour water (אֶצָּק־מַיִם/δώσω ὕδωρ) on the thirsty land, and streams on the dry ground/I will pour out my spirit (אֶצֹּק רוּחִי/ἐπιθήσω τὸ πνεῦμά μου) on your descendants, and my blessing on your offspring" (Isa 44:3).[80] But it also represents a striking reinterpretation of an image of restoration. John interprets "living water" as the Spirit, thus claiming that eschatological blessings have truly arrived but also allowing for the delay (or complete transmutation?) of the creation-wide experience of eschatological blessing that "living water" could denote. The lived-experience of eschatological blessing is available through the presence of the Holy Spirit, and thus the gift of the Spirit-as-living-water occurs in advance of (or perhaps fully place of?) the experience of *actual* water streaming forth from Jerusalem and nourishing the land.

This offer of living water provokes a division in the crowd (7:43): How could a man from Galilee (vv. 41, 52) be the source of such blessing? The division and debate do not derail Jesus, however, who, when he speaks again, makes a further claim that draws on the imagery of Sukkot: "Again Jesus said to them, I am the light of the world; the one following me will never walk in darkness but instead will have the light of life" (Πάλιν οὖν αὐτοῖς ἐλάλησεν ὁ Ἰησοῦς λέγων· ἐγώ εἰμι τὸ φῶς τοῦ κόσμου· ὁ ἀκολουθῶν ἐμοὶ οὐ μὴ περιπατήσῃ ἐν τῇ σκοτίᾳ, ἀλλ᾽ ἕξει τὸ φῶς τῆς ζωῆς).[81] As described above, light was a potent image associated with Sukkot. It was thematized in the ceremony that the Mishnah describes, a ceremony in which the people self-consciously counteracted the apostasy of their forbears, who bowed down to the sun (Ezek 8:16), and now asserted their

---

[80] The LXX of Isa 44:3 is striking with regard to John 7:37. For further discussion of water/Spirit imagery, see above on John 4:10–14, and Brown, *John*, I.178–179; 327–329.

[81] For modern readers, the *pericope adulterae* interrupts the flow of the narrative and its thematic indebtedness to Sukkot. On this passage, see Chris Keith, *The Pericope Adulterae, the Gospel of John, and the Literacy of Jesus*, NTTSD 38 (Leiden: Brill, 2009).

loyalty the Lord alone, whom they worshiped through the night in the bright light of candles set up in the temple and torches burning throughout the city.[82] A similar image was offered in the vision of Zechariah 14:7, which portrayed the day of God's kingship as one of ongoing light, even at evening time. Zechariah illustrates that the experience of such light as the gift of God was a particular hope of Israel's eschatological future. Isaiah cast a similar vision: "Arise, shine, for your light has come... darkness shall cover the earth ... but the Lord will arise upon you; his glory will appear over you" (Isa 60:1–2);[83] "The people who walked in darkness have seen a great light; those who lived in a land of deep darkness (LXX: "in death's darkness") – on them light has shined (Isa 9:1 MT)."

In the context of Sukkot, as in the context of other biblical descriptions of these conditions, light and darkness characterize God's presence and absence, the experience of restoration or of exile.[84] Jesus presents himself as the light of the world and thus as one who ushers in the promised experience of light and divine presence. Life "in the light" refers to both the ethical and soteriological conditions of a person's existence – a person can both walk in the light (ὁ ἀκολουθῶν ἐμοί) and "have" it (ἕξει τὸ φῶς τῆς ζωῆς).[85] As noted in regard to the water libation, Jesus' words in 8:12 do not claim that he replaces the specific observances of Sukkot; instead, he positions himself as the object toward which those observances point. A late first-century reader of John would not hear in Jesus' words a claim of replacement or annulment – he would hear a claim of fulfillment, a claim that Jesus meets the hopes that Sukkot had long nurtured. The remarkable assertiveness of Jesus' claim should be heard in this context: "I am the light of the world," recalls the voice of God – or God's Memra – declaring "Let there be light" (Gen 1:3).[86] The pairing of ἐγώ εἰμι with this particular predicate (τὸ φῶς τοῦ κόσμου) moves further in the direction of Psalm 27 ("The Lord is my light and my salvation," v. 1), as well as the texts from Isaiah that envision the light of the Lord dawning on God's people

---

[82] *m.* Sukk 5:2–3 locates the candles of the light ceremony in the temple's court of women, adjacent to the treasury where Jesus is located in 8:20.

[83] Quoting here from the MT. Cp. the specification of Jerusalem in the LXX: Φωτίζου φωτίζου, Ιερουσαλημ, ἥκει γάρ σου τὸ φῶς (cp. the illumination of the whole city in *m.* Sukk 5).

[84] On this dualism, see Ashton (208–214); Test. of Lev 19:1.

[85] See Thompson, *John*, 182–184.

[86] Cf. John 1:4–5, 7–9, and the discussion in Chapter 2.

(Isa 60:1–2; cf. 50:10) and shining as an everlasting light for them (60:20).[87] Most provocatively, Jesus' claim to be the light of the world implies that when the leaders of the people turn their backs to the sun and look instead to the presence of God as source of their light, they should now see Jesus in that role. As the Jewish leaders broke with the apostasy of their forbears in Ezekiel 8, Jesus presents himself as the sure source of the divine light. The one who follows after him will never (οὐ μή) walk in darkness (as the apostate leaders once did), but he or she will have the light of life. In John's view, the hope for the future that Sukkot kept before the people illuminates Jesus.

The imagery of Sukkot makes another appearance in these chapters when Jesus describes Abraham rejoicing at the sight of Jesus' day. Leading up to this statement, a vigorous argument has brought Abraham into view. First, the conflict centers on the status of Abraham's offspring (8:37, 39–40); second, Jesus' interlocutors resist his promise of life based on the simple observation that the great men of Israel, Abraham and the prophets, have all died (i.e., how could Jesus offer what even the patriarchs have not possessed?). Finally, Jesus brings Abraham back into the argument when he claims that the disbelief of the *Ioudaioi* reflects *not* fidelity to the patriarchs and their witness of God but rather the refusal to recognize Jesus and respond appropriately: "Your father Abraham rejoiced that he might see my day; indeed he saw and rejoiced!" (Ἀβραὰμ ὁ πατὴρ ὑμῶν ἠγαλλιάσατο ἵνα ἴδῃ τὴν ἡμέραν τὴν ἐμήν, καὶ εἶδεν καὶ ἐχάρη, v. 56). The *Ioudaioi* are incredulous that Abraham had seen Jesus' day, but in John's view, the relative youth of Jesus is no impediment to such a vision – "before Abraham was, I am" (v. 58). The implications of Jesus' claims to give life and to preexist Abraham are well understood by the *Ioudaioi*, who, perceiving the blasphemous implications, pick up stones to kill him.[88]

The striking aspect of Abraham's recognition of Jesus in John 8:56 is his joy.[89] This joy is often understood with reference to the

---

[87] Cf. Thompson, *John*, 156–60, who explains that the "I am" sayings of John are constituted not simply by their use of ἐγώ εἰμι, but more importantly by the specific predicates they take that signify things that give life. In addition to Exod 3:14 LXX, cf. also Deut 32:39 Isa 41:4; 43:11; 43:13, 15; 46:4; 48:12; 51:12; 52:6. Cf. Barrett, *John*, 336–337.

[88] Reading here with Thompson, *John*, 197.

[89] On this theme, see Menken, "Die jüdischen Feste im Johannesevangelium," 280–281.

Testament of Levi 18:11–14 and 4 Ezra 3:14, both of which record Abraham's joyful vision of end-time events. Numerous New Testament texts describe God granting the patriarchs and prophets visions of the age to come and the messiah through whom God will work.[90] Jubilees 16 joins these texts in understanding Abraham's joy at the birth of Isaac in terms of the blessings of the age to come, but it includes an often overlooked detail that associates Abraham's vision with Sukkot. In Jubilees, Abraham responds to the birth of the promised son by building an altar near a well and then celebrating a feast for seven days. With his servants, Abraham constructs booths and offers sacrifices,

> rejoicing with all his heart and with all his soul ... And he blessed his Creator who created him in his generation because by his [God's] will he created him for he knew and he perceived that from him there would be a righteous planting for eternal generations and a holy seed from him so that he [Abraham] might be like the one who made everything.[91]

According to Jubilees, Abraham's joyful celebration of the birth of Isaac was, in fact, the first observance of Sukkot (16:21), and it spilled over from Abraham's recognition of Isaac as the one through whom God will uphold the covenant. Importantly, the particular implication of God's faithfulness that Jubilees records is the merging of God's ways with human ways, the moment when God adopts a descendent of Abraham as a "righteous planting for eternal generations and a holy seed."[92] Abraham is like God – "he might be like the one who made everything" – because the promised future (which belongs only to God) will now be mediated through a particular human being. If this narrative serves as a context for understanding John 8 – and it is the only Jewish text outside of John associating Abraham's joy and Sukkot – it seems likely that in John 8:56 Jesus invokes the broad tradition of Abraham as an end-times visionary

---

[90] See Lk 10:24 = Mt 13:17; Heb 11:13; 11:17–19; 1 Pet 1:10–11. For further references, especially later rabbinic ones, see Str-B 2.525–26; for discussion, cf. Schnackenberg, *The Gospel according to John*, 2.221–223.

[91] Jub 16:25–26. The emphasis on joy in Jub 16 is more prominent than one brief quotation can demonstrate. Joy is described or commanded in 16:20 [2x], 25, 27 [2x], 29, 31.

[92] It is, of course, possible that Israel, and not a particular individual, could be this "righteous planting" and "holy seed." Cf. Isa 6:13; Ezra 9:2; Isa 11; Gal 3:16.

(4 Ezra; T. Levi) but does so through a particularly pointed reference to Abraham's joyful celebration at Sukkot of God's provision of a "holy seed" who would establish "eternal generations" (Jub 16:26). Abraham's joy at the merging of God's plan for redemption with the particular human lineage of Abraham – the joy that underlies his celebration of Sukkot – gives Jesus' claim its traction. The joy of Sukkot extended from (and should lead back to) a vision of Jesus.

When considered together, Jesus' statements and interactions with the *Ioudaioi* and the Jewish crowds at the festival position Jesus as the one who fulfills the hopes of Israel through a series of images that were bound up with Sukkot: At a festival that celebrated God's faithful provision of rain and looked forward to God's future provision of life-giving water, Jesus promises living water (viz., the Holy Spirit) to those who believe in him. With the memory of the elders of the people turning their backs on the rising sun and instead illuminating Jerusalem and the temple through the dark of night, Jesus now claims to be the light of the world. Amid stories of Abraham glimpsing God's good future and celebrating the festival, Jesus claims that he himself is the object of Abraham's vision and joy. These are, of course, controversial claims that supplant the place of the temple and altar (even if, after 70, the altar and temple lay in ruins). All together, the recurring point among Jesus' self-disclosures that take up the imagery of Sukkot is that he himself is the object and goal toward which Sukkot has long been oriented. The future has arrived – living water, light for the world, the object of the patriarch's joy – and those who believe in Jesus *in these terms* can find in him the continuity that brings together the Scripture, history, and tradition of Israel with its future.

In addition to John's portrayal of Jesus in terms of the imagery of Sukkot, these chapters also depict the controversy that accompanies acceptance of John's innovative vision of Jesus as the one through whom Israel might embrace its future. This is the second thread of the Gospel's narrative argument in these chapters. John's Jesus unapologetically presses his hearers to reorganize how they think and live around him. As we will see below (8:31–59), one of the most acrimonious debates in the Gospel emerges as Jesus confronts "the *Ioudaioi* who believed in him" with the radical implications of his messiahship. We will trace this thread as it rises prominently to the surface across chapters 7–10:21. First, we will consider the relationship between Jesus and Moses as a source of conflict; second, and relatedly, we will consider the origins of Jesus and of the the the *Ioudaioi*;

third, we will consider the message of Jesus' teaching on the Good Shepherd as it expresses the identity of Jesus as the one who enables Israel to embrace its future while also sharply criticizing the those whose vision for Israel opposes Jesus'.

Jesus and Moses

The relationship between Jesus and Moses stands out as one of the prominent threads running through the Fourth Gospel. In fact, it provides one of the comparisons by which readers are led to an understanding of Jesus: "The Law was given through Moses; grace and truth through Jesus Christ" (1:17). Throughout the narrative, John assumes that a true understanding of Moses opens out onto faith in Jesus, recording, for example, "We have found him whom Moses wrote about in the law – and the prophets too, Jesus the son of Joseph, from Nazareth'" (1:45); "If you believed in Moses, you would believe in me ... if you do not believe his writings, how will you believe in me?" (5:46, 47). Despite the deep connection that John envisions between Jesus and Moses, not all knowledge of Moses is the same. John is aware that that a mistaken view of Moses might harden a person against Jesus. Thus, Jesus warns that Moses will be the "accuser" of those who have wrongly hoped in him rather than the one about whom he wrote (5:45); he reframes the manna miracle (6:32) to correct (it would seem) a comparison of Moses and Jesus as equals rather than of Jesus as an eschatological successor.[93] For John, the charge, "You are his [Jesus'] disciple, but we are disciples of Moses!" (9:28) is both a rejection of Jesus and a tragically ironic misunderstanding of Moses.

In chapters 7–10, the typological relationship between Moses and Jesus rises more prominently to the surface and foments the growing hostility that Jesus faces. Chapter 7 describes persistent division and conflict about Jesus: The *Ioudaioi* are looking for him (v.11); the grumbling crowds are speculating – "He is good," but also, "No, he is deceiving the crowd" (v.12). After Jesus begins teaching, the Jerusalemites ask, "Do the rulers truly know that he is the Messiah? ... How can this be since we know his origins?" (7:26–27). As the crowd begins coming to faith, the people reason that Jesus' signs are sufficient proof of his identity: "When the messiah comes,

---

[93] So also John 3:14.

will he do more signs than this one has done?" (v. 31).[94] After Jesus declares himself to be the source of living waters, the crowds are convinced of Jesus' significance but again divided about his identity – Some say, "Truly he is the prophet" (ὁ προφήτης), but others conclude, "He is the Messiah" (vv. 40–41). Thus the crowd undergoes a division (σχίσμα, v. 43). These debates and divisions center on Jesus' identity, his origin/authority, and his status as either a truthful prophet or a deceptive teacher. As such, these debates are in part indebted to a comparison of Jesus with Moses, the true prophet whose commission from God is beyond doubt.

John brings the relationship between Jesus and Moses into focus in 7:19–24, where Jesus defends his right to heal on Sabbath by raising a comparison with the law of Moses, which allows a person to violate the Sabbath to observe circumcision.[95] Although Jesus' rationale (making a man whole) seems to fall short of the later rabbinic standard (enacting God's command for circumcision on the eighth day), it is not the novelty of Jesus' argument that sparks the conflict. Rather, Jesus' repeated declaration that he has come to do the will of he who sent him, and that he does not act on his own, provokes conflict. Thus, just before Jesus defends himself with reference to Moses, he says,

> If anyone wants to do his will [=God's/the one who sent me], let him recognize whether the teaching is from God or if I am speaking from myself (ἀπ' ἐμαυτοῦ). The one speaking from himself (ὁ ἀφ' ἑαυτοῦ λαλῶν) seeks his own glory, but the one seeking the glory of the one who sent him, this one is true and there is no unrighteousness in him. (7:17–18)

Immediately after Jesus' appeal to Moses, he continues with the same argument: "Then Jesus cried out while teaching in the temple and he said, 'You know me and whence I come. Indeed, I have not come from myself (ἀπ' ἐμαυτοῦ οὐκ ἐλήλυθα), but the one who sent me is true, and you do not know him (7:28).'" The next action in the narrative appears as the consequence of Jesus' repeated claims to not speak from himself but, instead, to represent God: "Therefore,"

---

[94] On the role of such expectations for the messiah, see Thompson, *John*, 173; Schnackenburg, *The Gospel according to John*, II.148.

[95] On observing God's command to circumcise on the eighth day, see Gen 17:12; 21:4 *m.* Shab. 19 (cf. Luke 2:21!). On (nearly) contemporary arguments as those in 7:19–24, although with the saving of life in view, see *t.* Shab. 15, 16. Cf. also *b.* Yoma 85a–b; Schnackenburg, *The Gospel according to St. John*, II.134.

John writes, "they sought to arrest him" (7:30). Why? Unlike in John 5 and 10, the Jewish authorities do not charge Jesus here with blasphemy. What makes him worthy of arrest? The most compelling logic for this hostile response to Jesus is that the narrative of John 7 records a controversial claim that many readers of John have been slow to recognize. Alongside the repeated charges that Jesus "deceives" and "divides" the crowds (7:12, 43, 47), John records Jesus claiming that he represents the one who sent him (vv. 16, 18, 29, 33) and that his words are not his own (vv.17, 18, 28). Chapter 7 is also specifically attuned to the character of Moses (7:19–24) and the possibility that Jesus might be a prophet (7:40, 52). In fact, the Jesus–Moses relationship provides a helpful key to the logic of chapter 7 and the growing conflict surrounding Jesus, since Jesus' self-defense echoes the defense Moses made in the face of the rebellion of Korah, Dathan, and Abiram: "Moses said, 'By this you will know that the Lord sent me to do all these works, that they are not from myself'" (Num 16:28).[96]

Read with an awareness of this context, readers can see that in vv.19–24 John presses the Jesus–Moses relationship by recording Jesus' defense of his actions in this Moses-like terminology.[97] But there is an added consequence of John framing the debate about Jesus' identity by means of a comparison to Moses: by presenting Jesus as a figure with a Moses-like authorization, the narrative implicitly communicates what is at stake in such a claim: Jesus presents himself as a new, authoritative prophet. Moses himself had spoken to Israel about God raising up such a figure who would perform signs and speak to the people for God (Deut 13:1–5; 18:15, 18–20). But the division caused by Jesus' teaching could easily suggest that instead of Jesus being the promised prophet, he might in fact be a deceiver of Israel. The consequence of such deception is death: "The prophet who acts impiously by speaking a word in my name that I have not ordered to speak ... that prophet shall die" (Deut 18:20); "...that prophet [ὁ προφήτης ἐκεῖνος] or that diviner by dream shall die [ἀποθανεῖται], for he spoke to lead you astray from

---

[96] Num 16:28: Καὶ εἶπεν Μωυσῆς Ἐν τούτῳ γνώσεσθε ὅτι κύριος ἀπέστειλέν με ποιῆσαι πάντα τὰ ἔργα ταῦτα, ὅτι οὐκ ἀπ' ἐμαυτοῦ. The Hebrew phrase "from myself" used here (מלבי) occurs in the MT only in Num 16:28 and 24:13; the Greek phrase (ἀπ' ἐμαυτοῦ) only in Num 16:28 and 4 Macc 11:3. Cf. T. F. Glasson, *Moses in the Fourth Gospel*, 30.

[97] In fact, Jesus has been speaking in this terminology for two chapters. On earlier use of "from myself," see 5:19, 30; 12:49 (ἐξ ἐμαυτοῦ); on "the one who sent me," see 3:34; 4:34; 5:23, 38; 6:29, 38–39; 6:57, 12:44–50).

the Lord your God" [ἐλάλησεν γὰρ πλανῆσαί σε ἀπὸ κυρίου τοῦ θεοῦ / כי דבר-סרה על-יהוה אלהיכם] (Deut 13:1–5). As Wayne Meeks has noted, it is this constellation of themes and the implications of Jesus deceiving and dividing the people that accounts for the three abrupt references to killing Jesus as he teaches in the temple (7:19, 20, 25).[98] John would have its readers recognize Jesus as a long-awaited eschatological teacher, one greater than Moses whose appearance was bound up with Israel achieving its hopes.[99] To this end, Jesus echoes the words and self-defense of Moses, and readers are reminded of Jesus' powerful signs (7:23, 31). But precisely at this point the nature of John's innovative claim is laid bare, because the signs and claims of Jesus can also be rendered presumptuous with reference to the same texts that would validate his identity as one sent from God (see Deut 13:5, 18:20). Jesus and his opponents are at loggerheads.

As these themes of chapter 7 play out in chapters 8–9, John records Jesus and the *Ioudaioi* speaking in terms that increasingly miss one another. We will look at these texts briefly, but the basic terms of the argument have already been determined by the way in which John has narrated that there is no *logical* argument that can begin with the commitments of the *Ioudaioi* to Torah and their particular eschatological expectations and then go on to belief in Jesus. The way of thinking of the *Ioudaioi* leads inevitably to the conclusion that Jesus was a false prophet, one who should die for dividing and misleading the people of God. For John, of course, Jesus is the sent one, the savior, the one of whom Moses wrote. But what is needed for such a recognition is an innovative commitment (or, in John's terms, a healed heart, 12:40), which would provide the ability to accept John's understanding of God's actions and Israel's hopes and then to allow that new understanding to re-signify the coherence of the whole tradition. The Moses–Jesus typology in John thus illustrates one possible way of understanding the tradition's new coherence and also the way in which Jesus' claims would have been heard as a tangible threat to a tradition that, at the end of the first century, was actively attending to the integrity of its way of life.[100]

---

[98] Meeks, *Prophet-King*, 58.
[99] Meeks goes into rich detail on this (see esp., *Prophet-King*, 318–319).
[100] On how the Jewish tradition was attending to the integrity of its own tradition, see esp. Cohen, "The Significance of Yavneh"; Marcus, "The Birkat Ha-Minim Revisited"; Neusner, *First Century Judaism in Crisis* (all cited in Chapter 1). I am

Chapter 7 concludes with the Pharisees and rulers opposing the possibility that Jesus might be "the prophet" (vv. 40, 52), and when the scene continues in 8:12, the Pharisees specifically oppose Jesus' claims to be "light of the world." John sustains the characterization of Jesus as one who, like Moses, speaks not "from himself" even as the debate moves on to various topics: witnesses (8:14–19; cf. 5:37–38), Jesus' departure/origins and lifting up (8:21–29), Abraham (8:33–59). Thus, "When the Son of Man is lifted up, then you will know that I am, and that from myself (ἀπ᾽ ἐμαυτοῦ) I do nothing, but just as the father taught me do I speak these things" (8:28); "You seek to kill me, a man who has spoken to you the truth that I heard from God" (8:40). "I did not come on my own (ἀπ᾽ ἐμαυτοῦ), but he [God] sent me" (8:42). The deadly hostility in John 8:37, 40, and 59 is a reaction not to Jesus' testimony about himself in general, but rather to the specific profile of Jesus' testimony, which is spoken in a context that is sensitive to Jesus' relationship to a Moses-like figure and also delivered in terminology ("from myself"/him who sent me") that specifically echoes the claims that legitimized the authority of Moses. This continues in chapter 9, when, after Jesus successfully heals on the Sabbath, the Pharisees undergo a σχίσμα (v. 16). The context for this division is their attempt to settle a perplexing issue (i.e., how could Jesus both violate the Sabbath and be from God?); the Pharisees ask the healed man to identify Jesus, and he answers in terms that exactly fit the conflict surrounding him: "He is a prophet" (v. 17). But this conclusion is closed for the Pharisees: "We know that God spoke to Moses, but this one – we don't know where he is from" (9:29).

In these ways the relationship between Jesus and Moses fuels the controversy that takes place during the festival of Sukkot. Jesus speaks in terms the hark back to Moses, a predecessor who, in John's logic, offers a vantage point from which one might understand the authority of Jesus. Moses illuminates Jesus' identity as an agent who has been sent and authorized by God, and who in fact does nothing on his own. To resist or believe in Jesus is (as with Moses) to take a position vis-à-vis the one who sent him. But the comparison with

<hr />

aware of the debates that surround these reconstructions (cf. Hakola, *Identity Matters*; Boyarin, *Border Lines;* "Justin Martyr Invents Judaism"). My claim here is not that there was an early organized rabbinate but, more simply, that at the end of first century the Jewish tradition was engaged in reflection and organization about its coherence.

Moses also illustrates for John the failure of the *Ioudaioi* with regard to their own tradition. Rather than seeing Jesus as the fulfillment of a promise and a long-hoped for figure, they interpret Jesus as a deceiver and pretender, whose risk to the unity of the people necessitates rejection and even death (7:19, 20, 25; 8:37, 40, 59; 9:22).

Derivation/Origins

Alongside of the Moses–Jesus typology – and related to it – runs another conflict related to the source from which Jesus and his interlocutors derive their identities. For John, a person's actions and beliefs are transparent to the power and ethical influence that operates in, over, and through his or her life – this is, in Leander Keck's words, a person's "of-ness."[101] In the present section of the Gospel, John develops the connection between actions/beliefs and a person's "of-ness" by setting in the starkest possible terms the nature of the choice that Israel faces in Jesus: freedom and truth, or slavery to sin and lies, and, with these things, an origin in God or in the devil. To consider John's view of a person's origins, we will first consider how a person's origin and identity are bound together in the Gospel of John and then we will consider how the connection between origin and identity relates to the acceptance or rejection of Jesus.

The Gospel raises the issues of the "of-ness" of its characters early on: John the Baptist's ministry of testifying to Jesus reflects that he and his ministry should be understood as "from God" (παρὰ θεοῦ, 1:6); and those who accept and believe in Jesus are reborn "not from blood, nor the will of the flesh, nor the will of a man, but from God" (ἐξ ... ἐκ ... ἐκ ... ἐκ θεοῦ, 1:13). Admission into the kingdom of God follows on the reorientation of one's life and his appropriation of a new "of-ness": a person must be born from water and spirit (τις γεννηθῇ ἐξ ὕδατος καὶ πνεύματος, 3:5); what is born of flesh is flesh, and of spirit is spirit (τὸ γεγεννημένον ἐκ τῆς σαρκὸς ... ἐκ τοῦ πνεύματος, 3:6; see also 3:8). Thus, in John, as people are chosen by Jesus and believe in him, they exchange one source of power operating in

---

[101] Cf. Leander Keck, "Anthropology and Soteriology in Johannine Christology," in Leander Keck, *Why Christ Matters: Toward a New Testament Theology* (Waco: Baylor, 2015), 73–89. On how a person's actions belie their parentage, cf. Philo, *Virt.* 207; Pseudo-Philo, *L.A.B.*, 33:5; Prov 23:15–25; (cf. Sir 22:3–5); Matt 5:44–48, 4 Macc 15.

their lives for another – they are no longer ἐκ τοῦ κόσμου (15:23; cf. 16:27; 17:16).

Along these lines, the impasse between Jesus and the *Ioudaioi* reflects the inability of the *Ioudaioi* to judge Jesus because they have not experienced a reorientation of their lives: "You are from below; I am from above. You are from this world; I am not from this world" (ἐκ τῶν κάτω ... ἐκ τῶν ἄνω ... ἐκ τούτου τοῦ κόσμου ... ἐκ τοῦ κόσμου τούτου, 8:23; cf. v. 47; 3:18–21). Interestingly, the Pharisees also judge (in John's logic, misjudge) Jesus because of the connection that *should* link a person's actions with the power and influence that works in and through him: "This man is not from God (παρὰ θεοῦ), because he breaks the Sabbath" (9:16; cf. v. 33). Together these statements about John the Baptist, and about those who do or do not believe, reflect a basic point of Johannine anthropology: a person's derivation (i.e., her origin/"of-ness") is not fixed, but is instead determined by the choices and commitments of her life.[102]

Jesus' life fits this pattern too: his faithful obedience to a divine commission is a window into his origin with God (e.g., 5:19–30; 19:36). But, in a way that is unique in comparison with other characters in the Fourth Gospel, Jesus' origin *is* essentialized and bound up with his nature. In other words, Jesus' sonship is confirmed by both his identity (who he is and where he is from) and his ethics (what he does), but other characters derive their "of-ness" based primarily on their ethics rather than from a predetermined (or semi-gnostic) account of identity that would precede the courses of the lives that they live.[103] This means that, as the Word of God, Jesus is not only from God in an ethical sense but also *with God* and, indeed, God (ὁ λόγος ἦν πρὸς τὸν θεόν, καὶ θεὸς ἦν ὁ λόγος, 1:1). Jesus' actions *further reveal* that both his identity and ethics derive from God: in revealing the Father's glory, Jesus' life reveals that he comes "from God" (1:14). Scattered descriptions of Jesus as the one who "has descended" from God join together the uniqueness of Jesus' identity (who he is and where he comes from) and the way in which

---

[102] For a recent presentation of this perspective, see the aforementioned work of Keck, "Anthropology and Sotieriology in Johannine Christology."

[103] For important discussion of these views, see Jeffrey Trumbower, *Born from Above: The Anthropology of the Gospel of John,* HUT 29 (Tübingen: Mohr Siebeck, 1992). See also Luke Timothy Johnson, "John and Thomas in Context: An Exercise in Canonical Criticism," in *The Word Leaps the Gap,* ed. J. Ross Wagner et al. (Grand Rapids: Eerdmans, 2008), 284–309.

his truthful witness (what he does) should make clear the place where he is from.[104]

While Jesus is "from God" both by nature and by action, the "of-ness" of all the other characters in the Fourth Gospel is determined by the lives that they live, specifically by the ways in which their responses to Jesus throw into relief the truthfulness of their lives. This unique characterization of Jesus is how John overcomes the challenges associated with Jesus' unlikely messiahship. For Jesus' opponents, particularly the *Ioudaioi*, Jesus' human origin presents a major stumbling block: "Is this not Jesus, son of Joseph, whose father and mother we know? How can he now be saying, 'I have come down from heaven?'" (6:42). "You are not yet fifty years old – you've seen Abraham?!?" (8:57). Even when they are eventually backed into a corner by Jesus' ability to violate the Sabbath *and* work miracles on it, the Pharisees refuse to acknowledge Jesus' heavenly origin: "This one – we do not know where (πόθεν) he came from" (9:29).[105] John has a ready answer for those repelled by the problems of Jesus' humanity, family, Galilean extraction, and most importantly his exalted claims about himself: "Do not judge according to appearances, but judge with right judgment" (7:24). That is to say: for most people, a Sabbath violation would reveal a fundamental disrespect for God, Torah, and tradition. But Jesus must be judged by a different standard because his identity precludes the possibility of actions inconsistent with the God of Israel and the true orientation of Jewish Scripture and tradition.

In the scene of Jesus at the festival of Sukkot (7–10:21), the question of origins rises prominently to the surface in chapter 8, which records Jesus defending his testimony about himself because, first, he knows both his origin and his destination (8:13–15); second, because the Father witnesses for the authenticity of Jesus' identity – that is, the Father witnesses for the *whence* of Jesus' words and actions (8:16–19; cf. 27); and, third, "the *Ioudaioi* who believed in him" have mistakenly entrusted themselves to the false belief that sonship of Abraham/sonship of God must entail a rejection of Jesus' uncompromising claims about himself (8:33–40, 41–45). It is this final argument that crystalizes John's bracing views on "of-ness"

---

[104] On Jesus' origins, cf. also John 1:18; 3:13, 31, 34; 5:19; 6:38; 7:28–29; 13:3; 16:27–28; 17:14–16; 18:36–37.

[105] In John, πόθεν consistently makes reference to heavenly/divine origins, see, e.g., 1:48; 2:9; 3:8; 4:11; 6:5; 7:27; 8:14; 9:29–30; 19:9.

and from which it is best to understand how John develops an account of a person's origins as a way to set in stark terms the nature of the choice that Israel faces in Jesus: freedom and truth, or slavery to sin and lies.

The heated exchange between Jesus and the *Ioudaioi* in John 8 is catalyzed by Jesus himself when he challenges "the *Ioudaioi* who believed in him" (v. 31) by stating that truth and freedom extend from him alone. As Jesus clarifies what this means (vv. 33–36), he explains that even offspring of Abraham (σπέρμα Ἀβραάμ) are held captive to sin, and thus it is possible to be the σπέρμα Ἀβραάμ and not enjoy the benefits and freedom of sonship. An audience familiar with Abraham's two sons – one born of a slave and the other of a free woman, one who did not remain "in the house" and one who inherited everything – would understand his logic: it is not enough to claim you are the seed of Abraham, you need to align yourself with the son.[106] Jesus concedes that his interlocutors are the offspring of Abraham, but then he voices what (in his mind) is a contradiction to true sonship: "I know that you are offspring of Abraham, but you seek to kill me because there is no place in you for my word" (v. 37) The force of this sentence suggests that the *Ioudaioi* are indeed offspring of the patriarch but, surprisingly, their errors align them not with freedom and sonship but with sin and slavery. What is at stake in the full acceptance of Jesus' word is *not* descent from Abraham – that is a given. Instead, what is at stake in the acceptance of Jesus is a place "in the house" of the one who is free from sin and can free others as well (vv. 35–36).[107]

Jesus' hearers ignore the distinction (or refuse to enter the argument) that Jesus makes about sons and slavery, and in 8:39 they reassert their paternity – "Abraham is our father!" In turn, Jesus' radicalizes his claims too: Jesus speaks the truth he heard from God, thus, the hostility of the *Ioudaioi* toward Jesus tells against their claims to paternity: Abraham was hospitable to the messengers of

---

[106] Paul applies a similar argument against the Judaizers (likely some of the form of "the *Ioudaioi* who believed in Jesus"?) in Gal 4:21–5:1. Adele Reinhartz (*Befriending the Beloved Disciple*, 91) interprets δουλεύω in John 8 and Gal 4 [esp. v. 9] in terms of true or false worship, not physical captivity. On the issues at play here, see further C. K. Barrett, "The Allegory of Abraham, Sarah, and Hagar," in *Essays on Paul* (London: SPCK, 1982), 154–170; also 169n31 (citing Gen R 53:11, Str–B III.575f); Jerome H. Neyrey, "Jesus the Judge: Forensic Process in John 8,21–59," *Biblica* 68.4 (1987): 509–542, adds *t.* Sotah 6:6 as a further noteworthy text.

[107] See Philo, *Virt.* 207.

God's word; by contrast, hospitality is far from the minds of the *Ioudaioi*, which are set on murder (cf. vv. 39–40).[108] From here the implications unfold rapidly. Jesus has claimed that the actions of the *Ioudaioi* are incongruent with those of Abraham. Therefore, they must have another father. The first protest of the *Ioudaioi* is an assertion of their loyalty to the tradition: "*We* are not begotten from sexual immorality" – that is, we are not like the τέκνα πορνείας whom Hosea decried (2:4, LXX 2:6), but we are the children of God (Hos 1:8–11 [υἱοὶ θεοῦ], 11:1 [τὰ τέκνα αὐτοῦ]). But Jesus confronts this as an errant claim because the hostility of the *Ioudaioi* – which at this point in the narrative is a hostility seeking to kill Jesus – cannot coincide with their acting under the influence and power of God. In John's logic, it is an impossible contradiction for the *Ioudaioi* to seek Jesus' death and to claim an identity that stands in continuity with the God of Israel.

When the narrator writes – and Jesus says – "You are of your father the devil, and you seek to do the [murderous, 44b] desires of your father" (8:44a), he is pressing the logic of his argument to its conclusion. A person's actions with regard to Jesus reveal the power determining his or her life. The *Ioudaioi* claim – as they have throughout the entirety of the Fourth Gospel – to represent accurately the interpretation of the Torah and fidelity to the Jewish tradition. That is, the *Ioudaioi* claim to have both God and Abraham as their father (8:39, 41). Their origin is secure, and they act according to their divine ruler and human exemplar. Bound up with the efforts of the *Ioudaioi* to lead faithfully the people of God is their hostility to Jesus. They view him as a false prophet, a presumptuous claimant to a role for which he is unfit, indeed, as "a Samaritan and demon-possessed" man (v. 48; cf. 7:20; 8:52; 10:20–21). The penalty for the presumption and deception Jesus represents is death, and in the narrative of John both Jesus and the *Ioudaioi* have recognized this as the threat implied by their disagreement (5:18; 7:1, 19, 25, 30; 8:37, 40; 11:53). If Jesus is not who he says he is, he deserves to die.[109]

---

[108] My phrasing is indebted to Neyrey, "Jesus the Judge," 524. See also Brown, *John*, I.357; Jason J. Ripley, "Killing as Piety? Exploring Ideological Contexts Shaping the Gospel of John," *JBL* 134.3 (2015): 605–635, esp. 630–631.

[109] Importantly, it is Jesus' (purportedly false) teaching, not any particular violation, that lies at the base of his trial in 18:19. Jesus' defense that he has taught openly (παρρησίᾳ, 18:20) is likely a defense that looks back to Deut 13:5–10, which describes the one who entices Israel to go astray as one who speaks in secret (λάθρᾳ).

But the testimony of the Gospel, and particularly the testimony of Jesus in John 8, is that he is an innocent man (8:46) who speaks the truth and comes not ἀπ᾽ ἐμαυτοῦ, as the false prophet does, but from God (vv. 43, 46). The persistent rejection and impulse to kill an innocent man derives, in John's view, from only one place – "the devil ... this one was a murderer from the beginning" (v. 44). From this perspective, the charge that the *Ioudaioi* have the devil as their father amounts not to an ontological statement but to an ethical one that draws out the implications of "ethical sonship" that are applied to characters throughout the Fourth Gospel.[110] For John, the *Ioudaioi* seek the death of God's emissary, one who has done no wrong (v. 46 – τίς ἐξ ὑμῶν ἐλέγχει με περὶ ἁμαρτίας;) but instead speaks the truth. Uncomfortable as it is to read twenty centuries later, John's theological account of the origins of such hostility – the hostility that could encounter God's word, name it as false, and seek to kill it – can only be located in the power of the devil exerting a controlling influence in the lives of particular people.

Before moving deeper into Jesus' accusation that the *Ioudaioi* act out the will of their father, the devil, it is important to consider how the understanding of origins sketched here finds its climax in John 8:47. In that place, Jesus answers his own rhetorical question ("If I am speaking the truth, why are you not believing in me?" v. 46) by stating, "The one who is from God (ὁ ὢν ἐκ τοῦ θεοῦ) hears the words of God. This is why you do not hear: you are not from God (ἐκ τοῦ θεοῦ)." This statement could certainly be read as a statement about the predetermined ontological derivation of the *Ioudaioi*. In that case, Jesus would be saying that they cannot comprehend him, and never could, because their origins preclude hearing or belief. Jesus certainly speaks here in dualistic terms – one is either from God or from the devil, from above or from this world. But, importantly, Jesus does not trace the resistance of the *Ioudaioi* to his words to a fixed, unchangeable ontology but to their contingent decision against

---

[110] See also the discussion of John 1:12–13 (see Chapter 2). On the ethical (not ontological) force of this language, see Pedersen, "Anti-Judaism in John's Gospel," 184–193; Thompson, *John*, 192. Although it is possible to see such sonship as referring to "the nature" of the *Ioudaioi*, readings that do so do not seem to express the particular logic of John, but rather a close and dangerous inference of John's language that becomes quickly available when the plotline of John is lost. The reception of John within Gnosticism testifies to the ease of such an inference – but it makes it neither inevitable nor correct. See Miroslav Volf, "Johannine Dualism and Contemporary Pluralism" *Modern Theology* 21.2 (2005): 189–217; Richard B. Hays, *The Moral Vision of the New Testament,* 426–429, 424 (cp. 154).

him and unwillingness to commit themselves fully to his word. To see this, it is important to allow 8:31 to frame the argument of the broader section we are considering.

The argument of 8:31–47 works on the logic that a person's decision to hear or resist the word of Jesus "actualizes and demonstrates their 'of-ness.'"[111] The argument presupposes that origins are not fixed; they can be altered by an act of radical trust in the words of God's messenger, or they can be exposed by a hostile rejection of the messenger. To see this, it will be helpful to view the argument of 8:31–47 in its broader outline:

> Claim #1: Jesus states: "If you remain in my word, you will truly be my disciples, and you will know the truth, and the truth will make you free" (8:31–32). Jesus is exhorting and confronting "the *Ioudaioi* who believed in him" (v. 31) to put full trust in his word.
>
> Claim #2: The *Ioudaioi* do not respond directly to the summons to trust Jesus' word. Instead, they challenge Jesus' claim about freedom. Are freedom and truth really at stake in entrusting oneself to Jesus' word? As noted above, Jesus carries forward the argument in terms of the status as sons and slaves (vv. 33–36).
>
> Claim #3: Jesus states that the paternity of the *Ioudaioi* is visible in their reception of God's messenger (v. 40). Their hostility reflects the sonship of a murderer and liar (v.44), rather than their love for God (v. 43). Jesus is stating that the reception of him by the *Ioudaioi* belies a paternity that is different than they assume. This implies that the claim of vv. 31–32 is correct: truth and freedom really are at stake in a decision about Jesus.
>
> Claim #4: In vv. 45–47, Jesus ties together claim #1 with claims #2–3: Contrary to their opinions of themselves (namely that their actions denote their sonship of Abraham and God [vv. 39, 41]), it is only by "hearing" the words of God (=believing in the words of God spoken by Jesus) that the *Ioudaioi* can truly be "from God." Their rejection of Jesus enacts the character of the devil rather than of Abraham.

---

[111] Keck, "Anthropology and Sotieriology in Johannine Christology," 83.

When seen within the framework of the argument, Jesus' statement, "This is why you do not hear: you are not from God" (v. 47), functions as the proof that would shock the *Ioudaioi* into accepting the claim of Jesus in 8:31–32. Jesus' words in this section aim to disprove the assumptions of the Jews about their paternity by linking their reception of him to their hostility and violence. Jesus' appeal for the *Ioudaioi* to enact true sonship works (1) by means of a daring call to trust in his word (8:31–32) and (2) by means of a demonstration of how the violence and accusations of the *Ioudaioi* disprove their assumption that they act in faithfulness. Contrary to their self-estimation, the inability of the *Ioudaioi* to hear Jesus' word reflects not their loyalty to God but rather the tragic determination of their actions by the enemy of God. This determination is ethical, not ontological, and can therefore be changed. The logic of 8:31–47, and 46–47 especially, rests on conviction that a person's "of-ness" – and particularly, his identity as one who is "of" the God of Israel – is determined by his willingness to receive Jesus.

How, then, does the viewpoint developed here illuminate the heated polemic of John 8? To reflect more deeply on the argument in this passage, we should begin by repeating the observation that in the immediate context of John 8, the charge of v. 44 that the *Ioudaioi* are "from your father the devil" is determined entirely by a context that is concerned with killing and falsehood. As the *Ioudaioi* falsely accuse and wrongly seek the death of Jesus, they position themselves under the power and influence not of God or of Abraham but of the devil, a murderer from the beginning whose mother tongue is lies. The Gospel acknowledges that an alternative interpretation of the facts is possible. When Jesus' accusation against the *Ioudaioi* ends, they immediately return the accusation: "Are we not correct in saying that you are a Samaritan and have a demon?" (v. 48). These charges that the *Ioudaioi* and Jesus are respectively acting under the influence of superhuman evil amount to more than abstract accusations or insults. Rather, in a context in which the faithful versus false leadership of God's people is at stake, such claims amount to theologically specific indictments that align their subjects (Jesus, the *Ioudaioi*) with the figure/power that in contemporary Jewish thinking was responsible for ensnaring Israel and leading the people away from their God.[112] Thus, to take a prominent example from Second

---

[112] For an overview of the devil/Satan in Second Temple Judaism (without developing that identity specifically in terms of Israel), see Paolo Sacchi, "The Devil in Jewish

Temple literature, The Damascus Document records the dominion of Belial within Israel in terms of Belial enticing and misleading Israel into calling what is unjust just:

> Belial will be set loose against Israel, as God has said by means of the prophet Isaiah, son of Amoz, saying: "Panic, pit, and net [are] against you, you who live on the earth." Its interpretation: They are Belial's three nets ... by which he catches Israel and makes them [the nets/snares/ injustices] appear before them [the Israelites] like three types of justice. The first [snare that will appear as justice] is fornication; the second, wealth; the third, defilement of the temple. (CD 4.13–18)[113]

In this passage, those who are led by Belial have their perceptions so broken that they no longer distinguish good from bad. In fact, those who are so led defile the holy spirit within them, speak against God's covenant, and are like those in the past who have made Israel stray (cf. CD 4.11–21). In another apocalyptic text, and this one particularly close to the Gospel of John, Revelation 12:9 envisions the messiah as victorious over "the ancient serpent, called the devil and satan, who deceives the whole world"; in Revelation 19, at the climactic victory of the lamb, the seer envisions the captivity of both God's superhuman opponent ("the beast") as well as "the false prophet, who did signs before him by which those who received the mark of the beast were deceived and worshipped its image" (19:20).[114] Other examples could be adduced.[115] The important thing to note (and this is reproduced in the citations in the preceding footnote) is that the power embodied by the devil/Satan/Belial is not an abstract power. To the contrary, the devil embodies the specific power that would mislead the people of God and hold them captive from the life to which God calls them. In John, the cosmic

---

Traditions of the Second Temple Period (c. 500 BCE – 100 CE), in Paolo Sacchi, *Jewish Apocalyptic and Its History*, trans. William J. Short, OFM; JSPSup 20 (Sheffied: Sheffield Academic Press, 1990), 211–232.

[113] Trans. altered from Martínez and Tigchelaar, *The Dead Sea Scrolls Study Edition*, I.557.

[114] These passages open up the scope of the devil's deception beyond simply Israel (though certainly it is inclusive of it).

[115] Jubilees 1:20, 21; 12:20; 7:27; 11:1–16 (on Mastema, cf. also 19:29); 16:33–34; T. Levi 19:1; T. Benjamin 7:1–2; T. Dan 4:7; 5:6 (several of these texts from the Testament of the Twelve Patriarchs echo Deut 30:15–20); 1QS 1.23–24; 2.4–19; 11Q13 2.2–25; 1QH XII; cf. also 2 Peter 2:15.

drama that plays out in the opposition of God and the devil corresponds to the very human drama of Jesus and the *Ioudaioi*, each
representing a vision for Israel's life with God while simultaneously
recognizing the life-or-death consequences of proffering a false
vision.[116]

It is, therefore, a methodological error to read John 8:31–59 in
abstraction from the claim–counterclaim that both parties are
allegedly under the power of the devil (or a demon). The power
under discussion in this acrimonious exchange is one that would
prevent Israel from following God. To those who place their trust
in a future for Israel different from the one Jesus offers, Jesus
threatens the deadly consequence of rejecting the truth (8:24, 32,
40, 44–46) and casts the violent persecution by the *Ioudaioi* of a man
who has committed no sin as proof of the falsehood of their way
(v. 45–46). Because they live within the same theological reality, the
Ioudaioi give as they get: scoffing at Jesus' presumptuous claims (vv.
52–57), relegating his views to the "obvious" error of Samaritanism
(v. 48), as well as the cosmic source of such error (vv. 48, 52), and
finally holding over Jesus the possibility that, from their view, he is
bringing upon himself the punishment for misleading the people of
God (John 8:59 cf. Deut 13:10).[117] All of this is to say that a reading
of John 8 that is narratively, theologically, and historically contextualized should recognize that *inherent to the charges in John that a
person or group acts under the power of the devil is an awareness
that the primary role of the devil or a demon is to prevent Israel
from embracing its identity as the people of God and to hold God's
people captive to the falsehood and violence that have always marked
the devil's ways.*[118]

John 8:31–59, and 8:44 in particular, interpret the resistance of the
Ioudaioi to Jesus – resistance that would lead Jesus' own people (οἱ
ἴδιοι) to plot for his death – as an expression of cosmic resistance

---

[116] See Judith L. Kovacs, "'Now Shall the Ruler of This World Be Driven Out':
Jesus' Death as Cosmic Battle in John 12:20–36, *JBL* 114.2 (1995): 227–247.

[117] Similarly, see Reinhartz, *Befriending the Beloved Disciple*, 92–95; Reinhartz,
"John 8:31–59 from a Jewish Perspective," in *Remembering for the Future: The
Holocaust in an Age of Genocide*, ed. John K. Roth et al. (vol 2; New York: Palgrave,
2001), esp. 794–795.

[118] I omit here the ways that this exchange might be contextualized within ancient
polemic. In this vein, see Luke Timothy Johnson, "The New Testament's Anti-Jewish
Slander and the Conventions of Ancient Polemic," *JBL* 108.3 (1989): 419–441; D. G.
James, "The Embarrassment of History: Reflections on the Problem of 'Anti-Judaism'
in the Fourth Gospel," in *Anti-Judaism and the Fourth Gospel*, 51–53.

superintended by the devil. In other words, in John's logic, when adherents to the Jewish tradition do not believe in Jesus, and particularly as they do so to the point of violent hostility to Jesus, it is not because the tradition is under the sway of some neutral authority or has simply opted out of belief in Jesus but because it has been led astray by the power that opposes the plans of God for his people and the world. This seems to be the uncomfortable (for us) logic of John.

Excursus: Johannine Narrative Logic about the Jewish Rejection of Jesus

To be sure, Jewish resistance and disbelief can be accounted for in ways other than the influencing role of the devil set out in John 8. Modern interpreters often describe the dynamics of this heated exchange with reference to the struggles of the Johannine community, and there is no reason to ignore the role of those struggles in generating polemical language.[119] The Gospel's own accounting for Jewish disbelief, however, names love for human glory and fear of others (5:44; 7:18; 12:42–43), simple inability to hear or recognize, as well as a superhumanly wrought inability of the *Ioudaioi* to accept Jesus due to either God's hardening or the devil's influence (8:44; 10:26–30; 12:39–40).[120] Taken together, there is in John no single causality for unbelief in Jesus, no simple point of origin that would predetermine the "of-ness" of a character. From a source-critical perspective, this mélange of causes for unbelief could easily reflect a variety of viewpoints that have been joined without harmonization.[121] But as they interact within the narrative of the Gospel, they also evoke the theological mystery of belief and unbelief in Jesus. In

---

[119] Cf. Miroslav S. Wróbel, "John 8:44 as *crux interpretum*," in *Rediscovering John: Essays on the Fourth Gospel in Honour of Frédéric Manns*, ed. L. Daniel Chrupcala, SBFA 80 (Milan: Edizioni Terra Santa, 2013), 403–421.

[120] Cf. Martin Buber's objection to Christianity: "The church rests on its faith that the Christ has come, and that this is the redemption which God has bestowed on mankind. We, Israel, *are not able* to believe this . . . We know more deeply, more truly, that world history has not been turned upside down to its very foundations – that the world is not yet redeemed. We *sense* its unredeemedness." Quoted here from Jürgen Moltmann, *The Way of Jesus Christ* (Minneapolis: Fortress, 1993), 28. It is interesting to think about Buber's statements in conversation with Reinhartz, *Befriending the Beloved Disciple*, as well as Jon D. Levenson, "The Agenda of *Dabru Emet*," *RRJ* 7 (2004): 1–26.

[121] On this determinism and the forces that may contribute to a range of views, see, respectively, Trumbower, 30–46; Martin de Boer, *Johannine Perspectives on the Death of Jesus*, CBET 17 (Kampen: Kok Pharos, 1996).

other words, John does not resolve the problem of unbelief, but opts instead to offer a description that is irreducibly complex while also being theologically clear.

Amid the complexity, however, John does signal a path for its readers to walk as they reflect on the unbelief of the *Ioudaioi*. In John's logic, God himself (along with human frailty, sin, and the devil, but also God himself) is involved in the relationship of the *Ioudaioi* to the devil. The imminent connection between the *Ioudaioi* and the devil certainly falls on the impulse toward violence and rejection of the truth of which Jesus speaks, and thus the relationship between the *Ioudaioi* and the devil cannot be referred directly to God but rather to the character of people whose evil deeds have oriented their lives away from the light and towards the darkness (3:19). Even so, there is a critical sense in which God cannot and should not be separated from the relationship of the *Ioudaioi* to the devil. To do so would not only deny creation by God's Word (πάντα δι' αὐτοῦ ἐγένετο, 1:3), but, more importantly, it would also cause readers to overlook the way in which the God of the Gospel of John intends to break the power of the devil and enable acceptance of Jesus as Messiah through the crucifixion, as John goes on to state:

> "Father," [Jesus said,] "glorify your name." Then a voice (φωνή) came from heaven: "I have glorified it, and I will glorify it."
>
> The crowd standing and hearing [these things] said it was thunder. Others said, "An angel has spoken to him."
>
> Jesus answered and said, "This voice was not for me but for you – Now is the judgment of this world. Now the ruler of this world will be cast outside. And I, when I am lifted up from the earth, I will draw all people to myself."   (12:28–32)

Here, in John 12, when Jesus envisions the expulsion of the devil (="the ruler of this world") from "this world" through his own crucifixion, the cosmic conflict and the drama of Jewish unbelief overlap, just as they do in 8:31–59.[122] The important difference between chapters 8 and 12 is that the latter passage envisions a decisive judgment against the devil. If we consider together John's claim that the devil is the father of the *Ioudaioi* and also that the devil

---

[122] Cf. Kovacs, "'Now Shall the Ruler of This World Be Driven Out,'" 233.

will be cast out of this world through the crucifixion of Jesus, then it follows that the Gospel ultimately deals with the hostile rejection of Jesus by the *Ioudaioi* through a judgment against the devil. The hostility that led the *Ioudaioi* to deny, reject, and seek the death of Jesus was, during Jesus' life, an enactment of the devil's character. By the crucifixion of Jesus, however, the devil's relationship to the world has been undercut. The ruler of this world is driven out. If this paradigm would suggest an ethical approach of believers in Jesus toward the *Ioudaioi*, then it would have to be that the appropriate response to hostile and dishonest rejection involves, first, a steadfast and persistent witness to the truth, including also the naming of evil as evil; and then, second, this would be combined with a willingness to follow God's judgment over evil not by enacting that judgment but by suffering and waiting on God's vindication of good through suffering.[123]

I do not put forward this view with any expectation that it could, or should, paper over the real acts and feelings of malice, rejection, and even calls to violence against Jews that through the centuries have taken their cues from the Gospel of John.[124] Nor am I of the opinion that such a reading goes any great lengths toward affirming expressions of Judaism that reject Jesus.[125] Nevertheless, it is a great shame upon Christianity that many followers of Jesus have abjectly

---

[123] See Miroslav Volf, "Johannine Dualism and Contemporary Pluralism," *Modern Theology* 21.2 (2005): 189–217, here 209–211.

[124] On the troubling way in which John's language has fueled Christian anti-Judaism, see Jeffrey Trachtenberg, *The Devil and the Jews: The Medieval Conception of the Jew and Its Relation to Modern Antisemitism* (New Haven: Yale University Press, 1943), esp. 11–31.

[125] For John, disagreement about the future of Israel and the possibility that God's people are living in falsehood requires theological description. (Only a few contemporary biblical scholars hazard into this territory today, among them Jon Levenson, who asks, "Why should Jews affirm that God has a commitment to the church that shall endure 'until he redeems the world'?" idem, "The Agenda of *Dabru Emet*," 22. cf. also Volf, "Johannine Dualism and Contemporary Pluralism.") We are in a historical moment that is justifiably wary of such description. To speak of the only tradition I know, the American Protestant tradition has not proven itself trustworthy to describe the theological and spiritual implications of Jewish unbelief. *But to what extent does an ethical reading of John in our historical, cultural, and theological moment require the rejection of the theological vocabulary that developed in John's context? And is such a rejection by modern scholars better characterized as a judgment against John or against our own inability to reason theologically about these matters?* It seems to me that, in general, contemporary Johannine scholarship has rejected John's vocabulary without contemplating its own inability to fashion a language that takes seriously the question of truth that is raised by the simple existence of Judaism on the one hand and Christianity on the other.

failed to grasp the argument and ethics that are implied by the narrative of John; in so doing they have falsely inferred and essentialized a hostility of Jews toward believers in Jesus and, through this false inference, perpetrated and justified violence. In the logic of the Fourth Gospel, dishonest accusations and violent rejections indicate the deeper problem of one's life deriving its "of-ness" not from God but from the devil. John does not countenance the possibility that a believer in Jesus could enact such dishonesty and violence. Indeed, it would seem to be that from within the thought-world of John dishonest accusation and violent rejection are *unimaginable* for believers in Jesus (cf. 1 John 3:4–18). But for us who can all too easily imagine Christians perpetrating (or tacitly approving) violence and dishonesty, it is possible that Jesus' damning judgment against the *Ioudaioi* who sought his own life should in our contemporary context exercise its judgment against the Christian community. Whether or not Christians have the moral sense to read John well, an honest appraisal of John's ethics should recognize that when the faithful leadership of Israel is at stake, then the Johannine response to a dishonest, hostile rejection is to name its falsehood and the spiritual power that would mislead the people of God, and to go on to suffer the power of that falsehood and violence in anticipation of God's vindication.

From this perspective, John's language of derivation (or origins, or "of-ness") provides conceptual categories for understanding Jesus and the fulfillment of the promises of Judaism that are (in John's view) available in Jesus. Those who are "of God" are those who have recognized and received Jesus, and who have allowed his claims to reorient their understanding of the traditions of Israel. By contrast, those who oppose Jesus, who accuse him of falsehood and blasphemy, and who seek his life are not "of God" but rather of the scriptural character known for deception, killing, and the misleading of Israel: the devil. Seen from within this thread of John's argument, the theological and historical texture of Jesus' charge against the *Ioudaioi* in 8:44 can be encountered within the logic of the Gospel and its uncompromising vision of Jesus as the one who opens a future for Israel.

John 10: The Good Shepherd

The third way in which John thematizes the conflict that belief in Jesus presents to the Jewish tradition is through Jesus' teaching on the good shepherd. This is the final interaction set within the scene of Sukkot that began in 7:1. In its immediate context, the teaching of 10:1–21 follows the healing of the blind man in chapter 9, and it is contextually appropriate to read 9:1–10:21 as a further iteration of John's well known pairing of a sign with a discourse that elaborates the significance of Jesus in view of the sign.[126] John 9 is framed with statements by Jesus that draw on the vivid imagery light and darkness, vision and blindness that run through the imagery of Sukkot.[127] It concludes with a confrontational charge: "I came into the world for judgment, that those who cannot see might see, and those who do see might become blind." The Pharisees bristle at such an accusation: "Are you saying that *we* are blind!?!" To which Jesus responds, "If you were blind you would not have sin, but now that you're saying, 'We can see,' your sin remains" (9:39–41). With this interaction, John sets up the discourse on the good shepherd by framing it within (1) the judgment that Jesus' presence inevitably calls forth and also (2) by accounting for the misguided perceptions of those who, in the broad scene of John 7–10:21, have misidentified Jesus *not* as the one sent from God who fulfills the hopes that the festival of Sukkot had long-nurtured *but rather* as a demon-possessed man (8:48, 10:21). Therefore, in the good shepherd discourse, the *Ioudaioi*, who have presented themselves as authorities over the crowds and temple administration, interpreters of the law, and those who control the synagogue are portrayed as unfit leaders of Israel in contrast to the true shepherd from God.[128] When we consider the specific claims of the good shepherd discourse with an awareness of this setting, then we can observe that John 10:1–21 draws together numerous strands within Israel's Scriptures in order to press forward the Gospel's presentation of Jesus as the unique, faithful shepherd of Israel.

The imagery of the shepherd discourse has a long history in biblical literature, in which the people of God are portrayed as sheep and God himself or the leaders of the people are described as

---

[126] See Karoline M. Lewis, *Rereading the Shepherd Discourse: Restoring the Integrity of John 9:39–10:21*, SBL 113 (New York: Peter Land, 2008), 11–20, 107–111, 129–145; Johannes Beutler, SJ, and Robert Fortna: *The Shepherd Discourse of John 10 and Its Context*, SNTSMS 67 (Cambridge: Cambridge University Press, 1991).

[127] Jesus' command for the blind man to wash in the pool of Siloam (9:7) is a further link to the festival (cf. *m.* Sukk 4.9–10); there may be other associations at work as well (see Franklin Young, "A Study of the Relation of Isaiah to the Fourth Gospel," *ZNW* 46 [1955]: 215–233, esp. 220–221).

[128] On these roles, see 7:32, 45–52; 8:13; 9:16; 9:22. N.B. that here "the synagogue" means the local institution described in the text. "The synagogue" ≠ Judaism.

shepherd(s).[129] In light of this, it is right to understand that the preceding conflict between Jesus and the *Ioudaioi*/the Pharisees in John 7–9 provides a foundation for what comes next: Jesus confronts his opponents on the topic of the rightful leadership of Israel. As he does this, Jesus takes up terminology that is, in a general sense, uncontroversial: the sheep/flock (πρόβατον/ποίμνη) should be read as God's people (or Jesus' people); the shepherd (ὁ ποιμήν) is God's chosen leader. Although there are other ambiguous terms in the discourse, these are not among them.[130]

Even by Johannine standards, however, the transition into the shepherd discourse is abrupt: the opening words of the discourse immediately presuppose an audience that can appreciate the importance of the shepherd approaching the people of God from the right source or direction. This is what Jesus emphasizes as the teaching begins:

> Truly, truly, I say to you: the one who does not enter through the door into the sheepfold but comes up by another way, this one is a thief and a bandit. The one entering through the door is the shepherd of the sheep.
>
> Ἀμὴν ἀμὴν λέγω ὑμῖν, ὁ μὴ εἰσερχόμενος διὰ τῆς θύρας εἰς τὴν αὐλὴν τῶν προβάτων ἀλλὰ ἀναβαίνων ἀλλαχόθεν ἐκεῖνος κλέπτης ἐστὶν καὶ λῃστής. ὁ δὲ εἰσερχόμενος διὰ τῆς θύρας ποιμήν ἐστιν τῶν προβάτων. (10:1–2)

In general terms, this statement is uncontroversial: the one who would approach God's people as their shepherd must have legitimate claim to do so. It is only for a legitimate shepherd that the one appointed to maintain entrance to the flock will open the gate (v. 3). When the shepherd leads them out of the sheepfold, then they will follow his voice, but when another (ἀλλότριος) calls to them, they will not follow the voice of that one (vv. 4–5).

Although the Pharisees do not understand Jesus' figurative speech (παροιμία; v. 6), it is perhaps best to understand the ignorance of the

---

[129] See John Turner, "The History of Religions Background of John 10" in *The Shepherd Discourse*, ed. Beutler and Fortna, 33–52; Joachim Jeremias, "ποιμήν, etc.," *TDNT* 6:485–502.

[130] Many of these terms – gatekeeper, hired hand, etc. – will be discussed below. For extensive treatment, see Barrett, *The Gospel according to St. John*, 367–378, and Adele Reinhartz, *The Word in the World: The Cosmological Tale in the Fourth Gospel*, SBLMS 45 (Atlanta: Scholars Press, 1992), 71–98.

Pharisees not as ignorance in general, but rather as a failure – or, as Brown suggests, an unwillingness – to grasp the significance of this teaching as it applies in the immediate context of Jesus' healing of the man born blind.[131] They are not prepared to recognize the significance of Jesus in terms of the shepherd whom God will appoint over his people. As we have noted, Jesus' opponents have been debating for some time the source from which Jesus comes and, therefore, the source that would authorize his teaching (e.g., "This one – we don't know where he is from"; τοῦτον δὲ οὐκ οἴδαμεν πόθεν ἐστίν, 9:29; see also 6:41–42; 7:17, 27; 8:14, 41, 48; 9:16.). In this context, the seemingly abrupt transition in 10:1 is, in fact, an effort to re-engage the argument about Jesus' origins within a new, scripturally significant framework – that is, within the framework of the unique legitimacy of the shepherd of God's flock. The implication of Jesus' teaching in 10:1–5 is that there is only one legitimate way to approach the people of God: the shepherd must come in through the door, that is, he must be authorized by God.[132]

Seen from within this context, 10:1–5 explains the legitimacy of Jesus' ministry and the reason why people turn to him: He is authorized to enter the sheepfold. He knows his own and can lead them out. Those who follow Jesus and ignore the voices of others do so because those other voices belong to strangers, unauthorized to summon and lead the flock. In 10:1–5, however, all of this is implicit. The discourse works by evocation and allusion.[133] Jesus does not specify his own role or the identity or role of the "thieves and bandits." Thus it is valuable to ask: If the specific, and even polemical, claims of the discourse are made only indirectly, then what is gained by narrating the ministry of Jesus in the veiled imagery of the legitimate entry of the shepherd and the illegitimate place of the one who has come by other means? Three benefits of this language stand out.

---

[131] See Brown, *John*, I.393. On the contested meaning of παροιμία in this context, see Reinhartz, *The Word in the World*, 49–73, 97–98; Lewis, *Rereading the Shepherd Discourse*, 2–7; Maloney, *Signs and Shadows*, 132–33; Schnackenburg, *The Gospel according to John*, 2.283–88.

[132] So also Reinhartz, *The Word in the World*, 81. I think Reinhartz overlooks the imagery of Israel implied by the language, but she is right that Jesus' legitimate entry into the world is signified by his coming from God. In general, I am puzzled by the way in which Reinhartz's "cosmological tale" omits a significant role for Israel. Could an ancient Jew (i.e., a *Ioudaios*, but also a member of the Qumran community, a Samaritan, etc.) conceive of God's plan for the cosmos *without* Israel?

[133] See Hays, *Echoes of Scripture in the Gospels*, 327.

First, the teaching of 10:1–5 is capable of accounting for the ministry of Jesus within the accepted terms of the Jewish tradition. John 10:1–5 emphasizes the importance of a divine commission for the one who would legitimately shepherd God's flock. By emphasizing this, John is able to link Jesus' most distinctive claim about himself (i.e., he is sent from God) with the scriptural expectation that the shepherd of God's people possesses a unique commission. This expectation itself goes back to Moses who, in praying for a successor, said: "Let the Lord, the God of the spirits of all flesh, appoint someone over the congregation who shall go out before them and come in before them, who shall lead them out and bring them in, so that the congregation of the Lord may not be like sheep without a shepherd." The appointed successor is, of course, Joshua (יהושע/Ἰησοῦς; Num 27:16–18).[134]

In the broader scriptural use of this imagery, the role of shepherd is occasionally attributed to God (e.g., Ps 23) or to an Israelite king or leader (e.g., David, 2 Sam 24:17), yet in a dominant stream of the tradition the identity of the shepherd is simply determined by the action of God deposing unfit shepherds and raising up in their places a faithful shepherd(s).[135] Jeremiah decries the leaders of the people in such terms: "Woe to the shepherds who have destroyed and scattered the sheep of my pasture, says the Lord ... I will attend to you for all your evil doings. . . I myself will gather the remnant of my flock ... I will raise up shepherds over them" (Jer 23:1–4). Ezekiel employs the same imagery, offering a vivid depiction of God's promise to appoint a new shepherd over the people. The prophet denounces the shepherds of Israel who have failed to provide for and protect the people of God: they took what was not theirs and left the flock vulnerable to wild animals (Ezek 34:1–10). As a result, the Lord himself assumes the role of the shepherd: the Lord searches for the sheep, the Lord watches over the flock, the Lord leads the sheep out of captivity and into the open space of the land of Israel (34:11–16).[136] The final act of God's intervention is the provision

---

[134] The directional language in Num 27 (first the shepherd leads the people out, then he leads them in) would fit with the leading of the flock out (10:3–4). In 10:9 this movement is reversed (the shepherd leads *in* and then leads *out*). Reinhartz overlooks the parallel between 10:3 and Num 27 and thus sees only contradiction (*The Word*, 82).

[135] See, e.g., Jer 23:1–4; Jer 50:1–8.

[136] N.B. The movement of the shepherd – leading out, gathering, leading in – is shared across Ezek 34, Num 27, and John 10:1–5.

of a new shepherd, David, to rule in their midst: "I will raise up over them my servant David. He will be their shepherd, and I, the Lord, will be to them as God and David [as] ruler in their midst" (34:23–24).[137] The critical element to observe for the purposes of understanding John 10:1–5 is the unique relationship that links God to the shepherd and even begins to blur the distinction between the activity of God and the activity of the shepherd. While the language of Numbers and Ezekiel (and other texts using this imagery) could certainly accommodate leaders/shepherds who take their leadership through expected channels, the force of the language is much more direct: the shepherd acts under a divine commission that interrupts the normal course of history. God acts to raise up a leader for the people.

A second advantage of this imagery for John's characterization of Jesus is that while it works within the imagery of the tradition of Judaism, it also emphasizes the eschatological role of the shepherd whom God will appoint. Again, this is not the case in every scriptural use of the shepherd metaphor. Nevertheless, promises for a coming shepherd are bound up with promises for the presence of God in the midst of the people and a return from the scattering conditions of exile. We have seen this clearly in Ezekiel 34. Shortly after that oracle, in Ezekiel 37, the well-known expectation for new life to come to the people of God concludes with the expectation of God's presence in the midst of the people and a single shepherd, David, ruling over them (vv. 23–24). Isaiah also envisions the powerful deliverance of Israel from captivity with the promise that at that time "he [God] will feed the flock like a shepherd, and he will gather the lambs in his arms" (40:11). The implications of such passages for John 10:1–5 are that those who hear and respond to the voice of the shepherd – for instance, the blind man who ignores the religious authorities and obeys the voice of Jesus – such ones are in fact living out the drama that Ezekiel and Isaiah described: They are responding to the voice of the shepherd that will arrive at the end time to lead the flock of God. The unique commission of Jesus in John's Gospel dovetails with Israel's expectation for a uniquely appointed eschatological leader.

A third benefit of this language for framing Jesus' identity before the Pharisees is that it is helpfully ambiguous. John does not rush the

---

[137] My translation here follows the LXX.

application of the imagery to Jesus – it is enough for the imagery itself to underscore the unique source, legitimacy, and eschatological role of the one who will lead Israel into its future. Neither does John rush the identification of the stranger (ἀλλότριος, 10:4) or the thief/ robber (κλέπτης/ληστής) who enters by another way. Adele Reinhartz has helpfully interpreted the terminology of the shepherd discourse within "the cosmological tale" of the Fourth Gospel – that is, within the cosmic story of God's redemption of the world and the opposition to that redemption by the devil.[138] When viewed in these terms, the shepherd discourse avoids the identification of Jesus' rivals with particular historical actors, and the result is that the Pharisees whom Jesus addresses become less important than the role that they occupy. When God's eschatological shepherd calls out to his sheep, his legitimacy will expose the illegitimacy of the one who would claim to lead the flock without a unique commission.

Laden as it is with significance, Jesus' initial teaching falls on deaf ears: the Pharisees "did not understand what he was saying to them" (10:6). And so Jesus draws again on the imagery of the shepherd to re-present his case to the Pharisees. This second telling presses further into the identity of Jesus as the shepherd who has the authority to approach the people of God.[139] Beyond simply repeating the claims of vv. 1–5, Jesus' *relecture* of this teaching in vv. 7–18 emphasizes the way in which his being sent from God, as well as his death and resurrection, legitimize and validate his role as the shepherd of God's people. That is, vv. 7–18 do not explain the allegory of vv. 1–5. Instead, they apply the imagery of vv. 1–5 to Jesus in a more direct way. As we will see, this allows Jesus to occupy more than one role in the metaphor, but each of the roles assigned to Jesus positions him as the eschatological leader of God's people. In this *relecture*, Jesus emphasizes, first, the way in which he secures *access* to the eschatological promises of God; second, the way in which those who oppose him are cast in the uncomfortable position of

---

[138] The cosmological tale of the Fourth Gospel is the level of the narrative that considers the mission of Jesus as an entry into the world from God (John 1:1–18 and passim; cf. Reinhartz, *The World*, 30–47). As such, the cosmological tale helps locate both the historical tale (the story of Jesus) and the ecclesiological tale (the "sub-tale" of the community) within the overarching activity of God in the world.

[139] I see John 10:7–18 as an instance of *relecture*, i.e., a deliberate deepening and development of the shepherd metaphor with reference to the text and metaphors of vv. 1–5. See Brown, *An Introduction to the Gospel of John* (New York: Doubleday, 2003), 291.

opposing God's actions for Israel; and third, the way in which his suffering and death vindicates him in his identity as the shepherd.

First, as Jesus re-engages the metaphor for his hearers, he assigns himself the role of the door: "I am the door of the sheep. All who came before me were thieves and liars, but the sheep did not listen to them" (vv. 7–8).[140] In the first occurrence of the door (v. 2), it signified the passage through which the shepherd gained rightful access to the sheep, in contrast to the illegitimate access of those who would come in by another way. Jesus' identity as the one sent from God means that he has access to the people of God through legitimate means – he comes "through the door," that is, from God. Those who have come in another way – that is, who have not come from God – were and are unqualified to care for the sheep. In 10:7, Jesus' relationship to the imagery of the door shifts: The focus is no longer on the *character* of Jesus or what qualifies him to enter the sheepfold as the shepherd (i.e., his commission from God); now the focus is on the *access* that he provides.[141] Just as the sheep pass through the door to join the larger flock and are led out of the door to the pasture that will nourish them, so Jesus claims to be the point of access through whom a person may enter the flock of God's people, and he also claims to be the passage through which the flock may enter into the open space that God has promised. As John's shepherd metaphor works within "an image field" that is determined by scriptural promises of God's gathering his people and leading them into the promised future, the significance of these claims lies near at hand: God's action to gather the people and lead them into their future is underway. Jesus is both the shepherd who is authorized by God to approach the people (vv. 2, 11) and also the one who, as the door (vv. 7, 9), offers access to the eschatological people of God and the experience of abundant life in the pasture that will nourish the sheep.[142]

Jesus' claim to legitimacy is quickly matched by his denunciation of all other figures who would presume to be the door – they are "thieves and bandits" (10:8). John is uncompromising on this: other

---

[140] On the textual problems in this passage, I am following Brown, *John*, I.385–387.

[141] Chrysostom's distinction is similar to mine: "When he brings us to the Father he calls himself a door, when he takes care of us, a Shepherd" (cited in Hoskyns, *The Fourth Gospel*, 373).

[142] On "pasture" as a symbol of eschatological blessings, see Ezek 34:13–16, 26–31; Jer 23:7. For further examples of early Christians thinking with such, see Marcus, "'The Twelve Tribes of the Diaspora,'" esp. 445–446.

than Jesus, there is no other point of access to the flock of God's people and the promised blessings God has assured them. As in the first instance (v. 1), the referent of "thieves and bandits" in v. 8 is not immediately clear. The further specification of the thief in v. 10 as one (sg,) who comes to steal, kill, and destroy (ὁ κλέπτης οὐκ ἔρχεται εἰ μὴ ἵνα κλέψῃ καὶ θύσῃ καὶ ἀπολέσῃ), and the explicit contrast of this figure with the life-giving and eschatological work of the shepherd (vv. 9–10) suggests that Jesus has in view the devil, who embodies murder and dishonesty and who persistently opposes the faithfulness of Israel.[143] Yet Jesus' words can also be extended to those figures who, with or without an intention to oppose God's purposes, set themselves against Jesus and thus represent an alternative construal of the future of Israel. In other words, the immediate referent for the thief is the devil, who, in the narrative of the Fourth Gospel, is totally oriented toward death and lies. As various human agents align themselves with violence, falsehood, or the scattering of God's people, they find their identities associated with the devil. As I have argued, such an association lies near at hand in 8:44, and it occurs throughout the Gospel in the characterization of Judas as "a devil" (6:70), an uncaring "thief" (12:6), one who has the devil/Satan enter into his heart (13:2, 27), and the "son of destruction (17:12). Further, such an association between those who oppose Jesus and the devil is likely implicit in the tragically ironic preference of the *Ioudaioi* for the release of Barabbas, a λῃστής, in place of Jesus (18:38–40, cp. 10:1, 8).[144] Seen from this perspective, Jesus' characterization of these figures in 10:8–10 communicates a judgment against other would-be leaders because their opposition to Jesus entails a deeper opposition to God. Human opposition to Jesus reflects a cosmic opposition to God by the devil.

In vv. 11–18, Jesus shifts for a third time. No longer is the focus on Jesus as the one who provides access to the people of God and passage into eschatological blessings, nor is it on Jesus' opponents and their dangerous likeness to those who oppose God. Instead, nearly all of Jesus' remaining teaching centers on his commitment to lay down his life for the sheep. Such devotion to the well-being of a flock may have been a commonplace expectation for shepherds,

---

[143] Reinhartz, *The Word*, 85–92.

[144] The definition of a λῃστής is complex, but the simple translation "robber" omits the political profile of such a figure. See J. J. Twomey, "Barabbas Was a Robber," *Scripture* 8.4 (1956): 115–119.

but in the specific conflict with the Pharisees in which Jesus' speech is set, the imagery holds theological implications as well.[145] John signals this by using language that draws in an additional scriptural context to the visions of an eschatological shepherd of God's flock that we have considered up to this point. Here Jesus introduces the specific image of a suffering shepherd, an image that is almost certainly indebted to Zechariah, who announced the death of God's shepherd as the catalyst for both the judgment of the nation and the restoration of a remnant: "Awake, O sword, against my shepherd, against the man who is my associate . . . Strike the shepherd that the sheep may be scattered; I will turn my hand against the little ones. In the whole land, says the Lord, two-thirds shall be cut off and perish and one-third shall be left alive" (13:6–8). By invoking this image of a shepherd who suffers, John includes in his vision of the eschatological shepherd of Israel not only the well-known leaders prophesied in Ezekiel, Jeremiah, and Isaiah but also the expectation that God's eschatological leader will suffer and die.[146] The characterization of Jesus as a shepherd who will die has two immediate implications in 10:11–18.

First, the suffering shepherd is loyal to and protective of the sheep whereas the hired laborer (μισθωτός) acts out of concern only for himself (vv. 12–13). From this perspective, Jesus' willingness to die for the sheep, and in fact his death for them, confirms his identity as the shepherd of the flock. His death is not a contradiction of his messianic status, as the crowds will suggest when they ask about the messiah remaining forever (cf. 12:34); instead of undermining Jesus' legitimacy, his death embodies his rightful claim to be the shepherd of Israel. Further, Jesus' willingness to lay down his life exposes the illegitimacy of those Jewish leaders who, in John's view, are bound by a concern only for themselves that closely resembles the self-protectiveness of the μισθωτός (cf. 5:44; 12:43). Thus Jesus' discussion of the good shepherd laying down his life (and taking it up again)

---

[145] Jesus' description of his death as "laying down his life" (τὴν ψυχήν μου τίθημι; vv. 11, 15, 17–18) will later be used to refer to the crucifixion and/or martyrdom (13:4, 37–38; 15:13).

[146] N.B. My argument is that John associates the good shepherd with a dying shepherd because this image lies at hand in Scripture. I do not claim that we have a quotation of Zech 13 here, although there is likely an allusion to Zech 13:7 in 16:32. See Maarten J. J. Menken, "Striking the Shepherd: Early Christian Versions and Interpretations of Zech 13:7," *Bib* 92.1 (2011): 39–59.

in vv. 1, 15, and 17–18 both affirms his identity and challenges the legitimacy of his opponents.

A second implication is related to the first: by dying, the good shepherd is able to gather and lead the people of God. Again, the necessity of death for such a regathering is a specific contribution of Zechariah's image of the shepherd.[147] Without such a vision, the death of the shepherd could easily rule out the association between the promised shepherd of Ezekiel, Jeremiah, and Isaiah, and the human figure of Jesus and his shameful death, but with Zechariah's vision the shepherd's suffering renders intelligible both Jesus' death and the response of only a remnant to the redemptive work of God (Zech 13:8–9). It is this latter point, in particular – the salvation of only a remnant – that John seems to be pointing to in the series of statements that relate Jesus' death to those (relatively few) who respond to him. This emerges in v. 14 ("I know my own and my own know me") and also in the repeated references to Jesus' own sheep, those who hear his voice, in vv. 15–16. As Jesus' teaching addresses the legitimacy of his role as the shepherd *and* the unimpressive response that he evokes, it looks to the expectation of Zechariah about the suffering shepherd, concerning whom Zechariah envisioned the response of a remnant *not* as a the disconfirmation of the shepherd's identity but rather an the response that legitimizes his role. Those who respond – "my own," "the sheep," "those who hear his voice" – even if they be only marginal in number, can still claim to stand in continuity with the expectations of Scripture. Indeed, in Zechariah's vision, they have better claim to legitimacy.

If the reading offered here is correct, Jesus' good shepherd discourse engages directly with the future of Israel in multiple ways: It does so by taking up the scripturally rooted expectation of an eschatological shepherd and casting Jesus in that role. Indeed, the imagery of the shepherd is uniquely suited to characterize the Johannine Jesus because: (1) in scripture the shepherd metaphor blurs the distinction between God shepherding Israel directly and doing so through a human agent; (2) Jesus' derivation from God aligns with the scriptural imagery of God himself raising up a shepherd through exceptional means; (3) the imagery can hold

---

[147] On the introduction of suffering into the profile of the messiah, see William Horbury, *Jewish Messianism and the Cult of Christ* (London: SCM, 1998); Boyarin, "The Suffering Christ as a Jewish Midrash," 211–216, 220–222.

together Jesus' genuine leadership of Israel, his suffering, and the response of relatively few people to his voice; and (4) the shepherd imagery is particularly oriented toward Israel's future – the fulfillment of eschatological promises. In addition to these ways that the imagery serves to characterize Jesus positively, the characterization of Jesus as the shepherd also (5) suggests that the opposition of the Pharisees to Jesus is bound up with a more troubling kind of opposition to God and his shepherd – the thief who steals, kills, and destroys (10:10); the wolf who scatters the people of God (v. 12). When paired with the healing of the man born blind and the conflict it evokes, the shepherd discourse offers a dramatic vantage point from which to interpret Jesus' ministry and the conflict surrounding him: "the Pharisees" (=the *Ioudaioi*) are convinced of their own legitimacy and the illegitimacy of Jesus. Unbeknown to them, however, they are debating the legitimacy of the one whose life embodies the multiple roles expected of the eschatological shepherd of Israel.

As we have considered John 7:1–10:21, this scene, set at Sukkot, concerns itself with the characterization of Jesus as both the one who brings Israel into its future *and* the way in which Jesus' significance for the future of Israel stands in direct conflict with the vision and leadership of the *Ioudaioi*. Together these aspects of the Gospel comprise the narrative argument that we have been tracing over the course of this study: Jesus offers to the people the fulfillment of the hopes that are rooted in Israel's Scriptures and nurtured in its traditions and practices. At Sukkot, John presents Jesus in this way by presenting him as the object toward which the practices and traditions of the festival are oriented. He is the source of living water, light, and joy – that is, he brings about the hope that Sukkot nurtured among the people for so long. For those who are able to see him in this innovative way, belief in Jesus entails strong continuity between the foundational commitments of the Jewish tradition and the hopes for the future. When read in the decades after 70 – that is, in a historical context in which the destruction of temple and altar and the leadership of the people by a violent faction of would-be rulers were all recent memory – the presentation of Jesus in John 7–10 stands out for the way in which it positions Jesus as the fulfillment of scriptural hopes as well as for the way in which it names and denounces the impulse to violence among those who oppose Jesus. Because of the Gospel's depiction of the life-or-death stakes of a decision about Jesus, the logic of these chapters can be difficult to grasp unless the implicit concerns of the argument be brought to the fore: for John, taking its cues from scriptural concerns about the faithful or false leadership of Israel, the acceptance or rejection of Jesus is a matter of freedom or slavery, truth or falsehood, light or darkness, life or death, God or the devil.

Conclusion

The narrative of John 5–10 is marked by hostile arguments, abrupt accusations, strong claims about Jesus' identity, and equally strong denunciations of those who oppose him. As we have noted, the setting for these various scenes is the principal feasts of the *Ioudaioi*: an unnamed festival (chapter 5), Passover (6), Sukkot (7–10:21), Hanukah (10:22–42).[148] As this chapter has demonstrated throughout, these observances do more work in the narrative than as simple occasions for Jesus to heal, argue, and teach. Instead, because so many foundational commitments of the traditions of Israel are concentrated within the principal feasts of the *Ioudaioi*, John is able to use these feasts to demonstrate the significance of Jesus in terms of the observances, stories, and hopes that shape the traditions of Israel. By describing Jesus' power to heal, his unique freedom on the Sabbath, his identity as the bread from heaven, his role as the source of eschatological water and light, and as the shepherd of God's people, John demonstrates how the festivals of the *Ioudaioi* might be understood as pointing to Jesus and fulfilled in him. Jesus' call for others to believe in him is a call for them to take a step nearer to the heart of their own tradition, to think and live in continuity with its past and to experience the life that it had long promised. Threaded within this presentation of Jesus is John's ongoing defense of him as the figure about whom Moses prophesied, the one whom Abraham foresaw, and whom Isaiah, Ezekiel, and Zechariah envisioned.

---

[148] I have omitted a discussion of this last scene, 10:22–39, because it would extend my already long treatment of this section without adding anything materially new to the argument. The setting at Hanukah and the repetition of shepherding language (10:26–27) suggests the continuation of Jesus' critique of the leadership of the *Ioudaioi*. See Wheaton, *The Role of Jewish Feasts,* 159–182; James C. VanderKam, "John 10 and the Feast of the Dedication," in *Of Scribes and Scrolls: Studies of the Hebrew Bible, Intertestamental Judaism, and Christian Origins,* ed. Harold W. Attridge et al. (New York: University Press of America, 1990), 203–214; Jerome Neyrey, " 'I Said: You Are Gods': Psalm 82:6 and John 10," *JBL* 108.4 (1989): 647–663; Thompson, *John,* 235–236; Hays, *Echoes of Scripture in the Gospels,* 318–320.

The flow of the narrative and its argument can be tortuous, but the challenge is clear throughout: Are the *Ioudaioi* faithful shepherds who love God and hear his voice, or do they presume and maintain by violence a position that is not rightly theirs? Is Jesus the one who embodies the eschatological future of Israel, or is he a deceiver of the people?

4

CRISIS: JOHN 11–20

The outline of this study presents the Gospel of John under three headings: the announcement of Jesus as the one who brings about the future of Israel (John 1–4), the debate over Jesus as the one who claims such a role (5–10), and finally the crisis engendered by belief in Jesus as the one who embodies the innovative means by which the people of God might live into their promised future in continuity with their storied past. In this sense, the crisis (κρίσις) described in John 11–20 is best understood as both the judgment and the division provoked by belief or disbelief in Jesus.[1] Faced with a decision about Jesus, Judaism cannot but undergo a κρίσις, a judgment about the truth or falsehood of its path and a commitment to a way of life that expresses belief in or denial of Jesus as the Christ. The claim of this study is not that the Gospel was conceived upon such a simple outline (or a similar one), but rather that "announcement," "debate," and "crisis" are capable of catching up the arc of the Gospel narrative. In the final section of the Gospel considered here, readers encounter κρίσις as a prominent narrative feature after the raising of Lazarus results in belief in Jesus even among the ranks of the *Ioudaioi* (11:45–46; 12:11). Belief in Jesus among the *Ioudaioi* and then the crowd continues when Jesus is lauded as "king of Israel" (12:13). In contrast to what has come before, these scenes record no debate between those who believe in Jesus and those who do not. Instead, they record the judgment and division that takes place as people and groups accept or reject Jesus and then live into the consequences of their decisions. In chapters 11–20, John presents both the positive and the negative possibilities entailed in a decision about Jesus: positively, Jesus and his followers are characterized as

---

[1] Bultmann, *John*, 111; cf. BDAG, 569. Cf. J. Louis Martyn, "Source Criticism and *Religionsgeschichte* in the Fourth Gospel," in *The Interpretation of John*, ed. Ashton, 129.

innocent sufferers who faithfully carry out the commission of the Father and take up their places in God's eschatological restoration of Israel; negatively, John describes the Jewish authorities as unqualified theological and political leaders; indeed, they persecute God's chosen one. As we will see, these are the paths of faithfulness or unfaithfulness that belief in Jesus opens up for readers of John.

Before exegesis, however, a word on approach: To this point, this study has pursued its thesis through protracted treatments of whole scenes. In this chapter, the approach shifts to shorter studies of a few significant texts, images, and themes in John 11–20. Specifically, this chapter shows how John sustains its characterization of Jesus as the one who brings about the future of Israel across the final section of the Gospel with specific attention to (1) the quotations of Isaiah in John 12:37–43, (2) Jesus' description of himself as the true vine (John 15:1–8), (3) the depiction of Jesus as a righteous sufferer throughout John 13–19, and (4) the way in which John's passion and resurrection narratives (18–20) both *invalidate* the legitimacy of the Jewish leaders and also *validate* Jesus in his messianic role. Attention to these areas demonstrates the significance of John's characterization of Jesus as the one who ushers in the future of Israel as a thread that runs throughout the whole Gospel.

John 12:37–43: The Message of Jesus and the Disbelief of the People

After several chapters of often-acrimonious debate, John dramatizes the division that belief in Jesus opens up within the Jewish tradition in chapters 11–12. Rather than narrating direct engagements of Jesus with the *Ioudaioi*, these chapters portray the breach opened up within the tradition as members of the crowd and even those who identify with the *Ioudaioi* transfer their allegiance *from* the way of the *Ioudaioi* and *into* belief in Jesus. In fact, it is the threat of increasing division within the tradition that occasions the Jewish leaders' plot against Jesus. Note, for instance, the sense of transferring allegiances in the language below:[2]

> Therefore, many from the *Ioudaioi*, coming to Mary and seeing what he did, they belived <u>into him</u>. But some from

---

[2] Cf. Ignace de la Potterie, S.J., "L'emploi de εἰς dans S. Jean et sens incidences théologiques," *Biblica* 43 (1962): 366–387.

among them departed to the Pharisees and they told them
the things Jesus did. Therefore, the chief priests and Pharisees gathered a council and said, "What should we do, for
this man is doing many signs. If we let him go on, all will
believe into him, and the Romans will take from us both the
place [i.e., the temple] and the nation." (Πολλοὶ οὖν ἐκ τῶν
Ἰουδαίων οἱ ἐλθόντες πρὸς τὴν Μαριὰμ καὶ θεασάμενοι ἃ ἐποίησεν ἐπίστευσαν εἰς αὐτόν· τινὲς δὲ ἐξ αὐτῶν ἀπῆλθον πρὸς τοὺς
Φαρισαίους καὶ εἶπαν αὐτοῖς ἃ ἐποίησεν Ἰησοῦς. Συνήγαγον οὖν
οἱ ἀρχιερεῖς καὶ οἱ Φαρισαῖοι συνέδριον καὶ ἔλεγον· τί ποιοῦμεν
ὅτι οὗτος ὁ ἄνθρωπος πολλὰ ποιεῖ σημεῖα; ἐὰν ἀφῶμεν αὐτὸν
οὕτως, πάντες πιστεύσουσιν εἰς αὐτόν, καὶ ἐλεύσονται οἱ Ῥωμαῖοι
καὶ ἀροῦσιν ἡμῶν καὶ τὸν τόπον καὶ τὸ ἔθνος.) (11:45–47)

Then, when the great crowd from the *Ioudaioi* knew that he
was there, they came, not only on account of Jesus, but also
to see Lazarus whom he raised from the dead. And the chief
priests took counsel together that they might kill Lazarus,
because many were, on account of him, departing from the
Ioudaioi and believing into Jesus. (Ἔγνω οὖν [ὁ] ὄχλος πολὺς
ἐκ τῶν Ἰουδαίων ὅτι ἐκεῖ ἐστιν καὶ ἦλθον οὐ διὰ τὸν Ἰησοῦν
μόνον, ἀλλ᾽ ἵνα καὶ τὸν Λάζαρον ἴδωσιν ὃν ἤγειρεν ἐκ νεκρῶν.
ἐβουλεύσαντο δὲ οἱ ἀρχιερεῖς ἵνα καὶ τὸν Λάζαρον ἀποκτείνωσιν,
ὅτι πολλοὶ δι᾽ αὐτὸν ὑπῆγον τῶν Ἰουδαίων καὶ ἐπίστευον εἰς τὸν
Ἰησοῦν.) (12:9–11)

Then the crowd that was with him when he called Lazarus
from the tomb and raised him from the dead was testifying.
Therefore the crowd went to meet him because they heard
that he had done this sign. Therefore, the Pharisees said to
themselves, "See, you are gaining nothing! Look – the world
goes out after him!" (μαρτύρει οὖν ὁ ὄχλος ὁ ὢν μετ᾽ αὐτοῦ ὅτε
τὸν Λάζαρον ἐφώνησεν ἐκ τοῦ μνημείου καὶ ἤγειρεν αὐτὸν ἐκ
νεκρῶν. διὰ τοῦτο [καὶ] ὑπήντησεν αὐτῷ ὁ ὄχλος, ὅτι ἤκουσαν
τοῦτο αὐτὸν πεποιηκέναι τὸ σημεῖον. οἱ οὖν Φαρισαῖοι εἶπαν
πρὸς ἑαυτούς· θεωρεῖτε ὅτι οὐκ ὠφελεῖτε οὐδέν· ἴδε ὁ κόσμος
ὀπίσω αὐτοῦ ἀπῆλθεν.) (12:17–19)

Importantly, even as the Fourth Gospel describes people believing in
Jesus, the response to Jesus by "his own" remains minimal at best.
Individuals reorient their lives around Jesus, but the tradition as a

whole and its leaders reject him.[3] The Gospel must therefore account for how Jesus' fulfillment of the future of Israel can sustain such a broad rejection. This is why John concludes the public ministry of Jesus by offering an account of the unbelief of the people of God that positions rejection of Jesus as the fulfillment of the word of Isaiah. As we will see in the discussion that follows, John's presentation of Jesus as the one who opens up the future for Israel benefits in two ways through these citations of Isaiah. First, John shows its readers that Jesus' rejection is the enactment of theological realities that are plainly described by Isaiah. After suggesting this, John undertakes a second, related but more ambitious task: namely, John shows readers how Jesus' troubling crucifixion and death are not marks of shame but rather a revelation of glory. Taken as a whole, John's quotation of Isaiah places Jesus and his sufferings at the heart of the Jewish tradition's view of God and the way in which God relates to and restores Israel.

First, in John's summary comments about Jewish unbelief in response to the ministry of Jesus, the Gospel cites Isaiah 53:1. As noted earlier, the aim of John's quotation is to demonstrate that Jesus' rejection is the enactment of theological realities described in Scripture. Isaiah 53 records the searching question of a figure who represents a group that has witnessed God's revelation but finds itself in the minority: "Lord, who has believed our message, and to whom has the arm of the Lord been revealed?" (John 12:38, quoting Isa 53:1). With these words, the prophet, and now the Evangelist through him, juxtaposes belief in the active power of God ("the arm of the Lord") with an admission that God's revelation has found only limited acceptance ("Lord, who has believed our message?").[4] This dynamic alone – the revelation of God and its lack of acceptance – would suffice as a scriptural paradigm for the ministry and rejection of Jesus. But it is likely that John's quotation of Isaiah 53 suggests a deeper engagement with the prophet.

---

[3] Cf. John 1:11–12; Richard Bauckham, "Individualism," in *Gospel of Glory: Major Themes in Johannine Theology*, ed. Richard Bauckman (Grand Rapids: Baker Academic, 2015), 1–19.

[4] The "arm of the Lord" describes God's action to deliver Israel. See, e.g., Deut 4:34; 7:19; cf. Klaus Baltzer, *Deutero-Isaiah*, trans. Margaret Kohl; Hermenia (Minneapolis: Fortress, 2001), 403.

Brevard Childs notes that "the confessing 'we' of the Old Testament is always Israel and not the nations,"[5] and thus just as Isaiah 53:1 records a minority of Israelites recognizing this humiliated figure as the "servant of the Lord," so John presents believers in Jesus as the minority among God's people who do not stumble over Jesus' humble origins or the unsettling necessity of his death.[6] The immediate context of John 12:32–34 has positioned the "we" of 12:38–43 in just this way: in those verses, Jesus discussed the necessity of his suffering and death, and the crowd expressed its disbelief with the question, "How can you say that the Son of Man must be lifted up [i.e., crucified]?" (12:34). With this question, the Gospel created a distinction between those who acknowledge "the arm of the Lord" at work in the ministry of Jesus and those who are unable to recognize the events unfolding before them as revelation. This is how John in 12:38 sets up the continuity between its community and Isaiah's "we": the Evangelist and the community he represents are those who entrust themselves to God's unlikely suffering servant rather than being those who "walk in darkness and have no light" (Isa 50:10 LXX; cf. John 12:35–36).[7]

John's quotation of Isaiah 53:1 is quickly paired with Isaiah 6:10. By reading these texts as descriptions of the same figure, John offers a scriptural framework for holding the central aspects of Jesus' ministry together (his suffering *and* eschatological significance [Isa 53]; the disbelief of the people [Isa 6]). The Gospel presents the rejection of Jesus by his own as the expression of a theological reality that had been described to Israel centuries before in Isaiah's description of the suffering servant, chosen by God but dishonored by his own.[8] Further, by pairing Isaiah 53 and 6, John doubles down on the absolute necessity of Jesus' rejection by the majority of God's

---

[5] Brevard Childs, *Isaiah*, OTL (Louisville: Westminster John Knox, 2001), 413.

[6] For a recent assessment of scholarship on this passage, cf. Daniel J. Brendsel, *"Isaiah Saw His Glory": The Use of Isaiah 52–53 in John 12*, BZNT 208 (Berlin: de Gruyter, 2014), 102–104.

[7] See Andrew Lincoln, *Truth on Trial: The Lawsuit Motif in the Fourth Gospel* (Peabody: Hendrickson, 2000).

[8] See Craig A. Evans, "Obduracy and the Lord's Servant: Some Observations on the Use of the Old Testament in the Fourth Gospel," in *Early Jewish and Christian Exegesis*, eds. Craig A. Evans and William F. Stinespring (Atlanta: Scholars Press, 1987), 221–236; Günter Reim, "Wie der Evangelist Johannes gemäß Joh 12,37ff. Jesaja 6 hat gelesen," *ZNW* 92 (2001): 33–46.

people. It was not simply Jesus' ignoble form that prevented his own from believing in him (53:2–3). It was divine necessity:

> They did not believe in him, that the word of Isaiah the
>   prophet might be fulfilled
> He has blinded their eyes
> And hardened their heart
> That they might not see with their eyes
> And understand with their heart
> And turn
> And I would heal them.

> οὐκ ἐπίστευον εἰς αὐτόν, ἵνα ὁ λόγος Ἠσαΐου τοῦ προφήτου
>   πληρωθῇ.
> τετύφλωκεν αὐτῶν τοὺς ὀφθαλμοὺς
> καὶ ἐπώρωσεν αὐτῶν τὴν καρδίαν,
> ἵνα μὴ ἴδωσιν τοῖς ὀφθαλμοῖς
> καὶ νοήσωσιν τῇ καρδίᾳ
> καὶ στραφῶσιν,
> καὶ ἰάσομαι αὐτούς. (John 12:40, quoting Isa 6:10)

A closer look at John's quotation of Isaiah 6 shows how John draws out this necessity.

In context, Isaiah 6:10 claims that Israel's rejection of its God has called forth a stunning divine response: To a people so completely bent on their own ways, the words of God's messenger will now only increase their resistance to God.[9] Whatever good future Israel might hope for can now only follow on the broad-scale rejection of God and the message of his prophet. When quoted in the Fourth Gospel, Isaiah's words signify that the failure of the Jewish leaders to believe in Jesus does not impeach the truthfulness of Jesus' witness. John would instead have its readers locate Jewish disbelief as the expression of a theological reality played out first in the ministry of Isaiah and now repeating itself at the climax of Israel's history in the ministry of Jesus. The precise nature of that theological reality is that the vast majority of God's own people are so staunchly turned against God that they will fail to heed the words of God's messenger

---

[9] On the context of Isa 6, cf. Childs, *Isaiah*, 54–60. On the Johannine adaptation of Isa 6:10, see Menken, *Old Testament Quotations*, 99–122; Painter, "The Quotation of Scripture and Unbelief in John 12:36b–43," in *The Gospels and the Scriptures of Israel*, eds. Craig Evans and William Stegner, JSNTSup 104 (Sheffield: Sheffield Academic Press, 1994), 429–458.

until they have undergone an overwhelming humiliation. The whole encounter of Isaiah 6 runs as follows:

> Then I heard the voice of my Lord saying, Whom shall
>   I send? Who will go for us?
> And I said, Here am I; send me.
>
> And he said, Go, say to this people:
> Hear, indeed, but do not understand.
> See, indeed, but do not perceive.
>
> Make fat (hiph. imp.הַשְׁמֵן; ἐπαχύνθη) that people's heart
>   (לֵב־הָעָם/ἡ καρδία τοῦ λαοῦ τούτου),
> Stop (הַכְבֵּד) its ears,
> And seal (הָשַׁע) its eyes –
> Lest seeing with its eyes
> And hearing with its ears,
> It also perceive with its mind,
> And repent and save itself (וָשָׁב וְרָפָא לוֹ)[10]
>
> I asked, How long, my Lord?
>
> And he said: Until cities lie waste without inhabitant, and houses without people, and the land is utterly desolate; until the Lord sends everyone far away, and vast is the emptiness in the midst of the land. Even if a tenth part remain in it, it will be burned again, like a terebinth or an oak whose stump remains standing when it is felled. The holy seed is its stump.   (Isa 6:8–13)[11]

Readers can recognize John's reasoning tracking with the troubling logic of Isaiah, especially in the form of the quotation John offers. Although John has just cited Isaiah 53:1 in a form that corresponds exactly to the LXX, the Gospel's quotation of Isaiah 6:10 departs markedly from the LXX as well as from the persistent tendency in the Jewish textual tradition to soften the language and theological implications of this passage. John offers here a free translation of the Hebrew of Isaiah 6:10. Most noticeably, John rewords the prophecy and sets the command for blindness (not a dull or fat heart)

---

[10] Cp. LXX: καὶ ἐπιστρέψωσιν καὶ ἰάσομαι αὐτούς. John shifts into the LXX's first person in 6:10 but retains the overall sense of the Hebrew.

[11] This translation follows the JPS, but where the JPS prefers the LXX, I have altered it toward the MT.

as the first imperative (cf. 9:39–41). John's specific phrasing ("he has blinded ... he has hardened") approximates the causative sense of the MT's hiphil imperatives ("Make its hearts dull ... seal its eyes.")[12] John's purposive ἵνα implies that the blinding and hardening of God serve to exclude God's own people from the experiences that could lead to their healing. In this way, John's ἵνα μὴ ἴδωσιν ... νοήσωσιν ... στραφῶσιν carries out the same function as the Hebrew פֶּן: "Make fat that people's heart ... *lest* they look ... listen ... comprehend, and turn." The uncomfortable logic of this command is that God would commission the prophet to deepen the resistance of the people. This difficult idea was blunted within the later Jewish tradition, as can be seen (1) in the shifting of the initiative to the people hardening *their own hearts* in the LXX and Peshitta; (2) in the transformation of this text by the Qumran community into an appeal for hearers to draw closer to God's word; and (3) in the Targum's tendency to single out for hardening a group within Israel that is already obdurate (in contrast to a righteous remnant).[13]

Throughout the Gospel, John has noted the human behaviors that occur alongside of this divine hardening: the love of human glory, the love of darkness, incredulity at the prospect of God's eschatological deliverance taking form in the life of an unlettered man from Galilee.[14] The apparent benefit of John appropriating the difficult logic of Isaiah 6:10 MT – that is, that God has made perception of and faith in Jesus *impossible* (οὐκ ἠδύναντο πιστεύειν, John 12:39) – is that this reasoning is uniquely capable of characterizing the theological reality of Israel's rejection of its messiah. The LXX's language, which portrays obduracy as the result of the exceptional sinfulness of a generation, suggests that a humbler, more teachable people might actually respond to God's messenger. (Indeed, this is how the Qumran community characterized itself in its reading of Isaiah 6.) For John, however, Jesus' own people rejected him not

---

[12] On the early Christian reception of Isaiah's "hardening" imagery, cf. Rom 11:7; 2 Cor 3:14; Mark 8:17; Lieu, "Blindness," 87–88, 90. On John's use of τυφλόω (not the LXX's καμμύω), cf. John 9:39–41; 1 John 2:11.

[13] The detailed discussion of this is in chapters 1–5 of Evans, *To See and Not Perceive: Isaiah 6.9–10 in Early Jewish and Christian Interpretation,* JSOTSup 64 (Sheffield: Sheffield Academic Press, 1989).

[14] See, respectively, 5:41–44; 12:43; 3:19–21; 6:41–51; 7:14–15, 26–27, 52. Cf. Donald Hartley, "Destined to Disobey: Isaiah 6:10 in John 12:37–41," *CTJ* 44 (2009): 263–287.

because of their exceptionally rebellious character, but rather
because they were (quite unexceptionally) similar to their forbears
addressed by the well-known obduracy texts of Isaiah 6, 29, and
Deuteronomy 29, among others.[15] For John, the rejection of Jesus
emerges from a theological conviction that Israel cannot render itself
sentient. The only way to break out of one's love for human glory or
darkness, or to escape incredulity in the face of revelation, is, in
John's view, to be reborn (3:5–7), to be drawn by the Father (6:44,
65), or to be healed (12:40).

When considered within the Gospel's presentation of Jesus as the
one who brings about the future of Israel, we can recognize in John
12:37–43 two ways in which the Gospel presents its readers with a
strategy for reimagining the coherence of Israel's Scripture as it
witnesses to a rejected messiah. The first we have considered at
length above: namely, that the story of Jesus' rejection by his own
is a story animated by the same theological realities that faced Israel
before it entered the Promised Land (Deut 29) and that faced them
again when Isaiah's proclamation fell on deaf ears (Isa 6). Like
Isaiah's, Jesus' message *had* to encounter rejection from a people
who (John would allege) are in the same condition as their forbears.
If we stitch this view together with what we have seen from earlier
chapters in John, then just as rejection precedes restoration in Isaiah,
so also can the fulfillment of God's eschatological promises to Israel
only follow upon the rejection of an appeal that comes from the one
sent by God. As they invoke this storyline, John's quotations of
Isaiah 53:1 and 6:10 do not write off the possibility of Jewish belief
so much as they render such unbelief in Jesus as both comprehensible
and analogous to the prototypical unbelief described in Isaiah. John
12:37–43 makes clear that the future of Israel is not invalidated by
the unbelief of Jesus' own people any more than Isaiah's ministry
was invalidated by the obduracy of the people in the year that King
Uzziah died. For those attuned to John's characterization of Jesus
as the one who would usher in the future of Israel, Jesus' rejection is
nothing less than the vindication of his identity.

The second way in which John 12:37–43 would have its readers
envision the coherence of the Jewish tradition around Jesus involves
John's astonishing claim that "Isaiah said these things because he
saw his glory and he spoke of him" (12:41). The first implication

---

[15] Evans (*To See*, 131) proposes Isa 56:10 and 42:18, 19.

of this statement is that Isaiah actually envisioned the ministry of Jesus.[16] Such an assertion has precedent in the Gospel.[17] But John's striking claim is that the glory Isaiah describes in the vision of Isaiah 6 and the oracle of Isaiah 53 is, in fact, the singular glory of Jesus. We can see here the second way in which John's characterization of Jesus presses for a re-imagination of the Jewish tradition: the implication of John's simple statement is that the glory of God is capable of expression in suffering and crucifixion. John has merged the identities of the figures described in these texts:

Isaiah 6:1

> I saw the Lord sitting on a throne, lofty and raised up (רם ונשא/ὑψηλοῦ καὶ ἐπηρμένου), and the house was full of his glory (τῆς δόξης αὐτοῦ).[18]

Isaiah 52:13–14

> See, my servant shall understand,
> and he shall be exalted and glorified exceedingly (ירום ונשא/ ὑψωθήσεται καὶ δοξασθήσεται σφόδρα.).
> Just as many shall be astonished at you –
> so shall your appearance be without glory (ἀδοξήσει) from men,
> and your glory (ἡ δόξα σου) be absent from the men (52:13–14)

Isaiah 53:2

> He grew up before him like a child,
> like a root in a thirsty land;
> he has no form or glory (ולא הדר/οὐδὲ δόξα),
> and we saw him, and he had no form or beauty.

---

[16] John's ταῦτα suggests this, but it is the additional connections that suggest John's intention to link the quotations in 12:38 and 40 in terms of a Christological vision in v. 41. On this, see Jonathan Lett, "The Divine Identity of Jesus as the Reason for Israel's Unbelief in John 12:36–43," *JBL* 135.1 (2016): 159–173; Brendsel, *"Isaiah Saw His Glory,"* 123–134; Hays, *Echoes of Scripture in the Gospels,* 284–285.

[17] See e.g., 1:18; cf. 3:13; 5:37; 8:58; 14:9.

[18] Trans. NETS. N.B.: The phrase "the house was full of his glory" is in the LXX only. See further Catrin Williams, "Another Look at 'Lifting Up' in the Gospel of John," in *Conception, Reception, and the Spirit: Essays in Honor of Andrew T. Lincoln,* eds. J. G. McConville and L. K. Pietersen (Eugene: Cascade, 2015), 58–70.

In the immediate context of John 12, the Evangelist has primed his readers to make the connection that is embedded in his simple assertion that Isaiah saw Jesus' glory: Jesus has discussed his crucifixion three times as his "glorification" (δοξάζω; 12:16, 23, 28); twice John describes crucifixion as "lifting up" (ὑψόω; 12:32, 34; cf. also 3:14; 8:28). The implications lie near at hand for a reader who is tracking with how John views the crucifixion as Jesus' exaltation and glorification: "the glory that Isaiah saw is . . . that of the exalted Christ, that is, the Christ who was 'lifted up' on the cross and crucified."[19]

The claim that the glory Isaiah saw was the glory of Jesus as he is described in both Isaiah 6 and 53 has far-reaching implications. The Evangelist would have his readers envision the exalted, glorified (i.e., crucified) Christ as the one Isaiah saw exalted and glorious upon the throne. And, as Jonathan Lett has shown, John's language suggests that the image can also be flipped, so that the glory of God's own throne room can, without any contradiction, find expression in crucifixion.[20] The result of this juxtaposition is the expression of John's view that "humiliation is not accidental to the glory of Jesus, for this glory is the kind that condescends in order to bring salvation, even if it requires shameful death."[21]

Thus, with the seemingly unpretentious claim that "Isaiah said these things because he saw his glory and spoke of him," the Gospel of John intimates how the Jewish tradition might rethink its coherence in terms of Jesus in a way that is innovative to the extreme. To think about Israel's God and the activities of God in history is, for John, not only to be able to entertain the possibilities of binitarianism and/or incarnation. It is, further, to be able to rethink the meaning of God's glory not as something that is exalted infinitely higher than humanity but also (or instead) to think of God's glory as something that is appallingly beneath human glory. The difficulty in

---

[19] Evans, 219, quoted in Lett, "The Divine Identity of Jesus as the Reason for Israel's Unbelief in John 12:36–43," 170.

[20] See Lett, "The Divine Identity of Jesus as the Reason for Israel's Unbelief in John 12:36–43," 170.

[21] Ibid. On the hermeneutic that enables the evangelist to undertake such a reading, see Richard Bauckham, "Glory," in *Gospel of Glory: Major Themes in Johannine Theology*, ed. Richard Bauckman (Grand Rapids: Baker Academic, 2015), 43–62; Margaret Pamment, "The Meaning of *doxa* in the Fourth Gospel," *ZNW* 74 (1983): 12–16. Contrast here Schnackenburg, *The Gospel according to St. John*, 2.398–410; Käsemann, *Testament of Jesus: According to John 17* (Philadelphia: Fortress, 1968), 4–26.

accepting such a claim is the difficulty of rethinking the identity of God.[22] Nevertheless, John's striking redefinition of glory makes it easier to understand why loving τὴν δόξαν τῶν ἀνθρώπων would make a person unwilling to identify with Jesus and thereby undergo expulsion from the synagogue (12:42). It is not simply because of the vanity or superficial faith of the Jewish leaders. It is because John presents the glory of God as manifest in Jesus' shame-filled rejection and death, and this strikes at the heart of the tradition's view of what glory is.[23] The Gospel of John here follows its Christology to its logical end, insisting that Jesus' ministry and mission (including his suffering and death) are consistent with his identity as the son of the God of Israel; because Jesus' death is glorious like God is glorious, it is capable of ushering in the redemption envisioned by Isaiah.

John 15: The True Vine and the Future of Israel

From the climactic summary of Jesus' public ministry in John 12, we jump now to Jesus' teaching in his Farewell Discourse. In its immediate context, John 15:1–8 records Jesus encouraging his disciples to be faithful and carry out his commandment even after he departs from them to be with the Father.[24] Jesus has reassured his disciples that they will not be left as orphans (14:18) because the Holy Spirit will come to them (14:16, 26); indeed, Jesus himself will continue to come to his disciples (14:23, 28). Despite all of this encouragement, however, the disciples still need consolation, and Jesus responds with a pronouncement of peace and exhortations for them to be neither troubled nor afraid (14:27) – his upcoming death at the hands of the ruler of this world ought not be interpreted as defeat, but rather as the enactment of love and obedience to the Father (14:30). The next section of the discourse, Jesus' teaching on the true vine (15:1–18), restates nearly all of these themes. The concern of this present section is to clarify the significance of the image that Jesus uses to communicate to his disciples the ways in which he, his disciples, and the Father are joined in a relationship and the obligations of life in that

---

[22] Cf. Richard Bauckham, *Jesus and the God of Israel:* God Crucified *and Other Studies on the New Testament's Chistology of Divine Identity* (Grand Rapids: Eerdmans, 2009), 54–55.

[23] Cf. Brendsel, *"Isaiah Saw His Glory,"* 149–151.

[24] On the nature and genre of this section of John, see Brown, *The Gospel according to John,* II.597–601; Peter Ahr, "'He Loved Them to Completion': The Theology of John 13, 14," in *Standing Before God,* 73–89.

relationship. I will argue that Jesus' identification of himself as "the true vine" (15:1) draws on imagery from Ezekiel 15–19 and Psalm 80 in order to portray Jesus as the chosen figure (i.e., the vine) through whom God will provide eschatological deliverance to Israel. By characterizing Jesus in these terms, the Gospel portrays Jesus and his disciples in terms that are (or should be) deeply encouraging to disciples faced with the challenging future of life in a hostile world without Jesus. It is of utmost importance for understanding the nature of Jesus' encouragement that readers understand how John's vine imagery evokes an array of texts related to Israel's faithfulness and focuses on a specific subset of them in order to describe the significance of Jesus to his followers so that they may know that *his* eschatological significance ensures their own place in Israel's eschatological future.

The bulk of the interpretive tradition interprets John 15 as supersessionist in character. Edwyn Hoskyns states this view clearly: "*I am the true vine* is … a formal denial of Jewish claims and the fulfilment of prophecy. Jesus, not Israel, is the vine of God; the disciples, not the Jews, are the branches of the vine. The synagogue is superseded by the Christian *Ecclesia.*"[25] In an important article on Israel in the Fourth Gospel, John Painter cites John 15:1 in order to refute the proposal that John describes how Jews might belong to "the true Israel" – if Jesus is the true vine, argues Painter, then the people of Israel no longer can be.[26] If Hoskyns and Painter (and the many they represent) are correct, then "the future of Israel" is not an object that Jesus brings his tradition into, but rather a reality that he swallows up. But there is one major obstacle to such a reading: It clashes with the portrayal of Jesus as a figure of eschatological fulfillment we have been considering throughout the Fourth Gospel.

---

[25] Cf. Hoskyns, *The Fourth Gospel*, 475. Brown, *The Gospel according to John*, II.670, 675; Barrett, *The Gospel according to St. John*, 473; Schnackenburg, *The Gospel according to St. John*, 3.104–107. Cp. with the emphasis on fulfillment in Marianne Meye Thompson on this passage (*John*, 323–326; and her "Every Picture Tells a Story: Imagery for God in the Gospel of John," in *Imagery in the Gospel of John: Terms, Forms, Themes, and Theology of Johannine Figurative Language*, eds. Jörg Frey, Jan G. van der Watt, and Ruben Zimmermann, WUNT 2/200 [Tübingen: Mohr Siebeck, 2006], 259–277).

[26] See John Painter, "The Church and Israel in the Gospel of John: A Response," *NTS* 25 (1978), esp. 112; cf. Severino Pancaro, "People of God in St. John's Gospel," *NTS* 16 (1970): 114–129; Severino Pancaro, "The Relationship of the Church to Israel in the Gospel of John," *NTS* 21 (1975): 396–405.

Specifically, the portrayal of Jesus as Word/Memra, king, the one sent from God, shepherd, vicarious sufferer, living water, bread from heaven, and even as Christ (= Messiah) should make interpreters hesitant to conclude that John shifts in 15:1 from a portrayal of Jesus as the *bringer* of deliverance and/or eschatological blessing to the people of God, and that John now intends to show how Jesus *replaces* the object (Israel) that all of these other characters and symbols serve. Placed within a narrative that consistently renders Jesus as the one who fulfills the hopes of Israel, John 15 ought to be considered in this narrative frame.

In fact, if one resists reading the vine imagery of 15:1–6, 16 against the general Scriptural background of Israel as an unfruitful vine/vineyard (e.g., Isa 5), then the strongest thematic and lexical connections between John 15 and scriptural depictions of the vine confirm the hypothesis that John 15 invokes God's deliverance of Israel through particular leaders characterized as vines or branches. One important source for this imagery is Ezekiel 17:1–10, which describes a great eagle (Nebuchadnezzar) planting a vine (King Zedekiah) in Israel that spreads out its branches (κλήματα) in its modest land. The vine is unsatisfied in its soil, however. It is drawn to the abundant waters of Egypt, where it is transplanted and seeks to bear fruit (φέρειν καρπὸν). In Ezekiel's oracle, the vine's effort to bear fruit on its own terms is an unqualified disaster. The result of Zedekiah's willingness to break his covenant with Babylon and turn to Egypt will be his death in Babylon (vv. 11–21). Only after this judgment does God commit to planting a new shoot in the land of Israel:

> I will transplant him on a high mountain.
> And I will hang him in a mountain of Israel high in the air.
> And I will transplant him,
> and he shall produce a shoot and bear fruit and become a
>   large cedar.
> And every animal shall rest under him,
> and every winged creature shall rest under his shade,
> and his shoots shall be restored.
>
> (Ezek 17:22–23)

Although Ezekiel's imagery shifts to a cedar tree (κέδρον/ארז) as he goes on to describe God's chosen leader, the prophet's ability to employ this imagery (vine/cedar) when describing individual leaders is important to note, as it shows that imagery for Israel can also be concentrated onto an individual figure without eclipsing God's commitment to the people as a whole.[27] A similar use of this imagery occurs in Ezekiel 19:10–14, in which the tribe of Judah is portrayed as a vine (ἄμπελος, v.10), whose shoots and fruit emerge in strength only to be cut down by the Babylonian conquest. Again, a key observation to make here is Ezekiel's use of vine imagery *not* for the entire nation but for a part of the whole. Yet we must ask: This way of using vine imagery would be convenient for John 15, but is there any reason to prefer it? In fact, there is. As Marianne Meye Thompson has observed, John 15 is the only New Testament text to use the term κλῆμα for "branch";[28] and six of the eleven uses of κλῆμα in the LXX occur in vine imagery employed in Ezekiel 15, 17, and 19.[29] Further, as in John 15:6, Ezekiel speaks of judgment against the withered, unproductive branches of the vine in terms of their being tossed into the fire.[30] Finally, Ezekiel is the only scriptural source from which John could have derived the rare usage of the verb καθαίρω to describe the "pruning" of vine branches (John 15:2; cf. Ezek 15:4: ἐνιαυτὸν κάθαρσιν/the yearly pruning).[31] Ezekiel thus accounts for the application of vine imagery to an individual figure as well as for some of John's specific terminology. The prophet vividly describes God's people lacking a vine that can lead them faithfully. They suffer dearly for this lack. But it is striking that Ezekiel does not develop the vine as an image of restoration. The closest he comes is the image of a cedar (17:22–24). Why, then, if the Fourth Gospel is following Ezekiel, does it present Jesus as "the true vine"? An answer lies at hand if we consider a further application of vine imagery to an individual leader of Israel in Psalm 80.

Psalm 80 is a prayer for God to come to the aid of the scattered and hard-pressed people of Israel (v. 1).[32] Three times the people cry out, "O God, restore us! Let your face shine upon us, and we will

---

[27] See, e.g., Isa 11:1 (cf. Isa 60:21); Dan 11:7; 11:20 LXX; Jer 23:5; 33:15; Zech 3:8; 4:12; 6:12. Cf. also Isa 53:2; Andrew Streett, *The Vine and the Son of Man: Eschatological Interpretation of Psalm 80 in Early Judaism* (Minneapolis: Fortress, 2014), 44–46.

[28] Other NT texts prefer κλάδος (see Rom 11:16–21). N.B. Here, and for the rest of this paragraph, I am indebted to Thompson, "Every Picture," 273–276; Thompson, *John*, 322–326.

[29] Cf. Num 13:23; Joel 1:7; Nah 2:3; Mal 3:19; Jer 31:32; Ezek 15:2; 17:6, 7, 23; 19:11; and Ps 79:12 (discussed below).

[30] Ezek 15:4–8; 19:14.

[31] The more common term for pruning is τέμνω (cf. Isa 5:6). On uses of καθαίρω similar to John, see Philo, *Agr.* 10; 4 Macc 1:29.

[32] Here and below versification will follow the NRSV for Ps 80 (=79 LXX).

be saved" (v. 3; cf. 7, 19).[33] The first half of the psalm records the people's present humiliation in the context of their former glory (vv. 4–6, 8–11). The psalm pictures Israel as a vine (גפן/ἄμπελος) transplanted by God from Egypt and flourishing in its land with its branches (κλήματα) stretching out to the sea (v. 11). But the vine is ravaged by wild animals (v. 12), so the psalmist prays:

> (14) Turn again, O God of hosts; look down from heaven,
>   and see;
>   have regard for this vine (גפן/ἄμπελος),
> (15) the stock that your right hand planted,
>   and upon the son [or branch] of your strength
>   (ועל בן אמצתה לך)/Cf. LXX: καὶ ἐπὶ υἱὸν ἀνθρώπου, ὃν
>   ἐκραταίωσας σεαυτῷ[!]).[34]
> (16) They have burned it with fire, they have cut it down;
>   may they perish at the rebuke of your countenance.
> (17) But let your hand be upon the one (על איש/ἐπ' ἄνδρα) at
>   your right hand,
>   the one whom you made strong for yourself
>   (על בן אדם אמצת לך)/LXX: καὶ ἐπὶ υἱὸν ἀνθρώπου, ὃν
>   ἐκραταίωσας σεαυτῷ)
> (18) Then we will never turn back from you;
>   give us life, and we will call on your name.
>   (Ps 80:14–18)

Andrew Streett has recently shown that Psalm 80 was often read in the Jewish tradition as an expression of royal hopes, and, in the Second Temple and rabbinic periods, as a prayer of eschatological and messianic hope.[35] Ancient readers capitalized on the association between the "son"/"son of man" figure in vv. 15, 17 and similar terminology in Psalm 2 (the king as God's son), Psalm 8 (the son of man as God's ruler on earth), Psalm 110 (the king sitting at God's right hand), and Daniel 7 (the son of man; Israel's oppressors as

---

[33] This refrain is slightly altered in each occurrence.

[34] This line ("and the son of your strength") is excised from the NRSV and the BHS. Streett (*The Vine and the Son of Man*, 17–20) helpfully argues for its authenticity and explains the translation of בן as "son" or "branch" with reference to Gen 49:22.

[35] See Streett, *The Vine and the Son of Man*, 49–114. N.B.: Not *every* Jewish text reads the Psalm messianically. L.A.B. always reads the vine as the people of Israel. Cf. Streett, 145–150.

beasts).[36] Thus it is no surprise that when the Targumist of the Psalms came to the term בֵּן in Ps 80:15 ("the son of your strength"), he replaced it with a title: מלכא משיחא (King Messiah).[37]

Psalm 80 describes God as the caretaker of the vine (ἄμπελος) and the branches (κλήματα) as extensions that are "sent out" (שׁלח/ ἐκτείνω). It is certainly possible to read Psalm 80 and consistently hold that Israel, and only Israel, is the vine of God (vv. 8, 14). But ancient readers also faced – and accepted – a further possibility embedded in the psalm's language: that the vine of God can be identified with a particular figure whom God will raise up for his people. Israel and the messiah can both be imaged as a vine, raised up by God, the former (Israel) by the latter (messiah). In the logic of such a reading of Psalm 80, the prayer for God to restore the vine of Israel (vv. 14–18) might be paraphrased as follows:

> Look down from heaven and see!
> Have regard for this vine (i.e., Israel/the messiah) –
> The stock that you planted (Israel/the messiah).
> Even the Branch that you strengthen [Or, the Son of Man
>   whom you strengthen] (i.e., the messiah) . . .
> Let your hand be upon the man at your right hand (the
>   messiah), whom you strengthen.
> Then we (Israel) will never turn back from you.

The advantages of reading John 15:1–8 under the pressure of these passages from Ezekiel and Psalm 80 is that each of these texts can position Jesus as a vine with a singularly important role in bringing about the future restoration of Israel. This reading maintains the Gospel's consistent focus on portraying Jesus as one who fulfills important eschatological roles related to the people of God. In addition to portraying individual figures as a vine, John and Ezekiel employ similar terms and imagery (preference for κλῆμα; καθαίρω as "pruning"). In Psalm 80, the role of God as the one who plants the vine parallels John's description of God as γεωργός (15:1); the prayer for God to have regard for his vine (= the man/son/branch/son of man) could easily suggest John's Jesus, who is consistently portrayed in each of those terms except "branch." This is fitting, since if John's lexicon is determined by Ezekiel and Psalm 80, then the vine's

---

[36] Streett, *The Vine and the Son of Man*, 82–89; 107–114; 115–125.
[37] See ibid., 153. 2 Bar 36–40 portrays the messiah as a vine.

κλήματα are the people and works that extend from the vine and embody its legitimacy.

What, then, of the phrase "true vine" (ἡ ἄμπελος ἡ ἀληθινή, John 15:1)? Does not Jesus' chosen designation, particularly its allusion to Jer 2:21 LXX, suggest that Jesus sets himself up in counterpoint to Israel instead of as one of its chosen leaders? On the reading offered here, Jesus' claim to be the "true vine" would indeed trigger this important field of biblical images.[38] With the statement Ἐγώ εἰμι ἡ ἄμπελος ἡ ἀληθινή, John's Jesus evokes the relationship of Israel to its God and the important question of how Israel will achieve a fruitful status again. But just as soon as he evokes this broad field of images, Jesus develops the image in a particular way, a way that is resonant with how Ezekiel and Psalm 80 employ the imagery. Jesus characterizes himself as the individual vine raised up by God for the deliverance of the people. Thus, when Jesus says, "I am the true vine," he does not claim to replace Israel. He claims to be the one who, as the psalmist prayed, is strengthened by God to bring Israel into its future.

This section began by considering the context in the Farewell Discourse of Jesus' statement "I am the true vine." It is a context in which Jesus is reassuring his disciples even while commissioning them to carry forward his commandment to love one another as he has loved them. When read within this context, Jesus' claim to be the true vine catches up the identity of Jesus and his disciples in a new and challenging way: Jesus is the one whom God has raised up to bring Israel into its future. He is the answer to the prayer of Psalm 80; he is the counterpoint to the withered, faithless vine of Ezekiel 17. Implied within this imagery is that the Father's regard for Jesus will be the means by which he will deliver the whole vine of Israel. As in Ezekiel and Psalm 80, the branches of this plant will invariably reflect the vine to which they are attached. Thus, the vine imagery in John 15 draws on this scriptural background to characterize Jesus in his unique role as the one who brings about the future of Israel, and it also draws on this background as a resource for Jesus' disciples to envision how their identities are intimately bound up with Jesus, the true vine, and the purposes of the God of Israel who has established him. John's description of Jesus as the true vine carries forward the aims of the broader discourse (namely, encouraging and commissioning the disciples) even as it does so in terms that make

---

[38] See Silke Petersen, *Brot, Licht, Weinstock: Intertextuelle Analysen johanneischer Ich-bin-Worte*, NovTSup 127 (Leiden: Brill, 2008), 286–313.

ambitious claims about the identity of Jesus and his significance for the future of Israel.

John 13–19: Jesus, David, and Righteous Suffering

As a literary unit, John 13–17 is concerned with the basic generic concerns of a Farewell Discourse: teaching, commissioning, and comforting Jesus' followers. John's passion narrative (chapters 18–19) is also influenced by the conventions of early traditions about Jesus' death. In turning to this section of the Gospel, the aim of this study is not to propose a novel reinterpretation; instead, it is to show how John's concern to portray Jesus' significance for the future of Israel extends even to these aspects of the Gospel narrative that are shaped by other concerns and generic conventions. The present section focuses on John's characterization of Jesus as the suffering, righteous king of Israel throughout the Farewell Discourse and passion narrative. This emerges especially through John's quotations of psalms that offer a scriptural paradigm for interpreting Jesus' betrayal and suffering. As the Gospel presents Jesus in this way, it accounts for Jesus' sufferings by identifying them with the sufferings of David.

There are seven marked quotations of Scripture after the concluding interaction between Jesus and the crowd in 12:36. These seven differ from others in the Gospel because in each instance the events occurring are said to "fulfill" (πληρόω) Scripture.[39] But what is it about Scripture that is "fulfilled" in each instance? And what exactly does it mean to "fulfill" Scripture? The first of these quotations (12:38, 40) we have already considered at length, concluding that John's characterization of Jesus' ministry as the fulfillment of the prophecies of Isaiah 6 and 53 functions, first, to account for Jewish disbelief and, second, to identify Jesus' crucifixion with the lifting up and glorification of God and the servant of God. In this passage, Jesus fulfills Scripture by embodying its ultimate point of reference. The fulfillments of Scripture in John's Farewell Discourse and passion narrative continue along this path: each one portrays Jesus' suffering as a perfect embodiment of the suffering experienced by the chosen king of Israel. Further, and as we will see in the next section, John's portrayal of Jesus as the chosen king of Israel relates

---

[39] See John 13:18; 15:25; 17:12; 19:24, 28, 36, 37. These last two quotations are governed by a single "fulfillment" claim, as in John 12:38, 40.

directly to the future of Israel, while it also lodges an incisive criticism against those leaders of Israel who reject Jesus in this role. The Gospel has, of course, suggested a royal identity for Jesus earlier in the statement of Nathaniel (1:49) and in the addition inserted into the crowd's quotation of Psalm 118:25: "Hosanna [Save us]! Blessed is the one who comes in the name of the Lord, *the king of Israel*" (ὁ βασιλεὺς τοῦ Ἰσραήλ, 12:13). John resists identifying Jesus with a popular king (6:15). (Indeed, Jesus' kingship in John's Gospel is one that violates nearly every standard image of a king.) Yet, as we will see here, despite John's clear interest in avoiding certain images and expectations that would come with designating Jesus as a king, the Gospel is interested in defining how Jesus' messiahship aligns with expectations for a messianic king.[40] It is through Jesus' suffering as the true king of Israel that he fulfills his identity as the one qualified to bring Israel into its eschatological hopes. As we will see, John's quotations of Scripture in the Farewell Discourse (the first three examples below) work to bind Jesus' betrayal and the opposition he faces to the betrayal and opposition of King David. John's quotations of Scripture in the passion narrative (the last four) portray Jesus' sufferings in terms that resonate with the sufferings of Israel's true king. Brief considerations of each text will bear this out. But before considering these specific texts, it will be helpful to note that John's portrayal of Jesus as the fulfillment of specifically Davidic expectations is not limited to the seven quotations considered here (the six Psalms are all Davidic; the Zechariah text foresees the restoration of David's house). The characterization of Jesus as a David-like figure is a function of John's broader tendency to portray Jesus as the speaker or central figure of the Psalms, the one that is their true point of reference. The Davidic characterization of Jesus in the Farewell Discourse and passion narrative thus presses further a Gospel-wide characterization of Jesus as God's chosen (often Davidic) leader.

John 13:18

The first way in which John characterizes Jesus as the righteous, suffering king of Israel is by drawing out the similarities between

---

[40] For a helpful presentation of the messiah as king in Second Temple Judaism, see Mavis Leung, *The Kingship-Cross Interplay in the Gospel of John: Jesus' Death as Corroboration of His Royal Messiahship* (Eugene: Wipf & Stock, 2011), 23–51.

Jesus' betrayal and David's. In chapter 13, Jesus concludes his washing of the disciples' feet with this suggestive claim, "You are clean – but not all of you" (v. 11). He comes back to this statement sentences later:

> I am not speaking about all of you, for I know the ones that I chose, in order that the Scripture might be fulfilled, "The one eating my bread has lifted up his heel against me" (ὁ τρώγων μου τὸν ἄρτον ἐπῆρεν ἐπ᾽ ἐμὲ τὴν πτέρναν αὐτοῦ). I am telling you this before it happens, so that when it does happen you might believe that I am he.   (13:18–19)

Jesus' words indicate that he has purposefully chosen a mixed company of disciples, and he has done so because his betrayal by a close associate fulfills Scripture. The Scripture is almost certainly Psalm 41:10 (LXX 40:10: ὁ ἐσθίων ἄρτους μου, ἐμεγάλυνεν ἐπ᾽ ἐμὲ πτερνισμόν). By referring to this text, Jesus makes clear that his betrayal will be modeled on the betrayal of David by his trusted friend. In fact, the citation of Psalm 41:10 likely implies a specific betrayal: A rabbinic tradition associates the betrayal mentioned by David in Psalm 41:10 with the treachery of Ahithophel, David's counselor who sided with Absalom and plotted the death of David by means of a nighttime raid (2 Sam 15–17).[41] The David–Ahithophel association bears striking resemblance to the Jesus–Judas association in the gospels, and it is not a coincidence that the citation of Psalm 41 triggers the next scene in the narrative, wherein the words of David find their fullest meaning as Jesus gives bread to Judas, who then departs into the night to carry out the betrayal. Most important for our purposes is how John 13:18 underlines the *intentionality* of Jesus' actions. Jesus has chosen his disciples with the goal of reenacting a specific drama. His suffering at the hands of "his own" (1:11) recapitulates the persecution and betrayal of David by his associates. In John's logic, the betrayal of Jesus follows the script of David's and, in so doing, offers the ultimate realization of what David once described when he suffered innocently as Israel's true king.[42]

---

[41] See *b.* San 106b; Ps 41:10; cf also *b.* San 7a (with no connection to Ahithophel); Schuchard, *Scripture within Scripture*, 114–117; Menken, *Old Testament Quotations*, 130–136; Daly-Denton, *David in the Fourth Gospel*, 79–80, 191–201; T. Francis Glasson, "Davidic Links with the Betrayal of Jesus," *ExpT* 85.4 (1974): 118–119.

[42] See further Hays, "Christ Prays the Psalms," 107.

John 15:25

The connections with David continue as Jesus draws on the words of Israel's former king to interpret the hostility he and his disciples encounter. Our earlier treatment of John 15 focused on how the image of the true vine portrayed Jesus as the righteous leader through whom God would restore Israel, and it did so with an eye toward the larger purpose of the Farewell Discourse, namely the commissioning and equipping of the disciples. In a similar way, Jesus' teaching about the hatred of the world (15:18–25) looks back to the Psalms to account for the suffering of Jesus and his followers (15:26–16:4). In other words, John 15:25 and 15:1–8 employ Scripture – indeed, even imagery from the Psalms – to the same ends: they characterize Jesus as a figure of specific significance with regard to God's care for and restoration of the people, and both texts also imply what it will mean for Jesus' disciples to be associated with such a figure. When 15:25 is examined closely, two features stand out: first, John's use of Scripture in v. 25 presupposes the identity of Jesus as the righteous leader of God's people (this agrees with what we saw in 15:1–8); second, John puts a finer point on this characterization by specifying that the hatred of the world will be a further enactment of the hatred David experienced when he writes that his rejection had to happen ἵνα πληρωθῇ ὁ λόγος ὁ ἐν τῷ νόμῳ αὐτῶν γεγραμμένος ὅτι ἐμίσησάν με δωρεάν (15:25).

The source of John's quotation is either Psalm 35:19 or 69:4. Both are prayers of David, which portray him as the righteous king of Israel who suffers unjustly and yet entrusts himself to God. But it is Psalm 69:4 (LXX 68:5) that serves as the most likely source for the citation in John 15:25, since the Gospel has already characterized Jesus as the speaker of this psalm when it portrayed him as the righteous sufferer who will be persecuted by his "brothers" (Ps 69:8) due to his zeal for the house of God (John 2:17, quoting Ps 69:9). Here again David's prayer serves as a prefiguration of the experience of Jesus and his followers: The undeserved animosity once directed at Israel's king by his brothers is fulfilled in the animosity experienced by Jesus at the hands of those who reject him and his Father. John's characterization of Jesus in this way, and specifically in a discourse concerned with the disciples and their life after Jesus departure, works to equip readers to understand the hatred they experience as a hostility that is derivative from the opposition that God's chosen leader faced from his contemporaries.[43]

John 17:12

The quotations of Scripture in John 13:18 and 15:25 portray Jesus' betrayal and the hatred that he and his followers experience as the ultimate embodiments of the prior experiences of David, particularly as readers encounter him in the book of Psalms as God's chosen leader who suffered the opposition of his people. This logic also undergirds the fulfillment of Scripture in 17:12: "When I was with them, I kept them in your name which you had given me, and I guarded them. And not one of them was lost except the son of destruction, in order that Scripture might be fulfilled."

As in 13:18, here John addresses the theological problem entailed by the betrayal of Jesus from within his inner circle. If Jesus is God's chosen leader and his disciples have a share in the Father through him (15:3–8; 17:10), then how could one of his close associates commit such an appalling offense?[44] As before, the answer that lies at hand is that it must have been so. John's term for Judas (ὁ υἱὸς τῆς ἀπωλείας) does not immediately lend itself to any particular Scriptural source. Hence, it is likely that in this case John understands the fulfillment of Scripture as an extension of his prior citation regarding the necessity of God's chosen king suffering innocently at the hands of his brothers. If this is so, then Psalm 41:9 (LXX 40:10), cited earlier in John 13:18, is the text in view in John 17:12: the only one whom Jesus has lost is the one who turned against him – that is, the son of destruction, Judas.[45] The loss of Judas from among the disciples follows the intention of Jesus as he reenacts (and indeed

---

[43] Cf. Daly-Denton, *David in the Fourth Gospel*, 207–208; Hays, *Echoes of Scripture in the Gospels*, 338; Menken, *Old Testament Quotations*, 139–145.

[44] See B. J. Oropeza, "Judas' Death and Final Destiny in the Gospels and Earliest Christian Writings," *Neotestamentica* 44.2 (2010): 342–361; U. C. von Wahlde, "Judas, the Son of Perdition and the Fulfillment of Scripture in John 17:12," in *The New Testament and Early Christian Literature in Greco-Roman Context: Studies in Honor of David E. Aune*, ed. John Fotopoulos, NovTSup 122 (Leiden: Brill, 2006), 167–182.

[45] There are other Scriptures terminologically closer to John's ὁ υἱὸς τῆς ἀπωλείας (e.g., Isa 34:5; 57:4; Prov 24:22 LXX) and also thematically closer (e.g., Jer 23:3–6; cf. Hays, *Echoes of Scripture in the Gospels*, 327, 436n100). My contention is that John 17:12 describes the troubling betrayal of God's anointed by a close associate. In 13:18, John turns to Ps 41 for understanding that problem.

fulfills) a paradigm that finds biblical precedent in the downfall of Ahithophel and other close associates of David.

We move now to John's quotations of Scripture in the passion narrative. In this section, the quotations continue to depict Jesus as God's chosen king who suffers innocently, but there is also a shift: from a concern with betrayal and opposition in the Farewell Discourse (the appropriate focus of a discourse that aims to commission and equip the disciples) to an effort to demonstrate the way in which Jesus' specific sufferings portray him as the eschatological king of Israel.

John 19:24

All of the canonical gospels record the division of Jesus' clothes among the soldiers who crucified him. And while each Evangelist is aware of the importance of Psalm 22 as it provides a framework for Jesus' suffering, it is only the Fourth Gospel that explicitly cites the scriptural source for these actions. John's quotation follows Psalm 22:18 exactly (LXX 21:19: διεμερίσαντο τὰ ἱμάτιά μου ἑαυτοῖς καὶ ἐπὶ τὸν ἱματισμόν μου ἔβαλον κλῆρον), which is another of David's prayers for help as he is assailed by adverseries. Similar to the Gospel's quotations of other psalms, John's quotation of Psalm 22:18 portrays Jesus as the central figure ("They divided *my garments* among them; and for *my clothing* they cast lots."). John presents Jesus as fulfilling in his own life the humiliation described (but never narrated at length) in the life of Israel's quintessential royal figure.

One advantage to reading John 19:24 within a broader, chapterslong characterization of Jesus as a David-like sufferer is that doing so obviates the need to propose more speculative theological symbolism for the division of Jesus' garments. Thus, there is no reason to suggest that here John unexpectedly portrays Jesus as a priest due to his seamless garment (Exod 37:4; Lev 16:4; *Ant.* 3.161); nor are the garments of Jesus forced to symbolize the church going out into the Gentile world (in the hands of the four soldiers) while also retaining an essential unity (in the un-torn garment).[46] The symbolism is much more likely to serve the purpose of connecting Jesus' innocent suffering to David's. This connection is explicitly cited in

---

[46] See Brown, *John*, II.920–922; Schuchard, *Scripture within Scripture*, 127–132.

John's marked quotation, and it carries forward the Davidic and royal themes of John's broader characterization of Jesus.

John 19:28

These themes continue in the brief quotation of Scripture in 19:28. The specific source is difficult to pin down because the quotation is so brief. John writes, "After this [the division of his clothes and instructions to his mother and beloved disciple], Jesus, knowing that all was now finished, in order to bring the Scripture to its complete fulfillment, said, 'I thirst'" (Μετὰ τοῦτο εἰδὼς ὁ Ἰησοῦς ὅτι ἤδη πάντα τετέλεσται, ἵνα τελειωθῇ ἡ γραφή, λέγει· διψῶ). The basic claim of the text is clear, and again the emphasis is on Jesus' intentionality: his awareness of the drama that is unfolding in the course of his crucifixion prompts him to express his need.[47] This self-awareness makes it likely that the Scripture Jesus fulfills comes from Psalm 69, wherein David laments the utter lack of mercy shown to him in his sufferings by stating,

> Insults have broken my heart,
> so that I am in despair.
> I looked for pity, but there was none;
> and for comforters, but I found none.
> They gave me poison for food,
> and for my thirst they gave me vinegar to drink (εἰς τὴν δίψαν μου ἐπότισάν με ὄξος). (Ps 69:21–22)[48]

The citation of this Psalm at 2:17, and its likely use in 15:25, reinforces the probability that Psalm 69 provides the context that make sense of Jesus' words.[49] Here again the prayers and experiences of the suffering King David are used to color the dying moments of Jesus and to press readers toward an interpretation of his suffering that recognizes the paradigm of the suffering, righteous king that, in John's view, is on display in the suffering and crucifixion of Jesus.[50]

---

[47] Cf. Brown, *John,* II.928.

[48] LXX 68:21–22. John alone quotes this verse; Mark 15:36 and Matt 27:48 allude to it (cf. Lk 23:36). My quotation here follows the clearer logic of the NRSV (=MT) in v. 21.

[49] See also Pss 43:2; 63:1; Ps 22:15. Brown, *John,* II.929; Hoskyns, *The Fourth Gospel,* 531.

[50] Those who offer Jesus wine (ὄξος, John 19:29) do not antagonize him, but the figures in Psalm 69:21 *persecute David* by giving him wine. John takes cues from Psalm 69 without reenacting it in a wooden way.

John 19:36–37

John interprets the moment of Jesus' death as the fulfillment of two scriptural texts. First, John finds the fulfillment of Scripture in the fact that the soldiers to do not break Jesus' legs (ἐγένετο γὰρ ταῦτα ἵνα ἡ γραφὴ πληρωθῇ· ὀστοῦν οὐ συντριβήσεται αὐτοῦ, v. 36). The passage cited here has three possible sources – two related to Passover, one related to God's care for a righteous sufferer:

> You will not leave any of it until morning, and you will not break a bone of it. (οὐκ ἀπολείψετε ἀπ᾿ αὐτοῦ ἕως πρωὶ καὶ ὀστοῦν οὐ συντρίψετε ἀπ᾿ αὐτοῦ.) (Exodus 12:10)

> They will not leave any of it until morning, and they will not break a bone of it, [but] according to the instruction of the Passover they will do it. (οὐ καταλείψουσιν ἀπ᾿ αὐτοῦ εἰς τὸ πρωὶ καὶ ὀστοῦν οὐ συντρίψουσιν ἀπ᾿ αὐτοῦ· κατὰ τὸν νόμον τοῦ πασχα ποιήσουσιν αὐτό.) (Numbers 9:12)

> Many are the afflictions of the righteous, but he [the Lord] rescues them from them all/The Lord watches all of their bones, not one of them will be broken. (πολλαὶ αἱ θλίψεις τῶν δικαίων, καὶ ἐκ πασῶν αὐτῶν ῥύσεται αὐτούς. /κύριος φυλάσσει πάντα τὰ ὀστᾶ αὐτῶν, ἓν ἐξ αὐτῶν οὐ συντριβήσεται.) (Ps 33:20–21 LXX; MT 34:19–20)

John's wording – ὀστοῦν οὐ συντριβήσεται αὐτοῦ – could easily reflect any of these passages, and it is likely that John's quotation alludes to both the Passover texts and the Psalm. In so doing, John (1) suggests that Jesus' death can be understood as a kind of ultimate paschal sacrifice, and (2) John also presses further into the characterization of Jesus as a suffering, righteous figure, because here in his death readers see the Lord protecting Jesus' body from disfigurement.[51] The form of the quotation supports this: the Gospel's wording resembles the quotations from Exodus and Numbers, and yet it also employs the future passive of συντρίβω, a rare verbal form that occurs in Psalm 33:21 LXX.[52] More important than the specific

---

[51] See further Brown, *John,* II.952–953; Christine Schlund, *Kein Knochen soll gebrochen werden: Studien zu Bedeutung und Funktion des Pesachfest in Texten des frühen Judentums und im Johannesevangelium,* WMANT 107 (Neukirchen: Neukirchener Verlag, 2005); Dodd, *Interpretation,* 233–234; Thompson, "The Bear Witness to Me," 278–279; Schuchard, *Scripture within Scripture,* 136–140; Hays, *Echoes of Scripture in the Gospels,* 317.

[52] Menken, *Old Testament Quotations,* 248–252.

verbal similarities are the images of the inviolable bones of the Passover lamb and the preserved bones of the righteous. There is one Jewish text predating John that associates Passover with the preservation of the righteous. Jubilees 49:13 reads: "They shall roast it [the lamb] in fire without breaking any of its bones within it because no bone of the children of Israel will be broken." In other words, for Jubilees, the unbroken bones of the lamb symbolize God's preservation of his people. Considered in this light, the fulfillment of Scripture in John 19:36 could be seen (1) to allude to Passover instructions – a very likely possibility given the Passover setting of the narrative; (2) John 19:36 may further suggest a meaning similar to Jubilees (and Ps 33 LXX): Jesus' unbroken bones are a divine corroboration of his righteousness. As the book of Jubilees could view the unbroken bones of the Passover lamb as proleptic sign of God's preservation of the righteous, so John's claim is that this fulfillment has begun on the cross, indeed, at Passover.

Decades ago, David Daube argued that the imagery of unbroken bones shared by Psalm 34, Exodus 12, Numbers 9, and the prophecy of restoration in Ezekiel 37 made it likely that these associations were generally available to Jewish readers: "[T]he inviolability of the bones of the Passover lamb was widely regarded as symbolizing the individual's hope as well as the nation's [hope] of a glorious future."[53] Daube cited no evidence for this claim, and, admittedly, the testimony of Jubilees stands alone as evidence for this association prior to John; thus it may be doubtful that an association of Exodus 12:10 and Numbers 9:12 with Psalm 34:21 was common in ancient Judaism. But what is less doubtful is that the Fourth Evangelist thinks about the significance of Jesus' crucifixion using scriptural images that are both vivid and eschatologically significant. An interpretation of John 19:36 that considers it as the fulfillment of the Passover and Psalm texts should be seen as a compelling hypothesis because it carries forward a way of reading that is distinctively Johannine, and also one that has (admittedly limitied) historical precedent. To read John as drawing on these various scriptural contexts would mean to recognize its development of the connection between the paschal lamb and the righteous sufferer: for John, as Jesus dies at Passover, Jesus individually embodies (or proleptically experiences) the preservation that God promises to all Israel. The

[53] David Daube, *The New Testament and Rabbinic Judaism* (University of London: The Athlone Press, 1956), 309.

citation of Scripture in 19:36 thus furthers what we have seen above. John cites a Davidic psalm – one associated with his persecution (1 Sam 21) – to emphasize that the preservation of Jesus' bones mark him out as a righteous sufferer. In so doing, John portrays Jesus as experiencing in his death a form of divine preservation that is central to Israel's eschatological hopes and that was likely associated with the paschal lamb.

The second interpretative statement John offers in response to Jesus' death is taken from Zechariah 12:10: the piercing of Jesus' side (John 19:34) fulfills the prophet's words: "they will look on the one they have pierced" (19:37). When we consider the context of the Zechariah quotation, we see that John's presentation of Jesus as the focal point of Zechariah's vision associates Jesus' piercing with the restoration of David's house. John puts forward this understanding of Jesus by means of a distinctive reading of the text of Zechariah: the wording of John's citation (ὄψονται εἰς ὃν ἐξεκέντησαν) reflects a translation of Zechariah 12:10 MT, which reads:

"They will look on me, whom they have pierced"

וְהִבִּיטוּ אֵלַי אֵת אֲשֶׁר־דָּקָרוּ

Two significant choices are at work in John's reception of this text. First, John has revocalized the MT's "on me" (אֵלַי) to "on whom"(אֵלָיו).[54] Second, John has retained the language of piercing that the LXX translators rejected.[55] John's presentation of Jesus' death thus reflects a striking reception of this scriptural tradition – an adherence to the vivid language of the Hebrew text, but also a christological reorientation of it.[56]

The significance of John's quotation of Zechariah comes to the fore on a consideration of the passage in its context. The Lord is speaking through the prophet about the restoration of house of David and, through it, all of Jerusalem when he says:

> And I will pour out on the house of David and the inhabitants of Jerusalem a spirit of grace and pleas for mercy, so that, when *they look on the one they have pierced,*

---

[54] Cf. Menken, *Old Testament Quotations,* 171. The rereading suggested here would follow the vocalization on display in Job 3:22 and 5:26, and thus the spelling of the word remains the same but the object changes ("on me"/"on whom [him]").

[55] See Menken, *Old Testament Quotations,* 168–178.

[56] Cf. John's similar adherence to the sense of the MT in John 12:40.

> they shall mourn for him, as one mourns for an only
> son, and weep bitterly over him, as one weeps over a
> firstborn.   (Zechariah 12:10)[57]

In the context of Zechariah 12, the restoration of David's house is emblematic of the restoration of Jerusalem, Judah, and the people of God. When the house of David is restored," [it] will be like God, like the angel of the Lord, going before them [the people of Israel] (12:8). God's restoration will open "a fountain for the house of David, and the inhabitants of Jerusalem" (13:1). John's association of Jesus with the figure of Zechariah 12:10 presents him as the pierced figure who enables David's restoration. By looking to him (cf. John 3:14; 8:28; 12:33–33), the people of God can enter into their long-expected restoration.[58]

The force of John's quotation of Zechariah 12:10 emerges more fully when it is considered as the closing quotation of the seven fulfillments citations of John 13–19. John has, as we have seen, an interest in portraying Jesus as king of Israel both through the specific language of kingship (1:49; 6:15; 12:13) and through Jesus' association with other, often Davidic, leaders of Israel (the shepherd; the True Vine), but the Gospel is equally interested in a portrayal of Jesus' kingship that can accommodate the fullness of rejection that Jesus faced, particularly in his betrayal, the ironic acclamation of him as "king of the *Ioudaioi*," and in his death. The quotations of Scripture in John's Farewell Discourse and passion narrative are the means by which John holds together Jesus' identity as Israel's true king with the utter humiliation of his rejection and death, and with the ongoing hostility that his followers will face. First, in the Farewell Discourse, the Fourth Gospel turns to Scripture to show how Jesus' betrayal and opposition are coherent with his royal significance insofar as Jesus' sufferings are the ultimate embodiment of a drama prefigured in the life of David (13:18; 15:25; 17:12). John then continues this work in the passion narrative with quotations of Scripture that associate Jesus' particular sufferings with those experienced by David (19:24, 28, 36). John's quotation of Zechariah 12:10 serves as the climax of its chapters-long effort to characterize Jesus as

---

[57] In keeping with the proposal that John (or John's source) works from the MT, the translation here follows the MT. The underlined text represents John's emendation.

[58] A messianic reading of Zech 12:10 is offered in *b.* Sukkah 52a.

a righteous sufferer like David.[59] Through this final citation, Jesus' death is presented as the fulfillment of Zechariah's description of a death that is a catalyst to restoration, specifically the restoration of Israel through the restoration of the house of David. Jesus dies as the pierced one – the dead, beloved son, toward whom Israel might look, and mourn, and then experience the opening of a fountain for a new life with God (Zech 13:1; 14:8; cf. John 7:37–39).[60]

John 18–20: Who Is the King of Israel?

We have seen that, beginning with chapter 11, John no longer records Jesus' interactions with the *Ioudaioi*, Pharisees, and chief priests in terms of debate. Instead, in chapters 11–20, John describes a division opening up in the Jewish tradition as people follow or oppose Jesus. This is dramatized in chapters 11–12 and presupposed in the narratives and themes taken up in 13–20. The nature of the division is Christological: John presents Jesus as the one who would bring about the future of Israel by presenting Jesus as the king who comes in the name of the Lord, as the figure described in Isaiah 53 and 6, as the True Vine, and as the Davidic, righteous sufferer. Each of these ways of viewing Jesus' identity also marks out a path on which the Jewish tradition must, in John's view, undergo a judgment about its truth or falsehood. The tradition cannot avoid the κρίσις about whether or not Jesus is who he claims to be.

John's narrative argument about the eschatological significance of Jesus for Israel comes to its climax in the final chapters of the Gospel. Here John (1) drives home the identity of Jesus as Messiah while also (2) presenting the Jewish leaders' rejection of Jesus as a rejection of God's kingship. In John's narration of these events, Jesus' embodiment of his messianic identity in his crucifixion and resurrection simultaneously exposes the falsehood of the alternative represented by the *Ioudaioi*.

As noted earlier, the Fourth Gospel requires of its readers a nuanced understanding of the title "Messiah/Christ." Jesus can,

---

[59] See here William Randolph Bynum, "Quotations of Zechariah in the Fourth Gospel," in *Abiding Words*, esp. 49–54.

[60] Cf. also John 4:13–14. Note that the validity of my interpretation does not depend on who "they" are in the words "*They* will look on the one *they* have pierced." See Menken, *Old Testament Quotations*, 178–179; Brown, *John*, II.954; and how John looks forward to this event in 3:14–17; 6:56–58; 7:37–39; 8:28; 10:14–18; 11:50–52; 12:32.

indeed, be called "Christ": ". . . grace and truth came through Jesus Christ" (1:17); ". . . these things have been written so that you might believe that Jesus is the Christ, the Son of God" (20:31).[61] Without interpretation, however, John finds the title inadequate to Jesus, particularly as it would imply military strength and/or restoration without suffering. Hence, the Evangelist distances Jesus from associations of messianic identity with royalty (6:15) or notions of a new Davidic kingdom (7:41–42) that would know no end (12:34). Marinus de Jonge's survey of how John handles messianic expectations is helpful here: "Christian believers may use and do use 'the Christ' as a designation for Jesus (1:41; cf. 7:41) – it is the central point the debate between Jews and Christians – but *this is a title that needs to be interpreted.*"[62]

This interpretation is exactly what John gives in the passion narrative. The Gospel has primed its readers to view the crucifixion as Jesus' glorification (12:23), as the event by which the ruler of the world is driven out (12:28–32); it has presented the exaltation (= crucifixion) of the Son of Man as the moment in which his identity will be revealed (8:28). John has described the suffering of the shepherd as the means by which God's people will be protected and gathered into one (10:11–16). It has presented Jesus' zeal for God's presence as the true cause of his death (2:17), and the lifting up (= crucifixion) of the Son of Man as the means through which eternal life becomes available (3:14–15). As noted earlier in this study, even when the Gospel comes closest to images of Jesus as a king entering Jerusalem (12:13–15) or fulfilling experiences once described by David (13:18 and passim), the Gospel consistently chooses images that subvert the idea of a messiahship that would be recognizable as glorious in human terms (cf. 12:43). Jesus enters Jerusalem on a humble donkey; he most closely approximates David in his betrayal and humiliation. In the quotation of Zechariah 12:10, John suggests that David's house is restored through the piercing of Jesus.

All of this makes John's embrace of kingship language in its passion narrative both perfectly fitting and deeply ironic. John's almost relentless application of this terminology to Jesus is yet another way in which the Gospel bends the language of kingship around the one it knows to be God's messiah. This begins with Jesus'

---

[61] See 1:41; 4:29; 9:22; 11:27.
[62] De Jonge, "Jewish Expectations about the 'Messiah' according to the Fourth Gospel," 252 (emphasis added). See also Maloney, *Johannine Son of Man*, 35–41.

presentation to Pilate, who opens his interrogation of Jesus sarcastically presupposing his kingship: "[So] you are the king of the *Ioudaioi*" (18:33).[63] Jesus accepts the title in his response ("My kingship is not of this world," 18:36). But it is an acceptance that Jesus nuances by stating that his royal power is not invalidated by betrayal or suffering. A worldly kingship would resist persecution at the hands its opponents, but the kingship of Jesus is not from this world, and that is why his followers do not struggle (ἠγωνίζοντο) against the *Ioudaioi* (18:36). Here, again, John is drawing out Jesus' identity as Messiah by relating it to his willingness to suffer. He *is* the king, but his kingship is proven by his, and his disciples', acceptance of suffering. As the narrative goes on, the very acts that would disprove Jesus' position as "king of the *Ioudaioi*" are, in fact, ironic validations of it. John presents Jesus as the Messiah who ushers in the future of Israel *through* suffering and dying. This takes dramatic form in 18:38–19:7.

The scene opens as Pilate's first interrogation of Jesus ends and he presents Jesus to the *Ioudaioi* as their king (18:39–40). The *Ioudaioi* ask for Barabbas' freedom and Jesus' death. From this point, Pilate's treatment of Jesus follows the logic of a "penal liturgy" that would mock Jesus' royal pretensions. In the Evangelist's hands, however, it is the hostility toward Jesus by his opponents, rather than Jesus' own royal claim, that is exposed as ultimately misguided.[64] John's effort to validate Jesus as the true king and to expose the failure of his opponents takes two specific forms in our pericope. First, as Per Jarle Bekken shows, the words and actions of the soldiers ("Hail, king of the *Ioudaioi*"; the crown of thorns; the purple robe, 19:2) reenact the Roman military practice of *appellatio imperatoria*. That is, John depicts the Roman soldiers mockingly lauding Jesus with an acclamation, crown, and act of enrobing reserved for a conquering emperor who had proven his worthiness in battle. "The *acclamatio* signified that they [the soldiers] looked upon their commander-in-chief as the personal *Victor* and *Imperator* proper."[65] However, what

---

[63] On this scene, see Martin de Boer, "Pilate in John," in *Narrativity in Biblical and Related Texts,* eds. G. J. Brooke and J. D. Kaestli, BETL 149 (Leuven: Leuven University Press, 2000), 141–158.

[64] See Joel Marcus, "Crucifixion as Parodic Exaltation," *JBL* 125.1 (2006): 73–87 (esp. 78, 87).

[65] Bekken, *The Lawsuit Motif in John's Gospel from New Perspectives,* 243–244. The specific clothing (a crown and a robe) are elements of this ritual; "Hail, Emperor" (*Salutare, Imperatorem*) was the acclamation that accompanied it (Bekken, 245).

the soldiers intend as a humiliating parody fulfills the terms of Jesus' kingship. The greater the abuse, the closer Jesus comes to his exaltation. Though they cannot possibly know it, the soldiers are in fact greeting, crowning, and enrobing the one to whom God has given all authority (5:22–23).

A second affirmation of Jesus as king in the midst of his suffering occurs in 19:5–6. After Jesus is humiliated by the soldiers, Pilate theatrically presents him to the chief priests and officers: "He brought Jesus outside, wearing the crown of thorns and the purple robe, and he said to them, 'Behold, the Man'" (ἰδοὺ ὁ ἄνθρωπος; 19:5). On a superficial reading, Pilate's presentation of Jesus simply declares, "Here he is!" (NRSV: "Here is the man.") Yet Pilate's words resound with deeper meaning. Francis Maloney has proposed that John's "Son of Man" statements, several of which refer forward to the lifting up of Jesus on the cross (3:13–14; 6:53; 8:28; 12:23, 32–34), find their ultimate expression in 19:5 as the Son of Man is fully revealed in the moment when Pilate *thinks* that he is the one judging Jesus but is, in fact, laying bare the truth of his own identity. Thus, for the believer who sees what is really happening in John 19:5, Pilate's words go beyond the superficial "Here he is" to an ironic affirmation of the true identity of the humiliated figure who stands enrobed before the crowd: "Here he is," Pilate declares, "the Son of Man."[66] John has pressed its readers to recognize the crucifixion as an act of exaltation, judgment, and revelation (cf. 3:13–21), and Jesus as the authoritative Son of Man (5:21–29). Here, through the guise of Pilate's declaration, the Evangelist signals to his readers that Jesus still possesses this authority and position (Dan 7:13–14), even as he experiences the extremes of humiliation.

It is, in fact, not only the narrative logic of John's numerous statements about the lifting up the Son of Man that suggests a deeper meaning within John 19:5. In Numbers 24:7 LXX, Balaam announces the coming of a man (ἄνθρωπος), a king, whose exaltation (ὑψωθήσεται) will set him above the kingship of Gog. Zechariah 6:12 envisions a messianic figure coming to restore the house of God, to be seated on and rule from a throne. "Behold, a man" (ἰδοὺ ἀνήρ), says the prophet as he looks upon the coming king. Though Pilate employs the term ὁ ἄνθρωπος rather than Zechariah's ἀνήρ, the broader imagery of God's deliverer referred to as a man, and a

---

[66] Maloney, *Johannine Son of Man*, 202–207. Bultmann, *John*, 350.

man with a particular commitment to the house of God (cf. John 2:17), suggests the likelihood that the Gospel's readers rightly recognize this added layer of meaning in Pilate's words. Philo and others who wrote in the broader, literary-historical context around the time of John exhibit an awareness of the designation "the Man" as a messianic title.[67] And, within the immediate context of John 19, the strong response of the crowd to Pilate's presentation of Jesus as "the Man" – they immediately call out, "Crucify him!" (v. 6) – likely picks up on messianic associations of the title. In other words, the crowd's words, "Crucify him," represent a rejection of Jesus by those who are viscerally offended by the use of *this* designation for *this* man. Yet, as they reject him in these roles (royal and messianic), Jesus' antagonists actually fulfill the conditions of his messianic identity. The reader of John knows what these characters do not: that messiahship entails suffering, and so the true king of Israel (and "Son of Man," and "Savior of the World") is, in fact, the one who is crowned, robed in purple, and stands before Pilate and the *Ioudaioi* in the vulnerability of his "sheer humanity."[68] He is ὁ ἄνθρωπος.

If Jesus draws closer to his messianic identity throughout his trial, suffering, and rejection by the *Ioudaioi*, his opponents, as they reject him, move further from an identity that is continuous with their own tradition. The Fourth Gospel demonstrates this as the hostility of the *Ioudaioi* toward Jesus leads them, first, to call for Barabbas (a λῃστής) rather than Jesus. And then it climaxes in the startling declaration of the *Ioudaioi,* who state, "We have no king but Caesar" (19:15). Many interpreters rightly note here the reversal of Israel's confessions of God as king in Judges 8:23 and 1 Samuel 8:7.[69] Two things are crucial to note, however. First, the rejection of God as king is concomitant with the rejection of Jesus.[70] As they reject Jesus, the *Ioudaioi* distance themselves from both the tradition's storied past and its eschatological future; they renounce the very God they claim to serve (5:37–38) and they offer their loyalty to Rome instead. Second, when the profession of 19:15 (to Caesar) is held together with the call of 18:40 (for Barabbas's release), the ultimate characterization of the *Ioudaioi* is not that they are tragically resigned

---

[67] Cf. Philo, *Mos.* 1:290; *Praem.* 95; Bekken, *The Lawsuit Motif in John's Gospel from New Perspectives*, 211–234.

[68] Again, the phrase is from Bultmann (*John*, 63).

[69] Cf. also Ps. 97:1; 99:1; Jos. *Ant.* 18.23; *War* 2.118; 7.410, 418; Meeks, *Prophet King*, 77–78.

[70] Cf. John 5:23.

to the political status quo (allegiance to Caesar), but that their eschatological hopes are simply incoherent. "Give us Barabbas" and "We have no king but Caesar" are poles apart in terms of a worldview, and yet for John they sum up the utter failure of the *Ioudaioi* to represent a valid option for the future of Israel because they both represent options that, by the late first century, had been disconfirmed as mechanisms for living into the eschatological hopes of God's people.

In many ways, the Gospel follows a traditional course in its passion narrative, but we have also seen that the themes John raises have a marked effect on the overall characterization of Jesus and the *Ioudaioi*. The arrest, suffering, and crucifixion of Jesus function positively in John as they describe Jesus entering fully into his identity as the suffering Messiah. These scenes also depict the *Ioudaioi* negatively, revealing (what John sees as) the full logic of their worldview, namely that a rejection of Jesus entails nothing less than a rejection of God as king. These are aspects of Jesus and his identity vis-à-vis the *Ioudaioi* that the Gospel has had in view since its opening chapters, which recorded the questions of the *Ioudaioi*, their uncertainties, and their hostilities toward Jesus, as well as Jesus' persistent teaching that his unique identity as the one sent by God (as Son, Son of Man, shepherd, king, etc.) entails also his suffering in this role.

As the narrative goes on, John 20 records the vindication of Jesus and those who believed in him.[71] The disciples are overjoyed at the sight of the risen Jesus (20:20). In their first encounter, Jesus greets them with declarations of peace (20:19, 21) and by breathing the Holy Spirit upon them. John's word choice here (ἐνεφύσησεν καὶ λέγει αὐτοῖς, λάβετε πνεῦμα ἅγιον; 20:22) is pregnant with meaning. Specifically, John recalls God's initial breathing of life into humans in Genesis 2:7 (ἐνεφύσησεν; cf. Wis 15:11), and, more prominently, the breathing of the Spirit onto the dry bones described in Ezekiel 37:9. We have seen already the importance of Ezekiel 37 and its context for John's presentation of Jesus as the one who will bring Israel into its prophesied future.[72] Here Jesus personally initiates the outpouring of the Spirit that Ezekiel had once described, as Jesus

---

[71] The *Ioudaioi* now recede into the background (cf. 20:19). This makes sense narratively: As characters, the *Ioudaioi* have no more development to undergo after 19:15.

[72] See above on 1:5, 14; 3:3–8; 4:1–42; 11:47–52.

gives to his disciples an experience of the long-anticipated future of Israel.[73]

When the Evangelist addresses the reader directly in 20:30–31, he admits why he has told *this* story and recorded *these* signs and not others. It was not for lack of material (20:30). It was, instead, "that you may believe that Jesus is the Christ, the Son of God, and that you may have life in his name."[74] Here the Evangelist fully embraces Jesus' identity as Messiah and Son of God (cf. 1:17–18). As we have seen, however, he does so only after an extended Gospel-long display of what it entails to think of Jesus in such terms. In the immediate context of the passion narrative and resurrection stories, it means that Jesus is the Messiah as the suffering and vindicated one. In the broader context of John's narrative, it means that Jesus is Messiah and Son of God in the scandalous particularity of a Galilean man (1:46; 6:42; 7:27, 42; 10:20–21); he is Messiah and Son of God as he embodies Israel's hope and offers to those who believe in him the experience of Israel's long-anticipated eschatological blessings (1:51; 2:19; 4:14; 6:35, and passim); finally, in John's view, Jesus is Messiah and Son of God as he both embodies a way for Israel to enter into its future *and* exposes the failure of the *Ioudaioi* and the stream of the tradition they represent to embrace the eschatological hopes at the heart of the tradition John and the *Ioudaioi* hold in common (12:13, 38–42; 15:1; 19:5, 15).

---

[73] John's use of ἐμφυσάω suggests the prominence of Ezek 37 for John 20:22, but see also Joel 3:1–5; Isa 32:15; Zech 12:10; Ezek 39:29.

[74] Here reading with the better-attested present subjunctive πιστεύητε. Cf. Brown, *John,* II.1056.

5

CONCLUSION: IMPLICATIONS FOR THE INTERPRETATION OF JOHN

[T]he unity of the Christian *ekklesia* with Israel must be affirmed; and, at the same time, some account must be given of why the manifest and bitter separation between church and synagogue, and the manifest rejection of Jesus by those to whom the interpretation of Israel's tradition formally belonged, did not constitute a fragmentation of the unity of God's act. What is clear in the New Testament is not that there can be a single systematic resolution to all this, but that these issues have a necessarily high priority, given the sort of thing the church is and the sort of thing its talking about God is ...

'Is it the same God' is a question not to be answered apart from the question, 'Is it the same hope' or 'Is it the same pattern of holy life?'[1]

***

As often in John, a particular narrative that takes up biblical imagery and subsequent interpretive traditions nevertheless can be understood by those unfamiliar with the milieu and, indeed, by those steeped in other religious contexts. But awareness of the scriptural context not only enriches the texture of the narrative; it also orients the reader to a particular narrative and to the God portrayed in it.[2]

This study has considered the Gospel of John as a historically situated narrative argument about Jesus as the figure through whom the eschatological hopes of Israel are realized. Detailed studies of numerous passages have shown that John's presentation of Jesus consistently turns to the Scriptures, traditions, ideas, and hopes that

---

[1] Rowan Williams, "The Unity of Christian Truth," in *On Christian Theology* (Oxford: Blackwell, 2000), 22, 23–24.
[2] Thompson, *John*, 64.

were common to Second Temple Judaism and bound up with how that tradition conceived of its eschatological future. John turns to these sources in order to interpret how the particular figure of Jesus embodies the hopes of Israel. By doing this, John shows how continuity between Israel's storied past and prophesied future becomes available through Jesus. As a gospel (a *bios*), John's argument necessarily takes the form of a narrative about Jesus' life. But the narrative is not an end in itself. It is the vehicle for this incisive, historically rooted argument about who Jesus is.[3] The aim of this conclusion is to sketch the interpretive significance of this reading as it relates to three areas of study.

The Historical Context of John's Gospel

Much recent scholarship interprets the Gospel out of a historical context that is fundamentally determined by the Johannine community's experiences of persecution and expulsion from the synagogue by Jewish opponents (or the perception/fear of persecution and expulsion by those opponents). To be sure, sociological experiences are an inescapable aspect of how people and groups approach the world. Yet the conclusions of this study point away from social trauma as providing a sufficient explanation for the argument made in the Gospel of John. In the view offered here, the primary historical condition that accounts for the Gospel of John is an *epistemological* crisis that requires a reappraisal of the coherence of the Jewish tradition. John's awareness of this crisis is undoubtedly bound up with the community's particular historical and sociological experiences. But the historical context of the Gospel as a whole should not be reduced to an account of one community's social trauma. The Fourth Gospel's ambitious effort to provide a narrative of Jesus' life that portrays him as the fulfillment of Jewish eschatological hopes calls for a more complex account of its historical context. Doing so does not deny the presence of polemic in John or even a conflict between Johannine believers in Jesus and other Jews (i.e., particulary those identifiable with the Gospel's *Ioudaioi*). As noted throughout this study, the Gospel's affirmations of Jesus as the one who fulfills

---

[3] Cf. Despite the flaws in his overall argument, Bornhäuser saw this correctly: "Der Evangelist Johannes bezeugt ein großes, heiliges Ringen Jesu mit den Pharisäern und "Judäern" um Israel. Und was er selbst als sein Gabe in seinem Evangelium gibt, steht gleichfalls in Diente deises Kampfes" (*Das Johannesevangelium*, 151).

Israel's eschatological hopes are often cast in terms that simultaneously negate some other figure as the organizing point for the Jewish tradition. Even at the moment of fiercest polemic, however, John's central concern is how belief in Jesus opens out onto the future of Israel and how unbelief leads the tradition further from its hopes. In other words, the argument is consistently determined by the question of how the tradition might move from its storied past, through its present, and into its prophesied future. Therefore, the best historical context for accounting for the Gospel of John is the context of the ongoing struggle of the Jewish tradition to arrange its present life with its past and future. The particular experiences of the Johannine community form one part of this broader context.

Is it possible to be specific about John's context beyond recognizing its interest in the pressing historical and theological questions facing late first-century Judaism? Though fixing the Gospel to a particular time and place is inherently difficult, there are certain settings that are particularly amenable to the general context described above. Klaus Wengst has argued that John's historical location must be a Gentile location in which Greek was the primary spoken language (hence the need for translation and transliteration in John 1:38, 41; cf. 1:42), and in which Jewish customs and ideas would require some explanation.[4] To complicate matters, however, Wengst also notes that John must come from a place in which a Pharisaic vision for Judaism would have sufficient organization and force that the evangelist could intelligibly refer to Jesus' antagonists as a single group ("the *Ioudaioi*"), which possesses a (locally) authoritative interpretation of Jewish practices *and* at least some degree of social power. Wegnst argues that these historical conditions were in place during the reign of Agrippa II in the Syrian regions of Gaulanitis and Batanaea (to the north and east of the Sea of Galilee). This particular location is supported also by the prominence in the Fourth Gospel of John the Baptist as a witness to Jesus – what better advocate for Jesus than a figure whose own ministry was independent of Pharasaic Judaism and operated also in the Transjordan? This setting appears possible also in light of the dispersion of Jewish Christians from Judea and into the region of Perea (south of Batanaea) with the fall of the temple in 70. The

---

[4] Wengst, *Bedrängte Gemeinde*, 75–81.

lynchpin of Wengst's argument is his observation that the nascent rabbinic movement enjoyed the support of Agrippa II, and therefore Batanaea serves as a favorable location for a late first-century community of Jewish Christians who lived in a Gentile region but under particular pressure from a Jewish community during the last decades of the first century.[5] It is not essential to Wengst's argument, but the possibility that John 1:28 might refer to Batanaea (βατανσία; rather than the text's Bηθανίᾳ) further supports this position: Micah 7 and Jeremiah 50 (cf. also Ps 68) envision Bashan (Hellenized as βατανσία) as the pastureland in which the people of God will one day flourish.[6]

In the setting sketched above, it would be easy to imagine expulsion from the synagogue (becoming ἀποσυνάγωγος) as the consequence of one's commitment to a radically innovative vision for the future of Israel. Such a social consequence would not require one to imagine late first-century Judaism as a monolith or to reconstruct a decisive council (Yavneh) that issued authoritative decrees (the Birkat Ha-Minim). The particular social context envisioned by the form-critical interpretation of John 9:22, 12:42, and 16:2, as well as other passages, is historically plausible regardless of the historical accuracy of *b.* Berakhot 28b–29a (cf. *t.* Berakhot 3:25) as reconstructions of a rabbinic Jewish council.[7] John's neologism ἀποσυνάγωγος and consistent designation of Jesus' opponents as "the *Ioudaioi*" suggest a historical and social location in which two groups of Jews (i.e., those who reflect belief in Jesus and those who draw their identity from the *Ioudaioi*) were acutely aware of the need for the Jewish tradition to reorganize its life in the decades after 70, and especially after the deaths or discrediting of many cultic, social, and political leaders in the decades before. According to John, in this charged environment there were profound social and personal consequences for proposing a differing vision for the future of Israel.

---

[5] Ibid., 82–93.

[6] See especially Douglas Earl, "'(Bethany) beyond the Jordan': The Significance of a Johannine Motif," *NTS* 55 (2009): 270–294.

[7] On the form-critical readings of John 9, 12, 16, and other passages, cf. Martyn, *History and Theology*, and Rensberger, *Johannine Faith.* See also Marcus, "Birkat Ha-Minim Revisited," *NTS* 55 (2009): 523–551; Boyarin, "Justin Martyr Invents Judaism," *CH* 70.3 (2001): 427–461; Boyarin, *Border Lines.* After *Border Lines,* I cannot argue that the Babylonian Talmud records historical tradition of a Yavnean council. After Marcus, however, I find the likelihood of intense, competing, and even hostile relations between some members of the Jewish tradition (e.g., the *Ioudaioi*) and some (also Jewish) believers in Jesus to be extremely likely in the period of 70–100, especially in Palestine and Syria.

An array of evidence reporting Jewish hostility toward the early Christian community can be found both in the New Testament (Acts 13, 14, 17, 18 [note, of course, that in Acts many *Ioudaioi* are not hostile]; Rom 15:31; 2 Cor 11:24; Gal 1:13; 1 Thess 2:14) and outside of it (Justin, *Dial.*, 16; 96, 110, 133, 137; Origen, *Homilies on Jeremiah*, 19.12.31). These texts combine with the witness of the Fourth Gospel to suggest that the Johannine community grew up within a historical and social location that both nurtured the community to take Jesus seriously as the one who brings about the future of Israel and also caused the community to face directly the consequences of such an idea from a group of Jews (=*Ioudaioi*) whose vision for Judaism had been determined by the pre-70 Pharisees, a vision that was on its way to developing into the rabbinic movement.[8]

The aim of this description of the general context for the Gospel as well as a further, and of course necessarily less certain, sketch of the particular time, place, and social location for the Gospel is to suggest a context that is adequate not only to the particular *Sitze im Leben* of various scenes of the Gospel but also to the historical and theological questions with which John as a whole concerns itself. John is a text that is embedded in a particular set of historical and theological questions. If Wengst is correct – and there is good reason to think he is – John's social, geographical, and historical context likely nurtured the overarching questions that drive its narrative, even if the Gospel is not, as a whole, reducible to those specific experiences.

All of this is to argue that a grasp of the general historical and theological questions that drive the Fourth Gospel is more hermeneutically significant than agreement about the particular experiences of rejection and social trauma faced by the Johannine community. To make this case it will be helpful to illustrate briefly the prominence of expulsion hypotheses as explanations for the historical context of the Fourth Gospel and to observe particularly how experiences of expulsion and persecution are regularly offered as the sole explanations for Johannine material. To do so, it is necessary to consider several of the most prominent contributions to Johannine scholarship from the past generation.

---

[8] I *do not* think it is accurate to identify in a simplistic way pre-70 Pharisaic identity, post-70 Pharisaic identity, and the early rabbinic movement. I find John's *Ioudaioi* to resemble the group Marcus Borg profiled as Pharisees in *Conflict, Holiness, and Politics in the Teachings of Jesus* (New York: Continuum, 1998 [New Edition]), 71–77).

In a touchstone essay on the Fourth Gospel, Wayne Meeks incorporates the insights of J. Louis Martyn and argues that after an initial stage of association between the Johannine church and the synagogue "the trauma of the ultimate rupture from the synagogue and the failure, in the main, of the mission [to the synagogue] left an indelible mark in the primary symbols of the group's identity."[9] In another important study, Meeks accounts for John's descent/ascent motif as a myth that interprets reality for the embattled Johannine Christians and offers a framework for the community as it struggles to understand its alienation.[10] For Meeks, the "indelible mark" of the Johannine community's rejection appears everywhere one looks: as he considers the Farewell Discourse, Meeks writes, "these chapters provide a poignant expression of the group's negative identity, their fear of being ὀρφανοί in the world (14:18)."[11] Decades later, Meeks continued to sustain such explanations of Johannine material:

> Many of the Gospel's stories of conflict reflect responses to the Johannine community's struggle to enunciate, by a daring reinterpretation of Jewish scripture and tradition, their understanding of Jesus' identity. [Meeks cites the Nicodemus episode and the attempt to stone Jesus in 10:22–42 as examples.] The struggle has both radicalized the Johannine Christians' interpretation and led to their being ostracized. The process of separation has also produced fear, which in this Gospel stigmatizes those who dare not speak openly about Jesus (7:13).[12]

In a memorable turn of phrase, Meeks suggests that John's Jesus does not reveal simply that he is the revealer (contra Bultmann), but John's Jesus "reveals rather that he is an enigma."[13] In a critical moment for Johannine hermeneutics, Meeks asks, "In what situation does a literary puzzle provide an appropriate means of communication?"[14] The answer Meeks leads his readers into is that a situation of profound social trauma calls forth a literary puzzle (John) and its enigmatic hero (Jesus). Many interpreters join Meeks in assuming the sufficiency of social trauma for understanding Johannine material.[15]

---

[9] Meeks, "Am I a Jew?" 183.   [10] Meeks, "Man from Heaven," 48–57.
[11] Ibid., 66.   [12] Meeks, "The Ethics of the Fourth Evangelist," 321–322.
[13] Meeks, "Man from Heaven," 57. Cf. Bultmann, "Die Bedeutung," 102.
[14] Ibid., 47.
[15] Although these works move in different directions, they all presuppose social trauma as the root context for the Fourth Gospel: Jamie Clark-Soles, *Scripture Cannot*

The exegesis of John in this study challenges the sufficiency of the social trauma hypothesis as the primary interpretive tool for contextualizing the Fourth Gospel. To be sure – and to give Meeks his due (and Martyn his) – experiences of expulsion and social trauma may certainly stand behind some scenes in John. They may account for the energy of the polemic in John 8, for example, or help explain a given term (e.g., ἀποσυνάγωγος) or motif (ἀναβαίνω/καταβαίνω). But when the explanation of these aspects of the text are transferred to the entire Gospel, the social trauma hypothesis shows that it cannot bear the weight of explaining the Gospel in the form that we know it. The Johannine believers do not, in fact, have a "negative identity." They are identified with Jesus as the one who fulfills key aspects of their tradition.[16] The Gospel evinces clear patterns of thought and a particular symbolic world, but it is not so inaccessible as to be called a "literary puzzle," nor does Jesus come across as a complete enigma. Instead, John presents Jesus as one who unapologetically makes innovative claims about himself. The scholarly tendency to interpret Johannine community experiences of social trauma as sufficient explanations for the form and content of the Gospel stems from a mistaken transference of genuine form- and source-critical insights regarding specific pericopae to the final form of the text. Interpreters wrongly read the historical experiences of the community that are preserved in the Gospel as not just contributing parts to the narrative whole but as tiny encapsulations of the meaning of the whole. The *Sitz im Leben* of John 9:22, 12:42, and 16:2 may be real experiences of persecution, but the Gospel of John is not *about* those experiences. It is about how Jesus is the one who can, in the significance and particularity of his own existence, bring Israel's past hopes and future expectations together, and it is about how Jesus'

Be Broken: The Social Function of the Use of Scripture in the Fourth Gospel (Leiden: Brill, 2003), esp. 207–315; Mary Coloe, *God Dwells with Us*, 10–11; Robert Kysar, "Anti-Semitism and the Gospel of John," in *Voyages with John*, ed. Robert Kysar (Waco: Baylor, 2005), 147–159; and see Robert Kysar, "The Expulsion from the Synagogue: The Tale of a Theory," in *Voyages with John*, 237–245); Jerome Neyrey, *An Ideology of Revolt*, esp. 33–35; David Rensberger, *Johannine Faith and Liberating Community*, 25–30; John T. Townsend, "The Gospel of John and the Jews: The Story of a Religious Divorce," in *Antisemitism and the Foundations of Christianity*, ed. Allan Davies (New York: Paulist Press, 1979): 72–89, cf. esp. 84–88; Gale Yee, *Jewish Feasts and the Gospel of John*, esp. 24–27. For a methodologically cautious adoption of this viewpoint, see James F. McGrath, *John's Apologetic Christology: Legitimation and Development in Johannine Christology,* SNTSMS 111 (Cambridge: Cambridge University Press, 2001), 34–68.

[16] Cf. the criticism of Meeks in Brown, *Community*, 59–62.

identity in this role forecloses the possibility of other ways of organizing Jewish life. What is needed is an approach to the historical context of the entire Gospel of John that is adequate to the whole without denying the validity of reconstructions as they relate to its various parts.

Doubtlessly, interpreters could offer differing accounts and emphases for John's context.[17] What follows here is one example of a more comprehensive, and also more complex, description of John's historical context that draws on various points of emphasis considered in this study: In the late first century, Jewish believers in Jesus (the Johannine community) experienced an epistemological crisis due to numerous factors. As a result of this crisis, they undertook concerted reflection on the Jewish tradition and their belief in Jesus, and they formulated the Gospel as a response, adopting and adapting traditions already accessible to them in order to tell the story of Jesus in a way that would demonstrate how they would resolve the crisis facing their tradition. The factors that were basic to the perceived epistemological crisis and their proposed solution included:

1. Jewish disbelief in Jesus as the Messiah, particularly disbelief within the group of the *Ioudaioi,* which, due to history and circumstance, was uniquely situated to inherit a leadership role with regard to (what scholars call) "common Judaism";
2. The particularity of Jesus' life (esp. his humanity and crucifixion);
3. The eschatological hopes of the tradition (as they are articulated both in scriptural and in extra-scriptural sources);
4. The events of recent history, including the Jewish War and the destruction of the temple.

Although the following two events are, as W. D. Davies once remarked, "on the twilight" of our historical knowledge, the community also recognized and responded to:

5. The nascent, but very real, emergence of the Pharisaic vision for Jewish life as one that offered a competing coherence to the post-70 Jewish tradition; and

---

[17] Paul Anderson ("On Guessing Points and Naming Stars," 311–345), offers four epistemic contexts important for John's Christology. These could, *mutatis mutandis,* be incorporated into an account of the Gospel's historical context.

6.   The experience of persecution and marginalization that members of the community knew firsthand, likely from other Jews who recognized the challenge of the Johannine innovation to the typical and/or emerging way(s) of construing the tradition's coherence.

The historical context of John is the community of Jewish believers in Jesus who experienced all of these things over the course of several years and eventually developed a response in the form of a narrative that presents Jesus as the one who embodies the hopes of Israel and exposes the falsehood of competing proposals. As argued in Chapter 1, John is a text primarily concerned with insiders, that is, with the community's understanding of how the various factors (esp. the six above) hold together within the tradition that would give meaning to Jesus' life and the life of his followers. The historical context that determines the final form of the Gospel is the context of a community's effort to articulate a coherent understanding of Jesus' messianic significance as it relates to Jesus' history, the community's past and present, the living tradition of Judaism in which it existed, and the biblical past and its prophesied future.

Excursus: Evaluation of the Works of Martyn, Brown, Smith, and Meeks

Because J. Louis Martyn, Raymond Brown, D. Moody Smith, and Wayne Meeks are particularly influential interpreters of John as I have come to understand the field, it will be helpful to clarify how my conclusions relate to their views of the Fourth Gospel and historical reconstructions of the Johannine community.

Martyn's contributions to Johannine studies have been the major catalyst for interpreters who see expulsion/social trauma as the primary context for Johannine material. Martyn prepared the way for this when, in his 1968 study, *History and Theology in the Fourth Gospel*, he shifted from viewing discreet scenes as instances of a two-level drama (e.g., John 9, 5, 7) to arguing that the community's life – and, presumably, its written gospel – embodies such a drama due to the ongoing presence of Jesus in the community through the paraclete. (This takes place in the transition into chapter 7 from chapters 1–6 in *History and Theology*.) Martyn further laid the groundwork for this reading in his 1970 article "Source Criticism and *Religionsgeschichte* in the Fourth Gospel," in which he proposed that the redaction and expansion of the "Signs Gospel" into the Gospel as we know it could be traced back to specific arguments and experiences with the synagogue. In other words, *expulsion was the catalyst for the redaction of community traditions/texts into what we know as the Gospel of John.* This article was only "a sketch" (his words), and I am not certain that Martyn would have approved of its insights being adopted in a programmatic way. Nevertheless, through these two works the foundation was laid for viewing expulsion/social trauma as the primary historical context for the Gospel.

Earlier in *History and Theology* (3rd edition, pp. 115–117), however, Martyn suggested that John takes up the challenge of reasoning about Jesus for an audience sensitive to scriptural arguments about his identity. To this end, the Gospel casts its bold claims about Jesus in terms that would be familiar to audiences who seek "midrashic" argument. Of course, John does this in a way that is utterly uncompromising with regard to the significance of Jesus. But the insight is important: John's extended engagements with Scripture, tradition, symbols, and expectations, do not always reflect a setting that is determined by trauma, but they do consistently reflect a context that is organized around pressing questions about Jesus' identity vis-à-vis Israel's eschatological expectations. In his 1979 essay, "Glimpses into the History of the Johannine Community," Martyn set forward a view that could easily support the position of this study: there Martyn proposed a complex set of social and historical tributaries that come together to make up the "final form" of the Gospel (i.e., the concerns of Johannine Christians, experiences and debates with a hostile synagogue, exposure to and cricitism of "crypto-Christians" [Brown's term], and the need to address other Christians beyond the Johannine community). Although this study has proposed a different account of the "tributaries," the complexity Martyn describes in his 1979 essay – and not one particular social trauma – is exactly what needs to be acknowledged with regard to the historical context of the Gospel in its final form.

Brown describes the historical conditions of the Fourth Gospel in detail in his study *The Community of the Beloved Disciple* (esp. pp. 59–91; cf. *John*, I.lxvii–lxxix). There he assigns the writing of the Gospel to "Phase II," i.e., a time in which a mixed set of influences came together, including contact with Gentiles and followers of John the Baptist, ongoing struggle with nonbelieving Jews (i.e., members of John's original tradition; this took form especially in episodes of persecution and denunciation), impatience with various expressions of inadequate Christian Judaism, and, finally, a desire for harmony with apostolic Christianity. This is a helpful, if at some points tenuous, reconstruction of the multiple concerns facing the Evangelist at the time of John's composition. Ultimately, Brown follows Schnackenburg in arguing that a text that was written in various editions may have various purposes [*John*, I.lxvii]. Hence, the Gospel's material about John the Baptist may refute late first-century sectarians of the Baptist; Jesus' replacement of the festivals may comfort Johannine Christians who have been expelled from the synagogue; and so on. The material derives from different sources and aims at different goals. Brown is therefore helpfully cautious about forcing a hypothesis of social trauma to do more explanatory work in John than it can be asked to do. But Brown's insight here comes at the expense of a more unified view of the historical context and narrative unity of John's final form. This study has aimed to offer an account of both the narrative unity and a historical context that would build on and improve Brown's work.

Smith cautiously advances the central importance of the conflict theory throughout his works. In the various essays in *Johannine Christianity* (Columbia: University of South Carolina Press, 1984), Smith refers to the traumatic experience of expulsion as the catalyst for Johannine theological development and the source of its polemical tone (*Johannine Christianity*, 21–24, 33–34, 181–182, 208–220; cf. also *John*, ANTC [Nashville: Abingdon, 1999], 33–38; *The Theology of the Gospel of John* [Cambridge: Cambridge University Press, 1995], 53–56). Yet Smith settles on a wider range of factors as responsible for the shape of the Gospel of John in its final form: "There are motifs in the Johannine literature that go beyond the controversy with Judaism and reflect a later stage in the development of the Johannine church. The farewell discourses seem to represent a principally inner Christian development, and to raise christological, eschatological, and ecclesiological issues arising apart from or subsequent to a break with the synagogue" (*Johannine Christianity*, 35; cf. "Judaism and the Gospel of John," in James H. Charlesworth, ed., *Jews and Christians: Exploring the Past, Present, and Future* [New York: Crossroad, 1990], 76–96). In the end, Smith's position is close to Brown's – namely, a desire to account for various aspects of the Gospel as products of various conflicts (a position I have no quarrel with), but also a lack of interest in viewing John as a text that makes a coherent argument (a position that I find insufficient to the narrative of the Gospel).

Meeks goes a step beyond these others in the way that he consistently turns to experiences of social trauma to explain Johannine material. In other words, in the writings of Martyn, Brown, and Smith, it is easy to see how a generation of scholars could *infer* the primacy of a social trauma for Johannine theology. (Martyn's work lends itself most directly to such an inference, though there is a shift toward a more complex historical background in his 1979 essay on John.) After Meeks, inference becomes assumption. Meeks's 1972 article "The Man from Heaven in Johannine Sectarianism" introduced "the sociology of knowledge" to Johannine studies. In that work, Meeks explored the social functions of Johannine symbolism, giving special treatment to the ascent/descent motif in the Fourth Gospel as a motif that secures the unique significance of Jesus against the claims and criticisms of other Jewish groups. "Jesus alone has access to heavenly secrets . . . the descent/ascent motif serves here [John 3:13] as a warrant for those secrets" (ibid., 53). Throughout the Gospel, the primary function of the ascent/descent motif is to account for why "the Jews" and those of "this world" cannot recognize Jesus (57–61). For Meeks, the ascent/descent motif functions as an etiology for the Johannine community: The motif creates a symbolic world that both explains and reinforces the community's estrangement from its parent community (68–71). After securing this understanding of the ascent/descent motif, Meeks takes an interpretive step similar to one made by Martyn: He takes his interpretation of one aspect of John and transfers it to the entire Gospel.

> The book defines and vindicates the existence of the community that evidently sees itself as unique, alien from its world, under attack, misunderstood, but living in unity with Christ and through him with God . . . One of the primary functions of the book, therefore, must have been to provide a reinforcement for the community's social identity, which appears to have been largely negative. (70)

What has happened is that Meeks's account of a motif has become a hermeneutic, one he would not fail to utilize in subsequent studies (see Meeks, "Am I a Jew?" 183, 185; "The Ethics of the Fourth Evangelist," 324–325). Many scholars, particularly those minted at Yale during his tenure, follow him in this.[18]

---

[18] I have in mind the works of Neyrey, Clark-Soles, and Rensberger (cited above, n. 15).

Having considered four of the most prominent interpretters of John in modern times, one can see that the decision to make social trauma the hermeneutical key to the Gospel of John traces its origins back to an interpretive move that was first taken by Martyn but then furthered and sustained by Meeks: Both of these scholars shift from explaining particular texts or motifs with reference to social trauma to explaining the Gospel *as a whole* as a text that emerges from a context that is fundamentally determined by social trauma. But it is Meeks who most fully models the decision challenged above, viz., that social trauma can serve as a *discrimen* for the Fourth Gospel, an imaginative act that is capable of ordering the material of the narrative and configuring it into a coherent and meaningful whole.[19]

The Theological Center of John

In 1999, R. Alan Culpepper reviewed the state of the question on Johannine Christology and noted that numerous major studies map the various titles ascribed to Jesus in the Fourth Gospel onto various stages of Johannine community experiences. The result of this approach, as he expressed it, was that a satisfactory account of Johannnine Christology has proven elusive due to the way in which historical studies of John's Christology have yet to be integrated with literary studies. Interpreters of John have many well-understood parts but little sense of the whole.[20] Two years later, Marianne Meye Thompson's study, *The God of the Gospel of John*, advanced interpreters' understandings of John's Christology by showing how it serves the purpose of revealing the identity of God, particularly as the God revealed by Jesus in the Gospel of John is the God of Israel.[21] But, organized as it is around theological themes (life, knowledge of God, worship, etc.), Thompson's insightful study does not undertake a description of how the various strands of Johannine theology/Christology serve to organize the literary whole

---

[19] David Kelsey outlines the role of a *discrimen* in his *Proving Doctrine: The Uses of Scripture in Modern Theology* (Harrisburg: Trinity Press International, 1999 [Orig., *The Uses of Scripture in Recent Theology* (Philadelphia: Fortress, 1975)]), 158–173. Since Kelsey's interest is in doctrinal uses of Scripture, the application of his analysis to Meeks's approach obviously has its limits.

[20] Culpepper, "The Christology of the Johannine Writings," in *Who Do You Say That I Am? Essays on Christology in Honor of Jack Dean Kingsbury*, ed. Mark Allan Powell and David R. Bauer (Lousiville: Westminster John Knox, 1999), 85–86.

[21] Thompson, *God of the Gospel of John*, esp. 48–55.

of the Gospel. If the main lines of the present study are correct, then two implications follow: first, Thompson's thesis about the basic orientation of John's Christology around the action of Israel's God in history stands out as a promising vantage point from which to approach John's Christology; second, Culpepper's search for an account of Johannine Christology that integrates historical and literary approaches might now have a helpful study demonstrating one form such an account can take. Reading John as a narrative argument about how Jesus might bring Israel into its future in continuity with its past offers a way of drawing together John's multifaceted Christology (including especially the many titles ascribed to Jesus) with a historically rooted theological question that runs through the Fourth Gospel and, indeed, the broader Jewish tradition of its time. Thus, this study builds on the works of Culpepper and Thompson, and it demonstrates a way of reading John that draws together the Christology of the narrative whole around the historical and theological question of how the Jewish tradition achieves coherence through faith in Jesus.

To this end, we have seen throughout this study that the Gospel's Christology regularly coordinates Jesus' identity with figures and symbols of eschatological importance. In numerous instances (e.g., as Memra, source of living water, bread from heaven), Jesus' identity is disclosed with language that other streams of the Jewish tradition did (or soon would) associate with the Torah and its life-giving role within Israel. These findings illuminate the way in which John's Christology draws on various symbols and figures in the Jewish tradition to articulate the unique role and significance of Jesus. Importantly, the Gospel presents its Christology in a way that is sensitive to the demands of its historical moment.[22] In contrast to Bultmann's well-known declaration that in John "Jesus reveals nothing except that he is the revealer," it should now be said that in John Jesus reveals that he comes from and returns to the God of Israel, and that he is the revelation of this God by the way in which he embodies particularly significant aspects of eschatological hope that had been nurtured in the Jewish tradition – namely, Jesus embodies God's word, God's commitment to nourish Israel through his own

---

[22] This statement of the literary/historical function of John's Christology does not deny that John's christological categories had a prehistory in the community (for an account of the conflicts operating in the Gospel's historical background, see de Boer, *Johannine Perspectives*).

presence, teaching, and the blessing of eternal life; Jesus is the source of the Holy Spirit, and he is God's way of providing for Israel a shepherd and vine who will lead the people into God's good future.

If the main lines of this study are correct, then interpreters of John are in a better position to recognize how the historical setting of John (i.e., the epistemological crisis outlined above) and the theological center of John (Jesus as one by whom the God of Israel leads the people of God into their eschatological future) are directly related to one another. John's historical context called forth an account of how those committed to the Jewish tradition might understand Jesus as one to whom people may entrust themselves in order to live in faithful continuity with Israel's storied past and prophesied future. The Gospel draws deeply (and often innovatively) on its tradition in order to characterize Jesus in exactly this way. As it does so, it organizes a Christology that functions as a historically rooted narrative argument.

John and Jewish–Christian Relations

The historical context and theological center of John discussed above lead into a third area, in which it is proper to ask: What does this reading of John imply for how the Gospel ought to be drawn into understanding Jewish–Christian relations? It is widely accepted that John is the absolute nadir of the New Testament treatment of Judaism.[23] Working out from this point, Christian and Jewish scholars regularly suggest that an ethical response to John's anti-Judaism can take one of two forms: (1) readers can historically contextualize John's anti-Judaism and then subject it to *Sachkritik* (usually to the love commandment), canonical criticism (expressing a preference for the argument of Romans 9–11), or they can refer John's anti-Judaism to the time-bound "contingency" of the text; alternatively, (2) scholars can confront John's anti-Judaism and condemn it without apology. The former approach is taken by Robert Kysar, D. Moody Smith, John Townsend, R. Alan Culpepper, and, with some important alterations, by Stephen Motyer; the latter approach is taken by Rosemary Radford Ruether and Michael

[23] See especially Ruether, *Faith and Fratricide: The Theological Roots of Anti-Semitism*, 116; Kysar, "Anti-Semitism and the Gospel of John," 156; Rensberger, *Johannine Faith and Liberating Community*, 139; Eldon Jay Epp, "Anti-Semitism and the Popularity of the Fourth Gospel in Christianity," *CCAR Journal* 22 (1975): 35–57.

Cook.[24] Adele Reinhartz, one of the few Jewish New Testament scholars to write on this topic, acknowledges the historical context of the Gospel's polemic but also locates it not only in one historical layer of the text but in the ideology present within every layer of the Johannine narrative.[25] She writes:

> It is not possible to explain away the negative presentations of Jews or to deny that the Johannine understanding of Jesus includes the view that he has superseded the Jewish covenant and taken over its major institutions and symbols. Any honest and engaged reading of the Gospel must surely acknowledge, and lament, the presence of these themes.[26]

One of the aims of this study has been to draw out the way in which John's presentation of Jesus often reflects a simultaneous commitment to the Jewish tradition *and* a strong criticism of those who construe the tradition differently. The positive aspects of John's Christology and its negative implications for those of the Jewish tradition (esp. *Ioudaioi*) who reject Jesus are interwoven with one another as aspects of John's narrative argument. Therefore, there should be no denying John's strong opposition to other ways of understanding the Jewish tradition.

Nevertheless, these two ways of interpreting John in the context of Jewish–Christian relationships do not address the central concern that John raises. If the thesis of this study is correct, then John's entire narrative argument is construed around the proposal that Jesus' life is good news for a people concerned with how the Jewish tradition might move into its future in continuity with its past. As we have seen in our exegesis, many of the terms, images, and symbols that John takes up to communicate this argument are rooted in a

---

[24] For references to the works cited here, see esp. n. 15 above. Culpepper's work at times dips into both categories; see R. Allan Culpepper, "The Gospel of John as a Document of Faith in a Pluralistic Culture," in *What Is John? Readers and Readings of the Fourth Gospel*, ed. Fernando F. Segovia (Atlanta: Scholars Press, 1996), 107–127; Michael Cook, "The New Testament: Confronting Its Impact on Jewish-Christian Relations," in *Introduction to Jewish-Christian Relations*, ed. Michael Shermis and Arthur E. Zannoni (Eugene: Wipf & Stock, 2003), 34–62; Michael Cook, "The Gospel of John and the Jews," *Review & Expositor* 84.2 (1987): 259–271.

[25] Michael Cook, "The Gospel of John: How 'the Jews' Became Part of the Plot," in *Jesus, Judaism, and Christian Anti-Judaism: Reading the New Testament After the Holocaust*, ed. Paula Fredriksen and Adele Reinhartz (Louisville: Westminster John Knox, 2002), 99–116.

[26] Ibid., 114.

discourse that has a broader historical context. Nowhere is an awareness of the context that grounds John's argument more vitally needed than in a reading of John 8:44 and 48 ("your father the devil," said to "the *Ioudaioi*"; "you have a demon," to Jesus). It was argued above that Jewish literature of this period consistently views the devil as the deceiver who leads Israel away from its God. To read John's language about being children of the devil or having a demon in abstraction from this historical context is to lose track of the true or false path for Israel that animates the terminology of John 8:44 and 48, in particular, as well as the Gospel's argument more generally.[27] The standard ways of assimilating John into reflection on Jewish–Christian relationships tend to read John in abstraction from the questions and conditions that undergrid its argument.

How should readers think about the ways in which John's Gospel has been read largely in abstraction from the historically rooted questions that shaped its argument? Without a doubt, it is Christian readers who bear responsibility for the failure to read John within the framework of its argument. Perhaps the Evangelist's use of strong terminology (in John 8:44) and/or his use of widely accessible symbolism (e.g., light and darkness) made it inherently likely that readers would lose awareness of the historically textured meaning of John's terminology. In other words, perhaps John lends itself to such misreadings. But an additional factor contributing to reading John in abstraction from the historical and theological questions that drive its narrative is the earliest reception of the Gospel. The first attempt to control the reception of the Fourth Gospel in the First Epistle of John shows a community that is clearly struggling with the basic implications of its Christology among believers, let alone with the more ambitious aspects of the Gospel's presentation of Jesus and his significance vis-à-vis the Jewish tradition, its Scripture, and its teleology as Israel. After this initial reception in 1 John, the Gospel went on to be received by groups that were conditioned by other questions and traditions: for example, among gnostics and into a

---

[27] Once one loses track of the historical and theological context that grounds a charge like "You are of you father the devil," it becomes inevitable that the interpreter will need to decide on her own what is the meaning of such a depiction. To read such a charge in abstraction from the set of broader historical and theological conditions that give such language meaning is to invite, or even require, the human imagination to undertake a theological task for which it is not qualified – namely, to decide apart from Scripture and its usage in a particular historical moment what it might mean to be associated with the devil or a superhuman expression of evil.

largely Gentile church during the second century. Thus, John was received into mainstream use by groups that were deaf to the questions and contexts that shaped the Gospel at the time of its composition.[28] The high cost of this reception history has been the severing of the Gospel from its original setting as a historically conditioned argument. Jews and Christians have paid dearly for this. This is obviously the case with regard to the ways in which John's particularized argument has been abstracted into more general anti-Jewish sentiment. But there are two other consequences of overlooking John's argument, and both of these have inhibited contemporary interpreters from thinking with John about Judaism.

First, interpreters of John have largely overlooked how the Gospel of John presents the crucifixion of Jesus as the dramatic act that can overcome Jewish unbelief, or at least the supernatural power behind it. The result is that readers of John typically construe John's view of "the *Ioudaioi*" around three observations but overlook the actual plot of the Gospel. The themes under which interpreters often reflect on the *Ioudaioi* are the following: first, interpreters survey Johannine polemic against the *Ioudaioi* by commenting on the Gospel's distinctive portrayal of the *Ioudaioi* as an often hostile monolith; second, interpreters lay out the possibility of hostile communal relationships (i.e., social trauma); and third, interpreters survey various ways in which Jesus takes up and fulfills/replaces symbols or hopes that were important in Second Temple Judaism. In organizing John's thinking about Judaism in this way, interpreters impose terms for thinking about John and Judaism that overlook the way in which John's plot frames the charged interactions of Jesus and the *Ioudaioi* so as to present the crucifixion as an act that might reverse unbelief.

In a Gospel that so obviously thematizes the problem of Jesus' broad-scale rejection by the *Ioudaioi*, it is crucial to note that the crucifixion of Jesus casts out "the ruler of this world" (12:31–32). The devil whose power once expressed itself through the violent rejection of Jesus no longer operates in the same way *after* the crucifixion. Indeed, it is the crucifixion that makes accessible the

---

[28] See Charles E. Hill, *The Johannine Corpus in the Early Church* (Oxford: Oxford University Press, 2004), 444; Rensberger, *Johannine Faith and Liberating Community*, 16–17. This detachment opens the way for supersessionist/mythologizing readings of the *Ioudaioi* in John's Gospel – a dynamic that Willie Jennings characterizes as a form of "Gentile hubris" (Willie Jennings, *The Christian Imagination: Theology and the Origins of Race* [New Haven: Yale, 2010], 167).

identity of Jesus and the eschatological promise of life that he offers. This is stated explicitly in John 3:14–15, 8:28, and 12:31–32. The quotation of Zechariah 12:10 in John 19:36 ("they will look on the one they have pierced") claims that the conditions of repentance are available now as a result of the crucifixion. It is, of course, possible to infer, as Martin Luther did late in his life, that after the crucifixion Jews prove themselves to be uniquely obstinate, since they do not believe, even now. But it is certainly more in line with Johannine thought to reason that, after the crucifixion, Jewish rejection of Jesus as the Messiah and Son of God must be accounted for *not* as a kind of embodied evil resistance, but rather as a struggle against minds and hearts that do not recognize the innovative and surprising resolution that Jesus embodies for those belonging to this tradition (2:17, 22; 12:16; 20:9). John suggests that such recognition might even require an act of healing by the God of Israel (12:40). Thus, after the crucifixion, the Jewish "no" to belief in Jesus cannot be traced back to the devil because the devil has been cast out; rather, after the crucifixion, the Jewish "no" to belief in Jesus must be referred ultimately to the God to whom both the Johannine community and its nonbelieving Jewish neighbors bear witness. It is necessary to add that, from within John's world of thought, violence in the name of Jesus is an unimaginable option, one that would disconfirm Jesus' messiahship and invoke the attributes of the devil (18:36; 8:44). Christians have a long history of choosing violence against Jews rather than the way exemplified by Jesus in John – that is, the way of truth-telling and willingness to suffer. Each time Christians choose hostility and violence, they reject the logic of John. Thus, the first consequence of reflection on John's relationship to Judaism in abstraction from the argument of the narrative is the problem of overlooking how John reflects on the seriousness of Jewish unbelief throughout the narrative with a view toward the revelatory importance of the crucifixion as (1) an eschatological act that breaks the power of the devil and ushers in new conditions for understanding the theological dimensions of the ongoing rejection of Jesus by the majority of "his own" and (2) as an ethical paradigm for suffering rather than responding to resistance, disbelief, or hostility with violence.

Second, failure to observe John's argument about how Jesus offers a way for the Jewish tradition to enter its future in light of its past has impoverished Jewish–Christian reflection by allowing one question (i.e., how should we understand John's ethically challenging view of the *Ioudaioi*?) to eclipse another question that is directly relevant to the historical and theological concerns of the text: namely, is our way of organizing our life before the God of Israel a truthful and coherent witness to the specific past we have inherited and the specific future toward which we live? The problem is not the desire to read John ethically and to exercise care in appropriating its viewpoints.[29] The problem is thinking that John's view of the Jewish tradition can be summarized without attention to this second question, one that is almost necessarily self-involving for the interpreter. In the Fourth Gospel, the Evangelist puts before his readers a very practical answer (belief in Jesus, including the social embodiment of such belief) to a very practical problem (how to sustain the Jewish tradition into the future in continuity with its past).[30] Interpreters of John inadequately consider the question of John and Judaism when they neglect this question that is central to the logic of the Fourth Gospel.

When considered from the angle of this study, the basic contribution of the Fourth Gospel to reflection on the relationship of Christianity to Judaism is the Gospel's presentation of Jesus as an innovative figure who mediates through himself continuity with Israel's past and future. John functions from within the Jewish tradition as an innovative proposal for its ongoing integrity. It presupposes the election of Israel, the validity of the Jewish tradition, and the tradition's faithful way of nurturing eschatological hopes. John's presentation of Jesus is an affirmation of the broader tradition, even as it presses forward an innovative proposal about it and, of course, argues against alternative ways of construing the Jewish tradition.[31] Johannine Christianity thus reflects an extended argument about how the late first-century Jewish tradition could live in fidelity to its past and into its future. When interpreters consider John's contribution to Jewish–Christian reflection primarily as the

[29] See R. Alan Culpepper, "The Gospel of John as a Document of Faith," 127. David Rensberger, "Anti-Judaism and the Gospel of John," in *Anti-Judaism and the Gospels*, ed. William Farmer (Harrisburg: Trinity Press International, 1999), esp. 152–157.

[30] See Rensberger, *Johannine Faith and Liberating Community*, 59–61, 113–116. In a different vein, see Andrew Byers, *Ecclesiology and Theosis in the Gospel of John*, SNTSMS 167 (Cambridge: Cambridge University Press, 2017).

[31] See further Reinhard Hütter, "'In': Some Incipient Reflections on 'The Jewish People and Their Sacred Scriptures in the Christian Bible' (Pontifical Biblical Commission 2001)," *Pro Ecclesia* 13 (2004): 13–24; Thompson, *God of the Gospel of John*, 208–217.

task of explaining historical and theological hostility rather than as the task of understanding a vigorously argued answer to a question that was (and for many remains) a central question of life before God, they distance themselves from a question that is central to the Gospel. Even today this question has the power to provoke searching criticism of the church that continues to read John and productive dialogue between Jews and Christians: Is our way of life a truthful and coherent witness to the specific past we have inherited and the specific future toward which we live?[32]

Conclusion

This study has argued that the Fourth Gospel is a narrative argument about how the Jewish tradition might live into its future in continuity with its past. As such, the Gospel's historical context reflects an array of influences and experiences, but at its core it is a context that is deeply engaged in an effort to conceptualize how Jesus offers an innovative continuity to a tradition facing a (perceived) epistemological crisis. John's theological center is closely related to this historical context: in a way that is as innovative as it is consistent, the Gospel's Christology characterizes Jesus as the one who embodies the eschatological hopes of the tradition. The Evangelist never states explicitly that his narrative serves an argument, yet he implies as much when he states that the Gospel narrative ("these things which were written") is intended to lead readers into faith in Jesus (20:31). Beyond the way that the Evangelist orients his own narrative toward a particular conclusion (and thus, as an argument), it is also historically appropriate to consider John as an argument when the Gospel is considered among other Jewish discourses of its time. This approach accounts for the Gospel's negative portrayal of the *Ioudaioi* and its positive portrayal of Jesus as a figure of unique significance in terms of Israel's past and future. To demonstrate these proposals, this study began by setting John within a broader account of Second Temple Judaism as a series of attempts by various groups

---

[32] The work of John Howard Yoder offers a helpful, and very Johannine, perspective for thinking about the possibilities of this question. See Yoder, *The Jewish-Christian Schism Revisited*, ed. Michael G. Cartwright and Peter Ochs (Grand Rapids: Eerdmanns, 2003), esp. 69–89. For critical assessments, see Peter Ochs, *Another Reformation: Postliberal Christianity and the Jews* (Grand Rapids: Baker Academic, 2011), 127–163; Daniel Boyarin, "Judaism as a Free Church: Footnotes to John Howard Yoder's *The Jewish-Christian Schism Revisited*," *Crosscurrents* (2007): 6–21.

to close the gap between various expressions of "Judaism" and the idealized entity of its past and future, namely "Israel" (Chapter 1). The study considered John's characterization of Jesus as a figure of primary importance in terms of Israel's past (i.e., as Memra; the one witnessed by Abraham: and in the writings of Moses and prophecy of Isaiah); it also considered John's Jesus as a figure of significance with regard to the tradition's eschatological future (the source of living water, true light, the bread from heaven, the Davidic figure whose suffering might initiate repentance) (Chapters 2–4). This concluding chapter has considered the significance of these claims for several aspects of the interpretation of John. If the path taken in this study is correct, then we have traveled in closer proximity to the historical argument of the Fourth Gospel than many interpreters have done throughout its long reception history. Yet success in this task only opens out onto a much more challenging one: to explore the contributions and criticisms that such a reading of John can provide to the communities that continue to be shaped by its voice.

SELECT BIBLIOGRAPHY

Ahr, Peter. "'He Loved Them to Completion:' The Theology of John 13, 14." Pages 73–89 in *Standing before God: Studies on Prayer in Scriptures and in Tradition with Essays in Honor of John M. Oesterreicher.* Edited by Asher Finkel and Lawrence E. Frizzell. New York: Ktav, 1981.

Alexander, Philip S. "'In the Beginning': Rabbinic and Patristic Exegesis of Genesis 1." Pages 1–29 in *The Exegetical Encounter between Jews and Christians in Late Antiquity.* Jewish and Christian Perspectives Series 18. Edited by Emmanouela Gryeou and Helen Spurling. Leiden: Brill, 2009.

———. "'The Parting of the Ways' from the Perspective of Rabbinic Judaism." Pages 1–26 in *Jews and Christians: The Parting of the Ways A.D. 70 to 135.* Edited by James D. G. Dunn. Grand Rapids: Eerdmans, 1992.

———. "What Happened to the Priesthood after 70." Pages 5–33 in *A Wandering Galilean: Essays in Honor of Seán Freyne.* JSJSup 132. Edited by Zuleika Rodgers et al. Leiden: Brill, 2009.

Anderson, Paul. "On Guessing Points and Naming Stars." Pages 311–345 in *The Gospel of John and Christian Theology.* Edited by Richard Bauckham and Carl Mosser. Grand Rapids: Eerdmans, 2008.

Ashton, John. *The Interpretation of John.* 2nd ed. Edinburgh: T&T Clark, 1997.

———. *Understanding the Fourth Gospel.* 2nd ed. Oxford: Oxford University Press, 2007.

Baron, Lori. "The Shema in the Gospel of John." PhD Diss., Duke University, 2016.

Barrett, C. K. *Essays on John.* Philadelphia: Westminster Press, 1982.

———. *The Gospel according to St. John.* 2nd ed. Philadelphia: Westminster, 1978.

———. *The Gospel of John and Judaism.* 1st American ed. Philadelphia: Fortress, 1975.

———. "The Lamb of God." *NTS* 1 (1955): 210–218.

———. "The Old Testament in the Fourth Gospel." *JTS* 48.2 (1947): 155–169.

Bauckham, Richard. *Gospel of Glory: Major Themes in Johannine Theology.* Grand Rapids: Baker Academic, 2015.

———. *Jesus and the God of Israel: God Crucified and Other Studies on the New Testament's Christology of Divine Identity.* Grand Rapids: Eerdmans, 2009.

"John and Qumran: Is There a Connection?" Pages 267–279 in *The Scrolls and the Scriptures: Qumran Fifty Years After*. JSPSS 26. Edited by Stanley E. Porter and Craig E. Evans. Sheffield: Sheffield Academic Press, 1997.

"John for Readers of Mark." Pages 141–171 in *The Gospel for All Christians*. Edited by Richard Bauckham. Grand Rapids: Eerdmans, 1998.

Bekken, Per Jarle. *The Lawsuit Motif in John's Gospel from New Perspectives: Jesus Christ, Crucified Criminal and Emperor of the World*. NovTSup 158. Leiden: Brill, 2015.

Betz, Otto. "To Worship in Spirit and in Truth: Reflections on John 4, 20–26." Pages in 53–72 in *Standing before God: Studies on Prayer in Scripture and in Tradition with Essays in Honor of John M. Oesterreicher*. Edited by Asher Finkel and Lawrence Frizzell. New York: Ktav, 1981.

Beutler, Johannes. *Das Johannesevangelium*. Freiburg: Herder, 2013.

Judaism and the Jews in the Gospel of John. SubBi 30. Rome: Editrice Pontificio Instituto Biblico, 2006.

Beutler, Johannes and Robert Fortna. *The Shepherd Discourse of John 10 and Its Context*. SNTSMS 67. Cambridge: Cambridge University Press, 1991.

Borgen, Peder. *Bread from Heaven: An Exegetical Study of the Concept of Manna in the Gospel of John and the Writings of Philo*. Leiden: Brill, 1965.

"The Sabbath Controversy in John 5:1–18 and Analogous Controversy Reflected in Philo's Writings." *Studia Philonica* 3 (1991): 209–221.

Bornhäuser, Karl. *Das Johannesevangelium: Eine Missionsschrift für Israel*. Gütersloh: C. Bertelsmann, 1928.

Boyarin, Daniel. *Border Lines: The Partition of Judaeo-Christianity*. Philadelphia: University of Pennsylvania Press, 2004.

"The Gospel of the Memra: Jewish Binitarianism and the Prologue to John." *HTR* 94.3 (July 2001): 243–284.

"The IOUDAIOI in John and the Prehistory of 'Judaism.'" Pages 216–239 in *Pauline Conversations in Context: Essays in Honor of Calvin J. Roetzel*. JSNTSup. Edited by Janice Capel Anderson, Philip Sellew, and Claudia Setzer. London: Sheffield Academic Press, 2002.

The Jewish Gospels. New York: The New Press, 2012.

"Justin Martyr Invents Judaism." *CH* 70.3 (2001): 427–461.

"What Kind of Jew Is the Evangelist?" Pages 109–153 in *Those Outside: Noncanonical Readings of the Canonical Gospels*. Edited by George Aichele and Richard Walsh. London: T&T Clark, 2005.

Brendsal, Daniel J. *"Isaiah Saw His Glory": The Use of Isaiah 52–53 in John 12*. BZNT 208. Berlin: de Gruyter, 2014.

Brown, Raymond. *The Community of the Beloved Disciple: The Life, Loves and Hates of an Individual Church in New Testament Times*. New York: Paulist Press, 1978.

An Introduction to the Gospel of John. New York: Doubleday, 2003.

The Gospel according to John. AB 29–29A. Garden City: Doubleday, 1966–1970.

Bultmann, Rudolf. "Die Bedeutung der neuerschlossenen mandäischen und manichäischen Quellen für das Verständnis des Johannesevangeliums." *ZNW* 24 (1925): 100–146.

——. "The History of Religions Background of the Prologue to the Gospel of John." Pages 27–41 in *The Interpretation of John*. 2nd ed. Edited by John Ashton. Edinburgh: T&T Clark, 1997. (Originally published as "Der religionsgeschichtliche Hintergrund des Prologs zum Johannes-Evangelium." Pages 1–26 in *Eucharisterion: Festschrift für Hermann Gunkel*. Edited by Hans Schmidt. Göttingen: Vandenhoeck & Ruprecht, 1923.)

——. *The Gospel of John: A Commentary*. Translated by G. R. Beasley-Murray. Philadephia: Westminster Press, 1971.

Burns, Joshua Ezra. "Like Father, Like Son: An Example of Jewish Humor in the Gospel of John." Pages 27–43 in *Portraits of Jesus: Studies in Christology*. Edited by Susan E. Myers. WUNT 2/321. Tübingen: Mohr Siebeck, 2012.

Byers, Andrew. *Ecclesiology and Theosis in the Gospel of John*. SNTSMS 167. Cambridge: Cambridge University Press, 2017.

Childs, Brevard. *Isaiah*. OTL. Louisville: Westminster John Knox, 2001.

Chilton, Bruce. "The Gospel according to John's Rabbi Jesus." *BBR* 25.1 (2015): 39–54.

Clark-Soles, Jaime. *Scripture Cannot Be Broken: The Social Function of the Use of Scripture in the Fourth Gospel*. Boston: Brill, 2003.

Coloe, Mary. "'Behold the Lamb of God': John 1:29 and the Tamid Service." Pages 337–350 in *Rediscovering John: Essays on the Fourth Gospel in Honour of Fréderic Manns*. Edited by Lesław Daniel Chrupcała. Milan: Edizioni Terra Santa, 2013.

——. *God Dwells with Us: Temple Symbolism in the Fourth Gospel*. Collegeville: The Liturgical Press, 2001.

Cook, Michel. "The Gospel of John and the Jews." *Review & Expositor* 84.2 (1987): 259–271.

Cowley, A. E. *Aramaic Papyri of the Fifth Century B.C.* Oxford: Clarendon Press, 1923.

Culpepper, R. Alan. *Anatomy of the Fourth Gospel*. Philadelphia: Fortress, 1983.

——. "The Christology of the Johannine Writings." Pages 66–87 in *Who Do You Say That I Am? Essays on Christology in Honor of Jack Dean Kingsbury*. Edited by Mark Allan Powell and David R. Bauer. Louisville: Westminster John Knox, 1999.

——. "The Gospel of John as a Document of Faith in a Pluralistic Culture." Pages 107–127 in *What Is John? Readers and Readings of the Fourth Gospel*. Edited by Fernando F. Segovia. Atlanta: Scholars Press, 1996.

——. ed., *Critical Readings in John 6*. BIS 22. Leiden: Brill, 1997.

Dahl, Nils. "'Do Not Wonder!' John 5:28–20 and Johannine Eschatology Once More." Pages 322–336 in *The Conversation Continues: Studies in Paul & John in Honor of J. Louis Martyn*. Edited by Robert T. Fortna and Beverly R. Gaventa. Nashville: Abingdon, 1990.

——. *Jesus in the Memory of the Early Church*. Minneapolis: Augsburg, 1976.

Dahms, John V. "Isaiah 55:11 and the Gospel of John." *EvQ* 53.2 (1981): 78–88.

Daise, Michael. *Jewish Feasts in the Gospel of John.* WUNT 2/229. Tübingen: Mohr Siebeck, 2007.

Daly-Denton, Margaret. *David in the Fourth Gospel: The Johannine Reception of the Psalms.* AGJU 47. Leiden: Brill, 2000.

Daube, David. "Jesus and the Samaritan Woman: The Meaning of Synchraomai." *JBL* 69.2 (1950): 137–147.

Davies, W. D. "Aspects of the Jewish Background of the Gospel of John." Pages 43–64 in *Exploring the Gospel of John: Essays in Honor of D. Moody Smith.* Edited by R. Alan Culpepper and C. Clifton Black. Louisville: Westminster John Knox, 1996.

de Boer, Martinus C. "Historical Criticism, Narrative Criticism, and the Gospel of John." *JSNT* 47 (1992): 35–48.

Johannine Perspectives on the Death of Jesus. CBET 17. Kampen: Kok Pharos, 1996.

"The Original Prologue to the Gospel of John." *NTS* 61 (2015): 448–467.

"Pilate in John." Pages 141–158 in *Narrativity in Biblical and Related Texts.* Edited by G. J. Brooke and J. D. Kaestli. BETL 149. Leuven: Leuven University Press, 2000.

de Jonge, Marinus. "Jewish Expectations about the 'Messiah' according to the Fourth Gospel." *NTS* 19 (1973): 246–270.

de la Potterie, Ignace. "L'emploi de εἰς dans S. Jean et sens incidences théologiques." *Bib* 43.3 (1962): 366–387.

"'Nous adorons, nous, ce que nous connaissons, car le salut vient de Jiufs': Historie de l'exégèse et interprétation de Jn 4,22." *Bib* 64.1 (1983): 74–115.

Dennis, John A. *Jesus' Death and the Gathering of True Israel: The Johannine Appropriation of Restoration Theology in the Light of John 11.47-52.* WUNT 2/217. Tübingen: Mohr Siebeck, 2006.

Devillers, Luc. "Le prologue du quatrième évangile, clé de voûte de la littérature johannique." *NTS* 58.3 (2012): 317–330.

Dodd, C. H. *Historical Tradition in the Fourth Gospel.* Cambridge: Cambridge University Press, 1963.

The Interpretation of the Fourth Gospel. Cambridge: Cambridge University Press, 1965.

More New Testament Studies. Grand Rapids: Eerdmans, 1968.

Dunn, James D. G. "The Embarrassment of History: Reflections on the Problem of 'Anti-Judaism' in the Fourth Gospel." Pages 41–60 in *Anti-Judaism and the Fourth Gospel.* Edited by R. Bieringer et al. Louisville: Westminster John Knox, 2001.

"Let John Be John." Pages 309–339 in *Das Evangelium und die Evangelien: Vorträge vom Tübinger Symposium 1982.* Edited by Peter Stuhlmacher. WUNT 1/28. Tübingen: Mohr Siebeck, 1983.

Earl, Douglas. "'(Bethany) beyond the Jordan': The Significance of a Johannine Motif." *NTS* 55 (2009): 270–294.

Epp, Eldon Jay. "Anti-Semitism and the Popularity of the Fourth Gospel in Christianity." *CCAR Journal* 22 (1975): 35–57.

Evans, Craig A. "Obduracy and the Lord's Servant: Some Observations on the Use of the Old Testament in the Fourth Gospel." Pages 221–236 in *Early Jewish and Christian Exegesis*. Edited by Craig A. Evans and William F. Stinespring. Atlanta: Scholars Press, 1987.

——— . *To See and Not Perceive: Isaiah 6.9–10 in Early Jewish and Christian Interpretation*. JSOTSup 64. Sheffield: Sheffield Academic Press, 1989.

Felsch, Dorit. *Die Feste im Johannesevangelium: Jüdische Tradition und christologische Deutung*. WUNT 2/308. Tübingen: Mohr Siebeck, 2011.

Ford, David. "Reading Backward, Reading Forwards, and Abiding: Reading John in the Spirit Now." *JTI* 11.1 (2017): 69–84.

Förster, Hans. "Die Begegnung am Brunnen (Joh 4.4–42) im Licht der Schrift." *NTS* 61 (2015): 201–218.

Freed, E. D. *Old Testament Quotations in the Gospel of John*. NovTSupp 11. Leiden: Brill, 1965.

Frey, Jörg. *Die Herrlichkeit des Gekreuzigten*. WUNT 2/307. Tübingen: Mohr Siebeck, 2013.

Fuglseth, Kåre Sigvald. *Johannine Sectarianism in Perspective: A Sociological, Historical, and Comparative Analysis of Temple and Social Relationships in the Gospel of John, Philo and Qumran*. NovTSup 119. Leiden: Brill, 2005.

Gärtner, Bertil E. *John 6 and the Jewish Passover*. ConBNT 17. Gleerup: Lund, 1959.

Giblin, C. H. "The Miraculous Crossing of the Sea: John 6.16–21." *NTS* 29.1 (1983): 96–103.

Glasson, T. Francis. *Moses in the Fourth Gospel*. London: SCM, 1963.

Hakola, Raimo. *Identity Matters: John, the Jews and Jewishness*. NovTSup 118. Leiden: Brill, 2005.

Hanson, A. T. "John 1:14–18 and Exodus XXXIV." *NTS* 23.1 (1976): 90–101.

Hartley, Donald. "Destined to Disobey: Isaiah 6:10 in John 12:37–41." *CTJ* 44 (2009): 263–287.

Hengel, Martin. *Die johanneische Frage: Ein Lösungsversuch*. WUNT 1/67. Tübingen: Mohr Siebeck, 1993.

Hill, Charles E. *The Johannine Corpus in the Early Church*. Oxford: Oxford University Press, 2004.

Hoskyns, Edwyn. *The Fourth Gospel*. London: Faber and Faber, 1956.

Johnson, Luke Timothy. "John and Thomas in Context: An Exercise in Canonical Criticism." Pages 284–309 in *The Word Leaps the Gap: Essays on Scripture and Theology in Honor of Richard B. Hays*. Edited by J. Ross Wagner, C. Kavin Rowe, and Katherine Grieb. Grand Rapids: Eerdmans, 2008.

Käsemann, Ernst. *Testament of Jesus: According to John 17*. Philadelphia: Fortress, 1968.

Keener, Craig. *The Gospel of John: A Commentary*. 2 vols. Grand Rapids: Baker Academic, 2010.

Keith, Chris. *The Pericope Adulterae, the Gospel of John, and the Literacy of Jesus*. NTTSD 38. Leiden: Brill, 2009.

Kerr, Alan R. *The Temple of Jesus' Body: The Temple Theme in the Gospel of John*. JSNTSup 220. Sheffield: Sheffield Academic Press, 2002.

Koester, Craig R. "'The Savior of the World' (John 4:42)." *JBL* 109 (1990): 668–674.

Symbolism in the Fourth Gospel: Meaning, Mystery, Community. 2nd ed. Minneapolis: Augsburg, 2003.

Köstenberger, Andreas. "The Destruction of the Second Temple and the Composition of the Fourth Gospel." Pages 69–108 in *Challenging Perspectives on the Gospel of John*. Edited by John Lierman. WUNT 2/219. Tübingen: Mohr Siebeck, 2006.

Kovacs, Judith L. "'Now Shall the Ruler of This World Be Driven Out': Jesus' Death as Cosmic Battle in John 12:20–36." *JBL* 114.2 (1995): 227–247.

Kuyper, Lester. "Grace and Truth: An Old Testament Description of God, and Its Use in the Johannine Gospel." *Int* 18 (1964): 3–19.

Kysar, Robert. *Voyages with John: Charting the Fourth Gospel*. Waco: Baylor University Press, 2005.

Larsen, Kasper Bro, ed. *The Gospel of John as Genre Mosaic*. SANt 3. Göttingen: Vandenhoeck & Ruprecht, 2015.

Lett, Jonathan. "The Divine Identity of Jesus as the Reason for Israel's Unbelief in John 12:36–43." *JBL* 135.1 (2016): 159–173.

Leung, Mavis. *The Kingship-Cross Interplay in the Gospel of John: Jesus's Death as Corroboration of His Royal Messiahship*. Eugene: Wipf & Stock, 2011.

Lewis, Karoline M. *Rereading the Shepherd Discourse: Restoring the Integrity of John 9:39–10:21*. SBL 113. New York: Peter Lang, 2008.

Lieu, Judith M. "Blindness in the Johannine Tradition." *NTS* 34 (1988): 83–95.

Lincoln, Andrew. *Truth on Trial: The Lawsuit Motif in the Fourth Gospel*. Peabody: Hendrickson, 2000.

Maloney, Francis J. *Belief in the Word: Reading the Fourth Gospel: John 1–4*. Minneapolis: Fortress, 1993.

The Gospel of John: Text and Context. Leiden: Brill, 2005.

The Johannine Son of Man. Biblioteca di Scienze Religiose 14. Rome: LAS, 1976.

John. SP 4. Collegeville: The Liturgical Press, 1988.

Signs and Shadows: Reading John 5–13. Minneapolis: Fortress, 1996.

"Who Is 'the Reader' in/of the Fourth Gospel." *ABR* 40 (1992): 20–33.

Martyn, J. Louis. "Glimpses into the History of the Johannine Community." Pages 149–175 in *L'Evangile de Jean: Sources, rédaction, théologie*. Edited by M. de Jonge. BETL 44. Leuven: Leuven University Press, 1977.

The Gospel of John and Christian History: Essays for Interpreters. New York: Paulist Press, 1978.

History and Theology in the Fourth Gospel. 3rd ed. Louisville: Westminster John Knox, 2003.

Mason, Steve. "Jews, Judeans, Judaizing, Judaism: Problems of Categorization in Ancient History." *JSJ* 38 (2007): 457–512.

McGrath, James F. *John's Apologetic Christology: Legitimation and Development in Johannine Christology*. SNTMS 111. Cambridge: Cambridge University Press, 2001.

McHugh, John. *A Critical and Exegetical Commentary on John 1–4*. ICC. New York: T & T Clark, 2009.

"In Him Was Life." Pages 123–58 in *Jews and Christians: The Parting of the Ways A.D. 70–135*. Edited by James D. G. Dunn. Tübingen: J.C.B. Mohr, 1992.

McWhirter, Jocelyn. *The Bridegroom Messiah and the People of God: Marriage in the Fourth Gospel*. SNTMS 138. Cambridge: Cambridge University Press, 2006.

Meeks, Wayne A. "Am I a Jew? – Johannine Christianity and Judaism." Pages 163–186 in *Christianity, Judaism and Other Greco-Roman Cults*. Edited by Jacob Neusner and Morton Smith. Leiden: Brill, 1975.

"The Ethics of the Fourth Evangelist." Pages 317–326 in *Exploring the Gospel of John: Essays in Honor of D. Moody Smith*. Edited by R. Alan Culpepper and C. Clifton Black. Louisville: Westminster John Knox, 1996.

"Equal to God." Pages 309–321 in *The Conversation Continues: Studies in Paul & John in Honor of J. Louis Martyn*. Edited by Robert T. Fortna and Beverly R. Gaventa. Nashville: Abingdon, 1990.

"The Man from Heaven in Johannine Sectarianism." *JBL* 91.1 (1972): 44–72.

The Prophet-King: Moses Traditions and the Johannine Christology. NovTSup 14. Leiden: Brill, 1967.

Menken, Maarten J. J. "Die Feste im Johannesevangelium." Pages 269–286 in *Israel und seine Heilstraditionen im Johannesevangelium: Festgabe für Johannes Beutler SJ zum 70. Geburtstag*. Edited by Michael Labahn. München: Paderborn, 2004.

Old Testament Quotations in the Fourth Gospel: Studies in Textual Form. Kampen: Pharos, 1996.

Moser, Marion. *Schriftdiskurse im Johannesevangelium*. WUNT 2/380. Tübingen: Mohr Siebeck, 2014.

Motyer, Stephen. "The Fourth Gospel and the Salvation of Israel: An Appeal for a New Start." Pages 83–100 in *Anti-Judaism and the Fourth Gospel*. Edited by R. Bieringer et al. Louisville: Westminster John Knox, 2001.

Your Father the Devil? A New Approach to John and the Jews. Carlisle: Paternoster, 1997.

Myers, Alicia D., and Bruce G. Schuchard, eds. *Abiding Words: The Use of Scripture in the Gospel of John*. Atlanta: SBL Press, 2015.

Neyrey, Jerome H. "'I Said: You Are Gods': Psalm 82:6 and John 10." *JBL* 108.4 (1989): 647–663.

An Ideology of Revolt: John's Christology in Social-Scientific Perspective. Philadelphia: Fortress, 1988.

"The Jacob Allusions in John 1:51." *CBQ* 44 (1982): 586–605.

"Jacob Traditions and the Interpretation of John 4:10–26." *CBQ* 41 (1979): 419–437.

"Jesus the Judge: Forensic Process in John 8:21–59." *Bib* 68.4 (1987): 509–542.

Odeburg, Hugo. *The Fourth Gospel: Interpreted in Its Relation to Contemporaneous Religious Currents in Palestine and the Hellenistic-Oriental World*. Uppsala: Almqvist & Wiksells Boktryckeri, 1929.

Painter, John. "The Church and Israel in the Gospel of John: A Response." *NTS* 25 (1978): 103–112.

"The Quotation of Scripture and Unbelief in John 12:36b–43." Pages 429–458 in *The Gospels and the Scriptures of Israel*. Edited by Craig Evans and William Stegner. JSNTSup 104. Sheffield: Sheffield Academic Press, 1994.

Pamment, Margaret. "The Meaning of *doxa* in the Fourth Gospel." *ZNW* 74 (1983): 12–16.

Pancaro, Severino. "People of God in St. John's Gospel." *NTS* 16 (1970): 114–129.

"The Relationship of the Church to Israel in the Gospel of John." *NTS* 21 (1975): 396–405.

Pedersen, Sigfred. "Anti-Judaism in John's Gospel: John 8." Pages 172–193 in *New Readings in John: Literary and Theological Perspectives. Essays from the Scandinavian Conference on the Fourth Gospel, Århus 1997*. Edited by Johannes Nissen and Sigfred Pedersen. JSNTSup 182. Sheffield: Sheffield Academic Press, 1989.

Petersen, Silke. *Brot, Licht, Weinstock: Intertextuelle Analysen johanneischer Ich-bin-Worte*. NovTSup 127. Leiden: Brill, 2008.

Reim, Günter. "Joh. 8.44 – Gotteskinder/Teufelskinder: wie antijudaistisch ist 'die wohl antijudaistischte Ausserung des NT?" *NTS* 30 (1984): 619–624.

"Wie der Evangelist Johannes gemäß Joh 12,37ff. Jesaja 6 hat gelesen." *ZNW* 92 (2001): 33–46.

Reinhartz, Adele. *Befriending the Beloved Disciple: A Jewish Reading of the Gospel of John*. New York: Continuum, 2001.

"The Gospel of John: How 'the Jews' Became Part of the Plot." Pages 99–116 in *Jesus, Judaism, and Christian Anti-Judaism: Reading the New Testament After the Holocaust*. Edited by Paula Fredriksen and Adele Reinhartz. Louisville: Westminster John Knox, 2002.

"Incarnation and Covenant: The Fourth Gospel Through the Lens of Trauma Theory." *Int* 69.1 (2015): 35–48.

"The Johannine Community and Its Jewish Neighbors: A Reappraisal." Pages 111–138 in *What Is John? Volume 2: Literary and Social Readings of the Fourth Gospel*. Edited by Fernando Segovia. Atlanta: Scholars Press, 1996.

"John 8:31–59 from a Jewish Perspective." Pages 787–797 in *Remembering for the Future: The Holocaust in an Age of Genocide*. Edited by John K. Roth et al. Volume 2. New York: Palgrace, 2001.

"The Vanishing Jews of Antiquity." *Marginalia Review of Books*. June 24, 2014: http://marginalia.lareviewofbooks.org/vanishing-jews-antiquity-adele-reinhartz/

The Word in the World: The Cosmological Tale in the Fourth Gospel. SBLMS 45. Atlanta: Scholars Press, 1992.

Rensberger, David. "Anti-Judaism and the Gospel of John." Pages 120–157 in *Anti-Judaism and the Gospels*. Edited by William Farmer. Harrisburg: Trinity Press International, 1999.

Johannine Faith and Liberating Community. Philadelphia: Westminster, 1988.

Ripley, Jason J. "Killing as Piety? Exploring Ideological Contexts Shaping the Gospel of John." *JBL* 134.3 (2015): 605–635.

Rowe, C. Kavin. *One True Life: The Argument of Rival Traditions.* New Haven: Yale University Press, 2016.

Rowland, Christopher. "John 1.51, Jewish Apocalyptic and Targumic Tradition." *NTS* 30 (1984): 498–507.

Schlund, Christine. *Kein Knochen soll gebrochen werden: Studien zu Bedeutung und Funktion des Pesachfest in Texten des frühen Judentums und im Johannesevangelium.* WMANT 107. Neukirchen: Neukirchener Verlag, 2005.

Schnackenburg, Rudolf. *The Gospel according to St. John.* New York: Crossroad, 1981–1990.

Schneiders, Sandra M. "The Lamb of God and the Forgiveness of Sin(s) in the Fourth Gospel." *CBQ* 73 (2011): 1–29.

Schröder, Jörn-Michael. *Das eschatologische Israel im Johannesevangelium: Eine Untersuchung der johanneischen Israel-Konzeption in Joh 2–4 und Joh 6.* NET 3. Tübingen: A. Franke Verlag, 2003.

Schuchard, Bruce G. *Scripture within Scripture: The Interrelationship of Form and Function in the Explicit Old Testament Citations in the Gospel of John.* SBLDS 133. Atlanta: Scholars Press, 1992.

Sheridan, Ruth. "Issues in the Translation of οἱ Ἰουδαῖοι in the Fourth Gospel." *JBL* 132.3 (2013): 671–695.

Retelling Scripture: 'The Jews' and the Scriptural Citations in John 1:19–12:15. BIS 110. Leiden: Brill, 2012.

Smith, D. Moody. *John.* ANTC. Nashville: Abingdon, 1999.

The Theology of the Gospel of John. Cambridge: Cambridge University Press, 1995.

"Review of *The Johannine Letters: A Commentary on 1, 2, and 3 John,* by Georg Strecker." *JBL* (119): 778–780.

Staples, Jason. "Reconstructing Israel: Restoration Eschatology in Early Judaism and Paul's Gentile Mission." PhD Diss., University of North Carolina at Chapel Hill, 2016.

Stone, Michael Edward. *Fourth Ezra.* Hermenia. Minneapolis: Fortress, 1990.

Streett, Andrew. *The Vine and the Son of Man: Eschatological Interpretation of Psalm 80 in Early Judaism.* Minneapolis: Fortress, 2014.

Swancutt, Diana M. "Hunger Assuaged by the Bread of Heaven." Pages 218–251 in *Early Christian Interpretation of the Scriptures of Israel.* Edited by Craig A. Evans and James A. Sanders. JSNTSup 148. Sheffield: Sheffield Academic Press, 1997.

Thatcher, Tom, and Richard Horsley. *John, Jesus & the Renewal of Israel.* Grand Rapids: Eerdmans, 2013.

Theobald, Michael. "Abraham – (Isaak) – Jakob. Israels Väter im Johannesevangelium." Pages 158–183 in *Israel und seine Heilstradition im Johannesevangelium: Festgabe für Johannes Beutler SJ zum. 70 Geburtstag.* Edited by Michael Labahn, Klaus Scholtissek, and Angelika Strotmann. Paderborn: Ferdinand Schöningh, 2004.

Die Fleischwerdung des Logos: Studien zum Verhältnis des Johannesprologs zum Corpus des Evangeliums und zu 1 Joh. NTAbh 20. Münster: Aschendorff, 1988.

Im Anfang war das Wort: textlinguistische Studie zum Johannesprolog. SBS 106. Stuttgart: Verlag Katholisches Bibelwerk, 1983.

Thompson, Marianne Meye. "Every Picture Tells a Story: Imagery for God in the Gospel of John." Pages 259–277 in *Imagery in the Gospel of John: Terms, Forms, Themes, and Theology of Johannine Figurative Language.* Edited by Jörg Frey, Jan G. van der Watt, and Ruben Zimmermann. WUNT 2/200. Tübingen: Mohr Siebeck, 2006.

The God of the Gospel of John. Grand Rapids: Eerdmans, 2001.

John: A Commentary. NTL. Louisville: Westminster John Knox, 2015.

"'They Bear Witness to Me': The Psalms in the Passion Narrative of the Gospel of John." Pages 267–283 in *The Word Leaps the Gap: Essays on Scripture and Theology in Honor of Richard B. Hays.* Edited by J. Ross Wagner, C. Kavin Rowe, and Katherine Grieb. Grand Rapids: Eerdmans, 2008.

Tomson, Peter J. "'Jews' in the Gospel of John as Compared with the Palestinian Talmud, the Synoptics, and Some New Testament Apocrypha." Pages 176–212 in *Anti-Judaism and the Fourth Gospel.* Edited by R. Bieringer et al. Louisville: Westminster John Knox, 2001.

"The Names 'Israel' and 'Jew' in Ancient Judaism and the New Testament." *Bjidr* 47.2–3 (1986): 120–140, 266–289.

Townsend, John T. "The Gospel of John and the Jews: The Story of a Religious Divorce." Pages 72–89 in *Antisemitism and the Foundations of Christianity.* Edited by Allan Davies. New York: Paulist Press, 1979.

Trumbower, Jeffrey. *Born from Above: The Anthropology of the Gospel of John.* HUT 29. Tübingen: Mohr Siebeck, 1992.

Turner, John. "The History of Religions Background of John 10." Pages 33–52 in *The Shepherd Discourse of John 10 and Its Context.* Edited by Johannes Beutler and Robert Fortna. SNTSMS 67. Cambridge: Cambridge University Press, 1991.

VanderKam, James C. "John 10 and the Feast of the Dedication." Pages 203–214 in *Of Scribes and Scrolls: Studies of the Hebrew Bible, Intertestamental Judaism, and Christian Origins Presented to John Strugnell on the Occasion of His 60th Birthday.* Edited by Harold W. Attridge, John J. Collins, and Thomas H. Tobin. S.J. New York: University Press of America, 1990.

Volf, Miroslav. "Johannine Dualism and Contemporary Pluralism." *Modern Theology* 21.2 (2005): 189–217.

von Wahlde, U. C. "Judas, the Son of Perdition and the Fulfillment of Scripture in John 17:12." Pages 167–182 in *The New Testament and Early Christian Literature in Greco-Roman Context: Studies in Honor of David E. Aune.* Edited by John Fotopoulos. NovTSup 122. Leiden: Brill, 2006.

Wengst, Klaus. *Bedrängte Gemeinde und verherrlichter Christus: der historische Ort des Johannesevangeliums als Schlüssel zu seiner Interpretation.* Neukirchen-Vluyn: Neukirchener Verlag, 1981.

Wheaton, Gerald. *The Role of Jewish Feasts in John's Gospel.* SNTSMS 162. New York: Cambridge University Press, 2015.

Williams, Catrin. "Another Look at 'Lifting Up in the Gospel of John.'" Pages 58–70 in *Conception, Reception, and the Spirit: Essays in Honor of*

Andrew T. Lincoln. Edited by J. G. McConville and L. K Pietersen. Eugene: Cascade, 2015.

Wróbel, Miroslav S. "John 8:44 as *crux interpretum*." Pages 403–421 in *Rediscovering John: Essays on the Fourth Gospel in Honour of Fréderic Manns*. Edited by Lesław Daniel Chrupcała. Milan: Edizioni Terra Santa, 2013.

Yee, Gale. *Jewish Feasts and the Gospel of John*. Zaccheus Studies, New Testament. Wilmington: M. Glazier, 1989.

Young, Franklin. "A Study of the Relation of Isaiah to the Fourth Gospel." *ZNW* 46 (1955): 215–233.

Zimmermann, Mirjam and Ruben Zimmermann. "Der Freund des Bräutigams (Joh 3,29): Deflorations- oder Christuszeuge." *ZNW* 90 (1999): 123–130.

INDEX